strategic leadership

INTRODUCING 'STRATEGIC LEADERSHIP, LEADERSHIP AND THE NEW AGENDA • • COMPETITIVE ANALYSIS AND VALUE IN THE MULTI-BUSINESS FIRM • STRATEGIC PROCESSES–TRANSFORMATION AND RENEWAL

strategic

GOVERNANCE AND RENEWAL' • STRATEGY,
THE CONTEXT OF BUSINESS IN SOCIETY
INNOVATION, STRATEGY AND ORGANISATION
PROCESSES – INNOVATION • STRATEGIC
• SOME FINAL THOUGHTS AND REFLECTIONS

leadership

governance & renewal

Brian Leavy
*Dublin City University
Business School*

and

Peter McKiernan
University of St Andrews

palgrave
macmillan

First published 2009 by
PALGRAVE MACMILLAN

Palgrave Macmillan in the UK is an imprint of Macmillan Publishers Limited,
registered in England, company number 785998, of Houndmills, Basingstoke,
Hampshire RG21 6XS.

Palgrave Macmillan in the US is a division of St Martin's Press LLC,
175 Fifth Avenue, New York, NY 10010.

Palgrave Macmillan is the global academic imprint of the above companies
and has companies and representatives throughout the world.

Palgrave® and Macmillan® are registered trademarks in the United States,
the United Kingdom, Europe and other countries.

ISBN-13: 978-0-230-20511-6   paperback
ISBN-10: 0-230-20511-9   paperback

This book is printed on paper suitable for recycling and made from fully
managed and sustained forest sources. Logging, pulping and manufacturing
processes are expected to conform to the environmental regulations of the
country of origin.

A catalogue record for this book is available from the British Library.

A catalog record for this book is available from the Library of Congress.

10 9 8 7 6 5 4 3 2 1

18 17 16 15 14 13 12 11 10 09

Printed and bound in China

contents

list of figures   vi

list of tables   vii

list of vignettes   viii

preface   ix

1   introducing 'strategic leadership, governance and renewal'   1

2   strategy, leadership and the new agenda   19

3   the context of business in society   69

4   competitive analysis and value innovation   125

5   strategy and organisation in the multi-business firm   167

6   strategic processes – innovation   203

7   strategic processes – transformation and renewal   243

8   some final thoughts and reflections   285

references   295

index   321

list of figures

3.1 The four Cs of strategic management.   73

3.2 Harmony among the three Cs.   74

3.3 Typologies of change.   75

3.4 Shell Global Scenarios to 2025, Shell
International BV.   94

3.5 Variable importance and uncertainty matrix.   119

7.1 Six stages of organisational decline and renewal.   245

7.2 Decline chain factors.   249

7.3 Triggering action.   254

7.4 Responses to decline.   254

list of tables

2.1 Managerial culture versus leadership culture   42

6.1 Contrasting principles of closed and open innovation   222

7.1 Symptoms of corporate decline   247

7.2 Main secondary causes of decline   250

7.3 Retrenchment strategies   259

7.4 Recovery strategies   261

list of vignettes

3.1 Strategies for teenagers with diabetes: Italy
     versus Scotland   70

3.2 Theory of the modern state   81

3.3 Commission on the year 2000   105

3.4 Generic scenarios; UK foresight   108

preface

Strategic Leadership: Governance & Renewal has been written to provide a thematic companion to support the case-based teaching of strategy at senior undergraduate, MBA and executive development levels. In putting it together, we have been guided by two main considerations with one overriding aim. The two considerations were to keep the focus on the bigger picture and make leadership our overarching theme, and the overriding aim was to help restore the 'CEO perspective' to the heart of strategy teaching, particularly where the strategy course is intended to be a programme's 'capstone module'.

So our primary orientation is towards the educational needs of the aspiring general manager rather than the strategy specialist. Our emphasis will be mainly analytical rather than prescriptive, and we intend the book to help stimulate debate in the classroom rather than pre-empt it. We also intend the book to be a resource to business executives, seeking to update themselves with an accessible treatment of the main topics and issues in strategy most relevant to their current and emerging needs. Finally, we hope the book will be a valuable resource to students on the lookout for suitable dissertation topics in the strategic management area, because it highlights throughout many of the debates and questions that continue to energise the field and also includes extensive referencing.

A number of acknowledgements are in order. Firstly, we would like to thank our students at DCU Business School and the University of St Andrews for providing us over the years with the lively and challenging classroom environments within which the ideas for this book have taken shape. One of us also owes a particular debt to editor Robert Randall and other colleagues on the editorial team of *Strategy & Leadership,* for all their support, encouragement and intellectual stimulation over the last five years, much of which is reflected in these pages. We would further like to thank the team at Palgrave Macmillan for helping us bring this book through to fruition: Anna Faherty, who showed the initial interest and gave us vital early encouragement; Martin Drewe, our publisher, who was a great support to us right throughout the process, along with his colleagues, Mark Cooper and Sarah Fry; and the staff of Macmillan Publishing Solutions for helping to get the project over the finishing line in a very professional, helpful and timely fashion. Senior researchers at St Andrews, Gary Bowman and Swapnesh Masrani, helped at various stages of production, and Barbara Lessels was instrumental in proofreading earlier drafts. Last but not least, we would like to thank our families, for always being there for us, especially when we most need them.

Permission acknowledgements

We thank the following publishers for their kind permission to allow us to draw freely in various sections of this book from the following previous publications: 'Organisation and competitiveness',[1] 'Creating value in the Multi-Business Firm'[2] and 'Creativity, the new imperative',[3] all published by Braybrooke Press in the *Journal of General Management;* 'Competing for hearts and minds: a corporate culture perspective on marketing'[4] and 'A more creative organisation *and* a better breeding ground for leaders',[5] both published by Mercury Publications in the *Irish Marketing Review; Key Processes in Strategy*,[6] published by Thomson Learning (now Cengage Learning); and 'Understanding the triad of great leadership: context, conviction and credibility',[7] 'Assessing your strategic alternatives from a market position and core competence perspective',[8] 'Outsourcing strategies: opportunities and risks'[9] and 'A leader's guide to creating an innovation culture',[10] all published by Emerald in *Strategy & Leadership*. We also thank *MIT Sloan Management Review* for permission to use the material in Table 6.1 which is taken from 'The era of open innovation'.[11]

We are grateful to Shirley Wright of the Global Business Environment at Shell International BV for editing our treatment of Shell's Global Scenarios in Chapter 3, and to Royal Dutch Shell plc for permission to use this content.

Notes

1 Leavy (1999).
2 Leavy (2001).
3 Leavy (2002).
4 Leavy and Gannon (1998).
5 Leavy (2003b).
6 Leavy (1996a).
7 Leavy (2003a).
8 Leavy (2003c).
9 Leavy (2004b).
10 Leavy (2005b).
11 Chesbrough (2003b).

INTRODUCING 'STRATEGIC LEADERSHIP, GOVERNANCE AND RENEWAL'

STRATEGY, LEADERSHIP AND THE NEW AGENDA • THE CONTEXT OF
BUSINESS IN SOCIETY • COMPETITIVE ANALYSIS AND VALUE INNOVATION
• STRATEGIC PROCESSES IN THE MULTI-BUSINESS FIRM •
STRATEGIC PROCESSES – INNOVATION • STRATEGIC PROCESSES – TRANSFORMATION
AND RENEWAL • SOME FINAL THOUGHTS AND REFLECTIONS

1 introducing 'strategic leadership, governance and renewal'

Normally, treatises on strategic management from the Euro-American domain are either generalist or functional. In the former, the big picture perspective is concerned with issues of leadership, the influencing of context, governance choices and decisions about the fundamental basis of competitive strategy and how these might shape the organisation. In the latter, the disciplinary perspective aims to provide succinct analysis of the building blocks of strategy (e.g. marketing, finance, human relations), with individual attention on the smarter, operational techniques that emanate from each and impinge on strategy formulation, choice and implementation. In the modern evolution of strategic management, the former's influence has been replaced incrementally by the persuasive techniques of the latter.

This book attempts to redress the balance. It adopts the lens of the Chief Executive Officer (CEO) and tries to address their most critical questions in a series of pressing strategic themes informed by a research-driven approach. It assumes that some knowledge of the strategy-building blocks has already been acquired and that some decision-making at middle management level has been exercised. Also, it assumes an appetite for broad, integrative thinking and original research rather than an exceptional hunger for more tools, frameworks, techniques or quick fixes. It is critical in its manner. However, it is accepted that this contribution may be a victim of its contemporary origins. As in other disciplines and in broader politics, issues in strategic management can take a pendulum swing from one extreme to another. In this attempt to move the pendulum back to its strategy origins, the book is another step in the evolution of a youthful domain.

How the strategy field has evolved over the years

The modern commercial strategy field as a self-conscious discipline has its roots in the early 1960s with the publication of Chandler's *Strategy and Structure* in 1962, Sloan's *My Years with General Motors* in 1963, Ansoff's *Corporate Strategy* in 1965 and the development of the well-known PIMS (Profit Impact of Market Strategy) research, initiated within General Electric in the 1960s.[1]

Since these early beginnings, there have been many developments in the strategy field. Most prominent among the concepts introduced during the 1960s and 1970s were the product life cycle,[2] the directional matrix,[3] the experience curve and the growth-share matrix, the last two developed by the Boston Consulting Group (BCG), under the leadership of Bruce Henderson (1973). These concepts have remained important elements in the strategist's toolkit through to the present day. The 1980s were dominated by the contributions of Michael Porter (1980, 1985, 1990), and his five forces, generic strategies, strategic groups, value chain and diamond concepts. The resource-based view of strategy rose to prominence in the 1990s, with the Prahalad and Hamel (1990) concept of core competency earning its own enduring place in the strategic management lexicon. More recently, Christensen's (1997) disruptive innovation, Prahalad and Ramaswamy's (2004) co-creation of value and Kim and Mauborgne's (2005) blue ocean strategy have been among the most influential ideas to emerge over the last ten years or so.

Such developments reflect the enormous growth in interest and research effort since the field's early beginnings. They are also reflective of the shifting nature of the strategy problem over time,[4] particularly for companies in the West, where much of the early thought leadership in the strategy field had tended to emanate. In the environment of the 1960s and 1970s, the primary interest was in strategies for growth, and the concept of strategy at the time became almost synonymous with diversification and vertical integration. Economies of scale and scope were seen to be the primary determinants of competitive advantage. With the onset of the low-growth 1980s and the influx of new 'world-class' competitors from the East into Western markets, many of them outperforming their larger Western rivals without the traditional advantages of scale or scope, the emphasis in the strategy field shifted more directly on to the issue of competitiveness, and more nuanced approaches to the understanding and development of sustainable competitive advantage were needed urgently. This was a context ripe for the seminal contributions of Michael Porter on competitive strategy.

The 1990s brought renewed growth in the global economy, but unlike the 1960s and 1970s, many of the new 'white space' opportunities were to be found beyond traditional industry boundaries, due to the liberalisation of markets, advancing globalisation and the impact of technological change, so that traditional approaches to growth through diversification were no longer to be relied on and new approaches were called for. It was a time in the research literature when, as Rumelt et al. (1991: 22) observed, 'both theoretical and empirical research into the sources of advantage' had 'begun to point to organizational capabilities, rather than product-market positions or tactics, as the enduring sources of competitive advantage'. The core competency perspective of Prahalad and Hamel (1990) provided a particularly appealing conceptual and practical alternative to strategists looking for new and more organic routes to growth in this emerging context.[5] Most recently, the threat of increasing market saturation and strategy convergence in existing markets, and the fresh opportunities for very substantial growth offered by the largest of the developing economies (China, India, Brazil and Eastern Europe) and by Internet commerce, have led to a shift in interest towards strategy, and business model, innovation. This is where the recent ideas of Christensen, Prahalad and Ramaswamy and Kim and Mauborgne seem to be offering some promise.

In parallel with this rich array of conceptual perspectives, that have served to enrich our capacity for strategic analysis over the years, there have also been very significant developments that have focused more closely on the relationship between organisational variables (such as leadership, structure, process and culture) and sustained competitiveness and growth. Back in the 1960s and 1970s, one of the most fundamental and widely accepted axioms of the strategy field was that 'structure follows strategy'.[6] Strategy was seen to be the primary determinant of growth and competitiveness, and this thesis had an enormous influence on how strategy was taught and practiced for more than two decades. Most of the early teaching of strategy tended to frame it as a two-step process of formulation followed by implementation. Formulation was seen to be largely a conceptual matter of economic analysis, while implementation was concerned mainly with the administration process of making sure that the structure was aligned with the strategy and the measurement and rewards systems were fully aligned to support both. Formulation was the primary creative task and strategic differentiator. When it came to the determination of sustained growth and competitiveness, organisational considerations were seen to be secondary.

The notion that organisational considerations were secondary began to be challenged in the early 1980s. The first 'wake-up call' came from the successful infiltration by Japanese competitors during the 1970s and 1980s into major internationalising markets like automobiles and consumer electronics, where Western companies had long been dominant. The primary explanation for their success seemed to have less to do with strategy, and more to do with organisational agility and execution. The realisation that certain key internal processes might be linked to growth and competitiveness, and that far from being subsidiary to strategy they might be part of its essence, gathered pace with the 'excellence crusade' of Peters and Waterman (1982), and their 'back-to-basics' assertion that execution was strategy. It was also fuelled by the growing influence of Quinn (1980), Mintzberg (1987) and others, highlighting the limitations of the two-stage model of strategy, with its tendency to artificially separate the thinking and action stages of the strategy process. One of the biggest weaknesses in the traditional view that organisation is subsidiary to strategy was that, essentially, it placed strategy before people, and economic rationality before passion. This underestimated the potential that high engagement, high commitment organisations have to outperform their rivals on a sustained basis.

Since the early 1980s, the search for insight into how to create the high engagement, high performance organisation, capable of retaining its capacity for entrepreneurship, adaptability and innovativeness as it grows, has spawned a strong literature stream in its own right. This has served to underline the strategic significance of organisation (in all of its key dimensions, including structure, process, people, leadership and culture) and its potential to be a competitive differentiator in its own right. From *In Search of Excellence*[7] and *The Change Masters*[8] right up through *Hidden Value*[9] to *The Future of Management*,[10] the search for an organisational model capable of harnessing the full intellectual, social and emotional capacities of the people who work within it has continued apace, whether we have been calling it the 'adaptive corporation',[11] the 'learning organization',[12] the 'living company',[13] the 'individualized corporation',[14] the 'horizontal organization'[15] or any number of 'built-to-last',[16] 'built-to-perform'[17] or 'built-to-change'[18] variants along the way.

In sum, the decades since the 1960s have witnessed the continuing development of conceptual frameworks for developing strategy, with new ideas being added to the strategy toolkit as the context for business has changed over time and new challenges have emerged, requiring fresh perspectives. Also, there has been a growing recognition that organisational variables are potentially strategic in their own right and need to be considered as integral to the central concerns of strategy and not as simply adjunct to them.

A third major development in the strategy field which has come to prominence particularly since the turn of the millennium is the renewal of interest in corporate governance and the role of the board in strategy development. In the wake of the stock market woes and corporate scandals of the early 2000s, long-running debates in the areas of corporate governance and corporate social responsibility have been given fresh impetus, and issues that played a relatively minor role in the development of the strategy field for most of the last forty years have been taking on new urgency and significance. Corporate governance has both an administrative/fiduciary and an entrepreneurial function, but for most of the history of the strategy field to date, the emphasis has been on the entrepreneurial, with boards typically playing relatively passive, ritualistic and supporting roles. More recently, the pendulum has swung very firmly towards the administrative/fiduciary end of the spectrum, with many now concerned that modern-day boards and management have become more timid, circumscribed and risk-averse than is desirable for the ongoing strategic health of any business. As Jack Welch put it in a recent CNBC interview: 'I see the almost fear of boards of directors who instead of coming in and saying: How big? How fast? – too often come to board meetings saying: Anything happen in the last month that could embarrass us?' As a consequence, issues of corporate governance have now, in themselves, also become more significant in current strategy theory and practice.

The teaching of strategy and the role for this book

As these developments were taking place, approaches to the teaching of strategy and its role in the business school curriculum, particularly in graduate programmes and in executive education, have also been changing.

Strategic management has long been considered a capstone course on many, if not most, MBA and executive leadership programmes. With the changes that have been taking place within the strategy field over the years, the capacity of most strategic management courses to perform this capstone role has become more open to question. Most MBA and related business programmes prior to 1980 sought to develop the unique perspective of the general manager through a case-driven capstone course that was typically titled Business Policy. The original and most influential template at the time for the teaching of business policy evolved through the work of Edmund Learned, C. Roland Christensen and Kenneth Andrews at Harvard Business School back in the 1950s and 1960s. The concept of corporate strategy was offered by them as their unifying concept, but their perspective on strategy remained one of a generalist. As they portrayed it, their 'idea of corporate strategy' was to be seen as 'a simple practitioner's theory', a 'kind of Everyman's conceptual scheme made for use in real life in unstructured, complex and unique situations', which 'when brought to its full power in intelligent use' would be 'capable of including the most extensive combination of interrelated variables involved in the most important of all business decisions'.[19] For them, corporate strategy was the unique answer that the leadership of any particular business should come up with through addressing four key questions affecting the future of the enterprise: What might we do (opportunities)? What can we do (competencies)? What do we want to do (ambitions and aspirations)? And what should we do (values, obligations and wider responsibilities to society)?

Now, it is recognised widely that 1980 represents a watershed in the development of the strategy field, with the arrival of Michael Porter, and the enormous influence that his work on competitive strategy has had on the discipline ever since. Mainly, this has been for the better, but it has come with some unintended drawbacks. Strategy prior to 1980 had breadth, but it was lacking in analytical depth and sharpness. The contributions of Porter, and others that followed, changed all that with a succession of major frameworks such as the five forces model, generic strategy, value chain, core competence, disruptive innovation and blue ocean strategy. All added considerably to the range of conceptual options available to the strategist. Along the way, however, teaching and research in the strategy field became more specialised and the perspective of the generalist receded into the background. Strategic management courses became more focused on the economics of strategy (or on the 'what we might do' and 'what we can do' questions), to the relative neglect of leadership, meaningful purpose, aspirations, values and obligations. Reflecting this shift, many involved in the teaching of strategy came increasingly from an economics background rather than a general management one as top management became 'noticeably absent from writings on strategy, somehow passed over in favour of techno-economic factors such as product life cycles, market share, experience curves, portfolio matrices and industry analysis'.[20] Meanwhile, in the world of practice, the role of the CEO continued to expand, and many of the most challenging issues facing company leaders began to extend beyond the specific confines of business strategy to much broader concerns with the kind of companies they wanted their organisations to be, and the kind of values they wanted them to be seen to stand for within their wider communities.

As a consequence of these developments, many strategy courses no longer serve the original capstone function of developing the generalist CEO perspective, even though this perspective is now more needed than ever. This has left a gap, which up to now has remained largely unfilled. *Strategic Leadership: Governance & Renewal* sets out to address this need. As Cynthia Montgomery (2008) has recently argued (in a special issue of

Harvard Business Review to commemorate the foundation of Harvard Business School), it is time to put 'leadership back into strategy'. It is time to recognise that 'strategy is not just a plan, not just an idea' but 'a way of life for a company', and one that the CEO must watch over 'day by day', not only as his or her 'greatest opportunity to outwit the competition', but also 'to shape the firm itself' (p. 56) and address the most fundamental of issues about 'the kind of company you want yours to become'.[21]

The approach taken here in helping to develop a more generalist perspective, and restore the capstone course on strategy to its original purpose, will be unified around the concept of leadership, while remaining strategic in orientation. It will continue to stress the importance of understanding the economic fundamentals of strategy and competitiveness in both the single business and multi-business contexts. However, it will also emphasise the strategic impact of key leadership processes through which CEOs more typically make their most valuable contributions in today's world – not just in developing an understanding of industry dynamics, but also in creating high-spirited organisations, developing a corporate management approach that adds value in the multi-business context, institutionalising the capacity for strategic innovation and renewal, leading successful transformation and building moral communities that can find the right balance between their commercial interests and their social obligations. In today's environment, we no longer view the defining role of the CEO as master-strategist or expect a single mind to do all of the thinking for our organisations. The role of the CEO is just as concerned with shaping the organisational context within which a compelling vision, moral purpose and creative strategy are most likely to emerge. Today's CEOs need to be able to lead in ways that are both economically convincing and emotionally compelling, by seeking to integrate commercial realities with human aspirations and societal obligations.

Strategy at the CEO level used to be about the bigger picture, but the ever-increasing specialisation of the discipline has seen the emergence of many standard strategy textbooks of larger and larger proportions, incorporating what can often seem like minitexts on marketing, finance, operations, human resource management, organisational analysis and other foundation disciplines. While these have an important role to play in teaching the basic building blocks of strategy to the very finest detail, we believe that many lecturers and post-experience students will now welcome a strategic leadership book with a renewed emphasis on the CEO perspective that brings us back to the bigger picture, one that is issue-driven, while also being informed by the latest ideas and research. This is what *Strategic Leadership: Governance & Renewal* aims to do. The thematic structure reflects this issue-driven philosophy, and the relative conciseness of the book reflects its focus on the bigger questions. A thematic structure is also seen to be appropriate because strategic management as a field of inquiry still lacks a unifying theoretical paradigm or central framework. It remains 'firmly grounded in practice', and continues to exist largely 'because of the importance of its subject' rather than due to any distinctive theoretical coherence.[22] As a resource for post-experience students, the book assumes a basic familiarity with the language of business and strategy. Students who are comfortable reading popular business publications like the *Financial Times*, the *Economist* or *International Business Week* should have little difficulty in following the treatment.

For teachers of strategy and leadership, this book aims to be a thought-provoking resource to support a case-based approach to developing the CEO perspective in postgraduate and executive education programmes. Reflecting the inductive emphasis in the case-driven pedagogy, the book will tend to lead with key questions and issues rather than with theoretical frameworks (Asking, for example, Should the roles of CEO and Chairman be separate? Are managers and leaders different, and is such a distinction strategically meaningful? Can corporate values be a source of competitive advantage? Should competitive strategy be position-led or competency-led, and when does it matter? Can the capacity for innovation and renewal be institutionalised, and if so, how? Is major transformation possible without a crisis to trigger it off?). At the same time, it will seek to engage with these questions in both a theoretically informed and empirically grounded way.

This thematic, issue-led, approach is designed to support the teaching role rather than pre-empt it. The general thrust will be analytical rather than prescriptive. The primary intention is to use some of the larger questions and debates that continue to energise strategic management research and practice to provoke thought and allow the students to ground their learning in case discussion and analysis, always informed by current theory. In using the book, teachers should find plenty of scope for asking their students what they think about the kind of issues being raised, encouraging them to draw on their experiential learning as well as on their studies to date. They will also find much room to offer insights of their own, drawing on their particular interests and areas of expertise.

The structure of the book

In line with the issue-led, thematic approach just described, the remainder of the book is organised around six major themes:

Strategy, Leadership and the New Agenda (Chapter 2)
The Context of Business in Society (Chapter 3)
Competitive Analysis and Value Innovation (Chapter 4)
Strategy and Organisation in the Multi-Business Firm (Chapter 5)
Strategic Processes – Innovation (Chapter 6)
Strategic Processes – Transformation and Renewal (Chapter 7)

Each of these six themes has its own dedicated chapter, and together they form the main body of the treatment. We present them in the belief that these are the major topics in strategy, leadership, governance and renewal that any postgraduate or executive student of business will need to be familiar with to be effective in a general management position today. *Strategic Leadership: Governance & Renewal* also contains two further chapters, a brief introduction here (Chapter 1), aimed at helping the reader to understand the book's overall positioning and philosophy, and a concluding chapter with some final thoughts and reflections (Chapter 8).

The following provides an overview of the chapters to come.

In the next chapter, Chapter 2, we open our thematic treatment of Strategy, Leadership, Governance and Renewal with a focus on 'Strategy, Leadership and the New Agenda'. The chapter begins with a brief examination of what we mean by strategy and leadership, and whether the two are largely synonymous when it comes to understanding the role of the CEO. We ask how 'strategic' a factor is leadership in itself? And we look at how our understanding of leadership as a strategic variable in its own right, has been changing over the last two decades. We examine the focus of some of the early theories on leadership, and offer a contextual perspective on leadership at the institutional level that shifts the attention beyond traditional concerns with traits and styles to performance in the arena. The provocative debate about whether managers and leaders are different provides us with a useful lead-in to examine the relationships between leadership, corporate culture and competitiveness, and we also look at the potential pitfalls of strong leadership and culture, highlighting the darker sides of both. We go beyond this to offer an indicative schema which draws out the contrast between managerial and leadership cultures, a distinction which is generating a lot of interest in recent times. In the latter part of the chapter, we examine the changing expectations facing CEOs in the new business context of the early twenty-first century, a context which has brought the topic of corporate governance right back to the forefront of strategy and leadership, and given fresh impetus to the various debates that surround it (such as whether the roles of CEO and chairman should be separated, the appointment and remuneration of directors, the internal/external balance of the board and the impact of new regulations on board impact and operations). We end the chapter with a look at the new agenda facing CEOs, and the additional demands and challenges that it brings.

In turning to 'The Context of Business in Society', in Chapter 3, we examine the role that the wider environmental context plays in the determination of strategy, and explore some of the thinking, tools and techniques that have been developed to help out with one of the most difficult of the challenges facing CEOs today. In pursuing this aim, we depart a little in both style and content from the kind of issue-led, thought-provoking and thematic approach that we use throughout the rest of the book. We do this in order to offer some direct didactic help to strategists in an area that company leaders so often tend to shy away from because the turbulence of modern business settings frequently makes the task seem pretty overwhelming. How can strategic leaders go about the challenge of trying to make sense of contexts with a complex weave of elements like globalisation, rapid technological change, shortening product life cycles, product proliferation, shorter market channels, increasing consumer sovereignty, revolution in telecommunications, shrinking distance, extensive migration, clashes of civilisation, climate disruption, greater secularisation, increasing affluence and increasing poverty?

While there is much about the 'art of the long view', or scenario development, that remains an art, nevertheless, the role of this chapter is to demonstrate how it can be possible to generate a good understanding of context with the judicious application of appropriate thinking, tools and techniques in a flexible, creative and imaginative way. We begin with a brief vignette that shows how important an understanding of context can be in strategy development and offer a four-factor model as a useful framework for contextual analysis. We then go on to put the turbulent environment of the early twenty-first century into longer historical perspective, underlining the point that waves of change of the kind that we now seem to be in the midst of are nothing new. We take a close look at the 'global scenarios to 2025' of Shell Corporation, a widely acknowledged world leader in scenario development, and use them to identify the variables likely to shape the next change wave. This examination offers insights on three change drivers, seven predetermined variables, and three alternative future scenarios. We end the chapter by identifying three components of contextual uncertainty that CEOs must learn to understand and cope with, and we provide an introduction to the philosophy, perspective and techniques of scenario development, designed to help set future strategic direction in the face of such opaqueness.

In Chapter 4, 'Competitive Analysis and Value Innovation', we return to the book's main issue-led, thematic style and examine such issues as what matters most in generating and sustaining above-average profitability, industry structure or company capability, and we also ask whether strategy innovation and the creation of uncontested new market space might now be becoming more important than either of them. To explore such issues, we examine in some detail the three main perspectives on business strategy development that have emerged over the last quarter of a century: competitive positioning, core competency and value innovation. While the chapter is built primarily around these three perspectives, for completeness, we begin with a look back at some of the earlier concepts used in competitive analysis prior to the advent of Porter, particularly the product life cycle, experience curve and growth-share matrix concepts, all of which had a bearing on what was to follow and continue to be seen as useful elements of the strategist's toolkit right up to the present time. We then concentrate on each of the three main perspectives which form the centrepiece of the chapter. We look first at the positioning and core competency views of strategy and examine where choosing between them might matter and why. We then go on to look at the most recent perspective, value innovation, and examine how it differs from the previous two. We also look closely at three major variants of value innovation: blue ocean strategy, disruptive innovation and experience innovation, and we compare and contrast. The chapter ends with a look at how the competitive landscape for many businesses is shifting from 'firm-to-firm' to 'network-to-network' or 'business ecosystem-to-business ecosystem' competition and we examine the implications for competitive analysis and business strategy.

The distinction between business strategy and corporate strategy becomes particularly relevant in the case of the multi-business firm, and this is the focus of Chapter 5. In 'Strategy and Organisation in the Multi-Business Firm' (MBF) we open by identifying the central challenge for corporate management in the MBF – how to create more value that the businesses themselves could generate as stand-alone entities with direct access to the capital markets in their own right. We highlight how over the last four decades the MBF track record in trying to address this challenge has been underwhelming at best, and often pretty dismal, with more value being destroyed than created in too many cases. Against this general background, however, there have been some notable successes, and it seems that the route to success in meeting the central challenge of the MBF has also been changing and evolving over time. So this chapter examines the changing shape of the MBF challenge and the various approaches that have been taken to address it up to the present time, beginning with an early emphasis on strategy, and shifting in more recent times to a greater emphasis on organisation, leadership and culture.

The earliest attempts, going back to the 1960s and 1970s, tried to meet this challenge through the use of strategy matrices, most notably the BCG's growth-share matrix, and its associated organisational innovation, the SBU (Strategic Business Unit), and we examine the early experience with the use of these concepts. One important limitation was the inability of the BCG Matrix and its various derivatives to deal with the issue of relatedness among the various businesses in the multi-business context. This is seen to be significant because one of the most consistent findings from the empirical research since the early 1970s is that related diversification is generally more successful than unrelated diversification. We examine whether indeed relatedness is the key to successful corporate strategy, and go on to ask, what kind of relatedness? The early focus in the literature tended to be on market or product relatedness, but, over the years, the dimensions of relevant relatedness have since been expanded to include competency relatedness and several other types on which coherent and effective corporate strategies might be based, and we examine this development and its implications. We then go on to explore the link between organisation and competitiveness in the MBF, asking does structure follow strategy or is structure becoming more strategic? In exploring this issue, we highlight four recent trends in the relationship between organisation and effectiveness in the MBF that point to new directions in the effort to build 'organisational advantage', and we draw upon the recent history of General Electric for indications of how a new management model for the MBF is likely to evolve. We finish the chapter with a brief examination of the HQ-Subsidiary relationship in the globalising firm, and how this relationship changes over time with changes in the role of the subsidiary in regional strategy. We also look briefly, in this concluding section of the chapter, at the recent swing in the centralisation–decentralisation dynamic within the MBF literature back from the radical decentralisation of the 1990s towards stronger integration, but without the level of dependence on hierarchical mechanisms or formal matrix structures that characterised earlier eras.

In Chapters 6 and 7, we turn our attention to two key strategic processes, innovation and renewal, that are as important to the CEO today as business and corporate strategy, especially in the rapidly changing business environment of the early twenty-first century. In the first of these, 'Strategic Processes – Innovation', we concern ourselves with two main issues: How can the capacity of a firm to innovate be institutionalised as it grows in scale and complexity? Also, how can new business ventures be incubated successfully within the established corporation? We begin our treatment of the first of these by asking if the key to the innovation advantage lies mainly in talent or in organisation. We examine how organisations might go about the challenge of how to become more ideas-driven, now that the competitive environment is putting a greater premium on innovation than ever before. This begins with developing a deeper understanding of the unusual person with unusual ideas, and of how to make our organisations more hospitable to them. We look at aspects of organisational structure, process and culture that seem key to the ability to foster creativity and innovation in organisational settings, including how to go about building a corporate culture and context for creativity, how to nurture and lead the creative process and how to go about trying to secure the right balance between creativity and efficiency. We then go on to explore the recent trend towards open innovation and examine its early impact and implications. In the final part of the chapter we take a close look at the organisational challenges facing well-established companies in trying to successfully incubate new businesses, particularly those in brand new market spaces, where a successful profit formula and business model have yet to emerge, and where the key success factors are likely to be very different from those pertaining to the core. We look at the track record of internal corporate venturing and examine such issues as why the pattern has tended to be so cyclical up to now, and whether corporate entrepreneurship is more effective when managed as a top-down or bottom-up process. We also examine a number of prominent questions still unresolved in the literature such as how much autonomy a new business venture should be given, how the leaders for such ventures should be chosen and rewarded and how far the approach to planning and accountability within such new businesses should be allowed to deviate from a company's mainstream processes and systems. We end with a look at the broader question of how seriously should we take the current 'growth imperative' to be, and ask whether many companies might be wiser to face up to futures of more modest growth than try to pursue internal corporate venturing activities of uncertain outcome with no clear skills to bring to the process.

In the second of these two chapters, *Strategic Processes – Transformation and Renewal,* we look at the leadership challenges facing once-successful companies which have become over-adapted to old circumstances and whose strategic recipes are losing traction in a changing marketplace. If many well-established companies find it quite difficult to incubate radically new businesses to help them maintain their dynamism as they grow, most find it even more difficult to reinvent themselves and renew their core business when this becomes the pressing need. What happens when companies go into decline? Why are they often so slow at taking the required action? Why is it so difficult for them to renew themselves? Why is financial crisis and change of leadership too often needed to bring about successful renewal? How do the dynamics of strategic transformation and renewal typically play out and how can the process best be managed? These are the kinds of issues that concern us throughout this, the last of our chapters dealing with the book's main themes. We begin our treatment of strategic transformation and renewal by taking a close look at what happens when any organisation goes into decline. We develop our analysis around a six-stage model (*organisational decline, triggers for action, diagnostics, retrenchment, recovery* and *renewal*), examining each stage in some detail. In the final part of the chapter where we turn to the dynamics of the transformation and renewal process, we begin by looking at the 'incremental versus punctuated (or cyclical) model of the change' debate in the literature, and go on to highlight some of the main aspects of the process dynamics, including the emergent nature of the process and the building of a momentum for change to self-sustaining levels. The debates around whether crisis and change of leadership are, or should be, necessary to trigger and secure successful renewal are also examined and the chapter ends with a look at some recent literature aimed at finding an alternative to the disruptive cyclical pattern, a literature focused on how to make our organisations more 'resilient'.

We conclude in Chapter 8 with 'Some Final Thoughts and Reflections' on where we see the strategy field today, in both theory and practice, in terms of both current position and future challenges. On the research front, we note, in particular, the recent emergence of the 'strategy-as-practice' perspective, and highlight how it seems to accord with the kind of outlook that we have taken here in *Strategic Leadership: Governance & Renewal*. In the final part of our concluding chapter, we return once more to the question of strategic and organisational resilience, featured at the end of Chapter 7. In addition to encapsulating one of the central challenges facing strategic management theory and practice as we face towards the future, the question of how to build the resilient, continuously self-renewing organisation also provides us with a useful way to draw together many of the key ideas and themes around which our book revolves.

Notes

[1] Schoeffler et al. (1974), Buzzel and Gale (1987).
[2] Levitt (1965).
[3] Ansoff (1965).
[4] Ansoff (1979).
[5] See also Hamel and Prahalad (1994).
[6] Chandler (1962).
[7] Peters and Waterman (1982).
[8] Kanter (1983).
[9] O'Reilly and Pfeffer (2000).
[10] Hamel (2007).
[11] Toffler (1985).
[12] Senge (1990).
[13] De Geus (1997a).
[14] Ghoshal and Bartlett (1998).
[15] Ostroff (1999).
[16] Collins and Porras (1996).
[17] Foster and Kaplan (2001).
[18] Lawler and Worley (2006).
[19] Bower et al. (1991: ix).
[20] Hambrick (1989: 5).
[21] Tilles (1963: 112).
[22] Rumelt et al. (1991: 6).

INTRODUCING 'STRATEGIC LEADERSHIP, GOVERNANCE AND RENEWAL'
• STRATEGY, LEADERSHIP AND THE NEW AGENDA • THE CONTEXT OF
BUSINESS IN SOCIETY • COMPETITIVE ANALYSIS AND VALUE INNOVATION
• STRATEGIC INNOVATION IN THE MULTI-BUSINESS FIRM •
STRATEGIC PROCESSES – INNOVATION • STRATEGIC PROCESSES – TRANSFORMATION
AND RENEWAL • SOME FINAL THOUGHTS AND REFLECTIONS

2 strategy, leadership and the new agenda

Introduction

Strategy and leadership are often treated as synonymous in practice. Even in theory, strategy was long seen as the defining responsibility of the CEO. In contemporary strategic management, while strategy and leadership still belong together, it now makes sense for us to consider them as two separate, but related, concepts.

For a start, we no longer see the defining role of the CEO as master-strategist or expect a single mind to do all of the strategic thinking for our organisations. Since the 1980s, the strategy field has been giving more attention to the role of leadership in shaping the organisational context and culture within which compelling visions and creative strategies will emerge.[1] In Gary Hamel's (1998) colourful phrase, the 'strategy oven' in many organisations now extends way beyond the CEO and senior management. A second reason for viewing these two concepts as related, but distinct, is the need to examine leadership as a potential strategic variable in its own right.

So how strategic is leadership? How has the emphasis on leadership been changing in the strategy field over the last two decades and why? Are managers and leaders different? What is the link between leadership and corporate culture, and between corporate culture and competitiveness? What are the downsides to strong leadership and culture? These are the kind of questions that will occupy us in the early part of this chapter, and along with this analysis, we will offer a contextual perspective on the strategic leadership phenomenon. It seems clear to all by now that the early years of the new millennium have been a significant turning point for business and its role in society. In the later part of the chapter we look at this development in the light of the return to centre stage of corporate governance, comparing and contrasting the recent experiences on both sides of the Atlantic, along with the responses, both legislative and voluntary. We will also examine briefly the evergreen debate about whether or not the roles of the chairman and CEO should be separate. We end the chapter with a look at the new priorities emerging for corporate leaders in the early twenty-first century, as the call for a new industrial order gathers pace. Among the most urgent are the needs to restore integrity to the free market system and credibility in its business leadership, and to put the issues of 'sustainability' and 'corporate social responsibility' at the heart of the CEO's agenda.

Strategy and leadership

How distinctive an asset is Herb Kelleher to Southwest Airlines or Richard Branson to Virgin? More generally, what is the relative importance of strategy and leadership? To date, the success of Virgin would seem to be more attributable to leadership than strategy – the Virgin approach, as Branson once described it, is that they often do things and work out afterwards what the strategy was. In contrast, both unique leadership and superior strategy appear to be behind the success of Southwest Airlines.

Over the years, in the strategic management field, our perspective on the relative importance of these two variables has ebbed and flowed. Up to the 1980s, using the right framework and choosing the right strategy was seen to be much more important than having the right individual at the top. In fact, leadership was 'noticeably absent from writings on strategy, somehow passed over in favour of more techno-economic factors such as product life cycles, market share, experience curves, portfolio matrices, and industry analysis'.[2] The early findings of the PIMS (Profit Impact of Marketing Strategy) research reflected this view, indicating that aspects of business strategy, such as product quality and capital intensity, tended to account for most of the variation in business performance leaving relatively little to be explained by leadership.[3] Adding to the argument was a finding by Lieberson and O'Connor (1972) in the early 1970s that CEO succession seemed to have little impact on financial performance.

This view changed dramatically over the 1980–2000 period. The rapid rise to prominence of industry revolutionaries like CNN and Wal-Mart was one major influence. The spectacular turnaround of major corporations such as Chrysler and IBM was another. The unprecedented boost in shareholder value created in companies like Coca Cola and General Electric was a third. Big personalities, the likes of Ted Turner, Sam Walton, Lee Iaccoca, Lou Gestner, Roberto Goizueta and Jack Welch, had returned to dominate the corporate stage. Outstanding leadership was seen to be less about strategic acumen and more about the ability to rekindle the entrepreneurial flame within a company, raise its aspirations through big, hairy, audacious goals, and create high-spirited, high performance cultures.[4] Contemporary research reflected the shift. For example, Peters and Waterman (1982: 26) saw the role of the CEO as primarily concerned with managing 'the values of the organisation' and Schein (1997: 5) with 'creating and changing cultures'. Overall, as the well-known economist, John Kay, characterised it, this period marked a general shift away from an emphasis on centralised strategic planning to one of vision and leadership.[5]

Most recently, in the wake of the stock market bubble and major corporate scandals, the importance of strategy is once again coming to the fore. Excessive faith in leadership, and the excessive rewards that this gave rise to, are seen by many to have been part of the problem. Though the rate of change has not relented, we are once again as interested in the strategic logic governing market leadership as we are in the personalities that head the industry pacesetters. CEOs like Lee Scott (Wal-Mart), Sam Palmisano (IBM), Jeff Immelt (GE) and Neville Isdell (Coca Cola) neither have, nor seek, the level of public recognition enjoyed by their predecessors. The era of the charismatic 'celebrity' CEO is on the wane, and quieter, more self-effacing and 'authentic' leadership is back in vogue.[6]

What the history of the field has shown us is that strategy and leadership are both important. The most effective corporate visions are economically convincing and emotionally compelling. Strategic management is concerned with two fundamentals: commercial logic and human aspiration. Traditionally, strategy tends to emphasise the first, leadership the second. Throughout this book we will be exploring them both and how they inter-relate.

Leadership – what is it?

According to Tichy and Cohen (2002: 10): 'The scarcest resource in the world today is leadership talent'. Few would disagree. But where should we look for the essence of outstanding leadership – personality, style or process? After thousands of studies, the answers remain vague and incomplete. Even recent gurus point to different directions. Goleman (1998: 93) sees the *sine qua non* of leadership as emotional intelligence and Collins (2001) finds the secret recipe in a paradoxical mixture of personal humility and intense professional resolve, while George et al. (2007), and Goffee and Jones (2005), emphasise the central importance of learning how to discover your 'authentic self' and 'managing authenticity'.

Traits and styles – the early focus

The early attempts to understand the nature of leadership concentrated on personal traits and behaviours. Outstanding historical leaders, like Washington, Gandhi and Churchill, were typically compared in the hope of finding the distinguishing personal attributes of great leaders. The implicit theory was that leaders are born, not made. The results were largely inconclusive. Later, the needs of the modern corporation shifted the focus onto middle management, and the basic competencies of the many, rather than the outstanding traits of the few. Interest also turned away from attributes to style. Leadership research became preoccupied with trying to establish which of the two main styles – directive or participative – was the most effective. The subsequent finding that neither style was superior, but each worked best in different circumstances, led to the development of the situational leadership theories of Fiedler (1967), and others.

Situational leadership – is leadership a transferable asset?

In 1983, John Sculley made a high-profile move from Pepsi to Apple. Ten years later, Lou Gestner made a similar move from RJR Nabisco to IBM. The second of these worked out, the first one didn't. Such examples raise the question, how transferable is leadership effectiveness across firms and industries?

One of the earliest beliefs in the management field was that the skilled executive, with the right professional training, could be equally effective across a wide range of organisations and industries. It was a belief that helped to fuel the conglomerate growth of the 1960s and 1970s. It was also one that interested the early situational leadership theorists, and they were divided on the issue. Fiedler (1965: 155) believed in horses for courses, because it was 'surely easier to change almost anything in the job situation than a man's personality and his leadership style'. Others were convinced that leaders had a much wider capacity to vary their styles to the requirements of the situation.[7]

More recent research tends to support the view that individual leaders are unlikely to be equally effective across industries, companies or even strategies, and migration across firms and industries remains uncommon. In one of the most extensive studies ever carried out, involving 300 chief executives, it was found that only 10 per cent or so had come from outside their company, and less than 5 per cent from outside their industry.[8] Kotter (1982), in a more intensive study, confirmed this view. According to these studies, leadership effectiveness depends not only on generic skills but also on firm- and industry-specific knowledge and relationships developed over time. For former CEO of Citibank, John Reed, the essence of leadership boils down to two things: 'We decide what to do, and we try to make it happen'.[9] Kotter (1982) found that the key to both lay in the ability to define a strategic agenda over time and develop a network of supporting relationships to carry it through. Industry-specific knowledge and connections were both found to be valuable.

Strategic leadership as performance in the arena – a contextual view

Kotter's study was among the first to move leadership research from relatively static concerns with personal attributes to a more dynamic focus on how the leadership game is played in the wider arena. Person-focused leadership theories can work well at middle management level, where the emphasis is on team dynamics and generic interpersonal skills, and such theories tend to be well covered by most good textbooks on organisational behaviour. However, something more is needed at the strategic level, where CEOs often have to be able to inspire the hearts and minds of hundreds, even thousands, of followers with little, if any, opportunity for face-to-face interaction with most of them. We believe that leadership effectiveness at the institutional level can be better understood in terms of three main elements – the context for leadership, the conviction of the leader and the dynamics of credibility over time and tenure.[10]

Context – defining the opportunity

Leadership impact at the institutional level is always shaped by context. To paraphrase Marx, great leaders do make history, but not always in circumstances of their own choosing. Former US president Richard Nixon (1982: 2) proposed that the formula for placing any leader among the greats had three elements, 'a great man, a great country and a great issue'. Without the second two, potential greatness will remain unrecognised and unfulfilled. Churchill once said of a talented predecessor that he was unfortunate to have lived at a time of great men and small events. In contrast, what, we might wonder, would have become of Napoleon, had he been born in less revolutionary times? In the movies, an Oscar-winning performance often begins with securing the right role. This is a truth that extends beyond Hollywood.

In the business world, leadership roles tend to be shaped by corporate history and the context of the time. If General Electric had chosen Stan Gault to be CEO in 1981, and Jack Welch had gone to Rubbermaid, how would they both be viewed today? In many ways, over the years, Gault's performance as a transformational leader was just as impressive as Welch's,[11] but then Rubbermaid is 'off-Broadway' compared to the corporate theatre that is General Electric.

Business leaders typically play out one of three main roles: builders, revitalisers or inheritors. The first two offer the greatest opportunity to make a personal mark, whether through building great enterprises as Bill Gates did with Microsoft or Ted Turner with CNN, or revitalising formerly great companies, as Roberto Goizueta did at Coca Cola or Michael Eisner at Disney. In contrast, the contributions of skilful inheritors, like David Glass at Wal-Mart, tend to be seen as less dramatic, making it difficult for them to stand out or to be seen as charismatic.

Conviction – fuelling the performance

Getting the opportunity to make an impact is not the same as making one. The individual leader must still have the talent and credentials to meet the challenge and the conviction to rise to it.

At CEO level, imagination and drive are likely to distinguish outstanding performance more so than professional expertise, which might be taken as a given. Yet many categorisations of the energy and enterprise of great CEOs are too generic, and fail to uncover the deeper wellsprings of inspirational leadership, which are always context specific. Take the idea of leadership vision, for example. Without context, it is little more than image or fantasy. This is one reason why many corporate mission statements turn out to be so ineffective and to lack 'gut-grabbing' meaning, as *Built to Last* authors Collins and Porras (1996) have often argued. Leadership that truly inspires is deeply rooted in values, convictions and principles of a more transcendent nature.

For psychologist, Howard Gardner (1997), the essence of inspirational leadership lies in the ability to create and act out compelling stories, particularly stories of collective identity, which appeal to both reason and emotion. As Thurman Arnold once said: 'Unhappy is a people that has run out of words to describe what is happening to them' – to which John Gardner added when quoting him: 'Leaders find the words' (Gardner 1993: 18). Great enterprises, like Wal-Mart, are built on potent founding stories, embodied in larger-than-life characters like Sam Walton. Talented inheritors, like David Glass, keep the spirit alive and maintain its momentum. In their turn, great revitalisers reinterpret shared legacy and make it relevant to new and formidable challenges. For example, in the aftermath of the '9/11' terrorist attack, the world watched mayor Rudolph Giuliani brilliantly rediscover the spirit and resilience of the 'New Yorker' and articulate it in a new and compelling way that helped rally the city at a time of great uncertainty and distress. Likewise, during his twenty-year tenure as CEO, we saw Jack Welch reinterpret the spirit of General Electric and rekindle the American dream within that country's leading business institution. It was an accomplishment that helped reaffirm to the wider business world that entrepreneurial flair need not be lost with scale, in spite of much historical evidence to the contrary.[12]

Credibility – keeping the stakeholders on board

All great leaders recognise credibility as the dynamic currency of leadership, yet it rarely figures in traditional theories. In our view any theory of leadership at the institutional level has to concern itself with how credibility is created and destroyed over time. There are a number of reasons.

To begin with, credibility is where symbol and substance meet in strategic leadership effectiveness. Much of the debate over whether leadership is more style than substance tends to miss a key truth. As a case in point, consider the fascination that John F. Kennedy continues to hold for most Americans, in spite of the brevity of his time in office, modest legislative record and subsequent revelations about his personal life. Veteran Washington correspondent, Helen Thomas (2000: 298) considers him her favourite president above all that have come since because of the new spirit that he brought to the country during his brief tenure at the top: 'He understood the past and he cared about the future. After all, who else set a goal to land on the moon in a decade?' What the 'Camelot' presidency illustrates is how symbol and substance can work together to transforming effect. A leadership style and story that embodies confidence and hope is itself a powerful, energising force.

The flow of credibility also depends on performance in the arena, and leaders are continually trading in this currency throughout their tenures at the top. The traditional focus on attributes and styles has tended to make us too preoccupied with how leadership capacity varies from person to person. However, it is just as important to understand how it varies in any given individual over time. There is some research to show that leadership effectiveness over lengthy tenures follows a curve, rising to peak performance before sliding into steady decline.[13] New leaders, it seems, first tend to grow in the job, and gain in both effectiveness and credibility as they develop.[14] Later still, most tend to 'grow stale in the saddle'.[15] One reason is that they eventually succumb to the 'success disease'. As credibility grows, the line between confidence and hubris often becomes very thin, as Jack Welch discovered several times during his tenure as CEO of General Electric, most notably during the Kidder, Peabody and the Honeywell episodes, and also in his retirement. A further problem develops when executives reporting to the CEO begin to act like acolytes or courtiers, an ominous sign that credibility has shifted to credulousness and too much 'happy-talk' is dominating executive discussion. These are not easy realities for successful leaders to recognise, and few face up to them in a timely fashion. One that did was the former president of

Honda, Kiyoshi Kawashima, who decided to step down early from his leadership of the company when he found that his most senior people had taken to agreeing with him more than seventy-five per cent of the time.

At the other end of the spectrum, credibility can be lost from trying to move too quickly in advance of key constituencies. Jac Nasser's failed attempt to reinvent Ford Motors as a consumer services company, in the late 1990s, is a dramatic example. At the time of his appointment as CEO, Nasser had been widely seen as the best in the industry. Yet, 'somehow during the course of his tenure he managed to create a lack of trust among virtually every constituency', according to one of his board members at the time.[16] Other leaders lose their effectiveness over time because their spirits get tired or their stories get old. Thomas Jefferson once described the US presidency as a 'splendid misery', and no incumbent aged more quickly in office than Abraham Lincoln, one of the greatest. In ways not widely recognised in traditional theories, leadership is a consumable asset and top leadership takes its toll.

Even where great leaders manage to remain strong in body and spirit over lengthy tenures, few are able to reinvent themselves and their stories when the original version no longer excites and emboldens their would-be followers. Margaret Thatcher still felt she could go 'on and on' at the time her political career ended in tears and she had failed to recognise that her story had run its course. As a further example, Ken Olsen of Digital was lionised in the business press for more than twenty years, but arguably he undermined a great legacy by holding on to the top job too long. Jack Welch recognised this particular danger at General Electric when he told a forum of Asian business leaders in 1999 that he was 'not retiring because I am old and tired' but because 'an organisation has had twenty years of me' and has to 'renew itself'.[17] The former visionary of the modern Canon, Ryuzaburo Kaku, was another. Speaking at the height of his success, he recognised that 'when such time comes that I have to deny the past, I inevitably would have to step down'.[18]

The contextual view and related perspectives

Our view of leadership effectiveness as located in the dynamic interaction of leader, organisational history and context over time has close links with other perspectives. For example, it sits quite well with those who like to look at leadership as a performing art or take a 'leadership-as-drama' approach.[19] In many respects, it is closest to leadership theory in the public policy literature, as the earlier reference to the Nixon formula clearly indicates, and it also reflects the kind of perspective captured in the following cameo of Indira Gandhi by John Gardner (1993: 44): 'Of her leadership, one could say that the historical context provided the opportunity and her family background schooled her for the role, but finally it was her own inner strength that made her a major and controversial figure for over two decades'. While this kind of contextual perspective remains underdeveloped in the business literature, it is heartening to see the rising interest in it, as evidenced in the recent extensive study by Mayo and Nohria (2005) and their addition of phrases like 'zeitgeist leadership' and 'contextual intelligence' to our conceptual vocabulary. Furthermore, like the institutional theorists, we see context working in two ways – defining opportunity, but also shaping role expectations.[20] The presidencies of George Washington and George W. Bush were very different, not least because of the changes in role expectations that have evolved over the last two hundred years. Moreover, like Neustadt (1990: 83), we recognise that the 'moving factor' driving credibility is not so much the changing image of the leader as what the followers see as happening 'to themselves'. Credibility is rooted in leader–follower dynamics.

Leaders and managers – are they different?

In trying to understand leadership as a strategic variable in its own right, one question that is always provocative is whether managers and leaders are different. Some see this as an argument over semantics. Jack Welch certainly didn't. Acclaimed by Fortune Magazine in November 1999 as the twentieth century's 'Ultimate Manager', the accolade may not entirely have pleased him. As he once put it: 'I simply dislike the traits that have come to be associated with "managing"', and 'never associate passion with the word manager' yet have 'never seen a leader without it'.[21]

It is curious how the study of leadership in the public and private sectors has run along parallel tracks for most of its history. 'The field of leadership has two 800-pound gorillas that look a lot alike and even sound much the same, but for some peculiar reason the two lugs have never met'.[22] Much of the reason lies in the leader/manager distinction.

Traditionally, public policy focused more on leadership – the business sector on management. 'We must not confuse leadership with status', according to public leadership guru, John Gardner (1993: 2), 'the top-ranking person may simply be bureaucrat number 1'.

Up to the end of the 1970s, leadership and management were largely equated in the corporate world. 'Leadership as good management' was 'the industrial paradigm of leadership'.[23] The distinction may have mattered little at the height of the command-and-control era, and would not have bothered Reginald Jones as much as it later did his successor at General Electric. As the 1980s progressed, leadership became a 'fixation' in both the public and private arenas, particularly in the United States.[24] Corporate America was reeling from the onslaught of international competition, especially from the Japanese. At the same time, public life was suffering from the 'malaise' of the Carter era, and even the presidency itself seemed to have become unworkable. It was a context made for the re-emergence of charismatic leaders, such as Lee Iaccoca and Ronald Regan, offering fresh hope at a time of great distress, and it brought renewed interest in the distinction between managers and leaders.

So what distinguishes management from leadership? For Bennis and Nanus (1985: 21) they are largely different mindsets. The manager is focused on doing things right (efficiency), the leader on doing the right thing (effectiveness). Such a distinction was not lost on the hapless Lyndon Johnson, who once exclaimed at the height of his Vietnam troubles that it would have been easy to do the right thing, if only one knew what the right thing was. For Bennis and Nanus (1985: 21) the corporate malady of the 1980s was the result of too many firms being 'overmanaged and under-led' – though it might also be argued that the dot.com/Enron malady of the late 1990s was an example of the reverse pathology. For Kotter (1990), management and leadership are more than just different mindsets, they are also distinct systems of action; management focused on coping with complexity and leadership on coping with change. Schein (1997: 5) sees culture as the key: 'If one wishes to distinguish leadership from management or administration, one can argue that leaders create and change cultures, while managers and administrators live within them'.

The most provocative contrast is that of Abraham Zaleznik (1977, 1992), who first opened the debate in a Harvard Business Review classic.

According to him, leaders and managers are fundamentally different personality types, and the former have more in common with artists and other creative thinkers than they do with the latter. For him, a crucial difference lies in the conceptions that they hold deep in their psyches of chaos and order:

> Leaders tolerate chaos and lack of structure and are thus prepared to keep answers in suspense, avoiding premature closure on important issues. Managers seek order and control and are almost compulsively addicted to disposing of problems even before they understand their potential significance. (Zaleznik 1992: 131)

Zaleznik's leaders are typically 'twice-born' personalities, stamped by early defining experiences, and their professional lives are often marked by a profound sense of separateness and the struggle for personal mastery. They tend to work from high-risk positions, relate to people through ideas rather than roles, and seek to harness the aggression in themselves and others rather than try to repress or deny it. In contrast, the managerial personality tends to develop through socialisation and become well adapted to the mores of organisational life. Steady stewardship and the preservation of good social relations tend to take precedence over the struggle for psychological and social change. It is not too hard to find the likes of Steve Jobs, Jack Welch or Richard Branson in the first of these categories. However, Zaleznik offered Alfred Sloan as archetypical of the managerial personality. That Sloan, who is generally recognised as one of the great strategists in the history of the automobile industry, can be said to be a manager but not a leader is the kind of assertion that continues to lend real edge to this debate.

One of the most interesting perspectives on this debate has been provided by James McGregor Burns (1978) in the public policy literature. Burns drew a distinction between two types of leadership, transactional and transformational, based on two different types of exchange relationship with followers. Transactional leadership is the most common type found in organisational life. It is rooted in a direct exchange relationship between leader and follower, and is relatively independent of history and context. Transactional leadership motivates by means of concrete exchanges, economic (salary/promotion) or psychological (mutual loyalty/respect), which are characteristic of the management process at all levels. Transformational leadership, on the other hand, operates out of deeply held personal value systems that cannot be negotiated or exchanged. Where transactional leadership induces, transformational leadership inspires. Transformational leadership reaches out beyond the immediacy of face-to-face interaction to infuse entire organisations with a collective sense of mission and purpose. For many, there are clear parallels with the Zaleznik perspective. Transactional and transformational leaders 'are qualitatively different kinds of individuals who construct reality in markedly different ways'.[25]

Leadership and corporate culture

Transformational leadership and corporate culture are inextricably linked, and it is no coincidence that interest in both has flourished since the early 1980s. Transformational leadership deals primarily with questions of values and identity, the central elements of corporate culture. Together, these concepts have brought the people dimension back to centre stage in what Ebers (1985) has characterised as the new 'Romanticism' in organisation studies. They have also brought a distinct break with the traditional strategic management model, drawing attention to the enormous under-utilisation of talent that had prevailed under the strategy-structure-systems approach, which gave too much primacy to control.[26] The traditional approach spoke to the needs of the business, not to the needs of people.[27] High-spirited, high performance companies, like Wal-Mart, Virgin, IKEA, Nokia, Honda, eBay, Google and many others, have shown just how competitive companies can become when they put the needs of people first.

Institutionalising founding charisma – corporate culture

What will happen to the Virgin spirit when Branson moves on? What will happen to the 'IKEA-Way' after Igvar Kamprad? How can such organisations keep the dynamic alive beyond the tenures of charismatic founders? Even during a founder's tenure such 'vibrant, almost cult-like', organisations often have to work hard to maintain their 'sparkle' in the face of the pressure for formalisation that comes with rapid growth.[28] For example, in 2003 IKEA had grown to over 70,000 employees worldwide, 20,000 of them with the company less than a year due to both expansion and attrition.[29] Today the employee total is over 90,000.

Notwithstanding the challenges, however, there are now many examples of organisations that seem to have successfully institutionalised their visionary capability, values-orientation and compelling sense of mission across a wide range of industry and national contexts.[30] They are typically characterised by enduring guiding philosophies derived from their entrepreneurial founders. Sometimes these are written down, but more often than not, like the 'H-P Way' at Hewlett-Packard, they just seem to be 'built in and understood', as Bill Hewlett himself once described it.[31] Likewise, the 'spirit of Hondaism' is seen to be open to many interpretations, not simply reducible to a fixed set of rules.[32] At Herman Miller, the award-winning furniture company, 'a very diverse group of individuals' is seen to share 'a set of common values', the roots of which may 'differ from person to person', but the 'spoken and understood expressions of it are remarkably coherent'.[33]

Within such companies, the leadership process itself is often perceived primarily in cultural terms. 'The first responsibility of a leader is to define reality', says Max de Pree (1989: 11), the former CEO of Herman Miller. 'One of my goals has been to create the most fun workplace since the Industrial Revolution', says Dennis Bakke of AES (formerly Applied Energy Services), adding that he and his co-founder, Roger Sant, also set out ' to elevate people's behaviour at work to a higher plane'.[34] A primary focus for CEO Meg Whitman is developing the work ethic and culture of eBay as a fun, open, trusting environment.[35] As O'Reilly and Pfeffer (2000: 244) put it, the leaders of companies such as these 'see their roles not as managing the day-to-day business or even making decisions about grand strategy but as setting and reinforcing the vision, values and culture of the organisation'.

Competing for hearts and minds – is culture a source of sustainable advantage?[36]

Companies like Virgin, Wal-Mart and IKEA all succeeded in spite of being late entrants into mature markets with no clear location or factor advantages. The common formula that seems to link them is rooted in corporate culture and reflects the capacity to achieve 'extraordinary results with ordinary people'.[37] How do such companies secure sustainable competitive advantage primarily through corporate culture?

Enhancing differentiation – the difference is culture

Michael Porter (1980, 1985) outlines two primary routes to competitive advantage, cost leadership and differentiation. By definition, most companies have to seek their fortunes through the second option. According to Porter (1985: 120), differentiation 'cannot be understood by viewing the firm in aggregate, but stems from the specific activities a firm performs and how they affect the buyer'. In our view, this value chain approach to differentiation is too reductive and provides just part of the picture. It gives us valuable insight into the anatomy of differentiation, but not so much into its physiology or psychology (to draw on the analogy used by Bartlett and Ghoshal (1990) in a related context). The corporate culture perspective helps to complete the picture. Strong culture companies seek to differentiate themselves not only through their discrete activities but also more fundamentally through their corporate identities.[38]

A good example, in its heyday, was The Body Shop. The Body Shop at its foundation did more than focus on a number of discrete activities in the value chain where it could differentiate itself most from the market incumbents. It set out to be a totally different kind of company. As Anita Roddick explained: 'It turned out that my instinctive trading values were dramatically opposed to the standard practices in cosmetics industry', so she looked at what the industry leaders were doing and walked 'in the opposite direction'.[39] Underlining this philosophy, the staff and franchisees were deliberately recruited by unconventional methods from unconventional sources. Previous experience in the cosmetics industry was definitely not a recommendation, nor was a conventional education. Her outlook was that she could train almost anybody to run a Body Shop, but what she could not influence was the soul. Her company prided itself on the 'feminine principles' that underpinned its distinctive business practices in a traditionally male-dominated industry, and she saw the customer's belief in The Body Shop's 'covert understanding of women' as its 'extraordinary edge'.

The case of the Body Shop is not unique. Many impressive differentiators have deliberately dared to be different in everything, and defined themselves by challenging the prevailing norms, recipes and conventions of their industries at the time of entry. For example, the maverick founders of Honda had set out to build an organisation that 'was different from others in Japan, or anywhere else', a technology-driven company that would always be a pioneer, never a follower.[40] Likewise, at CNN, Ted Turner set out to create a different kind of news organisation, vowing to 'do news like the world has never seen news before', building his dream around the talents of 'three renegades from independent television', breaking new ground in creating an open newsroom environment more akin to a 1930s newspaper city desk, and training fresh young talent to be 'video-journalists', a new type of news professional.[41] The founding vision at AES was very similar, as Dennis Bakke described it: 'We knew that we wanted to create a very different kind of company, that's for sure – The actual type of business wasn't really important, to tell you the truth'.[42] Perhaps nowhere is this spirit more epitomised than in the case of Virgin, which in industry after industry, has shaken up the established order with a different kind of business model and company culture. As Branson (1998: 444) has put it: 'Virgin is not a big company – it's a big brand made up of lots of small companies. Our priorities are the opposite of our large competitors'.

Time and again, when leaders such as Richard Branson or Dennis Bakke have been asked what makes their companies different, their answer is the people. 'The core thing is absolutely and utterly the people', Branson believes, and 'if those people are proud of the company they work for, if they respect it and are listened to, the company will thrive'.[43] Are there 'Virgin people' or 'AES people'? Yes, they believe, but in the sense of kindred spirits, not stereotypes. As Dennis Bakke of AES has stressed: 'Hiring the right people is essential. The whole system would fall apart if we didn't have a lot of people who were passionately excited by our values'.[44] Fitting in to the culture is also the key requirement at Virgin. 'We want people with a clear idea of why they want to be with us, who don't beat around the bush when it comes to expressing a vision they might have. The organisation doesn't like 'yes' people or political people', according to Will Whitehorn, Group Director of Corporate

Affairs.[45] Putting personality and values before diplomas is a common theme. Soichiro Honda took the view that 'if a theory led you to an invention, all schoolteachers would be inventors',[46] so he built his company on the technical talents of mavericks like himself who shared his passion for engines. Likewise, CNN was built upon the dreams of nearly one hundred 'wildly enthusiastic, totally inexperienced young collegians' who had to be converted into video-journalists almost overnight.[47] Such companies achieve extraordinary results from ordinary people not least because they are willing to trust them with extraordinary opportunities. 'At any other company I'd have to have an engineering degree to do my job. Who'd have thought I'd end up where I am today?' says former forklift driver, Tommy Brooks of AES.[48] His story is not untypical.

Strengthening corporate identity – competing for share of hearts and minds

Companies that differentiate themselves on culture tend to market themselves through corporate identity. 'Customers must prefer our products because they bear the name of Canon', said the company's former president, Ryuzaburo Kaku.[49] Those that are generally most effective in winning the hearts and minds of consumers typically see themselves as identified by an idealism and spirit of adventure that goes beyond the profit motive.

At Virgin, for example, Richard Branson has long believed that 'if you do something for fun and create the best product, then the profit will come'.[50] Many strong corporate identities have been built on similar values-first philosophies over the years. In the early 1950s, George Merck explained his company's stance to a public gathering in the following way: 'We try never to forget that medicine is for the people. It is not for profits. The profits follow, and if we remember that, they have never failed to appear'.[51] IKEA was also founded on a clear consumer-oriented mission. As Ingvar Kamprad once explained: 'Too many new and beautifully designed products can be afforded by only a small group of better-off people', so 'IKEA's aim is to change this situation' and in doing so 'make a valuable contribution to the democratisation process at home and abroad'.[52] A similar sense of purpose propelled The Body Shop through its formative years, a sense of mission in which trade was to be pursued not just for profit, but as 'an instrument for change for the better'.[53]

Such a renaissance spirit is not confined to companies in consumer products. It is also to be seen in many of the great differentiators in more industrial markets. Boeing continues to push the passenger aviation envelope with products like the 767 first and foremost 'because we're Boeing'.[54] This pioneering spirit has always been fundamental to the company's identity. As former CEO Bill Allen said when the company launched the breakthrough 707 back in the 1950s: 'Boeing is always reaching out for tomorrow' with people 'who live, breathe, eat and sleep what they are doing'.[55] The same kind of spirit is to be found in Schlumberger, technology leader in the oil field services industry. As once explained by the late Jean Riboud, former CEO and keeper of the company's spiritual flame for over twenty years, 'if we lose the drive and fear searching for new technologies or fear taking incredible gambles on new managers', then 'we will become an establishment' and go into decline.[56]

Generating a trust premium – promoting inclusive capitalism

Companies that are most successful at leveraging strong corporate identities in the marketplace tend to create an identity of interests among their key constituents, customers, employees, suppliers and shareholders. More often than not this reflects a deep commitment to a more inclusive form of capitalism than is yet the norm in most Western enterprises. It begins with a genuine commitment to create value for customers, and it extends to sharing the surplus among all of the stakeholders, not just the shareholders. The approach is not new. For example, in the Johnson and Johnson 'Credo', the statement of corporate values first drawn up in 1943 (Collins and Porras 1996: 59), the company specifies its commitment to its major stakeholders in the following order: customers, employees, community and shareholders; and the company showed that this was a lived philosophy during the Tylenol crisis in 1982. A similar ordering of priorities typifies most values-led organisations today, like Virgin, AES, Federal Express, eBay and many others.

Companies that can successfully position themselves in the hearts and minds of their customers based on clearly held values of inclusive capitalism tend to enjoy a 'trust premium' with all of their key constituencies, the economic benefits of which are becoming increasingly recognised.[57] As Rutledge (1997: 73) sees it: 'A good reputation counts for more than a smart strategy or clever tactics', and can give a company considerable, difficult-to-imitate, advantage in the marketplace.

This is the kind of trust premium that has long been enjoyed by Marks & Spencer, and one that is helping the company make a strong recovery from its recent woes. From the start, Marks & Spencer set out to create a strong identity of interests among its key constituencies, and its early commitment to fostering good long-term relationships with all of them was way ahead of its time. The company's founders set out to build their business on three great assets: the goodwill and confidence of the public, the loyalty and devotion of management and staff throughout the system and the confidence and cooperation of suppliers. These three great assets, the 'social capital' of Marks & Spencer, helped the company to fulfil its economic mission of providing high quality, well-designed merchandise at prices that few competitors could match, and do so with unparalleled success for many decades. Everything about the company's behaviour towards its major constituencies, including staff and suppliers, was seen to be consonant with its stated philosophy. The powerful message coming over to its customers was that 'we never exploit our staff or our suppliers, and we won't exploit you'.

A further strategic benefit of strong corporate identity is the opportunity it creates for brand extension. The trust premium that Marks & Spencer has long enjoyed with the general public in Britain has allowed the company to extend its operations into new commercial areas like financial services. Robert Colville, director of financial services at the time of the initiative, explained the rationale: 'It is not so much the Marks & Spencer label as it is the Marks & Spencer culture. The public trusts Marks & Spencer and co-owns the culture. They believe that we are straight and fair dealers'.[58] The same kind of trust premium has also allowed the Virgin brand to be extended to so many diverse markets, and at a fraction of the investment that companies with weaker cultures and identities would have to face. It also operates to great effect in eBay, the online auction market leader.

Potential pitfalls of 'strong' leadership and culture

While value-rich leadership and corporate culture can be potent sources of superior economic performance, they have their limitations, dangers, dark sides and potential excesses.

In the first instance, it is important to recognise clearly what it is about culture that is most strategic. As Barney (1986) points out, for corporate culture to be a source of sustainable competitive advantage, it must be valuable, rare and difficult to imitate. Some in the literature claim 'that there is nothing magical or elusive about corporate culture', and that norms promoting or impeding desired behaviours can be readily established and changed.[59] However, prescriptions based on such an instrumental view (culture as something that organisations *have*), because they focus on the more imitable aspects of culture, can, at best, only help weaker companies to close a performance gap. A more interpretative view of culture (as something that organisations *are*) sees the elements that are true sources of sustainable competitive advantage in organisations as deeply layered in the 'unique circumstances of their founding', the 'unique personalities of their founders' and the 'unique circumstances of their growth', since history defies easy imitation.[60]

Value-rich leadership and culture also have their dangers. As mentioned earlier, hubris, or what Miller (1990) has called the Icarus Paradox, is one of the biggest. The more successful leaders and their organisations become, the more invincible they are likely to feel, the more inward-looking they tend to get and the more resistant to change they become – which is often the source of their ultimate downfall.

Enron is the outstanding example in recent times, and a particularly sobering one for all of us in the business world, executives and academics alike. Before the fall, Enron had been acclaimed by Fortune Magazine as America's most innovative company for an unprecedented six years in a row (1996–2001), and CEO Ken Lay had been honoured with a Lifetime Achievement Award in 1998 for his 'unmatched vision, strategy and courage' in the energy industry. Enron featured as an exemplar in most of the leading strategy books around the turn of the millennium, including Hamel's (2000a) *Leading the Revolution*, Michaels et al. (2001) *The War for Talent*, Foster and Kaplan's (2001) *Creative Destruction* and

Kurtzman and Rifkin's (2001) *From GE to Enron: Lessons on How to Rule the Web*. Jeff Skillings, Lay's chosen successor as CEO, was a Harvard and McKinsey alumnus, and the company was teeming with talented MBAs from prestigious business schools. There are many reasons for a collapse as spectacular and shocking as Enron, but the 'common theme is hubris, an overweening pride, which led people to believe they can handle increasingly exotic risk without danger'.[61] There were too many leading, too few managing, and empowerment was out of control. By the end the writing was literally on the wall – 'THE WORLD'S LEADING COMPANY' was the self-congratulatory proclamation dominating the Enron lobby at the time that the whole edifice began to crumble.

What creates such hubris is still 'very much an enigma'.[62] Halting the slide into hubris has often called forth some imaginative and dramatic approaches. For example, in 1959, Akio Morita, the charismatic co-founder of Sony, hired a brash young opera singer, Norio Ohga, in order to push his engineers beyond their comfort zones in the search for higher fidelity technologies, and then later groomed him for succession.[63] At Schlumberger, the enigmatic Claude Baks, with no official title for thirty-five years, was given right of access to any meeting with the sole purpose of forcing people to think and help prevent the company 'from becoming an establishment'.[64] In the world of antiquity, absolute monarchs had their sage-fools to remind them of their vanities and human frailties.

At its best, strong corporate culture provides a level of engagement and social cohesion that generates extraordinary results from ordinary people. However, such cultures also tend to create their own pathologies over time. For example, they become resistant to change, even in the face of clear and urgent need for renewal.[65] Furthermore, the same forces that foster cultural cohesion can also inhibit innovation, leading too readily to 'groupthink and a pressure to conform to the dominant view'.[66] Cultural homogeneity is reinforced by recruitment and promotion policies. Promotion from within tends to be the norm, with recruitment confined mainly to entry-level positions. Many applicants self-select, and new recruits are often young, inexperienced and at their most malleable. New hires that fail to respond to the early indoctrination-through-socialisation process typically do not stay long. As one employee of Marks & Spencer once observed, 'you have to receive your inoculation', and 'if you get a violent reaction, you'd better go'.[67] Strong culture organisations tend not to embrace the diversity of talent and outlook that many see as key to continuous innovation and renewal, so that 'what could be a rainbow' risks becoming 'monotonously monochromatic'.[68]

Furthermore, value-rich leadership and culture are very powerful influences that have insidious potential if abused. They tend to encourage the kind of emotional identification traditionally reserved for faith or country, so that lay-offs can be shattering as the 'Black Friday' episode at Coca Cola in 1957, for example, demonstrates.[69] They also represent the most covert face of power, the power to control another person's definition of reality and their world-view.[70] How far can charismatic leaders and their organisations be trusted with such power? Some radical theorists warn us that 'the social construction of reality should never be regarded as a disinterested affair',[71] and ask us to reflect on how the meanings that attach to words like 'strategy' and 'leadership' in our prevailing culture have been shaped to serve the interests of a greedy elite.[72] Others encourage us to remain quite sceptical about the 'liberation through submission' promise often implicit in charisma and culture.[73] Some have gone so far as to characterise the notion of charismatic leadership as an 'alienating social myth' that de-skills followers, both intellectually and emotionally, by fostering unhealthy dependency and uncritical devotion.[74]

We do well to remember that great achievements often spring from the most venal of motives, and that visionary leaders are rarely paragons of either virtue or emotional maturity. Many are the antithesis of the well-rounded, emotionally intelligent personality that is often the implied ideal in much of the management literature.[75] Some have even been at their most compelling when they were sailing close to the edge. For example, it is public knowledge, that Ted Turner was suffering from manic-depression at the height of the CNN adventure, but would there have been the same adventure without the psychosis? According to Maccoby (2000: 72–5), most charismatic leaders are narcissists, with both productive and pathological tendencies. Narcissists tend to 'have compelling, even gripping, visions for companies' that attract a following, and 'crave empathy from others' while they are 'not noted for being particularly empathetic themselves'. They can also be 'brutally exploitative', tend to 'have few regrets', and are prey to over-reaching, hubris and self-destruction. Steve Jobs, in his first time around at Apple, is the classic example. Former colleagues remember him as a leader with whom 'the highs were unbelievable but the lows were unimaginable'.[76]

In these days of widespread rhetoric about company devotion to its people, it is important to recognise that fear remains a very powerful motivator in organisational life and an important dimension of charisma.[77] Talented people in many of today's organisations continue to be stimulated to out-of-their-skin performances by psychologically abusive leaders who mess with their minds and play games with their egos.[78] It is also wise to note that the spirit that mobilises visionary organisations to high performance may not always reflect the brighter side of the human experience. At one point in their long-standing rivalry, when its competitor declared its intention to take over industry leadership in motorcycles, Honda set itself on a revenge mission to 'crush, squash and slaughter Yamaha'. It was hardly the most spiritually uplifting, but it certainly was emotionally compelling, and in the end devastatingly effective, forcing Yamaha into a humiliating retreat.

Strategy and organisation in a 'leadership culture'

Before concluding on leadership and culture, let us return again briefly to the Zaleznik perspective on leaders and managers, because of the wider implications it has for strategy and organisation. In his classic article, Zaleznik (1977) did not just claim that leaders and managers are different in psychological make-up. He also suggested that the kind of organisational culture that tends to evolve around them is also different in quite profound ways. In many respects, what we have seen happening over the last twenty years has been a dramatic shift away from the managerial culture to the leadership culture in both strategic management theory and practice.

How do these cultures differ? Below, we develop indicative profiles, guided by the literature, that show the contrasting tendencies of the two cultures in terms of strategy, organisation and mindset (see Table 2.1). The inherent tension between two tendencies is the dynamic that now lies at the heart of strategy and leadership in most organisations today.

Table 2.1 **Managerial culture versus leadership culture**

Managerial culture	Leadership culture
Ideology	
Rational	*Romantic*
Strategy	
Analytical	*Adventurous*
Necessity	Challenge
Fact-driven	Values-driven
Convincing argument	Compelling story
(Guru: Michael Porter)	(Guru: Gary Hamel)
Organisation	
Machine	*Living system*
Contractual	Communitarian
Instrumental	Moral
Hierarchy	Network
Centralised	Decentralised
Self-regulating	Self-renewing
Mindset	
Mr Spock	*Capt. Kirk*
Logical	Intuitive
Efficient	Enterprising
Adaptive	Inventive
Composed	Edgy
Solutions	Fulfilment
(GE in the 60s/70s)	(GE in the 80s/90s/00s)

Source: Adapted from Leavy (2003b)

The key features of the managerial culture are well known from traditional theory and practice, and this was the prevalent culture in Western business up to the early 1980s. It is one with its deepest philosophical roots in the rationalism of Locke and Hume. It emphasises the analytical in its approach to strategy development, defining its goals mainly from business necessities, and relies on convincing, fact-based, argument to bring people on board. It sees the organisation as a commercial machine, contractual in nature, instrumental in purpose, hierarchical in structure, centralised in decision-making and self-regulating in operation. It is a culture personified by the Star Trek character, Mr Spock, logical, efficient and adaptive, and one that prides itself on its capacity to solve business problems in a composed and confident manner.

In contrast, the key features of the leadership culture have really only come into full relief in the Western business theory and practice over the last twenty years.[79] Its philosophical roots are in the romanticism of Rousseau and Wordsworth. It is a culture that puts more emphasis on the adventurous in its reach for the future, developing compelling strategic narratives that are emotionally engaging as well as intellectually exciting.[80] The organisation is seen as strategic in its own right and viewed as a living system, communitarian in nature, moral in purpose, networked in structure, decentralised in decision-making and self-renewing in operation. It is a culture personified by Captain Kirk, intuitive, enterprising and inventive, one with edge and attitude, primarily concerned with the fulfilment of human potential.

Around the time that General Electric was replacing 'a legend with a live wire', as *The Wall Street Journal* described the Jones-to-Welch handover, Western business began a long transition from the managerial to the leadership end of the spectrum, a transition that was to be played out in full relief with the GE itself, a process we will examine more closely in a later chapter. The period up to1980 was strongly underpinned by the rational perspective. By the early 1960s, the modern corporation was already being seen as the major instrument of social and economic progress in most developed economies. Organisation rather than individual flair was believed to be the crucial determinant of long-run success. Business schools were founded in the expectation that management could be developed as a science. The dominant metaphor for the organisation itself was the efficient machine. Each part was replaceable, even the top leadership, with minimum disruption to its overall functioning. The concept of strategic planning was introduced to help institutionalise the entrepreneurial process, so that it was no longer seen to depend on the ephemeral imagination, intuition and flair of the gifted individual. Strategy was largely seen as a problem of market and product positioning. The sharpest analysts with the most penetrating understanding of the underlying rules of the game seemed best set to achieve and sustain superior corporate performance. Strategy making was largely conceptual. Tools and techniques predominated. Management and organisation were about disciplined execution.

The early 1980s brought the beginning of a new romantic era in reaction to the excesses of the rational era. The managerial culture was seen to have taken all the emotional engagement out of business, resulting in the chronic under-utilisation of human potential. The overall picture, as summed up by Anita Roddick of The Body Shop, was one of 'huge corporations dying of boredom caused by the inertia of giantism', full of 'tired executives in tired systems' whose 'only sense of adventure is in their profit-and-loss sheets'.[81] The tendency of the bureaucratic organisation to substitute means for ends became very pronounced in the case of many formal strategic planning systems. They seemed to demand more and more data and form filling, often resulting in paralysis by analysis, and too often becoming the passion-killer of the business.

The romantic era brought new excitement into this pretty colourless scene, charismatic leaders with big, hairy, audacious goals, 'democratising' the strategy process, rekindling the entrepreneurial flame, empowering functionaries to be businesspeople, rewarding talent and contribution and building high-spirited communities. However, in the years since the Enron scandal, we have become more aware of the pathologies of romantic excess and irrational exuberance, when faith becomes blind, image dominant, logic abandoned, discipline ridiculed and sceptics marginalised. Enron demonstrated these pathologies at their most extreme, but many of the exemplars of the romantic era untouched by scandal, such as The Body Shop and AES, have since returned to some of the more traditional management practices and skills in order to secure their future commercial prospects. Furthermore, the excessive faith in leadership and charisma that characterised the romantic era is now coming home to roost, as evident in the alarming rise in CEO turnover since the late 1990s.[82]

What this short history shows is the duality at the core of strategic management: its rational and romantic nature.[83] In our view, strategic management should be viewed as a humanity as well as a science. We need to see it encompassing spirit and emotion, as well as intellect and technology. While the central concerns of strategic management are changing over time, its essence remains the generation of a sense of confidence, stability and direction in the face of uncertainty and change. Strategic leaders need to be able to do this with all the rational-economic logic and strategy technology that they can muster. They must also strive to do it with a sense of purpose and adventure, if they are to fulfil the human potential at their disposal. The rational Mr Spock and the romantic Captain Kirk are both needed on the bridge of the modern enterprise. This is the kind of perspective on strategy and leadership that we are aiming to foster and develop throughout this book.

Strategic leadership in the twenty-first century – A new agenda

If the 1980s and 1990s saw a much needed re-infusion of the adventurous spirit into the strategic management field, the first decade of the 2000s has so far brought a fresh dose of realism back into the picture, particularly in the wake of the Enron and other corporate scandals, as we have noted earlier. This has been accompanied by renewed interest in corporate governance, bringing back to centre stage the relationship between a company's leadership and the board, where a similar balancing act must also be performed between the entrepreneurial and stewardship functions.

Corporate governance and its return to centre stage

We don't need to confine ourselves to modern business examples to deepen our understanding of the key issues at the heart of the governance challenge. Indeed, some of the most insightful examples can be drawn from history and from other domains. One such can be seen in the evolution of the early Christian church, where in the middle decade of the first century AD, St Paul found himself having to grapple with two rival ethnic groups among the early disciples in Rome – the Judeans and the Greeks – as he struggled to forge a more unified Christian identity. His New Testament letter to the Romans concerns the reconciliation of this internal ethnic conflict and the significant governance problems it presented for the early Church, whose unified spiritual vision and identity were in danger of being terminally damaged by serious infighting. Drawing on social identity theory for insight, Esler (2003: 242) asserts that

> " Paul emerges as a skilled entrepreneur of identity. Within a broad framework of seeking to make more secure the super ordinate category of Christ-follower in relation to sub-categories of Israelite and Greek in the Roman congregations, he pushes the Israelite sub-group ... in a certain direction by reminding them who they are and the historical path that got them there.[84]

Paul was operating in a context of Roman imperialism. At the time, the empire stretched from present-day England, across the Mediterranean to the Nile hinterland and came with its own legal jurisdiction and military might. This context, the ethnic infighting, the potential for excessive behaviours and the general governance issue that Paul faced in establishing the Church in Rome, destined to grow into the largest multinational organisation on earth, are echoed in contemporary business contexts and boardrooms.

Governance in the contemporary era[85]

Corporate governance is the process of serious decision-taking at the controlling heart of an organisation. For most practical purposes, this means the board and the CEO are the ultimate arbiters. Over the course of history, significant shifts have taken place in the balance of corporate ownership, and thus in the structure and composition of boards. In the early experience of joint stock companies,[86] such as that in sixteenth century Florence or in the East India Companies of the late seventeenth century, wealthy individuals made up the majority of shareholders and stock was traded on open markets. Over time, shares increasingly became consolidated in the hands of institutions, such as large pension funds, and the effects were to be seen in significant changes in the composition and behaviour of corporate boards. Where previously, boards had been chosen by key shareholders, whose prudence and hands-on monitoring provided valuable 'checks and balances', the tendency of the large institutions was to shift their investments when CEOs were not performing and the cost of dismissing them was high. As shareholders were becoming more passive in their stewardship, the composition of boards became increasingly incestuous, with 'cronyism' widespread.

These developments have come at a price. Recent research shows that responsive governance can generate up to 8.5 per cent higher returns than management autocracies,[87] while McKinsey (2002) in a global survey found that investors are prepared to pay a premium for well-governed companies, up to 40 per cent in weakly regulated markets, such as Russia or Morocco. But, governance is a complex affair with observation, litigation and academic analysis concentrating on the board's role and composition; the appointment, responsibilities and accountability of directors;

the proportion of executive to non-executive directors; board structures; the combined role of board chair and CEO; internal controls, financial disclosure; and transparency versus the loss of strategic intelligence. Importantly, not all these aspects have been linked to superior performance.

Much of the discussion on governance has surrounded commercial organisations and competing theories are offered as explanation. One is 'agency' theory. This sees the governance issue in terms of the relationship between the principals (the shareholders) and the agents (professional managers) to whom the running of the company is entrusted. Protocols are needed to help keep the latter's interests sufficiently in line with those of the former.[88] Usually, compensatory schemes, good structures and legal penalties are enough to protect shareholder interests,[89] including the policies of balancing executive interests on the board with independent, non-executive presence, and separating the roles of chairman and CEO to diffuse power. An alternative is 'stewardship' theory, in which the relationship between executives and principals is viewed in terms of shared goals and collective identity.[90] It applies most readily to the organisations in the not-for-profit sector, but also to commercial firms where there are strong relational connections, or close demographic and social ties between the CEO and the owners, such as family and/or local companies.

These two competing theories present a spectrum, with lots of variation in the balance between the agency and stewardship orientations to be found in practice. There is no clear evidence to suggest that either one is directly linked to superior financial returns. Lately, all variants have been subject to heavy scrutiny due to recent corporate scandals and shocking evidence of executive excess.

Board behaviour – What went wrong?

What gives rise to such behaviour? How do former pillars of the community, like lay preacher Ken Lay, or the shining alumni of some of our most prestigious business schools and management consultancies, like Jeff Skillings, end up going so far off the rails? How much of it is personal, and how much of it is social and systemic? Four theories of group action can help us to find some answers. First is the psychological concept of 'risky-shift', which helps explains why individuals are quite prepared to make decisions in group settings that they would never make acting alone. According to this theory the answer lies in the perception that they are sharing the risk and are willing therefore to take on more of it. The second is 'group polarisation' where people who participate in intense dialogue can often come away with views much more extreme than those they begin with, and so become more willing to endorse riskier strategic actions or tactics.

The third theory is 'group think'.[91] This is where people working in a group tend to become over-adapted to each others' ways of thinking over long periods of working together, and the deviant thought and deviant thinker eventually lose their influence. Many believe this explains the reluctance or inability of the Bush Administration to correctly interpret information on Iraq's weapons of mass destruction in the run up to the invasion in 2003. The fourth theory, de-individuation, concerns the submersion of one's own identity to a group or institution, the effects of which are most dramatically illustrated in the Waco and Jonestown tragedies, though such cult-like behaviour is also to be found in the corporate boardroom.

How far then are the recent corporate scandals, such as Enron, products of particular actors in particular companies at a particular point in time, and how far can we attribute them to some underlying weaknesses in our overall approach to corporate governance? What have we been doing since to turn this situation around? It is interesting to compare recent experience in both the UK and America. When we delve into what went wrong, the reasons seem to be many and varied, but soft signals of impending crisis had been around for nearly two decades in both countries. Their relative experiences and customs have led to different philosophical approaches in dealing with the governance challenge, more principles-based in the UK and rules-based in the United States.

The UK experience – recent corporate scandals and the response

In October 1990, Polly Peck, one of the UK's top public companies with net assets of £845 million and 17,227 employees, collapsed. Insolvency experts from Coopers and Lybrand and Touche Ross were appointed joint administrators, but at the time they failed to reveal the labyrinthine links they already had with Polly Peck through various consultancy, auditing, shareholding and advising ties into the company, its offshore activities and its flamboyant chairman, Asil Nadir. This public non-compliance with the code of practice of the Institute of Chartered Accountants in England and Wales (ICAEW) sparked no action from the professional body until it was forced by public and political pressure to hold an inquiry. It did so behind closed doors and imposed meagre sanctions on the Coopers and Lybrand directors involved.

In the wake of this incident and a further one at Coloroll, the Cadbury Committee was established in May 1991 in response to growing concern in the financial sector over the low level of confidence in financial reporting and the conduct and power of auditors. The suspicion was that accounting standards were loose, directors were not reviewing the controls in their business systematically and auditors were not standing up to their clients due to the intensity of the competition in their own industry. The Committee was chartered to investigate the accountability of UK corporate boards to their shareholders and broader stakeholders.

No sooner had the Committee met than two further dramas began to unfold. The first was when serious criminal activity was exposed at the Bank of Credit and Commerce International (BCCI), a major international bank founded in Pakistan in 1972. It was closed by the Bank of England in 1991. At its peak, it operated in 78 countries, had over 400 branches and claimed assets of $25 billion. Regulators found evidence of money laundering, bribery, terrorist funding, arms trading, tax evasion and smuggling. It was structured elaborately to avoid ready detection, with a unique web of multiple hierarchies linked to a seemingly impenetrable number of holding companies and other organisations that sheltered its founder Agha Hasan Abedi. Liquidators Deloitte and Touche sued BCCI's auditors Price Waterhouse and Ernst and Young and won a settlement of £130 million in 1999. The second drama concerned the pension funds of the Mirror Newspaper Group, which were gratuitously siphoned off by its owner, Robert Maxwell, in the early 1990s, and much of the money invested into companies in which he had a personal interest. In all, about £450 million went missing and, as in Polly Peck, the auditors Coopers and Lybrand were again implicated and admitted 59 'errors of judgement'. Clearly, the commissioning of the Cadbury inquiry was a timely one.

In addition, a broader, more pervasive, concern added to the momentum. The public was becoming outraged increasingly over excessive director compensation, involving a dazzling array of salaries, bonuses, golden hellos, golden goodbyes, share options, travel benefits, pensions and low-interest loans – especially when these incentives were not related visibly to overall company performance. Since many of these international companies operated in developing countries, where poverty was widespread, the implications of poor governance were not solely a national concern but also one with much broader economic and social consequences.

The Cadbury Report

Cadbury reported in December 1992, launching a 'Code of Best Practice' with nineteen clear principles on two pages covering, among other things, the regularity of board meetings; the board's effective control over management; the restraint of unfettered power by any one person or persons – especially where the board chairman is also the CEO; the role, independence, relationship, power and appointment by the board, as a whole, of non-executive directors – specifically, that the majority should be independent; effective controls for the running of the company; the length of director contracts; transparency over director fees and benefits; the objectivity and the professional relationships with auditors and the establishment of an audit committee with at least three non-executives; a remuneration committee dominated by non-executives; reporting responsibilities, qualifications and assumptions. The Committee was realistic in its efforts:

> " No system of corporate governance can be totally proof against fraud or incompetence. The test is how far such aberrations can be discouraged and how quickly they can be brought to light. The risks can be reduced by making the risks in the governance process as effectively accountable as possible ... Although the great majority of companies are competently run and audited under the present system of corporate governance, it is widely accepted that standards within the corporate sector have to be raised.[92]

The Report was welcomed as a landmark in the UK governance agenda for its robust investigative process and workable conclusions. It set an important non-mandatory tone in recommending that listed companies declare their compliance to the code or explain why they had not done so, thereby laying the groundwork for self-regulation. Cadbury saw the building of trust obviating the need for regulation. The Committee's focus on the board as the imprimatur of serious decisions and on properly formed sub-committees (remuneration, audit and nomination) were pioneering yet central contributions to good governance. Moreover, the resolution of board composition and power issues by the emphasis on independent non-executive directors and the separation of the roles of chairman and chief executive provided sufficient 'checks and balances' to ensure a workable system.

Such was the impact of the Committee's work that it inspired the formation, and influenced the outcome, of an international panel[93] on governance championed by the Organisation for Economic Co-operation and Development (OECD) and involving 28 other countries. The OECD acknowledged that there was no single model of corporate governance for all contexts, the capitalist cultures of the UK and US saw the main ingredients as the board and the shareholders, while the continental European model laid the stress on partnership between capital and labour. Nevertheless, the OECD was able to identify common elements from among the diverse perspectives across member countries and develop its own set of principles:

> " The Principles build on these common elements and are formulated to embrace the different models that exist. For example, they do not advocate any particular board structure and the term 'board' as used in this document is meant to embrace the different national models of board structures found in OECD countries ... The Principles are non-binding and do not aim at detailed prescriptions for national legislation. Their purpose is to serve as a reference point. They can be used by policy makers, as they examine and develop their legal and regulatory frameworks for corporate governance that reflect their own economic, social, legal and cultural circumstances and by market participants as they develop their own practices.[94]

The OECD principles are designed to be adaptive to different contexts and include:

- The protection of shareholder's rights;
- The equitable treatment of shareholders, including minorities;

- The recognition of the rights of stakeholders and active co-operation with them;
- The timely and accurate disclosure of all relevant materials;
- The responsibilities of the board in strategic guidance, management monitoring and accountability to the company and shareholders.

These principles soon became the international reference point for advisors, policymakers, strategists, investors and city institutions. They form the basis for an extensive programme of co-operation between member and non-member countries and underpin the corporate governance component of World Bank and IMF reports on the observance of standards and codes. Specifically, they develop the Cadbury approach to embrace all stakeholders (as well as shareholders). The Principles were reviewed thoroughly in 2004 to capture trends in member and non-member countries, with more focus placed on the development of a corporate governance framework that contributes to economic development and the efficient operation of markets.

With such influence played by Cadbury in the development of the OECD principles, it can be argued that the UK initiative had become internationalised. British legislators continued to press on with a series of further studies, such as those of Greenbury, Hampel, Turnbull, Higgs and Smith, designed to tackle particular governance issues in more detail. This overall effort led to a serious review of UK company law, with most of the combined recommendations eventually being incorporated into the Company Law Reform Bill of 2005. The UK's Trade and Industry Secretary at the time this bill was coming into being, Patricia Hewitt, stated that there was no need for the UK to rush into the kind of legislative requirements contained in the American Sarbanes-Oxley Act. Policymakers in the UK and Europe had succeeded in holding firm to a principles-based approach to governance. The story in America was to be quite different.

The US experience – recent corporate scandals and the response

It seems hard to believe now that Enron was one of America's most admired companies almost right up to the time of its demise. At its pinnacle, Enron had over 21,000 employees with sales of over £70 billion and played a leading role in the global electricity, natural gas and communications markets.

We now know that this one-time corporate star was held together by a complex web of company/subsidiary ownership structures with questionable financial relationships that eventually came to embroil it and its auditors, Arthur Anderson, in scandal. Furthermore, in order to secure key international energy contracts, it is alleged to have used bribery, corruption and political favours from the Clinton and Bush administrations. Despite urging their investors and fellow employees to keep supporting the stock, key executives were quick to off-load much of their own before this house of cards came tumbling down. The share price dropped from $90 to $0.30 cents during 2001 and Enron collapsed finally at the end of November that year. The employee pension fund was left completely bereft, adding to the general distress and public outcry.

The Enron-Anderson debacle sparked a flurry of regulatory activity in the world's most significant capital market. Thirty-five different corporate reform bills passed through both houses of the US Congress in rapid time. In June 2002, massive accounting fraud at Worldcomm, involving an overestimate of profits of $3.8 billion over the previous five quarters, also compromising its auditors – again, Arthur Anderson – exacerbated the concern and ended with the largest bankruptcy in US history. Congress accelerated policy by combining the bills of Representative Oxley and Senator Sarbanes in the Sarbanes-Oxley Act (SOX) in late 2002. The New York Stock Exchange, the Securities and Exchange Commission (SEC) and the NASDAQ followed with their own specifications forcing all organisations that trade on US markets to incorporate the SOX provisions.

The Sarbanes-Oxley Act

The major provisions of the Sarbanes-Oxley Act included the certification of financial reports by Chief Executive Officers (CEOs) and Chief Financial Officers (CFOs); a ban on personal loans to directors and executive officers; transparency of CEO and CFO emoluments; insider trading checks; auditor independence and restriction of other services checks; harsher punishments for financial misdemeanour; and a detailed declaration of internal controls. Further checks and balances were provided, requiring a higher percentage of independent directors and specifying more tightly the membership and qualifications of directors on the audit and remuneration committees. The Act has since been criticised for its cost of compliance, its undue burden on directors, its reliance on criminal sanctions and its focus on a rules-based approach rather than one that lays the emphasis on principles. Critics had argued that it had been rushed through in a climate of crisis rather than one of reflection. However, the content had been under debate for a decade or more and it could be claimed that the scandals at Enron and Worldcomm served mainly to accelerate the process. To understand the background to this reform of corporate governance more fully, it is worth reviewing the context leading up to these major changes.

Hostile takeovers were a common feature of Corporate America in the low-growth 1980s and companies felt pressed into trying to maximise market value as their main line of defence. The easiest way was to cut costs, and the generous fees of the lawyers and accountants became prime targets. Having been the custodians of good corporate conduct for years, these professional firms were forced suddenly to compete for business. At the end of the 1980s, many were in a much weaker commercial position than their clients. The following decade brought a technology-driven bull market which, as former director of market regulation at the SEC, Bill Hyman,[95] described it,

> " represented the largest single misallocation of investment capital I have seen, or am likely to see, in my lifetime. Capital was allocated to ideas that did not deserve it, to companies that did not deserve it (or which, when they did deserve it, could not profitably deploy all they received), and finally, to many corporate executives who should not have been trusted with it. Many of these people, lionized by adoring media, comported themselves publicly, in a manner that should have been a tip off to any investor not blinded by his own greed.

Executive compensation reached heights normally reserved for genuine risk-taking entrepreneurs, not the stewards of public company assets. Investors, analysts and other stakeholders were caught up in the bull market hubris. The bubble was waiting to burst and Enron and Worldcomm were simply the most prominent examples amid thousands of corporate casualties at the time.

The outcome to date in both contexts

The contrasting experiences on both sides of the Atlantic provide distinct approaches to the corporate governance process. The European principles-based approach relies on voluntary compliance and is premised upon the development and preservation of high moral standards and the sustenance of trust. The American rules-based approach relies on conformity to detailed provisions and is accompanied by punitive penalties for any miscarriages. The US Government was forced to act quickly after the Enron-Anderson scandal at the end of 2001 and SOX reported just eight months later. The UK Government also had to move fast in launching an independent review – the Higgs enquiry in April 2002 – but for a different reason. The new American regulations had major implications for policymakers well beyond the United States, leading Philippe Hapeslagh to express the hope 'that the largest European companies, many of whom have a US listing, will not invoke their own forced compliance with Sarbanes-Oxley as reason to desert the fight for a common European principles-based approach'.[96]

In the case of the UK, as Sir Adrian Cadbury (2002) highlighted in a follow-up analysis of the impact of his Committee's principles and codes on UK corporate governance protocols, there had been a swift response by companies on compliance. For example, one of the key recommendations made by his Committee was that there should be a well-defined procedure for board directors seeking to employ sound professional advice. In fairly rapid order, such processes were instituted in the majority of the top 1550 firms on the London Exchange. Furthermore, in the Heidrick and Struggles biennial survey of corporate governance in European companies in 2005, there was clear evidence of speedy convergence to the 'comply or explain' codes. The UK, the Netherlands and France were the best 'coded' countries while Switzerland had leapt up the ratings from ninth place in 2001 to second in 2005. Only Belgium, Italy and Sweden had broad differentials between best and worst companies. However, in 2007, the top five countries above the European average were the UK, the Netherlands, Switzerland, France and Sweden. While the UK led the group, Portugal, ranked 10th in 2003 and 6th in 2007, recorded the greatest progress in the last five years. Although Belgium and Italy also showed progress, the downgrading of Spain (from 6th in 2005 to 8th in 2007) and Germany (from 7th in 2003 to 9th in 2005 and 10th in 2007), indicates a degree of 'inertia and indifference' in some countries. Nonetheless, the decade of investigation, reporting and debate seems to have paid off in Europe.

Meanwhile, over in the US, there has been a broad acceptance that SOX was necessary but after much debate over the costs of its implementation to US commerce as a whole, not just to individual firms. Some put the total cost to corporate America at beyond $4 billion. On the other hand, it could be countered that such a tough legislative approach, parachuting Government back into the boardroom, was necessary to renew investor confidence in equity dealings, and restore integrity to the markets.

Also, there have been more subtle changes afoot. First, before the Act, most boards comprised the CEOs of other firms. In the following years, their composition became more diverse. In particular, they have included more qualified accountants, as their role on the audit committee is an imperative of the legislation. Second, the role of the CFO had become critical, as, along with the CEO, they had to sign off each periodic report filed with the SEC. A third change concerned the interaction between directors and corporate officers. The legislative pressures bearing down on directors forced them to 'raise their game' and become more analytical and interrogative of data and affairs. Previously, corporate officers would have viewed such questioning as intrusive rather than as prudent and dutiful. Fourth, some close observers[97] argued that the heroic changes made by organisations to comply with SOX needed to work their way more fundamentally into the basic identity of the business to become sustainable. Fifth, CEOs began to lose their jobs more rapidly due to poor performance than at any time in past, while expectations on them have grown considerably in both range and complexity. As Hyman (see note 93) put it, corporate leaders 'are magnets now for politically correct attacks by political candidates, plaintiff's lawyers and [once-adoring] media. Humility is the order of the day, and the new CEO is a servant leader rather than a celebrity.'

Should the positions of the CEO and Chairman of the Board be separate?

One of the major implications of the renewed interest in corporate governance structures and procedures on both sides of the Atlantic over the last decade is the fresh impetus which has been given to the debate over whether or not the positions of CEO and Chairman of the Board should be separated. This has implications, in particular, for the practice still prevailing in the United States. In comparison to the UK and European traditions, the way that boards are structured in the US has concentrated power in a single pair of hands with the combination of roles of chair of the board and CEO. In 2003, the Economist[98] estimated that 75% of companies in the Standard and Poor 500 were still structured in this way. This high level is reinforced by a 2005 survey, indicating 81% of top 100 companies[99] and another in 2006 indicating 81% of leading 160 US companies[100] holding a joint CEO and Chairmanship. In contrast, in the UK, 96% of FTSE-250 companies in 2005 had a separation of Chairman and CEO.[101]

In the USA, influential commentators like Jeffrey Garten (2002b) have called for change to accompany the SOX and SEC progressions, pointing out that keeping the two roles combined raises conflicts of interests and makes it tough for other board members to monitor the performance of their CEOs and hold them accountable, where they also occupy the chair. For some time, Intel has been one of the more prominent exceptions on the US scene, and Andy Grove,[102] its legendary former CEO and advocate of the separation option, explained his company's thinking in the following way:

> The separation of the two jobs goes to the heart of the conception of a corporation. Is a company a sandbox for the CEO or is the CEO an employee? If he's an employee, he needs a boss, and that boss is the board. The chairman runs the board. How can the CEO be his own boss?

The Cadbury Committee in the UK came out strongly in favour of keeping these positions separate, and by 2006, over 70% (and rising) of UK-quoted companies had complied with this advice. But many US corporations were slow to yield. They defended the CEO-centric approach by pointing to the counterweight that strong independent members with diverse backgrounds can provide. This 'firewall', they argued, was reinforced by the greater independence given to the audit, compensation and nomination committees under the SOX-NASDAQ-SEC rubric, guaranteeing to hold the most powerful CEO to account. Taking this viewpoint further, Dalton and Dalton (2005: 9) suggested that, though there are many ways to strengthen the independence of the board without having to split the roles, it is less easy to substitute for the singular virtue of the combined model, where:

> " A single strong leader, at the board level or otherwise, can protect against a critical concern when relying on groups for decisions, action, or performance – a tendency referred to as the 'risky-shift'. This is essentially driven by recognizing a group's propensity for the diffusion of responsibility and its limited accountability.

In the case of the combined model, any potential ambiguity over who is accountable disappears. Research has yet to find unequivocal evidence that can link the separation of the roles to superior financial performance and, until this happens, it is likely that the majority of US companies will continue to keep these positions together. However, advancing globalisation, particularly in the area of international Mergers and Acquisitions (M&A), will surely keep the US-European clash of perspectives on this issue to the forefront and keep the debate alive.

A new agenda for corporate leadership

The return of corporate governance to centre stage is just one of the more obvious ways in which the current context for strategic management has been shaping up to be very different from that which prevailed over the 1980s and 1990s. Many now believe that the early years of the new century represent an inflection point for business and its leadership, requiring new perspectives and priorities.

In his recent book, *The Politics of Fortune*, Jeffrey Garten (2002b), Dean of Yale School of Management, identified the new priorities for business leaders in the post-9/11 and post-Enron era; among them are the restoration of integrity to the financial markets, sustainability of free trade, reduction of global poverty and expansion of corporate citizenship. All of these will require the business leaders of today to broaden and deepen their engagement with their wider society, politically and socially as well as commercially.

For example, restoring integrity to the markets remains a priority if business leaders are to regain their reputation and standing with the wider community, and while regulation has a role to play in this regard, the perspective, values and character of the men and women who lead major corporations is at least as important. Sustaining free trade can be done only with business and government working in more active partnership to ensure that international trade is fair as well as free. A commitment to reduce global poverty will be crucial to create the growth markets of tomorrow in rapidly expanding regions like India and China, and to earn the legitimacy to participate in them.[103] Expanding corporate citizenship will be key to securing and retaining the commitment and loyalty of all major stakeholders, not just shareholders but also customers, employees, suppliers and local communities. If 'enterprises are not committed to anything beyond making money', why should they expect their key constituencies to make anything other than 'transactional commitments' to them?[104]

Clearly, the onward march of liberal democracy that assisted the rapid spread of globalisation is no longer to be taken for granted in the face of increased fragmentation, trade barriers, security threats, ideological resistance to the spread of Western ideals and the perception of corporate exploitation of both labour and resources in the underdeveloped regions of the world. To counter these developments and help ensure that potential benefits of globalisation are widely and fairly realised, a new level of partnership with Government and Non-Government Organisations (NGOs) will be essential. Governments must continue to co-operate with each other to monitor business practice, to counter trafficking in money, people and illicit goods, to harmonise policies on energy security and global warming and to assuage the threat of terrorism. A more intense and continuous dialogue among CEOs, governments and pan-global institutions, like the G8, IMF, World Bank, will be required if free trade is to develop in a sustainable manner.

This trade dialogue should broaden into the area of global poverty. The World Bank estimates that 25% of the 4.8 billion people in the developing world had only $1 per day to live on, and another 50% had less than $2 per day while, in 2003, 20% of the global population enjoyed 85% of the world's income. A strong, committed business-government axis could lead the way in pressing for the lowering of the barriers to trade in advanced economies like the US and EU aimed at protecting producer interests in areas such as food, steel and textiles, where poorer regions of the world should normally have a comparative advantage. There is something of a double standard here, as Garten (2002b: 127) points out:

> the rich nations are sending capital (in the form of AID) to the developing world to develop their industries, but blocking the international markets for the products that could be sold. Lacking overseas markets, these poorer countries cannot attract adequate investment. It is a vicious downward cycle.

So the new agenda for leadership goes well beyond concerns with regulation and corporate governance to the wider responsibilities involved in the evolution of a new industrial order. There are those who wonder just how far and fast this new industrial order is evolving when it comes to caring about the environment and the kind of societal legacy to be passed on to the next generation. As Senge and Carstedt (2001: 25) put it: 'Judging by its impact on natural and social capital, so far the New Economy looks more like the next wave of the industrial era' rather than a truly post-industrial one, and this should concern us all, 'because the basic developmental patterns of the industrial era are not sustainable'. This is particularly acute in the context of advancing globalisation. As Hart and Christensen (2002: 54) point out:

> Affluent societies account for more than 75% of the world's energy and resource consumption and create the bulk of the industrial, toxic and consumer waste; if the developed world's model of commerce and consumerism were to become the standard everywhere, it would require the equivalent of more than four Earths to supply the raw materials, fossil fuels and waste sinks that would be needed. Clearly a different model is called for.

As some see it, what will be required is not just a different model, but a fresh way of looking at the world. According to Senge and Carsted (2001: 26) leaders in the business world and related domains will have to learn to work within a fusion of three world views: rationalism, naturalism and humanism, if we are to make real progress in moving towards a post-industrial model based on sustainable development:

> Rationalism, the belief in reason, has dominated society through-out modern times. It remains the dominant perspective in business and education. Yet, it has limits. It cannot explain the passion that motivates entrepreneurs committed to a new product idea nor the imagination of scientists testing an intuition. Nor does it explain why a quiet walk on the beach or a hike in the mountains may inspire both. These can only be understood by seeing how naturalism, humanism and rationalism infuse into one another. Naturalism arises from our innate sense of being part of nature. Humanism arises from the rich interior life that connects reason, emotion and awareness – and ultimately allows us to connect with one another. Epochs in human history that have nurtured all three have stood out as golden ages.

The new agenda for business leaders, together with the principles-versus-rules debate in corporate governance reform, brings the link between strategy and corporate social responsibility (CSR) further into prominence, raising again the long-standing question about whether, and to what extent, a business should be philanthropic. Back in the early 1970s, when CSR first came into vogue, Milton Friedman (1970) made the argument that the primary social responsibility of a business is to make a profit, and if philanthropic contributions are to be made, these should be left to the individual shareholders, not 'usurped' by management. As Porter and Kramer (2002, 2006) see it, this remains the basic position against which any case for a management role in corporate philanthropy must be made, and neither of the categories under which most corporate philanthropy is still practised, communal obligation and goodwill building, provides much in the way of a convincing counter-argument. For them, however, a more compelling category is what they call strategic philanthropy, i.e. when it is targeted at improving the 'competitive context' of the firm as defined by four basic elements: factor conditions, the context for strategy and rivalry, demand conditions and related and supporting industries (as developed in Porter's book, The Competitive Advantage of Nations, 1990).

An impressive example of strategic philanthropy, and one in line with Garten's new agenda item, reducing global poverty, is the recent 'i-community' initiative of Hewlett-Packard in the Kuppam region of Andhra Pradesh in India. It is one of several such 'living lab' projects at HP that are aimed at using company know-how and investment to help advance the process of economic development in poorer regions of the world, like southern India, while also opening up new market opportunities and stimulating innovation. The overall hope in this particular project was to help 'turn the Kuppam region into a thriving, self-sustaining economy where greater access to technology permanently improves literacy, creates income, and provides access to markets, government services, education and health care', through building a local 'ecosystem of public and private partners' and applying the 'rigour and processes of a well-managed company to problems that need to be solved'.[105] The project is also driving innovation within HP, not just in products and services, like the solar-powered digital photography 'photo-studio in a backpack' unit, developed specifically for this initiative, but also in scaleable, community-focused, business models and solutions, all with much wider potential application. As the project's main architects, Debra Dunn and Keith Yamashita (2003: 52) explain:

> HP has also been a beneficiary, gaining knowledge and contacts that will make the company a stronger competitor in the global economy, The Kuppam i-community will lead to new kinds of technology solutions that will prove valuable in India and other areas too ... Many of the online services we're developing are similarly promising for applications beyond Kuppam. In addition to the new products, we are creating intangible assets – like new networks and increased familiarity with new markets – that will have an important impact on our bottom line.

Involvement in the project has also proven to be highly motivating for the HP executives most closely involved, particularly those with roots in the region, and a major spin-off for the company has been the impact on leadership development. 'More can be learned in three years in a living lab than in virtually any leadership development programme or graduate course', and 'teaching leaders new ways to lead may be one of the largest competitive benefits of the initiative'.[106] Some might argue that philanthropy ceases to be philanthropic when a company like HP ends up 'doing well' while also 'doing good'. However, one of the central insights in the new agenda for leadership is that this kind of distinction loses its significance in today's increasingly interconnected business environment. To recall a phrase penned by Herman Melville over a century and half ago in his great novel Moby Dick: 'It's a mutual, joint-stock world, in all meridians'.

Strategic management is once again at a crossroads.[107] The aftershocks of greed and scandal urge a Paul-like reappraisal of the responsibilities of business and the role that it should play in our society and environment. It will no longer be enough just to make a profit and 'do no harm'. With more and more of society's resources at its command, business as an institution must become a much more active force for good. In rising to this challenge, deeper understanding of context and the role of business leadership in the shaping of a new industrial landscape become capabilities of growing strategic significance in their own right.

Summary

In this chapter we examined the relationships between strategy and leadership, and between leadership, culture and performance. We began by asking how 'strategic' leadership is as a variable in its own right, and also by examining the relative importance of strategy and leadership, and how this has been changing over time. Strategic management, we suggested, rests on two fundamentals: commercial logic and human aspiration. Strategy focuses on the first, leadership stresses the second.

We then went on to examine the nature of strategic leadership and its links with corporate culture and competitiveness. We began this part of the chapter by briefly revisiting some of the early attempts to isolate the essence of outstanding leadership in terms of attributes, styles and contingencies, and assessed the importance of specific organisational and industry experience to leadership effectiveness. Then we presented our own perspective on leadership as performance in the arena, highlighting the significance of three main elements: context, conviction and credibility, and we compared our view with related perspectives. We stressed the importance of understanding how leadership effectiveness varies not only from person to person but also within the same person over time. We then went on to examine the debate provoked by Zaleznik's assertion that managers and leaders are different, and highlighted the parallels with the transactional/transformational leadership typology of James McGregor Burns. Transformational leadership then led us naturally into an examination of the relationship between leadership and corporate culture, and the process of institutionalising charisma. Then we went on to distinguish between instrumental and interpretative views of culture and to examine how strong corporate culture can become the source of sustainable competitive advantage. Also, we examined some of the potential pitfalls and pathologies of strong leadership and culture. Then we returned to the Zaleznik distinction between managers and leaders to examine its wider implications for strategy, organisation and culture. When seen in historical context, this discussion led us to highlight the rational and romantic duality at the core of strategic management, and the value of considering the discipline as both a science and humanity.

In the final part of the chapter, we turned to the emerging new agenda for strategic leadership in the post-Enron, post-9/11, context. We looked at why corporate governance has returned to centre stage in strategic leadership and examined the main features of recent corporate governance reform on both sides of the Atlantic. We ended the chapter with a brief examination of the new priorities facing business leaders in the years ahead. One of the keys to meeting these new expectations successfully will be the enhancement of contextual awareness and acumen. How strategic leaders might go about developing this capability will be the main focus of our next chapter.

Notes

1 Bartlett and Ghoshal (2002).
2 Hambrick (1989: 5).
3 Schoeffler et al. (1974).
4 Collins and Porras (1996).

5 Dearlove (2003).

6 Collins (2001), Badaracco (2001), George et al. (2007).

7 Tannenbaum and Schmidt (1958).

8 Shetty and Perry (1976).

9 Huff (2000: 57).

10 Leavy and Wilson (1994), Leavy (1996b), (2003a). The discussion that follows draws freely from Leavy (2003a).

11 Graves (1992).

12 Peters and Waterman (1982), Foster and Kaplan (2001).

13 Eitzen and Yetman (1972).

14 Hambrick and Fukutomi (1991).

15 Miller (1991).

16 Tim Burt, *Financial Times*, (29/11/01).

17 Colvin (1999: 97).

18 Ackenhusen and Ghoshal (1992: 17).

19 Vaill (1989), Starrat (1993), Czarniawska (1997), Pitcher (1997).

20 Biggert and Hamilton (1987).

21 Lane (1989: 3).

22 Kellerman (1999: 1).

23 Rost (1993: 94).

24 Kellerman (1999).

25 Kuhnert and Lewis (1987: 649).

26 Ghoshal et al. (1999).

27 Waterman (1994).

28 Bryman (1993: 294).

29 Kling and Goteman (2003).

30 Collins and Porras (1996), O'Reilly and Pfeffer (2000).

31 Collins and Porras (1996: 36).

32 Mito (1990: 1).

33 de Pree (1989: 82).

34. Berman (1998: 177–8).

35 Pudney et al. (2001).

36 This section draws freely from Leavy and Gannon (1998).

37 O'Reilly and Pfeffer (2000).

38 Leavy and Gannon (1998).

39 Bartlett et al. (1995: 4).

40 Ehrlich et al. (1991: 2).

41 Bibb (1996: 167–76).

42 Wetlaufer (1999: 112).

43 Garten (2002a: 115).

44 Wetlaufer (1999: 115).

45 Dick and Kets de Vries (2007: 25).

46 Sakiya (1982: 54).

47 Bibb (1996: 176).

48 Berman (1998: 179).

49 Ackenhusen and Ghoshal (1992: 9).

50 Dick and Kets de Vries (1995: 13).

51 Collins and Porras (1996: 48).

52 Bartlett and Nanda (1995: 2–4).

53 Bartlett et al. (1995: 1).

54 Collins and Porras (1996: 81).

55 TIME, 1954: 46.

56 Bower et al. (1991: 418).

57 Fukuyama (1996).

58 Bower and Matthews (1996: 16).
59 O'Reilly (1986: 16).
60 Barney (1986: 660).
61 McClean (2001: 55).
62 Kets de Vries (1990: 752).
63 Nathan (1999).
64 Bower et al. (1991: 413).
65 Schein (1997).
66 Pfeffer (1992: 42).
67 Bower et al. (1991: 348).
68 Hamel (2000a: 253).
69 Pendergrast (1994).
70 Lukes (1974).
71 Clegg (1990: 143).
72 Knights and Morgan (1992).
73 Hopfl (1992: 29).
74 Gemmill and Oakley (1992).
75 Kets de Vries and Miller (1985).
76 Dumaine (1993: 46).
77 Hopfl (1992).
78 Dumaine (1993).
79 Leavy (1995), Collins and Porras (1996), Ghoshal and Bartlett (1998), Lewin and Regine (2000), O'Reilly and Pfeffer (2000), Tichy and Cohen (2002).
80 Fryer (2003), Guber (2007).
81 Campbell (1994: 664).
82 Wiersema (2002).
83 See Leavy (1995) for a fuller development of this argument.
84 Paul does this by creating an 'I' voice identifying himself with the Israelites and their problematic issues with Mosaic law (see Romans 7.15–19).
85 Governance in this section refers specifically to the models of liberal democratic capitalism in the West. It is recognised that there are other variants of corporate governance around the world e.g. Japan (kereitsu) and Korea (chaebol) that include broader stakeholder interests. They have many things in common with continental European structures, but they are not covered directly here.
86 With characteristic foresight, Adam Smith noted in the 'Wealth of Nations' that 'The joint stock companies which are established for the public spirited purpose of promoting some particular manufacture, over and above managing their own affairs ill, to the diminution of the general stock of society, can scarce ever fail to do more harm than good.' (Books IV–V).
87 Gompers et al. (2003: 3)
88 Jensen and Meckling (1976).
89 Demsetz and Lehn (1985).
90 Sundaramurthy and Lewis (2003).
91 Janis (1972).
92 Cadbury (1992: 7.2–7.3).
93 Sir Adrian Cadbury sat on this panel and continued to advise the renewal panel in 2003–04.
94 (OECD Report, 1999: 15).
95 Bill Hyman's remark is taken from his plenary address to the EURAM annual conference in St Andrews, Scotland in May 2004.
96 In Albert-Roulhac and Breen (2005, 20).
97 See, for instance, the Report by DeLoitte, Touche, Tohmatsu, 'Under Control: Sustaining Compliance with Sarbanes-Oxley in Year 2 and Beyond', DeLoitte Development (2005).
98 Economist, 'The way we govern now', 9 January 2003.
99 Shearman & Sterling LLP (2005), 'Trends in the corporate governance practices of the 100 largest US public companies'.

[100] Business Roundtable (2006), 'Fourth Annual Business Roundtable Corporate Governance Survey'.
[101] Pass (2006: 470).
[102] Quoted in Garten (2002c: 13).
[103] Hart and Christensen (2002).
[104] Senge and Carstedt (2001: 34).
[105] Dunn and Yamashita (2003: 48–9).
[106] Dunn and Yamashita (2003: 53).
[107] Carter and McKiernan (2004).

INTRODUCING 'STRATEGIC LEADERSHIP, GOVERNANCE AND RENEWAL'
STRATEGY LEADERSHIP AND THE NEW AGENDA • THE CONTEXT OF
BUSINESS IN SOCIETY • COMPETITIVE ANALYSIS AND VALUE INNOVATION
• STRATEGY AND ORGANISATION IN THE MULTI-BUSINESS FIRM •
STRATEGIC PROCESSES – INNOVATION • STRATEGIC PROCESSES – TRANSFORMATION
AND RENEWAL • SOME FINAL THOUGHTS AND REFLECTIONS

3 the context of business in society

Introduction

This chapter examines the role that environmental context plays in the determination of good strategy. Context often fails to get sufficient attention in the strategy process because the turbulence of modern business settings can often make the task seem overwhelming. How can sense be made of contexts with a complex weave of elements like globalisation, rapid technological progress, shorter product life cycles, product proliferation, shorter market channels, increasing consumer sovereignty, telecommunications revolution, shrinking distance, extensive migration, clashes of civilisation, climate disruption, greater secularisation, increasing affluence and increasing poverty?

This chapter begins by stressing the importance of context in shaping the domain in which strategic decisions are made both now and for the future. The vignettes illustrate the weaving of context, content, culture and cognition as inseparable parts in the strategy decision. By examining each and by considering their harmony together, it is hoped that better strategic decisions will result. From this baseline, the chapter builds to consider the notion that one of the best ways to understand the present and future context is to harness the power of history in the search for patterning from the past, through to the present and out to the future. Social and political patterns are examined and the route to the context of the present can be identified clearly. How these patterns might play out for the future is the issue to which the chapter turns next. The focus is not on hard forecasts of the future but on softer, scenario modelling that generates pictures or stories of the future that inform decisions in the present. Shell's global scenarios are used to illustrate the formation of different futures from patterns of the past coupled with emergent, current trends. Attention is then focused on how managers can grasp the risk element in exploring future pathways. For each component of risk, the chapter offers a suitable and proven empirical technique and this ends with a comprehensive treatment of scenario planning and how scenarios can be developed to inform managers of the likely terrain ahead of them so their current decision-making can be better informed. Scenario planning is not presented as a panacea for understanding what is ahead but a way of dealing with complexity over the long term.

The importance of context

The good news is that it is possible to generate a good understanding of context with the judicious application of appropriate thinking and the competent tools and techniques applied with a flexible, creative and imaginative manner. There is much in the armoury of the future strategist than can help, e.g., environmental scanning, simulation and games, road mapping, state-of-the-future index (SOFI) analysis, field anomaly relaxation and causal layered analysis. Below, we focus on some of the more popular techniques and trace their chronology as a family of tools.

First, by visiting Vignette 3.1, we examine why an understanding of context can be so important to strategy development.

VIGNETTE 3.1

Strategies for teenagers with diabetes: Italy versus Scotland

Throughout the 1990s, the Scottish medical community was concerned about the increased rates of diabetes among its teenage community. Moreover, performance indicators from across Europe indicated that its success rate for treatments was not an enviable one. For instance, Italian clinics scored 20 percentage points higher using exactly the same doses of insulin from the same manufacturer. Initial investigations by the medical fraternity could not find out the reasons for this marked disparity, despite their lengthy enquiries that focused heavily upon the numbers of doctors and nurses involved and their team ethos. To help solve the puzzle, the medics were joined by experts from social anthropology and strategic management.

To better understand ethnographic material, anthropologists have studied the features and characteristics surrounding social and cultural phenomena. This contextualisation provides form for their interpretation. To limit the extent of the contextual environment under study, they examine connections (and disconnections) that link the phenomena to its surroundings. Thus, context becomes a set of such connections woven into a pattern surrounding a problem (context derives from the Latin verb *texere*, to weave). If a pattern of connections could be found around the Italian clinics that was different from that around the Scottish ones, perhaps the problem could be identified and resolved.

To better understand competitive success, management experts have modelled the linkages between three key elements of strategy – context, content and the process of strategy. Outer context relates directly to the environment surrounding the organisation and this is frequently split into immediate task components involving competitors, suppliers, buyers, entry barriers etc., and a general environment of political, economic, social and technological variables that prevail upon the sector at a meta level. Strategists try to harmonise this context with the content of the strategy (e.g. organic growth) and the process by which this is carried out within the organisation (e.g. formal and rational).

The new team analysed the key features of context surrounding the clinics in Italy and Scotland and the network of connections from this context to each clinic. They observed the process by which treatments were conducted by monitoring the chain of events from initial diagnosis, through prescription, through the dosage regimen, through consultation attendance to the lifestyle of patients. Further studies of the clinic's management, team operations and prevailing culture fortified the data.

As the data was modelled, significant findings emerged. First, the much-vaunted Mediterranean diet fed to teenagers in Italy contained good amounts of slow burning carbohydrates that enabled the steady absorption of the insulin into the patient's blood stream. In Scotland, the mixed diet of fizzy drinks and mutton pies did little to help the absorption. Second, the dominant religion framing the outer context of the Italian clinics was Roman Catholicism. The powerful role of mothers in Roman Catholic families in Italy ensured that a punitive discipline surrounded a regular drug dosage and clinic attendance for their offspring. In Scotland, more liberal family ties meant that dosage was unsupervised generally and clinic attendance was spasmodic. Finally, families in Italy tended to see diabetes as their problem and not that of the patient. Whole families and extended families attended the clinic with the patient, offering both immediate and enduring support. In Scotland, teenagers often attended clinics alone and bore their disability in a private fashion thereafter. As a consequence of this research, policy changes on family attendance and dietary requirements followed swiftly in Scottish clinics and these acted to improve their performance significantly in the European league tables. Scottish teenagers with diabetes now enjoy hearty and healthy lives.

Source: Adapted by McKiernan from Greene et al. 1999

Context, content, culture and cognition

The initial medical team was a talented bunch but their training constrained their vision and forced them to focus on a narrow internal domain in the hope of solving the problem. Psychologists refer to this as cognitive inertia, which, if not treated, can prevent the generation of alternative views or those 'outside the box'. The medics focussed on what they knew and on what was familiar to them, i.e. the treatment of diabetes. Understandably, they did not explore what they did not know or what was outside their traditional cognitive frame of reference, not least the context external to the organisation and its connections to the organisation. Even for experienced managers familiar with its importance, the study of context is a tough game. Converging industries, rapid advances in computer and information technologies, globalisation, migration, environmental and demographic changes have painted context as a complex, turbulent sphere that is better to avoid than to understand.

Yet, the relationship between the environmental context, strategy content and strategy process lies at the heart of the underlying analytical architecture of modern strategic management. This relationship is premised upon their coalescence or 'fit'. The three should be in balance, each with the others, as the organisation should 'fit' its external context. However, we suggest three minor adaptations to this approach. First, the substitution of culture for 'process' is proposed. Here, the definition of culture is broad and encapsulates much of the operational side of the organisation but stresses the crucial role of the prevailing culture in the successful implementation of strategy. Second, the term 'fit' suggests that any two conceptual features can be engineered to a degree of exactness in every case and that their coalescence can be made perfect. Even if this was plausible theoretically, the realities of strategy in practice do not allow for this perfection in design. Hence, we suggest replacing the word 'fit' here by 'harmony' thus allowing for closeness rather than perfection (and we will be exploring the dangers of too much fit or 'over-adaptation' in later chapters). Finally, we suggest the presence of a fourth variable, that of cognition that links the other three in the mind of the strategist (See Figure 3.1). Cognitive freezing and the ability to hold the past, present and future in one 'moment of time' are important concepts in this chapter, and we will return to them later.

For illustration, we focus on the first three here. Put crudely, contextual conditions can lie on a scale between stable and dynamic; strategy content can be designed or planned deliberately or allowed to emerge and adapt while cultures can vary between bureaucratic and entrepreneurial.[1]

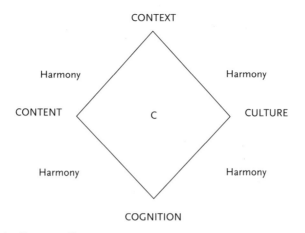

Figure 3.1 **The four Cs of strategic management.**

In stable contexts, conventional deliberate planning can work well. Forecasting is reasonably accurate and guides the three- or five-year plan through structured and regular meetings and bulletins. For example, it is no surprise with hindsight that the relative environmental stability from the mid-1950s to the onset of the oil price shocks of 1973 marked the heyday of systematic corporate planning and the emergence of the hallmark texts of Ansoff (1965), Argenti (1968) and the giant contribution from Steiner (1969). Moreover, such planning can be carried out efficiently through bureaucratic structures that allow for 'systematic' monitoring and control in regular fashion. Change is an exception and not the norm.

On the contrary, in unstable environments, e.g. those moving at pace, those containing shocks or those whose driving variables elicit a complex patterning, a more adaptive and flexible strategic approach, capable of fast response, is required to cope with the complexity and the multitude of threats and opportunities that arise. Equally, the most efficient cultural medium for strategy implementation is one marked with enterprise and creativity; so internally the organisation is used to dealing with, and taking advantage of, the types of shock it faces. Moreover, people are not fazed easily by the extent of change with which they have to endure. Change becomes the norm rather than the exception.

Such alignment patterns of the three variables create the harmony necessary for designing and delivering effective strategy. Clearly, in fast changing

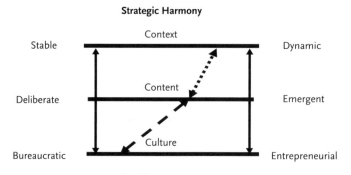

Figure 3.2 **Harmony among the three Cs.**

contexts, neither a planned strategy nor a bureaucratic culture is capable of the quick reactions and responses needed to survive. The cumbersome pace of things and the agnostic approach to change will prevent the taking of timely, appropriate action. Even in a stable environment, an adaptive strategy and an entrepreneurial culture may yield increasing frustration among the creative employees and responses could represent simply change for the sake of change.

The generic model in Figure 3.2 helps find the balance among the strategic variables. The solid lines represent harmony. The dashed lines illustrate disharmony and a position where strategy content has been adjusted pretty well to the changing context but the slow moving culture has been left behind. Over the last twenty-five years, the pace of change and the complexity of variables that make up environmental contexts have shifted the context types from stable to dynamic. The challenge for many consultants and senior managements has been to realign strategy with this shift, moving it from deliberate/planned to become more adaptive and learned. That has proved to be the easy part and such a shift can be accomplished relatively quickly through intensive, facilitated, sessions in the boardrooms, at boot camps or away days. The time amounts to weeks and months rather than years.

However, the biggest difficulty for many organisations has been in trying to make the cultural shift from bureaucratic to entrepreneurial. Cultures, in either a simple form or a multi-layered one, represent the organisational DNA by capturing the events, experiences, decisions, techniques and people of the past and manifest these in the present through commonly held belief systems or ways of doing things. This sensitive milieu cannot be altered easily or quickly. Hence, for many organisations in recent years, their attempts to realign the three variables following sudden shifts in their outer context have stumbled over the shaping of new, entrepreneurial cultures.

There is an important law in cybernetics – the 'law of requisite variety' that refers to the ability of a biological organism to change when faced with changes in its environment. If the organism is used to change and variety within itself, then when it is faced with external change and variety, its inbuilt coping mechanisms are ignited and they help it to make the adaptation and survive. However, if it is not used to change within itself, its underdeveloped coping mechanisms will not assist its survival when exposed to external change and it will perish. The analogy can be extended to organisations – those with entrepreneurial cultures are likely to survive better when exposed to contextual change than those with slow-moving bureaucratic ones.

Cultural changes can be accomplished through a number of change management processes (see Figure 3.3). First, incremental change of the Japanese 'kaizen' (or continuous innovation) type allows for small, marginal changes on a regular basis, e.g., annual product or service quality

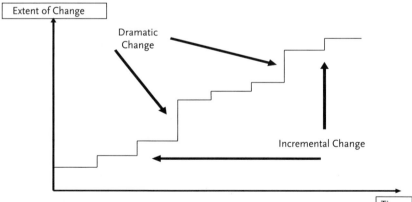

Figure 3.3 **Typologies of change.**

innovations. The changes are relatively small in proportion to total activity and so do not challenge or threaten existing cultural territory. Nor are they dramatic when considered in isolation but, over a five-year period, they can amount to significant overall repositioning for the organisation. Such a process helps build internal coping mechanisms, though the amount of change may still not be sufficient in high tempo contexts.

Second, cultural change can be achieved in a more dramatic manner. This tends to be most evident in organisational turnarounds (a subject we examine in much more detail in a later chapter) when, after long periods of inactive drifting by indigenous managers, external agents like financial institutions or creditors intervene by insisting on the wholesale replacement of top management, thereby knocking out the guardians of the old ways of doing things. Their replacement by new blood with new ideas and methods is accompanied normally with sweeping changes across the organisation, e.g. downsizing of the labour force, pruning of product/market activities etc. The net effect is to remove dramatically the old cultures and replace them with a newfound sense of enterprise. Such drama need not await the threat of turnaround but be triggered by contextual events like the threat of take-over, entry to core markets by powerful competitors, new legislation and so on. Each can provide senior management with an opportunity to 'change the way that things are done around here'.

Finally, cultural change can be accomplished using a combination of the above processes. Ironically, Japanese firms like Honda found kaizen to be an important means of internal change energy but not sufficient alone to keep up with the pace of external change in modern contexts or to leapfrog the innovations of competitors. Hence, their solution has been to intersperse continuous change with periods of dramatic change at regular intervals. Because change is expected within the firm, introducing sharp change does not have the same adverse impact as it would on an organisation without the embedding of incremental change. The dramatic events become part of the cultural 'expectation' of future change and are absorbed into the system. Consequently, the organisation can achieve significant advances in the extent of change possible over a long period.

Contextual change – the 'long view'

Much anxiety is generated by the hyperbole often used when characterising the turbulence and complexity in contemporary environmental contexts. Organisational leadership seems taxed as never before. Such challenges invite leaders to acquire new coping skills and continually upgrade the ones they possess. The call is for ambidextrous, multilingual, interdisciplinary individuals who can handle the intellectual and physical pressure that complexity brings, cope with 360-degree relationships and balance their work–life domains. The demand for these characteristics may appear to be a recent phenomenon. However, history tells us that change on a dramatic scale is nothing new to the world. Studies in political science, industrial history, international sociology and education show that our predecessors have experienced, and adapted to, change on a grand scale.

Waves of change in social history

History is analysed often in terms of distinctive periods of time (e.g. Marx, Foucault) or modes of organising that are different from each other. Though major paths of continuity exist through the periodic stages, e.g. the persistence of the great religions (Islam, Christianity, Buddhism, Judaism, Hinduism), political, economic, social and technological features of each can be grouped as relatively homogenous within each. Wave studies suggest several popular segmentations.[2] The first wave was the *agricultural society* from the mid-sixteenth century to the late nineteenth century in the Western world. Social groups settled in villages and cultivated land with systematic farming practices. Land became the basis for decentralised local economies and political influence, where villages were managed by elite groups or authoritarian individuals. Family life was embedded in the communities and housing grouped around a common meeting place, e.g., open space, hall, church, school. Farm and family lives merged. This organised experience, with its homogenous, seasonal pattern was a stark transition from the previous society of small, migrating groups of hunter-gatherers relying on knowledge, instinct and adaptability for survival.

The second wave was marked by the shift to *industrial society* from the early nineteenth century to the middle of the twentieth century. New industrialists challenged the dominance of the farming communities. Scientific breakthroughs meant that mechanisation and specialisation became the bywords for efficient organisation. These penetrated the quiet rural farming practices and replaced some of the labour element causing mass migration to growing urban conurbations. In the US, only 2 per cent lived in urban areas in the first wave as opposed to 75 per cent in the second wave. Factories had become the lean means of production and rows of street dwellings emerged to house their workers. Railways connected the growing urban conurbations and cities. The corporation grew as the powerhouse of change that could coordinate the many skills with the range of capital sources required to make them productive. Men dominated the labour force. Shifts from old autocracies and monarchies to new centralised hierarchical bureaucracies based on democratic process populated the public sector. The nation state was the dominant organising form at the national level. A factory and family split emerged; there was alienation, anonymity, increased crime, oppression and repression as well as hope, equality and opportunity. This world was removed significantly from the peaceful village communities of the first wave.

By the middle of the twentieth century, the industrial wave was embedded across the globe, but the invention of the modern computer and the movement of labour from manufacturing to service sector economies in the West, ignited a third wave, the *information society*. Marked by differentiated global economies, this age has witnessed the rise of new industries, e.g. electronics, ecology, telecommunications, space science and molecular biology. Associated organisations metamorphosed from their industrial images into flat, flexible, fluid, enterprising, team-based units and provided high-quality products and services to a discriminating customer base. Such sectors and systems favoured women in the workforce and work–life balance broke the old employment cultures with more part-time and flexible routines. Globalisation enabled larger corporations and major brands to dominate market segments. Multinational corporations (MNCs) became larger than many nation states, and international bodies (e.g. UN, OPEC, EU, WTO) assumed greater powers. The nuclear family that dominated the second wave began to disintegrate as more people lived alone. Local units thrived as technology allowed home working – bringing home and work back together. More significantly, cheaper travel and the revolution in telecommunications exposed more people more quickly to different cultures than at any time in history. This major cultural experience marked out the era sociologically and placed great demands on the way things were done, said, managed and organised. Leaders were warned of a 'clash of civilisations'[3] at the same time as the second wave clashes with the first. The speed of this change, collapsed into fifty years at the end of the twentieth century, was the major reason why many consider it to be the most dramatic transition ever.

Some now argue[4] that a fourth wave is already upon us – the *knowledge society*. This may stretch out from the millennium to 2050 and its characteristics have yet to be defined clearly. Driven by greater scientific and technological progress, increasing globalisation, damaging ecological time bombs, the battle for energy reserves, virtual communications and cultural and religious divergence, experts continue to speculate on its shape and its outcomes. Speculation takes the form of detailed long-view scenarios produced mainly through a Western lens. These sense-making imaginings have great strength in their ability to reduce uncertainty and promote better thinking so that strategic issues can be addressed in a credible manner. We illustrate how they work below.

Clearly, the speed and extent of the first wave differed greatly across the world. In the early phases, those who could not adjust to close community living had space in which to opt out and continue their hunter-gatherer existence. There was time to adjust and there was plenty of precedent to follow the initial settlements through the medium of storytelling. The transition between waves one and two was relatively gradual and, as before, precedents established by the early movers helped to lower considerably the uncertainty that followers might have to face. So, for example, most of continental Europe could look to the early British experience of the industrial revolution for guidance. The transition between waves two and three was more dramatic but occurred when the world was used to considerable change and upheaval following the impact of the two World Wars and the general acceptance of the outcomes of the advancement of science. Uncertainty was the norm rather than the exception and the speed with which business organisations adapted suggests that they had developed coping mechanisms to help make sense of the change around them. The current switch from the information to the knowledge society poses separate problems in terms of both the unknown and the unknowable. Its novelty and instantaneous spread across the globe mean the absence of precedent. Further, the added complication of a change in the form of political governance makes for a trickier adjustment.

Waves of change in political history

> " We are at a moment in world affairs when the essential ideas that govern statecraft must change. For five centuries, it has taken the resources of a state to destroy another state...This is no longer true, owing to advances in international telecommunications, rapid computation, and weapons of mass destruction. The change in statecraft that will accompany these developments will be as profound as any that the state has thus far undergone.[5]

The knowledge era is accompanied by the emergence of the Market State as a new form of governance (see Vignette 3.2). This evolution has been hard fought, fractious and competitive. But, states are challenged to alter the pathway by rethinking their role, practice and policy.

As the liberal democratic model became the favoured form of governance, states looked to market mechanisms to allocate scarce resources. Consequently, the traditional boundaries between government and business underwent rapid and significant transformation. As more governments followed the efficiency model, downsizing strategies meant that traditional activities were outsourced in areas such as healthcare, education and the prison service. At the same time, an expansion in the power and wealth of many leading business corporations helped them to prove a variety of services, to employees, including personal health schemes, pension schemes, counselling, lifelong learning and philanthropy. These were once the province of public agencies that had become inefficient. The ability of the corporations to sustain this activity will rest on whether or not the rise in economic power of MNCs can be sustained. The trends seemed favourable.[6] In 2002, only 47 of the largest 100 economies in the world were nation states, the rest were MNCs (for example, Wal-Mart with annual sales of \$250bn was right up in the seventeenth place). The 63000 MNCs employed over 90 million people.

This displacement of the old nation state by global organisations, along with the increasing power of the latter, inevitably invites questions over the relative domains of activity and how well MNCs are managed. The shock crashes of Enron, Worldcomm, Vivendi and Parmalat in the early 2000s signalled the call for greater corporate social responsibility in the powerful MNCs backed up by stronger legislation from national and transnational institutions, like the European Union. So, in the new market state, businesses may provide more of the original functions of the nation state but they come under more scrutiny from public and civil authorities in the process. The trends indicate that they will have to continue to handle this duality as they pick up the social and philanthropic duties in communities that have been jettisoned by governments. Ecology, environment, public health will have to be counterbalanced with the search for new markets, product innovation and profitability. Increasingly, corporate strategies will have to embrace the success of the society in which firms operate as a precursor to their own individual market aspirations. Corporate governance and corporate strategy will have to coalesce as the knowledge society, in tandem with the Market State, develops.

VIGNETTE 3.2

Theory of the modern state

Princely States (1494–1572)
Evolved in Italy during the European Renaissance and replaced the feudal lords as Princes offered people protection in return for taxes and local territorial power. This represents permanent Government, where the state confers legitimacy on the dynasty. Key date: Peace of Augsburg 1555

Kingly States (1567–1651)
Premised upon a divine right to rule, Kings did the same things for their subjects as Princes. This represents absolute monarchy that confers legitimacy on the state. Key date: Peace of Westphalia 1648

Territorial States (1649–1789)
Premised upon an aristocratic leadership that expands the nation's interests internationally through professional armies and navies. The state manages the country efficiently. Key date: Treaty of Utrecht 1713

State-Nations (1776–1870)

Premised on freedom and democracy, this new order united peoples around national, ethno-cultural identities. Imperialism progressed as national identities were exploited. The state forges the national identity. Key date: Congress of Vienna 1815

Nation States (1861–1991)

Prominent after the Civil War in the USA and after World War I in Europe, as old empires died.

Premised on the state providing greater welfare benefits for people, different forms of governance arose in the emerging nation states – communism (Lenin and Stalin in the Soviet Union), fascism (Hitler and Mussolini in Germany and Italy) and parliamentary capitalism (Churchill and Roosevelt in the UK and USA). A Cold War ensued between the former and latter. Capitalist models saw governments and business working in harmony through market regulation and social programmes. Key date: Treaty of Versailles 1919.

Market States (1989–onwards)

The Anglo-American form of liberal-democracy championed free-market economics and the market state emerged to maximise the chances for peoples to better themselves and to ensure the existence of market structures for wealth and prosperity. Governments see the efficient workings of markets as the best way to provide prosperity so deregulation and privatisation, together with public–private partnerships, mark the policy agenda. Key event: Fall of the Berlin Wall 1989.

Source: Bobbit (2002)

Making sense of the knowledge society and the market state

So how do executives make sense of the beginnings of the new wave, characterised by a knowledge society and a market state? How do they anticipate possible futures? How do they reduce their feelings of uncertainty about the future? One approach is to understand better the variables that will form the first period of the next wave by tracing their history to help determine their likely trajectory and impact.

Strategists intent on the long view embrace scenario planning (see below) to help them make sense of complex future contexts. To build their scenarios, they identify the key variables likely to play a significant role over a specific future time period. Then, these are analysed according to the certainty or uncertainty of their outcome. Some are certain or predetermined and some are uncertain. Scenarios are built around the uncertain variables.

In a prominent survey, the UK Cabinet Office[7] reviewed eighteen respectable generic scenario studies looking out as far as 2050. The main variables analysed were (a) economic issues (14), of which globalisation (however defined) was the key concern; (b) technological issues (13), of which the IT revolution was among the main issues; (c) environmental (13), issues of which climate change and energy crises loomed large; and (d) social issues (10), of which demographics and the clash of cultures were in the vanguard.

Clearly, these variables are not mutually exclusive. Their interactions cause complexity as the future context unfolds. But if we analyse them and their potential interactions and build the results into scenarios, surprising outcomes should be minimised and 'future shock' limited to things that cannot be foreseen easily – things that are unknowable or unforeseeable (such as sudden shocks with 'force ten' impact).

Royal Dutch Shell plc is acknowledged widely to be a world leader in scenario development and a closer inspection of their global scenarios will provide an understanding of the variables that will help shape the next wave.

Global scenarios to 2025 – the Shell perspective

For over thirty years, Shell has produced generic global scenarios to guide its divisional executives in their strategy making. Throughout the 1990s, it examined the concept of TINA – there is no alternative to the progress of globalisation, the march of new technologies and free market economics, in its three-year scenario cycles. These scenarios tried to articulate the dilemma between the efficiencies of *market-centred worlds* with *the values* and *social cohesion of communities* so asking the question:

> 'will the resolution to dilemmas arising from globalisation be dominated by global elites or by the people of the heartlands?'.[8]

Three drivers of the next wave

By 2005, the tension between these two variables above still teased policy-makers. But, in the meantime, there had been major incursions on Western lifestyles brought about by two crises, both of which were foreseeable if you knew where to look for the signals. First, the 9/11 incident brought a brewing discontent with these lifestyles, and the *market* and *territorial* state behaviours (especially US ones) that exported them, to the surface. The shock was catastrophic and the causal responses long term and global. Second, the major misappropriation of resources at Enron, and the criminal stewardship by Arthur Anderson, rocked the business world with similar intensity. It depleted trust sharply amongst investors, governments, employees and the general public in the workings of the free-market. Expectedly, Western citizens demanded that their states take the lead in providing physical security and restoring the integrity to markets.

Hence, to make sense of the initial period of the new wave, the scenario builders added a third driver of change to the two drivers of globalisation and community progress – the power of the state to control, through regulation or coercion, terrorism and market governance. These three drivers work separately towards different outcomes – efficiency, social cohesion and justice/security. All three may be desired but their common achievement is prevented by degrees of mutual exclusivity between them, e.g. it is difficult to be completely free, conform to group norms and be coerced at the same time. For scenario planners and strategists, this suggests a series of compromises or, in this case, a 'trilemma' between the three main drivers of change, to use a term coined by Shell. Hence, a series of three plausible futures can be built that imagines two of these happening at the expense of the other, such as, for example, one that includes some globalisation and lots of security but little social cohesion.

Seven predetermined variables of the next wave

But these drivers are not the only variables that would impact the next wave. Variables that can be known with greater certainty, or predetermined variables, enter each scenario in their own way. For these scenarios, Shell had seven main predetermined variables:

(1) The US, China and changing globalisation patterns

Globalisation is a widely used phrase with multiple meanings, from the pervasive spread of free market economics to the social criticisms of the net effects; through political state changes and power shifts from state to MNC; to normalisation and diversity in culture; to ecology of the planet, with sustainable development at its fore. The first three are embedded in closely related systems but the latter two take different approaches. However, common interpretation surrounds the gravitation of economies and social processes to some global operating norm in supply, demand and institutional spheres.

Once again, history tells us that the process of globalisation is nothing new. Therborn (2000) hypothesises at least six waves: from the initial diffusion of world religions and the formation of transcontinental civilisations (fourth–seventh centuries AD); to European colonial conquests in the fifteenth century; to the European global wars between Britain and France in the eighteenth century; to European imperialism in the latter half of the nineteenth century culminating in World War I (WWI); to the superpower, ideological era of the USA and USSR after WWII to the mid-1980s; to the current financial and cultural era dominated by free market economics and democratic freedoms. In between these phases, there were distinct periods of de-globalisation. For instance, after the global spread of religions and their holy languages, there followed a rise in local languages as high cultures adapted the global to the local. This caused regional fragmentation, especially between the twelfth and sixteenth centuries. The shrinking trade after WWI is another case of reversal. As Therborn (2000: 163) observes, 'globalisation is neither a unique, recent phenomenon nor something intrinsically irreversible.'

The Shell scenario builders acknowledged this history. They assumed high degrees of globalisation to continue with some backlash from nations intent on protecting themselves and going it alone. The process does not affect each country or region equally, so its progress has variable speed. However, the beginnings of the new wave are premised on globalisation being influenced heavily by the US and China.

The US has much stronger long run growth rates than Europe or Japan making trade and foreign direct investment (FDI) with the US critical to any integration in the OECD. Underpinning this is a 50 per cent increase in America's population by 2050 compared with a slide for many European countries. In addition to this generative power, the US plays an increasing role in legal and regulatory terms internationally. China's share in world trade doubled from 1993 to 2003 (from 2.2% to 5.2%) and recent growth rates are the highest in the world's recorded history. It is assumed that China will become the world's manufacturing centre due to low labour costs, market size and plant modernisation. Though the internal market is vast, it is still fragmented with many local entry barriers. China has adopted many World Trade Organisation (WTO) endorsed trading rules but faces broader governance issues as business expands.

For the beginnings of the new wave, Europe is the alternative super-power to the US in GDP terms. Despite political differences on foreign policy, the US and Europe have large trading exchanges that link them inextricably and a systemic social history that stabilises the relationship. Years of warfare have led to consensus-based decision-taking like the policy of 'mutual recognition' on global governance and the use of 'soft power' when dealing with internal conflict. So Europe is expected to play a stable and influential role over the scenario period. Interestingly, India is assumed to have a smaller impact than either China or Europe in the first part of the new wave as its modernisation drive has not been great and the weight of the agricultural sector has held it back (60% of its labour force but only 22% of GDP). High growth rates have been driven largely by outsourcing, mainly in the IT, medical and financial areas, and by thriving indigenous telecommunications and pharmaceutical sectors. Ethnicity, the caste system and language make policy reform much more difficult than in China. Hence, over the next twenty-five years India's full effect is unlikely to be felt:

> To stay a stable peaceful society, India has to be a muddle and a mess. It is a miracle that, proceeding in the way that it has done, it has come as far as it has, trebling its per capita income. But there will not be growth convergence between China and India... China will again become a viable Great Power. India may become just a Great Democracy.[9]

(2) African futures

As a vast continent, rich in resources and diverse in cultures, Africa has around 11 per cent of the world's population. Estimates suggest that about 20 per cent of the world's oil needs could come from West Africa between 2005 and 2015, making its mineral resources key to the advance of globalisation. But, many African states have failed to convert these resources into sustained growth and social development:

> " For its part, Africa must accelerate reform. And the developed world must increase and improve its aid and stop doing those things which hinder Africa's progress.[10]

Major differences in language, religion, politics, social processes and allegiances stemming from colonial heritages make it tough for scenario builders to make sense of the signals coming out of Africa. The challenges are great: increasing poverty in the sub-Saharan region with half its 700 million people existing on less than $0.65 a day; increasing corruption adding 20 per cent to the cost of goods and deterring foreign investment; environmental stress as 20 per cent of its vegetated land is classified as degraded; increased violence and warfare; resource depletion with a major exodus of about 80,000 of the brightest brains per annum; handicapped by the continued AIDS crisis with 60–70 per cent of total world infection on the continent.

But hope continues to spring from a rise in multiparty competitive elections over the last decade empowering civil groups, the emergence of new political leaders and the success of the novel peer-review mechanism, where 24 countries (75% of the population) have agreed to work together to review each other's weaknesses.

With rich natural endowments, underperformance and civil conflict, robust institutional development is essential to Africa's future. Major efforts have begun internally with transparency agreements in the extractive industries (EITI) and externally with the Millennium Challenge Accounts, where US investment is directed to effective sources only.

> " If Africa is to take responsibility for its own development, it must be given greater influence in decision-making which affects it most directly and must be able to exert much greater pressure on the rich world to honour its commitments to the poor people of Africa.[11]

For the new wave, Africa represents both challenge and hope. It has a crucial role to play in the process of globalisation but the extent of this role will depend on how the international community relates to its poorer neighbour in trade and institutional terms.

(3) Change from nation states to market states

Bobbit's genealogy (see Vignette 3.1) suggests that we are entering a seismic change in the evolution of the state from nation to market state. Global recognition of human rights, intercontinental weapons of mass destruction, transnational threats (e.g. AIDS, terrorism, climate change), significant global financial transfers and the telecommunication revolution have meant that states struggle to guarantee citizens their rights, safety or autonomy.

> " The state is not declining, nor is the nation dying, but the relationship between the two is changing and the particular version of the state that has dominated the developed world for more than 100 years is undergoing a profound change.[12]

The trend for nations to cede direct control of resource allocation and their organisation to markets in the new wave is assumed to continue over the next twenty-five years. However, states are unlikely to fade away or become bit-part players of a wider global game. Rather they will intervene in a variety of new ways, such as, for example, by contributing to the fight on poverty by squashing debt. Moreover, states have a selfish interest in promoting value added in their economies, through the avenue of tax returns, and will continue to invest in those areas directly linked to economic outputs like education, R&D and international regulations on standards and trade. Finally, states have important roles to play in creating the right kind of regulatory frameworks that help check excesses when market forces or corporate governance fail in areas such as pollution, corporate manslaughter and the like.

(4) Demography and migrations

Demographics tend to be *de rigueur* predetermined variables for the scenario builder as they can be known better than most other variables. Several issues need attention. First, these variables have a long reach and so it is typical to extend their 'forecast' beyond the realms of the time frame under study. Second, despite general trends at the global level, there are major differences at the country and down the regional levels (for example, in 2005, the population of Scotland was projected to decrease slightly over a fifty-year time period but this masked the expectation of a steeper decline for the city of Aberdeen alongside a fair-sized increase in the case of Edinburgh). Finally, demographics and migration tend to work through their interaction with other variables. For instance, they directly and strongly influence economic growth, energy demand and the pace of change in society. Moreover, migration tends to be treated as a temporary adjustment until a new equilibrium is achieved.

The Shell global scenarios to 2025, published in 2005, assume:

- A world population increase of 1.4m to 7.9 bn by 2050 (20% up on 2005 levels)
- The population for developed nations levels off at the year 2050 and then declines
- Africa grows by 1.6 per cent and Europe falls by 0.3 per cent
- Migration flows keep North American growth at about 0.7 per cent
- Urban communities expand from 3.2 bn in 2005 to 4.6 bn by 2025 and the shift is greater for developing nations increasing the number of slum dwellers
- Rural communities remain static at 3.3 bn
- Despite rapid increase in migration in the 1990s from the Eastern Europe and China, this will run its course by 2025.
- The main immigration countries will be US, Russia, Germany, Ukraine, France, Canada, Saudi Arabia and Australia
- Brain drain in Russia as population slides from 145m in 2000 to 114m in 2050
- China will be the main source of migrants and their remittances

These assumptions are based upon the best estimates from the UN, OECD and the World Economic Forum in 2005 and so represent the best available knowledge. Their impact on other variables is worked through the scenario logics and so their particular influence may not be seen clearly in any final scenario set.

(5) Economic growth

Such rates are notoriously difficult to judge, even in the hands of experts, as they are influenced by many other factors whose trajectory cannot be known easily, e.g. different incentives, market structures, MNC location decisions. Consequently, each plausible scenario contains an assumption about the prevailing growth rate that helps to bring it about. Shell created three scenarios with growth rates of 2.6 per cent, 3.1 per cent and 3.8 per cent, largely explained by productivity growth. Again, within each, there is regional difference with China and India growing two to three times faster than the rest of the world, the Eurozone lagging behind the steady rate of the US and Japan dwindling away as yesterday's success story.

The US performance is down to better demographic profiles and structural features. However, it needs to grow at 3 per cent and more to close its current account deficit (6% of GDP in 2004) caused mainly by a savings short fall (less than 2% of GDP). Japan has a high proportion of ageing people and faster ageing slows economic growth. Hence, the IMF estimates that Japan's real growth will slump by 0.8 per cent from 2000 to 2050.

(6) The search for energy security

The emerging structural energy supply gap is a major cause for concern at the start of the new period. Driven by events with defined underlying trajectories, e.g., the war in Iraq, demand from China, tensions in oil producing states and terrorist attacks in Saudi Arabia, the oil price rose by over 100 per cent from 2002 to 2005. Long-term assessments assume that the new level will be sustained. This is due to the structural adjustments required to cope with three key discontinuities:

(i) *Re-linking*

The balance of demand and supply is out of line with excess demand for energy coming from high growth nations like China and India and from an increasingly affluent middle-class consumer. Prices will remain high to bring the equation into balance.

(ii) *Energy security*

There are two aspects to this story. First, the obvious terrorist threats to supplies whether in the soil, during transportation, during process, storage or at points of sale. Carbon-based products make soft targets. Second, recent major corrections in the assessment of oil and gas reserves, their general state and access to them – especially in the Middle East - and the gradual release of reserves over time rather than profit taking, have cast doubt on the reliability and flexibility of global supplies. To meet current demand, major infrastructure investment is required at higher and higher risks.

(iii) *Carbon*

Regulatory and market developments have enabled carbon to be considered an independent commodity, though, when emissions are considered, its price is a negative one. Shell assumed that the energy system would operate as an energy and carbon one with increased public pressure for growth and lower pollution, especially in Europe.

All three discontinuities will herald new legislation and governance regimes for states and international institutions. In particular, a low-carbon world means dramatic revision to lifestyles, tight regulation of markets, investment in alternative technologies, reconsideration of nuclear power and ecology policies on a global scale.

(7) The energy and carbon industry

Balancing economic growth and lowering carbon emissions is a huge challenge for humankind over the next fifty years. Clearly, an increased global population, established and affluent middle-class consumers and the growth of the BRIC[13] nations (especially China) place huge demands on planet earth and its resources.

> " National decisions made now and in the longer-term future will influence the extent of any damage suffered by vulnerable population and ecosystems later in the century.[14]

Two main issues concern the planners:

(i) *Climate change*

Over the last million years, the earth's climate has moved through a cycle consisting of long ice ages interrupted by short but warmer interludes. Scientists have shown from tree rings and ice cores how these periods are marked out by variations of about 10 per cent of light in the Northern hemisphere and in atmospheric gases. Ruddiman (2003) found major discontinuities in the cycles of methane and CO2 about the same time as our farming ancestors adopted policies of 'slash and burn' to clear forests for the organised growing of vegetation and the rearing of animals. If they had not dumped so many gases into the atmosphere, Ruddiman argues that current temperatures would be down to glacial levels. Human activity kept these levels in check up to the twentieth century. But, the balance has been tipped of late by massive deforestation, huge greenhouse gas emissions and expanding population. Pre-industrial CO2 emissions were 280 ppm, current levels are at 380 ppm and rising. Experts argue that at 1000 ppm, the damage will be so great that major relocations of peoples will be necessary. A level of 500–50 ppm will require significant effort but could be managed. But predictions see this level by 2050 and a continued rise thereafter.

Whatever scenario comes about, a strategic urgency around the planet is a vital component. Hence international cooperation and accompanying legislative frameworks are core ingredients of that strategy. The Kyoto protocols were an example of such an effort but without the US and China, its impact could be minimal.

(ii) *Biodiversity*

Sustainable development depends on the efficient functioning of specific plant, animal and marine ecosystems. But humankind's polluting interventions have destroyed many natural habitats, some to extinction and others to the point thereof. Again, history shows us that care for biodiversity in environments is not new and can be traced back to third-century India (Emperor Asoka) and seventh-century Sumatra to more recent incursions in the John Muir inspired national parks of America. Biodiversity was made legal bound on the signatories of the 1992 earth Summit in Rio via the Convention on Biological Diversity and the Framework Convention on Climate Change.

For an energy major like Shell, biodiversity has figured strongly in its past operational strategies and, expectedly, the 2005 scenarios give it prominence. They assume increasing pressure on the ecosystems and an increasing reliance on cooperative and legal frameworks.

Three global scenarios to 2025

After consideration of the drivers of change and the predetermined variables, scenario builders can begin to create the stories of the future.

Shell constructed three plausible stories[15] from their reflections of the main variable above:

Low trust globalisation

(a legalistic, 'prove it to me' world)
Market and security driven so the trade-off is with social cohesion. The absence of market solutions to the crisis of security and trust, rapid regulatory change, overlapping jurisdictions and conflicting laws lead to intrusive checks and controls, encouraging short-term portfolio optimisation and vertical integration. Institutional discontinuities limit cross-border economic integration. Complying with fast evolving rules and managing complex risks are key challenges.

Open doors

(a pragmatic 'know me' world)
Market and community driven so the trade-off is with security. The latter is assumed to be 'built in' with compliance certification. The story describes a world of regulatory harmonisation, mutual recognition, independent media, voluntary best practice codes and close links between investors and civil society that encourage cross-border integration and virtual value chains. Networking skills and superior reputation management are essential.

Flags

(a dogmatic 'follow me' world)
Community and security driven so the trade-off is with market efficiencies. The story describes a future of zero-sum games, dogmatic approaches, regulatory fragmentation and national preferences. Conflicts over values and religion give insiders an advantage and put a brake on globalisation. Gated communities, patronage and national standards exacerbate fragmentation, and call for careful country risk management.

Clearly, none of these three scenarios will come about in their entirety. The skill of the planner is to use them to improve thinking, so better strategies can emerge for the operating companies of the Shell organisation. All three stories will influence strategy design, as the company will have to defend against some of the future outcomes and take advantage of others. Moreover, in this set of stories, the Shell planners have broken from past tradition and created a scenario space[16] into which the stories fall. This space allows for the emergence of other futures within the confines of the three driving forces – markets, communities and security. Hence, other combinations of these issues can be imagined and might come about.

The important learning in this set of scenarios is a better understanding of the tensions among the three drivers of change (see figure 3.4). Balancing the relationship between efficient market forces, social cohesion and the need for security is a timeless issue for civilisations. However, the gravity of the task in a borderless world, under environmental destruction, is huge. That is the challenge for executive leadership whether in private, public, not-for-profit or religious sectors. The challenge has never been greater but the uncertainty attached to strategy is much reduced with a thorough exploration of context. The next section explains how this can be done.

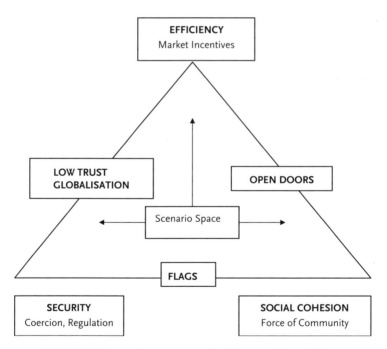

Figure 3.4 **Shell Global Scenarios to 2025, Shell International BV.**
Source: Van der Veer (2005)

Understanding contextual uncertainty

Much of the above discussion is premised upon the turbulent nature of modern environmental contexts facing organisations. The drivers of change and the predetermined variables will shape a very different future context to which organisations have to adapt and in which they have to operate. How do executives cope with the uncertainty that these changes bring?

To help, Van der Heijden (2005) argues that this uncertainty can be reduced to three components:

- Risk, where patterns from the past exist and prediction is possible.
- Structural, where no patterns exist but the event can be imagined from causal chain analysis.
- Unknowable, where there is no pattern nor causal chain imagination.

Risk is an easier concept to deal with as its perception can be reduced by well-established techniques. Structural issues require more perseverance but the techniques can be mastered with good tutelage and practice. These techniques will help prepare an organisation for the impact of 'unknowable' variables by inculcating the need for flexible design in mental and physical resource configuration and the need for rapid response by adaptivity. However, no organisation can know the time, the place or the impact of such variables.

(1) Risk

Risk can be assessed by the attachment of probabilities to the occurrence of future events from an analysis of past behaviour and the elements that form that behaviour. There are many analytical tools associated with this approach, forecasting being the best-known and most frequently used.

Forecasting

The use of forecasting can be traced back to the oldest civilisations with the ancient Egyptians predicting the richness of harvests from the level reached by the Nile in flood season and the Oracle at Delphi attracting a pilgrimage of high-level decision makers of the time. But it was the Keynesian revolution in macroeconomics in the 1930s that spawned the systematic development of modern forecasting techniques. These spread from origins in Scandinavia to the UK in the 1950s and then to other advanced economies. In the relatively stable context of the 1950s and 1960s, the technique enjoyed great success. This was halted swiftly by the unforeseen or undetected shocks in the 1970s from oil price shocks and the break down of the Bretton-Woods Agreement. Despite these set-backs, forecasting has continued to develop both in method and application, from simple extrapolation to time series, structural modelling and complex econometric systems.[17]

Forecasting has the benefit of objectivity – by allowing the data to speak; of simplicity of output – with single points making interpretation and planning easier; of consolidation of the existing knowledge base in one system; of accuracy over the short term and in stable environmental periods. Hence, forecasting still performs a crucial role in opening up our future gaze and much business decision-making is premised upon good use of the technique.

However, forecasting has its fault lines as the famous economist Paul Samuelson (1966: 92) pointed out: 'Wall Street indices predicted nine out of the last five recessions!' There are a number of problems. First, because point forecasting is limited in range, it can illuminate only a narrow part of the opaque future. The ground on either side of the point forecast is left dimly lit. To rectify this, the technique needs fortification from complementary tools. Second, forecasts will fail because of a particular cognitive trap built into the mechanistic routines that assumes that past patterns will always produce a good blue print for the near future. History shows that structural changes happen and these break the extant patterning and render probabilistic forecasting helpless. This issue is made worse by close networks in which forecasters exchange views and build their knowledge base. Fiedler (1977:62) emphasises 'the herd instinct among forecasters makes sheep look like independent thinkers.' Third, forecasting hits problems of accuracy when it tries to reach into mid or deep futures as the underlying assumptions on the key variables can break down easily over such time frames. The result is a set of forecasts that resembles a 'horse's tail' – a series of revisions that fall off as the prediction is taken further into the future. Again, this problem is exacerbated in fast-moving contexts because often, the time needed to collect data and to analyse and interpret it does not exist, rendering meaningful policy advice impossible.

Fourth, forecasting rarely captures the 'soft' elements that are often the basis of societal change, such as beliefs, values, cultures, spirituality, human relationships and so on. Such features of the future landscape do not lend themselves easily to quantification and tend to be absent from the majority of modelling systems. Indeed, as Schoemaker (1997: 47) points out, reality 'often includes elements that were not or cannot be formally modelled such as new regulations, value shifts and innovations'.

Hence, used with care, forecasting is an essential facilitator for understanding the risk element of environmental uncertainty, especially over the short term. Unfortunately, its flaws render it increasingly ineffective in fast-changing contexts where it needs special support from other processes to improve its navigational effectiveness. Fast changing contexts consist of both predictable or predetermined elements and unpredictable ones. Forecasting deals well with predictable elements such as demographic variables like birth and death rates, ageing populations in different countries and the like. However, it deals poorly with the unpredictable elements that cannot be ascertained from prior historical data. These elements fall into two categories. First, those that can be ascertained from careful cause–effect analysis that helps explain the impact of potential structural interventions. These can be handled with the application of a number of qualitative techniques of which scenario planning is perhaps the most powerful (see below). Second, history warns us that surprise elements that shock our systems will always occur. We have no way of knowing when and how, but preparation and flexibility remain the best defence.

Trend Impact Analysis (TIA) and Cross-Impact Analysis (CIA)

TIA and CIA can be considered as hybrid techniques dealing with the management of uncertainty by risk analysis and introducing probabilities to make forecasts more realistic *and* to model potential structural impacts and their effects through sensitivity analysis (CIA).

Traditional probabilistic forecasting assumed the future as an extrapolation of the past and lacked an integral algorithmic component for the reasoned treatment of divergence or shocks. TIA was developed in the early 1970s. It seeks to modify simple extrapolations by making projections with inbuilt curve-fitting techniques. Then, through the use of expert judgement, a set of probabilities is given to a generated set of unprecedented future events for both their timing and impact in the future. The adjusted extrapolations are then produced.

CIA is a variant on this probabilistic massaging process. It was developed by Gordon and Helmer in 1966 and tested in the application of the game 'Futures', prepared for the 100th anniversary of the Kaiser Aluminium and Chemical Company. Like TIA, it attempts to build perceptions of experts into the forecasting process through the attachment of probabilities to initial event occurrences. Originally programmed by Gordon and Hayward at UCLA in 1968, many software adaptations followed including Battelle's EXPLOR-SIM and Duperrin and Gabus's SMIC in the 1970s. Godet has noted that the latter has been applied to projects as varied as aircraft construction, geopolitical futures and nuclear power.

The allocation of probabilities of events goes beyond TIA by setting both a priori probabilities to future events *and* setting the conditional probabilities of the subsequent cause–event stream triggered by the main event. The following example in Gordon (1994: 2) gives the idea: 'If the use of transportation and construction increases six fold (say event 1), what is the likelihood of increased government intervention in the innovation process resulting from the demand for consumer protection and pollution control (event 2)?' These cross impact calculations help construct the cross impact matrix of the variable set which is then calibrated through computer modelling. This sensitivity modelling allows individual judgements on events to be simulated and changed several times to examine the relevant outputs.

Clearly, both TIA and CIA refine traditional forecasting through the combination of hard data with softer human judgement, despite the latter being turned into numbers through probabilities. Further, the disaggregation provided by CIA in its focus on cause–event chains facilitates deeper thinking on these events and their relationships. Moreover, by allowing probabilities to change, the sensitivity analysis is helpful to planners faced with a variety of 'what if?' type questions. Nevertheless, by relying on human judgement both techniques invite associated biases and limitations of worldviews to enter the modelling process. Moreover, the greater the number of probabilities to be estimated, the greater the amount of fatigue that can set in, since, for example, a 10×10 matrix needs 90 conditional probability judgements. Technically, as CIA relies on the interactions between pairs of events, it may not reflect the realities of the real world where multiple event interactions are commonplace. However, used in conjunction with other methods, such as, for example, TIA, Delphi and scenario planning, or CIA, Delphi and simulation modelling, their impact on unravelling current and future contexts is a powerful one.

(2) Structural

Structural changes create uncertainty, and forecasting is not effective due to the lack of patterning from the past with which to attach a probabilistic method. Structural interventions such as major inventions, significant mergers between key players and some natural disasters alter the nature of the patterning and open up the potential for multiple futures depending upon how the events are perceived and interpreted through the multiple lenses of those observing them. The outcome is likely to be virgin territory with few clear signposts and no global positioning system with which to navigate.

Several techniques have been developed to deal with structural changes and we describe the main ones below.

Delphi method

After WW II, the need to make a close link between military operations and technological development became clear to many US military experts and politicians. To meet this end, the RAND[18] Corporation was established in 1946, focusing initially on defence-related concerns but diversifying later into social issues. Forecasting's limitations soon became apparent as the teams tried to tackle complex problems with numbers before any precise scientific laws had been established upon which to build their modelling assumptions. Hence, in the early 1950s, 'Project Delphi'[19] investigated the most efficient and reliable use of groups of experts. Later, two researchers from RAND, Helmer and Rescher (1959) published 'On the epistemology of the inexact sciences' in which they argued that because there were areas in which science had yet to develop its laws and boundary conditions, expert opinion was a vital and legitimate source of data.

Researchers[20] developed the final technique based upon a 'Dialectical Inquiry' approach. This consists of three parts: Thesis, where an opinion is formed on a complex topic; Antithesis, where a conflicting opinion is gathered and Synthesis, where a new consensus is established that becomes the new thesis on the topic. Creative thinking and the avoidance of 'group-think'[21] are crucial aspects of the process. Understandably, the method was used first in long run (e.g. thirty-year) technology forecasting on issues like automation, space progress and weapon systems. Thereafter, its use was extended to business interests like new product market assessment and then to the public good, such as health care and education. Its accuracy in fortifying business forecasts seemed exceptional for the time. As Basu and Schroeder (1977: 23) claim:

> " The Delphi Method predicted the sales of a new product during the first two years with accuracy of 4–5% compared with actual sales. Quantitative methods produced errors of 10–15% and traditional unstructured forecast methods of about 20%.

Two Delphi methods are in active use today—the standard 'paper and pencil' version and the broadband digital conference version. Both approaches depend on groups of experts, carefully chosen for their insight and experience about parts of the complex problem but who need not be experts on the whole problem. Research[22] shows that groups as low as four can work well but a size between fifty and one hundred is usual for larger projects. Such experts do not gather together but operate in isolation and anonymously. For example, to explore the future transportation system for a large city, several panels were established comprising planners, academics, technologists, climatologists together with representatives of public transport users, operators, car drivers, delivery drivers, commuters, employers, parents of schoolchildren and so on.

In the standard approach, a Delphi team designs the survey questions that are administered to panel experts and returned for analysis. Conditioned by the results of the first survey, a second survey is designed and fed to the panel experts for revision and this process repeated until consensus is reached. Three rounds is usually the limit before new ideas dry up and participants get bored. The digital version brings the panellists together before and during the iteration process to capture their interactive thinking on key issues. For the city transport issue, a standard approach allows cost effective and rapid engagement of panellists across the city concerned, adjacent cities and towns and outlying rural areas. The responses can be handled centrally by the city planning officers or outsourced to specialist consultants. The results feed into the planning process or into the building of scenarios for the future of the city region.

The Delphi method can lead to rapid consensus and is effective when experts are geographically dispersed; when a topic is so complex that many subject inputs are required to master it; when the topic is controversial and anonymity is needed to enable the experts to speak openly; and when dealing with a specific, single dimension issue. In addition, it has been referred to as the method of last resort[23] when no other approach can cope with the extent of complexity subsumed in the problem.

On the downside, and expectedly, many argue that the collection of opinion and not hard data is unscientific. Moreover, its success is premised upon both the quality of this opinion with its potential for bias and subjectivity. Additionally, it is imperative that the opinion-based data must be analysed in an unbiased manner by the facilitating team. More serious, even the experts struggle with major paradigmatic and structural changes and their knowledge of the unknowable is as weak as that of the forecaster. However, when reinforced by cross-impact analysis and/or used as an input to other modelling techniques it can provide a substantial contribution to future observation.

Morphological analysis

The Delphi approach fares well with one-dimensional future issues. Modern day morphological analysis (MA) was developed by Fritz Zwicky (1948) in the middle of the twentieth century as a systematic method for structuring the total set of relationships in multi-dimensional issues that do not lend themselves easily to quantification. However, earlier applications can be detected as far back as the thirteenth century in the work of Ramon Lull, and later on in the endeavours of von Goethe, Lagrange and Faraday.

The name stems from the Greek word 'morphe' meaning to study shape or form, and so MA examines the structure and layout of the parts of an object and how these come together to make the whole. It has been used extensively in biology to examine the structure of organisms, in geology for rock formations and in linguistics to study words as they make up the parts of a complete language. Zwicky (1948: 121), a Swiss-American astrophysicist and aerospace scientist, describes it so:

> " Our aim is to achieve a schematic perspective over all of the possible solutions of a given large scale problem. Naturally, not all of the solutions which we are thus led to visualise can be carried out individually in all detail. Because of unavoidable limitations on time and means a choice must obviously be made, and preference must be given to some specific solutions.

He applied MA to classifications of astrophysical objects, the development of jet and rocket propulsion systems, technological forecasting, product creation and legal issues surrounding space travel and colonial affairs. But, with greater computer power available cheaply towards the end of the twentieth century, its inclusive processing of a multitude of variables and their interactions was made easier. Hence, it enjoyed a revival from the 1990s in areas like futures and policy studies.[24]

The method has the same logic as the Delphi technique above. First, the problem statement is formulated precisely, as in, for example, the future of digital cities. Second, all the variables that may have an impact upon the problem are specified, such as demographics, transportation, digital infrastructure, education, digital business and commerce, governance, community development and so on.

Third, a massive multidimensional matrix or box is created containing all the possible solutions to the problem (see Figure 3.3) representing what Zwicky (1948: 8) called 'complete, systematic field coverage'. The consequent matrix leads to a fourth stage whose purpose is to establish which of the configurations is feasible for the creation of a solution space and which can be eliminated. This approach allows an exploration of all the boundary conditions. For the digital cities, this would involve placing all values of the variables within the matrix, thus forming thousands of possible configurations, and questioning their feasibility, for example, advanced ageing population; poor integrated transport; high levels of digital communications; moderate education; high levels of e-governance; high levels of e-business and low community development.

That combination is feasible and exists in many European cities. However, low levels of digital infrastructure and high levels of e-governance and e-business would not be a logical combination in a modern city. The latter is not possible without the former being in position. Hence, this combination is likely to be rejected from the solution space.

Finally, all the feasible solutions are examined and the optimal ones selected and readied for application. Besides feasibility tests, selection among these options is helped by two further checks: the assessment of suitability, or does the solution fit with existing knowledge, resources and ways of doing things? And that of acceptability, does the solution provide rewards/returns at the levels of risk that are appropriate? Normally, a solution passing all three tests comfortably will be the preferred option for application. For digital cities, solutions with high levels of digital infrastructure and education, coupled with a balanced population and strong community development will excite investors, social workers and planners.

Clearly, MA by combining analysis and synthesis (see Delphi above), is a helpful means of investigating complex issues that are tough to handle in a quantitative way. Like the Delphi Method before it, there is a transparent audit trail at each stage of included and excluded variables and the reasons for these decisions. In some cases, the social scientists' test of replication may be possible. Moreover, by using the totality of all combinations, MA may expose novel solutions not considered previously due to the limits of human processing on such a scale. Inherent dialogue deepens human understanding of each solution and its components and so enhances organisational learning through knowledge transfer.

The technique can be dismissed easily by many strategists and planners due to perceived information overload, its abundance of possibilities and its exaggerated structure. More importantly, like the Delphi Method, it relies on human inputs of knowledge and judgement. Bias, error and guesswork can distort the process ('garbage in, garbage out') and dilute the results if left uncontrolled. These effects can be compounded through political manoeuvring. For instance, huge budgetary allocations and influential promotions can rest upon the final choice, with agents tempted to substitute personal gain for logic in these final debates.

Both Delphi and MA counter the limitations of forecasting by introducing expert opinion into a systematic process that is capable of handling complex issues that are not resolved easily by number crunching. Each can be used to help to focus thinking on the kind of structural issues that can wreck the soundest forecast. They can be used in conjunction to reinforce each other and as prelude to, and a part of, other processes such as scenario planning (SP). SP, by combining forecasting of the predictable variables with a thorough analysis of the variables likely to cause structural uncertainties (like resources, cultures, technologies, regulations and so on), is probably the best means of exploring complexity in the surrounding context. Moreover, by using a variety of data collection methods including expert opinion, it has the potential to ease the impact of unknowable variables (or Force ten impacts) by creating a heightened awareness of contextual drivers. Hence, we will devote the remainder of the chapter to it as we explore the emerging context for strategic leadership in the twenty-first century.

(3) Structural and unknown

'Time is a three-fold present: the present as we experience it, the past as a present memory, and the future as a present expectation.' St Augustine, Confessions, Book XI, AD 397

Complex contexts require a detailed understanding of the patterning of key underlying variables as they emerge from the past, through the present to the future. The concept of time inherent in such an analysis is not simply a chronological one. Understanding the past and making sense of the present to imagine the future involves a compression of time. Above, Augustine accompanied this three-fold present with a human capacity to experience a consciousness that extends beyond normal awareness where the soul embraces the present (*distensio anami*). Memory helps humans recall the past to the present at the same time as perceiving of the constructed present around them. In addition, humans have a startling capacity to capture the future through expectation and imagination. Hence, all three elements can be stored in the mind as if they were a 'moment in time'.

Scenario planning is a process that combines stories or images of plausible future environments with the practical strategic means of providing for them today. Much of the imagined future is based upon an analysis of past patterning of major variables, together with potential structural shifts, and much of the strategic means to cope with alternative futures is derived from a historically evolved resource base. Augustine's *'distensio anami'* is integral to the mindset of the scenario planner. This is a crucial point. Scenario planning is more about thinking (e.g. analysis, synthesis, imagination, reflection and preview) than about the project management of a set of strategic assets towards an end goal.

Scenario planning

To understand the power of this type of thinking, it is valuable to reflect upon Vignette 3.3, on the Commission on the Year 2000, and witness how its members made such good sense of complex events in the 1960s that they were able to paint a reasonably accurate picture of the world forty years later. Also, it illustrates that despite the awesome array of mental talent available, simple biases can lead to major errors of perception. It is interesting to conjecture what such errors might be in the 2025 Shell scenarios above. Previous versions have been accused of being too Western and capitalist focused, too hierarchical and too removed by their generic nature to be of much use. But, what have they missed?

VIGNETTE 3.3

Commission on the year 2000

'In reading an old document that dates from the 1930s, I was first struck by the excellence in methodology and then by the similarity between its projections and those of today. I found missing in it only the subject of adolescents and beatniks.'[25]

In 1965, a group of influential US thinkers and academics formed the **Commission on the Year 2000** to contemplate the world in 2000. Thinking about the future was not a legitimate or respectable pastime in those days, with France and Britain among the few other nations daring to ponder their future fates in national studies.[26]

A significant study on *Recent Social Trends* - a report of the President's Research Committee covering issues such as income distribution, poverty, education, health and urban trends was produced some thirty-three years previously (see quote above). The extrapolation of these social trends was accomplished through time-series forecasts, and the stability of the social phenomenon made the predictions pretty accurate, if pessimistic. By the 1960s, much of these issues had been subsumed, as St Augustine might have said, into 'present memory' and they made up much of the prevailing context when the new Commission gathered.

There were differences between the two projects. First, the new Commission grappled with several structural changes, e.g. the changing pattern of technology from machine to human, the rapid diffusion of goods and privileges in American society, significant shifting of society into a post-industrial world and the relationship of the US to the rest of the world. The complexity and dynamism of these changes meant that forecasting tools were ineffective and the team had to design a better way to peer into the future. Second, the Commission's ambition was not to predict trends but to create a self-consciousness about the anticipation and consideration of future problems, especially those impending from current policy decisions, and to examine broader, alternative solutions. To do this, they tried to sketch out several alternative futures rather than point forecasts. Finally, the context of the world of the 1960s – with the dilution of European empires, the 'white heat of technology' and the emergence of the manufacturing might of Japan, was different significantly from the late 1920s.

The Commission's report was published in a 400-page issue of Daedalus[27] in the summer of 1967. Their intellectual ponderings had enduring properties and a reading of the report thirty years later would not present many surprises about the contemporary world. The Commissioners shed light on issues of great significance to the world – the structure of the post-industrial society, the inadequacy of Government structures, the communications revolution, environmental degradation, the breakdown of the old international order, the increasing violence in society, the changing age distributions and increasing hedonism and tension within cultures. Clearly, the power of their conversations and the employment of softer methodologies – the use of metaphor, historical analogy and narrative, enabled them to deal with a complex array of issues over a long period of time.

Moreover, Hermann Kahn and his colleagues at the Hudson Institute wrote eight papers for the Commission. In one of these, Edmund Stillman created three scenarios for the future of the Soviet Union (*Stagnating USSR*, *Bismarkian* – a retreating USSR and *Young Turk* – new blood replacements for old regimes). Hence, the scenario language and method was a prominent force in helping Commissioners understand and preview the future so to anticipate the impact of policy decision made in the present.

Despite the combination of hard and soft methods and the employment of the new scenario techniques, the Commission didn't get everything right. They failed to deal with the changing role of women – one of the most crucial changes in social history in the latter part of the twentieth century. This might have been due to the virtual absence of women on the Commission and due to a focus on economic and political affairs rather than social dimensions. Most labour in manufacturing-dominated industrial society was male. The post-industrial shift to service sectors (e.g. health, education, financial services) has a labour force that is more female than male. This marked change has major ramifications for family size, separation, divorce, single parenthood and co-habitation.

With social change of secondary importance and a shared optimism that blacks would integrate easily into American society, the Commission was silent on the role of minorities and missed the development of a large underclass that existed with exclusion in conditions of relative poverty. Also, they missed the rise of the counter-culture, driven by the rock and roll, drugs and sex scene of the swinging sixties – perhaps due to the age (most of whom were in their forties and fifties) and class differences of the Commissioners. More significant, their blindness to the rise of Japan as the new economic powerhouse for the next few decades was cured only by the supportive scenario work of Hermann Kahn and Anthony Weiner[28] who advised the Commission.

Daniel Bell (the chairman of the Commission) and Stephen Graubard (1997) claim that the Commission's work is best judged against the serious studies of societal change like Ogburn's[29] *Recent Social Trends* and not against hyperbolic and sensational views of the future, like future shocks and mega trends. Unfortunately, the 'imperfect art' of future studies allows easy access to such sensationalists.

What do scenarios look like?

Scenarios are different stories about how the future might (not should) evolve. Imagine them as postcards that describe business conditions surrounding the organisation in twenty years' time and sent back to you by a future business analyst so you can read them today. These scenarios are possible futures of how the world today could unfold, none of which is likely to come about exactly. However, they will treat the uncertain elements that drive future conditions in an internally consistent way so that they will be plausible for the reader. Moreover, they should also surprise readers by challenging their assumptions about how the world works and so alter their mental model. They may even shock them into taking action now.

Generic scenarios (see below) are built by several organisations (e.g. United Nations, Chatham House, CIA, Economist, World Energy Council, World Business Council for Sustainable Development) and can be used to guide local, more customised scenario exercises. Shell and the Foresight Group within the UK's Department of Trade and Industry (DTI) produce some of the more respected versions. An illustration of the DTI ones is shown in Vignette 3.4. The four alternative scenarios of change in the UK over the next twenty to thirty years were devised in 2002 after a three-year process by researchers at SPRU[30] in consultation with stakeholders in business, government and academia. Like the *Recent Social Trends* and *Commission on the Year 2000* projects (see Vignette 3.3), these scenarios have 'social values' as a key driver of future change. From individual at one end to community at the other, the axis accounts for social and political priorities and the consequent economic activity. The second driver is 'systems of governance', ranging from autonomy, where power is held at a national level, to interdependency, where power shifts increasingly to macro institutions (e.g. EU, UN) and to micro ones (e.g. regional councils). These change drivers form two axes and the resultant scenarios emerge in their respective quadrants.

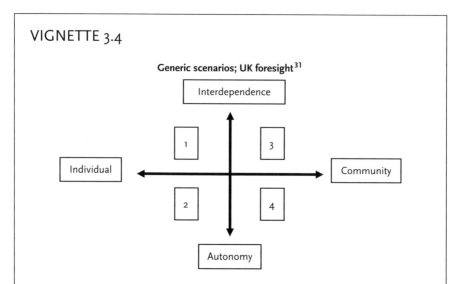

VIGNETTE 3.4

Generic scenarios; UK foresight[31]

1 World markets

People want to improve their own lives and are less concerned about equality and the effects that this may have on society. Business is globally focused and competition is intense resulting in few dominant firms and brands. Government becomes more international with EU, WTO gaining power; devolution in UK.

2 National enterprise

People value their freedom in a strong and independent UK. Business has a regional focus (e.g. UK and Europe) as instability in remote markets acts as a barrier to entry. Patriotism rules and UK remains peripheral to EU but US ties strengthened. Policies protect key sectors.

3 Global responsibility

People are community minded, both nationally and internationally. Business attempts to balance profit-seeking behaviour with social responsibility making active partnerships with Governments and consumer groups. Government is strong in healthcare, education and social services. EU expands and coordinates.

4 Local stewardship

People identify with local communities and focus on regional-level resource management. Business serves local needs and wants, causing fragmentation in many sectors. Small and local is beautiful. Different outcomes ensue for different parts of the UK as local issues shape growth and change. Shared, sustainable value systems mean the 'greening' of politics. EU has loose association with regions.

There are three main uses for scenarios. Firstly, they can be aimed at influencing *social or political affairs* and are developed for public consumption. Examples include scenarios for the future of a country (Ireland or Scotland), region (Connaught or Grampian) or organisation (Irish or British National Health Service). Here, new ideas can be generated and communicated to a large audience against possible future contexts, e.g. new policies on inward investment. Second, they can be developed for *strategic decision support* within organisations, such as entering key markets, rehearsing critical decisions against a series of outcomes and assisting strategy formulation through a thorough environmental analysis. Scenarios will help keep the conversation focussed on what *might* happen rather than on what *should* happen. Finally, scenarios can be used for *learning and development* in organisations. Group learning can enjoy a neutral space for developing a shared vision, rather than be hindered by political agendas, e.g. police and drug dealers, prison officers and inmates. The scenario process depends upon the inclusion of many voices to generate information and ideas and to build 'ownership' of the output. Ownership inspires motivation and energises aspirations in the implementation challenge that lies ahead. With neutral space and a shared vision, the scenario process has proved useful in conflict resolution.

The origins of scenario planning

The first formal systems for exploring possible future states found their origins in the battle zone, where anticipation of enemy action and reaction was crucial for survival, to anticipate surprise and to gain success. What if we reach the outskirts of the city and our water supply is poisoned? What if the enemy manages to traverse the ice-capped mountains and attack from the rear? Answers to such 'what if?' questions require *foresight* to build the possible future states that might unfold, and *planning* to prepare the resource base for any consequent strategic action.

Contemporary scenario history dates from the US military during WW II and the establishment of the RAND Corporation in its immediate aftermath (see the Delphi technique above). In the 1950s, its 'systems theory' approach was extended from defence studies into social issues like urban decay and poverty. One of its influential thinkers, Herman Kahn (see vignette above), left to set up the Hudson Institute in 1961, where his foresight studies speculated on the 'World of 2000'. Kahn's future conjectures were based primarily upon the analysis of the long-term trends, e.g. population growth, and their impact at key stages in societal development. On prompting by freelance writer Leo Rosten, he coined the term 'scenarios' for the resultant futures – a term used in Hollywood for the complete script and shooting directions of a motion picture. Kahn stressed non-fictional films in his analogy, as these were the basis for the imaginative stories he had in mind for the future. Ironically, in 'thinking the unthinkable' about thermonuclear warfare, the Dr Strangelove character in Kubrick's 1963 film of the same name, was based on Kahn.

Hudson's research attracted a variety of MNCs including Corning, IBM and Shell. The Shell Corporation is credited widely with the first commercial applications of Kahn-based scenario planning (SP). By 1965, Shell had introduced its global 'Unified Panning Machinery' (UPM) that described, in great detail, the process that oil followed from extraction all the way to the retail petrol outlet. However, as discontinuities appeared on the sector horizon, including the price of oil and the availability of alternative fuels, the forecasting-based UPM struggled to cope. So, in 1969, Shell experimented with different approaches of looking at a fifteen-year horizon. Pierre Wack, working for Shell Francais, capitalised on Kahn's work and introduced scenarios into the planning process as a better way of thinking about the future than forecasting.[32] Early scenario planning ran alongside the more traditional UPM on an experimental basis for several years.

In the early scenarios, Pierre Wack and Ted Newlands led a small team that examined the price of oil at a time when dominant thinking in the company concluded that supplies were secure and resources plentiful, largely because the oil majors were in control. At this time, the main technique for future prospecting was the type of probabilistic forecasting embedded in the UPM. This held reasonable accuracy over the short run but broke down seriously thereafter. Wack questioned Shell's thinking, asking what the outcome might look like if control were ceded to the producing nations. This team developed a crisis scenario premised upon the producers taking power and restricting supply. This unthinkable outcome transpired and triggered the oil crisis of 1973 and again in 1979. The scenario approach gained credence by stretching company thinking beyond the confines of the forecasting paradigm to the imagination of what deep futures could look like. Planners, faced with increasing complexity in their external contexts, had to embrace uncertainty rather than predictability and scenario planning provided the tools.

When should scenario planning be used?

The Shell example above illustrates the conditions for scenario usage. First, *uncertainty* in the way of environmental discontinuities was high. The price of oil could not be known easily in the face of a switch from a buyer's to a seller's market, the unknown strategies of Middle Eastern producers and the market for alternative fuel supply. Second, the *pace of change* in the market was beginning to accelerate such that soon, there would be no spare crude oil supply capacity. Third, the *complexity of the decision* was great. To build a refinery requires massive capital investment in the face of a set of unknown environmental factors. Finally, the *planning horizon was long*. An oil refinery may have an active service life of thirty years or more. Forecasting could not contemplate such an extent or scope. If the conditions of uncertainty, complexity, pace and length are key issues then scenarios are to be preferred to forecasting-based methodologies. Equally, if the organisation is engaged in emergency survival activity, if its prevailing thinking is short term, if numbers dominate the decision-making process, if no one has time for strategy or if there is no sponsor or home for scenarios, then their development will be futile and their use will be limited.

Types of scenarios

The various groups of scenarios can be defined by architecture, content or methodology used to develop them.[33] In terms of architecture, perhaps the most frequently used are *explorative* scenarios that trace the key trends from the past, through the present and into the future. They then describe the future consequences of these traced pathways. They are relatively easy to develop if data is available on the trends, and intelligence can be gathered on their likely trajectory. So they move from the present to the future in much the same way as forecasting would do but with a softer, more qualitative methodology. Alternatively, scenarios can be built from the future back to the present. These are called *anticipatory* scenarios and work by identifying a key future event with a significant impact and then work the pathway back to the present by asking 'how did this event come about?' Sometimes when past and current data are not widely available, say on new technologies, or when the complex interaction of many key variables makes extrapolation futile as in the case of deep future country studies, *normative* scenarios can be used. They are built around a key indicator and allow the indicator to drive other events, by asking, for example, what a nation's economy would be like if its GDP were to grow by 3 per cent per annum over a fifteen-year period.

Content definitions include *generic* scenarios that deal with an issue at the meta level, e.g., global geopolitical scenarios. These are useful as background in building and testing more specific 'nested' scenarios, e.g. for an industry or market segment. The latter are most useful in informing the development of business strategy. Scenarios can also be defined by their methodology. They are distinguished by how much emphasis they place on a specific approach, e.g. TIA, CIA or Morphological Analysis.

Good scenario builders will always use strong social science protocol in their development and the best techniques of delivery. As Pierre Wack (1985: 76) has said: 'Scenarios will either help decision makers or be of little use to them, depending on how they are constructed and presented … in the same way, two architects can create a well- or poorly designed building, even though they both use the same construction materials.'

Benefits and drawbacks

Clearly, any technique that provides assistance in making sense of complex contexts has value in its own right. It enables early strategy preparation; rehearsals for potential impacts of structural and 'unknowable' variables; performs judicial duties in due diligence situations; aids flexible deployment of resources; prevents cognitive freezing on particular recipes or ways of doing things; unifies teams around common goals; stretches ambition; generates new ideas and innovations and helps solve seemingly intractable problems in-between fractious grouping in neutral space. However, perhaps the greatest contribution lies in the process of SP and how it enables executives to think about environments and how they might shape them to their own ends.

It can be argued that SP helped provide the practical facilitation for a major turning point in the perception of complex contexts by organisational executives. Received teaching on business and management courses, like the MBA, and accompanying publications from the 1960s taught of a context 'out there', separate from the organisation. Traditionally, this was split into two arenas. First, the near or micro context represented a familiar domain of competitors, customers, suppliers and potential entrants. It could be understood through simple engineering analysis, using the likes of Porter's Five Forces, and the organisation could influence and shape it. The evidence from strategy studies on the reconfiguration of the value chain, by outsourcing and the like, suggests that they did it well and often. Second, a far or macro context, consisting of what, in 'strategy 101', we refer typically to as PESTLE (Political, Economic, Socio-demographic, Technological, Legal, Environmental) type forces, was removed from the grip of the executive and could not be influenced. In this 'modernist' view, uncertainty, caused by complexity and the rate of change amid the environmental forces, belonged in the environment itself. It was assumed that executives countered this enemy by reaching for more and more information to try to understand it. Moreover and fundamentally, it was assumed that these forces impinged on their prey with equal magnitude. In reality, this was not the case, as what was one executive's uncertain territory was another's risk-free domain. As Hatch (1997: 89) has characterised it: 'The term "environmental uncertainty" turned out to be quite misleading – environments do not feel uncertain, people do.'

Organisational theorists[34] had questioned the 'outside-in' paradigm, arguing that conditions in the environmental context cannot be separated from perceptions of those conditions. Uncertainty and the environmental perception lie firmly in people's heads. As a corollary, this 'social constructionist' view allows for executives to create or enact their own environments and respond to these visualisations as if the imaged contexts were exerting their own forces upon them. Perhaps the outcome is the same for both modernists and constructionists as the organisation and its environment harmonise, but the theoretical and practical underpinnings are quite different. The latter, via proactivity, means that more of the context can be shaped and influenced.

It can be argued that scenario thinking, by forcing executives to think deeper about contextual complexity and to understand it better, provided them with the confidence to carry out this shaping activity for their own futures and respond accordingly. In some cases, many have moved to creating their own futures and designing strategic responses to achieve them. The notion that these complex contexts were a given for organisations to navigate gave way slowly to the notion that organisations could imagine their own future contexts and help bring them about.

Scenario planning also has its sceptics. In 2000, the US Hart-Rudman Commission investigating 'American security in the 21st Century' was concerned that many future studies had failed to pick up soft signals that had caused startling outcomes later. It explored twenty scenario studies and found 70 per cent were surrogates of the 'intuitive logics' (see the appendix) of 'Shell' based methodology. Further, the 9/11 Commission in 2004 blamed the failure to spot the surprise attacks on the World Trade Centre on a lack of imagination in such future studies, despite the availability of warning signals.

True, SP methodologies may be to blame. First, many projects fail to spot weak signals due to a common focus on popular elements such as global economics, the information revolution and the like. These are studied regularly and at such a high level of abstraction. Their ready availability in the popular blossoming of SP resulted in their incorporation into most studies. Such mimicry could be due also to the common usage of the 'intuitive logics' method or its poor facilitation. Second, many general scenarios have been criticised for being too hierarchical, individualist and Western-biased (particularly the Shell scenarios), thus limiting their global applicability.

Third, the mental inertia of scenario actors can constrain their ability to 'think out of the box' and cause them to ignore signals or trends. Such inertia is built up over periods of time as recipes or ways of doing things. They can be reinforced if these ways have led to considerable success in the past. This is a form of cognitive inertia or freezing and can manifest itself in the reception of the scenario process and in its facilitation within organisations. This can be strong within individuals, such as dominant CEOs, and within groups, especially if there have been periods of relative stability in a sector, as, for example, under government shelter policies, or where there is a particular ethos of conservativeness embodied in a profession, like, say, accountancy.

Fourth, MacKay and McKiernan (2004) argue that, as the majority of methods follow Kahn in tracking issues from the past, perceptual errors and biases in perceiving of history cause fatal flaws in the resultant scenarios. Two biases seem to carry the responsibility for foresight error. First, the 'hindsight' bias is a phenomenon that occurs after an event. It leads people to overestimate the likelihood that they could have predicted its outcome before its occurrence as easily using foresight, as it was using hindsight after its occurrence. Second, 'creeping determinism' is a phenomenon that can lead unknowingly to misinterpretation, self-fulfilling prophecies and escalating error through an inherent human tendency to gravitate towards deterministic explanations of history that result from the process of retrospection itself. Taken together, these amount to a foresight bias and this results from a shallow perception of history as people take for granted what they think 'they know, they know' about the past. Such bias builds up in the mind like carbon deposits in an engine and is hard to erase.

Finally, in stable environments, and over the short term, the application of SP is likely to be inferior to forecasting. So overestimation of the merits of the more qualitative SP approach may lead to a lack of due appreciation for forecasting, and the value of including this more quantitative companion in the overall scenario development process, which it can usefully reinforce at the data interpretation and scenario-building stages.

For its future, SP requires continuous modifications to its building process to counter its genetic limitations. In particular, single method approaches will gain from reinforcement by other future techniques, such as morphological analysis, trend impact analysis or cross impact analysis. Finally, more applied research is needed into how scenarios inform strategy and how that strategy is enacted effectively in organisations. Many a boardroom wall is lined with well-built scenarios that have failed to secure the level ownership needed to bring their impact all the way through to strategy implementation.

Summary

This chapter has emphasised the need to understand the variables that shape the current and future context of business so that managers can make better strategic decisions in the present. This context has an impact on the content of strategy and on the culture in which that strategy has to be implemented. More important, the dynamic and complex make-up of a prevailing context ought to feed a creative cognition or mindset and avoid its ossification. Frequently, stable contexts lead to repetitive actions and can close minds and prevent executive groups from questioning or observing the patterns or events that emerge around them until it is too late to take effective action. One way of avoiding this danger is to identify a series of scenarios about how the future might evolve and to seek signposts that illustrate which scenario or its descendant is happening. Strategies can be rehearsed for each scenario if it should occur; hence any change in the signposts can be accommodated by a flexible approach to resource allocation.

These scenarios are constructed through an analysis of driving forces that shape the future. Many of these can be understood from the patterning of history; and others, more contemporary, can be detected by sharp antennae that scan the horizon in search of soft signals. Each of these driving forces has its own trajectory and each interacts with other forces thus introducing a complexity into the mix. The uncertainty in this complexity can be reduced by resort to a number of tools and techniques of which scenario planning is a powerful technique. In whatever guise, scenario planning must be fortified by other techniques, such as forecasting, historical analysis or Delphi studies, to counteract its inherent weaknesses. For many executives, immersion in the scenario process itself will be sufficient learning to heighten attention to the soft signals of future events that can impact upon strategy design and implementation. Once the major underlying variables are understood, the strategic response should be equipped flexibly to take advantage of opportunities and defend against serious threats. In some cases, executives may feel that enough confidence has been gained from the process and the scenarios themselves that they can shape their own future.

To do this, executives need a substantial depth of experience of contextual analysis and a strategic vision that is both long and peripheral.

A recent RAND study in 2003, noted the distinct lack of executives carrying these skills into leadership positions. It called for bold initiatives between governments, universities and foundations to produce tomorrow's leaders. This aim needs a sound intellectual base grown from worldly experience, shaped by cross-sector exchanges and made fertile by 'portfolio careers'. These leaders require the breadth in their perception of events and depth in their understanding of languages and cultures. This chapter has departed slightly from the approach in the remainder of the book by going into greater detail empirically in order to assist in the transfer of a specific skill set in future thinking for executives and managers. The scenario-based content is included to challenge existing cognition or 'worldly views' and to aid in the building of flexible strategic responses.

To help further, we add an appendix that provides an in-depth analysis of the main competing scenario planning processes. This section is designed to avoid the many pitfalls of the process and to lead to a greater understanding of the drivers of the future than is possible without the use of the technique. The results of its implementation should be better harmony between context, content, culture and cognition and the stronger foundations of the resilient organisation.

Appendix – scenario planning methodology

How are scenarios created? As Vignette 3.4 shows, building stories about the future is an imperfect art. The main requirements are the same as those for other forms of art, such as painting, sculpting or writing. They are tutoring and application. The former is relatively easy to acquire from the many good sources available, including primers, such as Schwartz (1991) and Van der Heijden (1996), established academic programmes, at universities like Oxford, St Andrews, Strathclyde and Warwick, and specialist expertise from several consultancy firms. The success of application is relatively harder as it involves the acquisition of experience of the 'doing' (the 'practice-making-perfect' dimension) together with an artistic talent for the 'doing' (the gift) manifest in creativity and imagination. Consequently, the low initial barriers to entry mean a mixed field of abilities, stretching from well-meant amateurism to seasoned professionalism. Further, with such a mix of planners comes a broad variety of methodologies, tempered by source organisation and geography. We focus here on the main Anglo American method based upon 'Intuitive Logics' and compare this with that of the French School.

Intuitive Logics (IL)

Intuitive Logics (IL) is an open-ended method relying on ideas generation and future imaging. In fact, as Martelli (1996: 280) observes: 'It could be said that Intuitive Logics is a residue: what is not Morphological Analysis, Trend Impact or Cross Impact Analysis is Intuitive Logics.' IL is designed to challenge the mental mind-maps of decision makers and in particular, those engaged in the process. It begins by trying to achieve transparency and focus on project specification between the client and the scenario facilitators, so that all involved can own and comprehend it. This might be, for example, 'scenarios for petrol-driven cars in Ireland in 2020'. This project is not about diesel-driven vehicles; it is not about vans, lorries or motorcycles; it is not about Scotland or England; and it is not about 2015 or 2030.

Once the project is well scoped, the IL method involves an extensive collection of data on the main variables (sometimes known as 'drivers') that contribute to changes in the environmental context surrounding the project scope, in this case, engine technology, alternative fuel developments, Irish government transport policy, EU and global emission agreements, demographics, oil prices, consumer purchasing patterns, 'green politics', cultural attitudes and so on. This data can be gathered from extant publications, by using, for example, the CAFÉ technique,[35] group-based interviews (e.g. Delphi), individual interviews with experts ('mover and shakers', extraordinary people, sector analysts and people in key 'power' positions) using semi-structured interviews around proven, taxing questions (such as the 'Seven' questions[36]). The data can be summarised and analysed within a workbook from which the consequent scenarios will be developed.

From the analysis, the main change variables are ranked by importance and uncertainty. This division creates two identifiable spaces. First, the forecasting space encircles the important and certain variables. These will occur in any story of the future and, because their outcome is reasonably well known (as in the case of many demographic variables), their

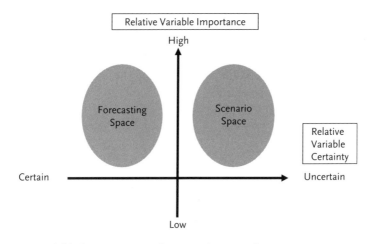

Figure 3.5 **Variable importance and uncertainty matrix.**

extrapolation or roll-out can be accomplished via forecasting or techniques like TIA and CIA. This quantitative approach represents the scientific side of the scenario-building method. Second, the space for scenario-building encircles the important and uncertain variables (see Figure 3.5). Their future development is rolled out across the time frame under investigation (in this case to the year 2020). The roll-out is influenced by patterning from the past, through the present to the future and follows a cause–effect pathway. There can be several roll-out paths leading to different views of the future. Other techniques, such as morphological analysis can enter to strengthen this process. Because of the complexity involved in working out the futures of single variables, and the means by which they might interact with other variables and 'unknowns', this part of the scenario-building process is the 'imperfect art'.

The scenario stories frameworks are created by the team and sometimes articulated by specialist scenario writers, such as novelists, commentators, journalists or poets. The stories are subjected to a battery of tests for issues like plausibility, internal consistency, surprise and gestalt. Revision occurs until the final stories, with signposts and warning signals, are robust enough to inform subsequent strategy or policy debates.

The primary difference between IL and competing methods for producing scenarios is that IL does not rely on predetermined, formalised procedures, but rather on a diversity of tools and techniques that can be chosen from the scenario planner's toolbox, thus enabling customisation of method to project scope, purpose, time and cost.

Although other organisations, like GE and the French firm SEMA, produced their own variants during the 1970s, the IL approach, as developed within the Shell Corporation, gained more commercial exposure over the following decade. This was due largely to the contemporary groundbreaking articles by Wack (1985) and the enterprise of ex-Shell personnel who set up consultancy organisations including Schwartz at GBN in California, Price at the University of St Andrews and Van der Heijden at the University of Strathclyde. They spread the scenario 'gospel' in blue-chip companies and then into a diverse range of public sector clients including governments, health services and NGOs. The broad client base helped develop the use of SP from its origins in informing strategy-to-ideas generation, team building and the search for solutions to intractable problems such as those between management and unions. Subsequent books by Schwartz (1991) and Van der Heijden (1996) became 'best-sellers' and helped reinforce the movement.

After a spell in the doldrums, SP recaptured its former glory at the turn of the new century with the growing complexity brought by globalisation and by the ICT and transport revolutions to the corporate strategy process. Consequently, there has been an explosion in SP books and academic and practitioner articles. SP is firmly rooted in most strategic management processes, especially where these require credible 'due diligence' elements, such as public sector planning, mergers and acquisitions. Significantly, in recent times, the SP terminology has metamorphosed into 'scenario learning' and 'scenario thinking' with the realisation that this was not just another planning technique but a cognitive process capable of context generation.[37]

French school

Due to its long association with Shell, and its early adoption by the likes of GE, the IL method is seen usually as the Anglo-American approach. However, SP travelled a different pathway in France. The Second World War had left the country in distress and there was a felt need to galvanise society and recreate La France from the grass roots. Gaston Berger founded the *'Centre d'Etudes Prospectives'* (CEP) where he developed a scenario approach to long-range planning entitled 'La Prospective' (LaP). He believed that the future was not part of a 'pre-determined temporal continuity' but something that could be shaped to the benefits of mankind (see below). *La Prospective* emphasises positive futures to entice politicians to think about how to improve France's future. By the 1960s, the approach had encapsulated education, the environment, urbanisation and regional planning. Pierre Masse incorporated the approach into the 4th French National Plan (1960–5) and it figured in subsequent iterations. Bertrand de Jouvenal joined CEP from his own 'Futuribles' group in 1966. He focussed on influencing key political groups in 'scientific utopias'[38] and on specifying the way in which these futures could improve the lives of ordinary people. Michel Godet, head of the futures group at the French defence firm SEMA, carried this work forward beyond the 1970s with the development of fresh tools and techniques. Like IL, the approach is a multi-method one (including Delphi, MA, TIA and CIA) but made distinctive by its comprehensiveness, quantification and mechanistic nature.

Berger and Godet constructed a mathematical and computer-based probabilistic approach which they claim to be unique for its integrated approach and the use of mixed systems analysis.[39] Three computer programmes (MICMAC, MACTOR and SMIC) focus upon the three main elements of the process – the identification of key variable, the roles of actors and their strategies and the building of scenarios and their probabilities. Particular strengths lie in the ability of MICMAC to identify indirect variables that could be missed by more human approaches, such as IL, because they are counterintuitive. Further and crucial to the process, MACTOR helps develop and interpret the actions and reactions of key actors as they game play, influencing key issues in shaping the environment. The approach tightens the cause–effect chain analysis by making variable linkages transparent. Hence, it scores highly on logical consistency measures. Unusually, with such heritage and sophistication, the approach has not had the same global exposure in the SP field as the more esoteric IL approach.

Both the Anglo-American (IL) and French School (LaP) scenario methods stress the role of actors throughout the process of scenario building. Coates (2000) claims that their speculations and conjectures are heralded more in US approaches but are supplanted with factual data in European studies, especially German ones. Moreover, European approaches focus more on the scenario process and less upon the actual scenarios, their strategy outcomes and users of the work. Coates blames this result on the overt role that academics have on futures work in Europe. The global focus of the Anglo-American School marks it out from the more nationally based French one. Further international differences exist simply because scenario building is rooted systemically in the culture within which the process is enacted. Ironically, their acceptance depends on an acknowledgement of their own complex context.

Notes

[1] Mintzberg and Waters (1985).
[2] Toffler (1980), Lackney (1998).
[3] Huntington (1997).
[4] Lackney (1998).
[5] Bobbit (2002: xxi).
[6] Gabel and Bruner (2003).
[7] Cousens et al. (2002).
[8] Van der Veer (2005: 9)
[9] Desai (2003: 18)
[10] Commission for Africa (2005).
[11] Commission for Africa (2005).
[12] Shell Global Scenarios to 2025 (Van der Veer, 2005).
[13] BRIC – emerging nations of Brazil, Russia, India and China.
[14] US National Research Council (2001: 1).
[15] For more information on Shell's approach see www.shell.com/scenarios
[16] Van der Veer (2005: 8).
[17] Clements and Hendry (1995).
[18] An acronym for research and development.
[19] As inspired by the legendary Greek Oracle at Delphi.
[20] Gordon and Helmer (1964), Dalkey (1968).
[21] Janis (1972).
[22] Brockhoff (1975).
[23] Fowles and Fowles (1978).
[24] Coyle and Yong (1996).
[25] Fred Ikle, Commission member.
[26] The *Futuribles* Project of Bertrand de Jouvenel in Paris and the Committee of the Next Thirty Years by the UK's SSRC.
[27] The Journal of the American Society of Arts and Sciences.
[28] In a quirk of irony, their own book is called 'The Year 2000'.
[29] The President's Committee that produced *Recent Social Trends* was directed by William Ogden of the University of Chicago).
[30] Science and Technology Policy Unit, University of Sussex, England.
[31] DTI (2002).

[32] Wack (1985).
[33] Martelli (1996).
[34] See, for instance, Weick (1979).
[35] The 'Construction Alternative Futures Explorer' developed by Professors Colin Eden and David Langford at the University of Strathclyde in Scotland.
[36] See, for example, Van der Heijden (2005).
[37] Fahey and Randall (1998).
[38] de Jouvenal (1967).
[39] Godet (2001).

INTRODUCING 'STRATEGIC LEADERSHIP, GOVERNANCE AND RENEWAL'
STRATEGY, LEADERSHIP AND THE NEW AGENDA • THE CONTEXT OF
BUSINESS IN SOCIETY • COMPETITIVE ANALYSIS AND VALUE INNOVATION
• STRATEGY AND ORGANISATION IN THE MULTI-BUSINESS FIRM •
STRATEGIC PROCESSES – INNOVATION • STRATEGIC PROCESSES – TRANSFORMATION
AND RENEWAL • SOME FINAL THOUGHTS AND REFLECTIONS

4 competitive analysis and value innovation

Introduction

Which matters most in generating and sustaining above-average profit-ability – industry structure[1] or company capability?[2] Is strategy inno-vation, and the creation of uncontested market space, now becoming more important than either?[3] Is the traditional obsession with competi-tion rather than customers a recipe for strategy convergence?[4] Is the com-petitive landscape, as it is evolving today, one where customers face more choice that yields less satisfaction, while strategists have more options that yield less value?[5]

In this chapter we will be looking at such issues as we examine the major perspectives on competitive strategy that have emerged over the last forty-five years. We begin the chapter with a review of three concepts that played a major role in the early development of the strategy field during the 1960s and 1970s, and form an important part of the evolution of modern competitive analysis. All three, the 'product life cycle', the 'experience curve' and the 'growth-share matrix' all continue to provide valuable insights through to the present day. We then go on to examine the three main perspectives on strategic analysis that have come to dominate the field since the early 1980s: competitive positioning, core competency and value innovation. The first two are associated with the work of Michael Porter (the positioning view), and C.K. Prahalad and Gary Hamel (the core competency view), and we discuss each of them in turn before com-paring them to try to identify where the difference between them might matter most in practice. In our treatment of the third perspective, value innovation, we examine three of the most prominent and promising variations on this theme: the 'blue ocean strategy' concept of W. Chan Kim and Reneé Mauborgne, the 'disruptive innovation theory' of Clayton Christensen and the 'experience innovation'/'co-creation of value' ideas of C.K. Prahalad and colleagues. We end the chapter with a look at the growing importance of business networks in strategic analysis and the trend leading beyond 'firm-to-firm' towards 'network-to-network' competition, and we examine the implications.

Strategic analysis – early concepts and perspectives

It is now widely recognised that the publication in 1980 of Michael Porter's landmark book, *Competitive Strategy*, represented a watershed in the field of strategic analysis. Up to then, the main tool used for strategy development in the classroom and in practice was what we now refer to simply as Strengths, Weaknesses, Opportunities and Threats (SWOT) analysis. The task of identifying which SWOT were likely to be the most significant strategically remained largely one of personal judgement. There were few analytical frameworks available at the time to help make such judgements more rigorous and systematic. This was to change very significantly after 1980.

Before going on to examine the three main perspectives that have emerged since 1980, and how they relate to each other, it is important, for completeness, to review briefly three concepts from the pre-1980 period: the product life cycle, the experience curve and the growth-share matrix. Together they came to provide a foundation for what was to come later, and they are still viewed as useful tools in the strategist's toolkit.

The product life cycle

The concept of the Product Life Cycle (PLC) draws on a biological analogy. The idea is that market demand for many products can be usefully thought of as going through four distinct phases: introduction, growth, maturity and decline, as depicted in the now-famous 'S-shaped' curve. Levitt (1965) was one of the first to demonstrate the strategic power of the concept in his classic article: 'Exploit the product life cycle', and the PLC continues to be widely used in strategic analysis. The first major implication of the PLC is that firms should focus on optimising returns over the full life cycle, rather than simply year-on-year. PLC thinking recognises how investment needs and profit potential vary across the different phases of the cycle, and how product and market development activities in the early stages of the lifecycle should be viewed as strategic investments, not simply as costs on the current profit and loss account.

Over time, many others have helped to tease out further the strategic implications and imperatives governing each phase of the cycle, not least of which is the supply–demand relationship over the life of a product. In the introduction stage, demand has to be created and many products simply fail to take off. As Levitt (1965) put it, for many products the curve is not an S-shape, but a sharp decline into oblivion. The growth phase, for the products that get this far, is typically characterised by demand leading supply. The leading early entrants all focus on ramping up capacity rapidly to grow with the market and maintain their leadership positions. Even the smaller firms with the higher cost bases are profitable at this stage in the market's development as industry margins remain quite strong all round. Eventually, the growth begins to slow down as the market approaches saturation, and replacement demand begins to exceed the new. Typically, at this stage, capacity overshoots demand as the industry players take time to absorb the transition. The onset of market maturity is usually followed by some degree of shakeout and consolidation, and the firms that are left shift their focus onto costs, or increasing segmentation, in an effort to protect margins as the competition intensifies. Eventually, the demand for many products goes into decline as new products arrive on the scene offering a quantum shift in the price-functionality relationship (the automobile for the horse and buggy, etc.) and what Joseph Schumpeter (1934) has dubbed the process of 'creative destruction' sets a new PLC in motion.

Recent work with the PLC concept has focused on examining more closely the dynamics of innovation at industry level and how the basis of competition varies as the cycle progresses.[6] What we know from much of this work is that the technological trajectory in many industries, particularly those involving assembled products as in the automobile, consumer electronic and office machine industries, follow a fairly general pattern over time. We also know that product and process innovation are related in predictable ways. Many new industries begin with a period of technological ferment when the rate of product innovation is at a peak. The opportunities offered by the birth of the new industry attract a large and diverse number of players, each hoping that its particular version of the new product will find most favour with the emerging market. What happens at this early stage, when viewed at the level of industry dynamics, is that scores of separate independent experiments are being carried out to find the version of the product, or particular package of functionalities, that will ultimately come to enjoy the widest level of user acceptance. This initial stage is followed by the emergence of a dominant design as the industry standard, and this is usually a prerequisite to market growth. It is only when the future trajectory of the technology becomes predictable enough that the leading firms will be ready to make the major commitments to ramping up production and be able to generate the economies of scale that will help drive costs and prices down sufficiently to enable the emergence of a mass market. At this stage in the PLC, speed to market with product enhancements and innovation to make the process more efficient tend to become among the most important drivers of ongoing competitiveness, as the success of Dell in the later phases of the personal computer industry's PLC most readily illustrates.

The emergence of the dominant design typically brings a change to the rules of the competitive game, with the focus shifting more and more onto process innovation and incremental product improvement. It usually heralds a drastic reduction in the number of viable players, as those with product designs least compatible with the dominant one get selected out. The emergence of the internal combustion engine in the automobile industry and the sealed refrigeration unit in home appliances are two well-known examples of this common pattern. The payoff for technology pioneering can often be substantial, as the early histories of companies like Polaroid and Xerox clearly attest. However, the costs and risks associated with being early to market with a radically new product can be very high, and the lion's share of the rewards often ends up flowing elsewhere, because the pioneer proves unable to establish its version of the technology as industry standard. This risk is particularly great where there are resourceful followers waiting in the wings, ready and able to move in and consolidate the new market when the time is ripe.[7] There are many factors that may lead to one or another version of an innovation becoming the eventual industry standard, and technical superiority is not always decisive. The success of Matsushita over Sony in establishing VHS as the standard in the video-recorder industry, and Microsoft's success with MSDOS in personal computers are two of the classic examples. The battle between Sony and Microsoft in the videogame industry is a more recent illustration of the same dynamics at play.

In many industries the version of the product that eventually wins mass market approval often turns out to be quite different from those that were launched to try to establish a market in the first place. The question of which company will benefit most from any radically new product often turns on factors of the technology protection regime operating in the industry and the importance of complementary assets. As Teece (1986: 287) has pointed out, 'many patents can be invented around at modest costs', and 'trade secrets' can be quickly uncovered through reverse engineering once a product is out in the market. In many industries, resourceful followers can have their own version of a new product on the market before a dominant design has emerged. The existence of complementary assets, like an established brand, distribution system or company-owned service network can prove decisive in determining whether the follower's design will ultimately become the dominant one at the expense of the product pioneer. There are many classic examples of innovators that have lost out in this way, like EMI in scanners, Xerox in office computers and DeHavilland in jet aircraft.

While the PLC is traditionally depicted as a four-phase cycle, and broad strategic implications have been drawn for each of the phases, some of the more recent work with the concept has concentrated on key transition points within the phases at the two ends of the cycle. For Geoffrey Moore (1991, 2005) the transition from early introduction to market take-off is rarely a smooth progression, particularly in technology-driven industries. It usually requires the successful crossing of the market 'chasm' that opens up between the small group of early enthusiasts, the true 'techies' that are ever on the lookout for the next 'cool' device and the real beginnings of more broadly based demand. The key to successfully crossing the chasm rests on being able to find those with the most pressing practical need for the new functionality, or as Moore (2004: 89) more colourfully depicts them, the 'pragmatists in pain' with a 'nasty problem' for which the new technology offers the sole solution. These are the only early adopters with strong enough incentive to help the new technology diffuse more rapidly. The question of how a new growth dynamic (often a disruptive one) can come to be injected into the later phases of the PLC is one that we will return to under the broader theme of value innovation later in the chapter.

The experience curve

The Boston Consulting Group (BCG), under the leadership of Bruce Henderson, contributed two of the most influential strategy tools of the 1960s and 1970s, the experience curve and the growth-share matrix, and the key insights underpinning these two concepts continue to inform strategic analysis right through to the present.

The notion of 'economies of experience' had already been around in the economics literature for some time,[8] and the concept of the production learning curve, to which the effect is related, had been widely used since the Second World War. However, during the late 1960s Henderson and his colleagues were the first to quantify the experience effect, extend it to the business model more broadly, not just to production, and promote it as a tool for developing strategy.[9] They demonstrated that in many industries unit costs could be seen to decrease with cumulative volume in a predictable and exponential fashion. In the then newly emerging semiconductor industry, for example, the price per unit fell from $25 to $1 as the industry's cumulative volume grew from 2 million to 2 billion units over the 1964–72 period (a similar experience effect is evident today in the case of solar photovoltaic technology). The main implication that Henderson and his colleagues were to draw from this insight was that any market leader, with the highest cumulative volume in its industry, should enjoy a significant cost advantage by virtue of being further down the experience curve than any of its competitors at any particular point in time. This advantage was assumed to be sustainable, as long as market leadership could be maintained.

This experience effect advantage (which is quite distinct from economies of scale, though both are often enjoyed by market leaders) was seen to offer a number of strategic benefits. The market leader could set prices and dictate the pace of competition. For example, it could use its lower cost, experience-based advantage to price below the unit costs of late arrivals and deter them from entering or burn them away early, as BIC was able to do in the branded disposable ballpoint pen market. It could also use the advantage of its higher margin to outspend rivals in areas like marketing and product development in order to further consolidate its market leadership.

In reality, experience-based strategies have delivered mixed results over the years. There have indeed been many examples of companies that have achieved sustained economic success with this type of approach, including Lincoln Electric in arc welding, Bausch & Lomb in contact lenses, and Texas Instruments in calculators. More recent examples might also include the likes of Dell in personal computers and Ryanair in the airline industry, where the experience effect is seen to operate at the level of cumulative volume leadership with a particular kind of business model (not necessarily market leadership on an overall basis). On the other hand, the business literature is also full of stories of experience-based strategies that failed to live up to initial expectations, like Du Pont in the titanium industry, or Monsanto in acrylonitrile. So while experience-based strategies can be very potent sources of sustainable competitive advantage, it is important to recognise, as Ghemawat (1985) points out, the conditions under which such strategies tend to succeed or fail.

To begin with, the strength of the potential experience effect tends to vary from industry to industry, being very strong in the semiconductor market and much weaker in activities like retailing. Across the broader front, the effect has been found to range from 40% to zero, with somewhere around a 15% effect being most typical. The impact also tends to vary over the product life cycle, being strongest during the rapid growth phase when the rate of increase in cumulative volume is at its highest and becoming progressively weaker as the market hits maturity. So that even in industries like semiconductors, where the effect tends to be strongest, the impact can be undermined by ever-compressing product life cycles. In industries where the experience effect is strong and the technology protection regime quite weak, pioneering firms may find themselves particularly vulnerable to second-movers, with deeper pockets and lower development costs, that are willing to seize the investment initiative and be more aggressive in building capacity and buying market share in anticipation of enjoying the experience-effect advantage further down the road. On the other hand, it can be very risky to attempt any such pre-emptive strategy before a clear dominant design has emerged, as the sought-after advantages may end up being linked to a losing technology and ultimately prove to be worthless.

Perhaps the most serious limitation with traditional experience-curve thinking is the implicit assumption that all companies learn at the same rate (in other words, that the effect is related to the cumulative volume produced, independent of time). Ray Stata (1989: 64), co-founder of Analog Devices, was among the first to question this assumption: 'How else can we explain the success of the Japanese automobile industry which learned faster than the US industry with substantially less cumulative volume' over the 1970s and 1980s. A more current view of competitiveness, in line with the growing interest in the link between learning and competitive advantage at the centre of the recent interest in the 'learning organisation', is that the experience effect depends on both learning opportunity (cumulative volume) and learning efficiency (a time-related, firm-specific, dimension).[10]

The growth-share matrix

Henderson and his BCG colleagues also developed the concept of the Growth-Share (G-S) matrix as a further aid to strategic analysis in both the single business and the multi-business contexts.

The G-S matrix, in effect, brings the PLC and experience-curve perspectives together into a single two-by-two matrix to help identify appropriate business strategies or balance of strategies, by market stage and competitive position. The horizontal dimension of the matrix represents relative market share and the vertical dimension, market growth. The first incorporates the experience effect and the second a compressed version of the PLC (with introduction-growth and maturity-decline condensed into two main categories). The G-S matrix identifies four different growth-share positions, each with its own strategic imperative. High relative market share is taken to be synonymous with market leadership (i.e. only a relative market share greater than one – when compared to the biggest competitor – qualifies as high on the horizontal axis). The crossover point between low and high market growth on the vertical axis is more open to judgement, and the overall rate of growth in the economy is sometimes chosen as a reasonable figure for marking this transition.

The different strategic positions and their implications are as follows. The two most attractive positions are Cash Cow and Star. A cash cow is a market leader in a low-growth market. As the market leader it is assumed to enjoy a significant cost advantage from being ahead of all competitors on the experience-curve effect. A cash cow earns above-average Return on Investment (ROI) for the industry and is very profitable, but has limited opportunity for further growth because the market is mature. It is a net generator of cash that can be used to fund more attractive growth opportunities elsewhere on the matrix. The strategic imperative for the cash cow is to reinvest enough of its profits to maintain its leadership position, before drawing off the surplus to apply to other, more attractive, opportunities for growth.

A star is also a market leader, and is also assumed to be enjoying the benefits of the experience effect, but this time the market is at an earlier, higher-growth stage in its PLC. The business is also seen to be earning above-average profits, but the strategic imperative is to continue to grow at least as fast as the market, or else it will lose market share and put its leadership position at risk. A star typically needs to reinvest all of its profits in order to keep pace with the market and may even need additional capital to fund the further expansion of capacity ahead of growing demand (in situations where it might be generating profits of say 20% but the market is growing at 30%, for example). Stars are rarely net generators of free cash flow, and may even be net users until market growth begins to slow down. When the market matures, a star would normally be expected to transition to the cash cow position.

The more challenging positions in the matrix are the Question Mark and Dog. The question mark is a product or business with low share in a high-growth market. As a market follower it is assumed to be in a relatively weak, high-cost position. The strategic imperative here is to decide whether or not this business can be propelled into a star, and this will usually require significant investment. This is often characterised as a 'double-or-quit' judgement. The G-S matrix offers little comfort to market followers. question marks that do not successfully challenge for market leadership eventually slide into the dog category when the market matures. Dogs are market followers, and high-cost players, in a low-growth market earning below-average returns and enjoying the bleakest of prospects. The strategic prescription for a dog is to divest, if a suitable buyer can be found (maybe the cash cow in the same market seeking to further consolidate its leadership position) or if not, to harvest (i.e. let it run down rapidly and release the tied-up capital to fund better opportunities elsewhere on the matrix).

The G-S matrix contained some valuable insights, and became popular as a way to think systematically about corporate strategy in the multi-business firm. In this context it also became known as the business portfolio matrix. One of its most attractive aspects for corporate strategists was that it offered a framework for balanced, self-funded growth. Properly planned, the surplus cash generated by cash cows could be used to fund the investment needs of stars, minimising the requirement for further external funding and allowing management to retain the highest level of discretion over future strategy. It also had some limitations as a corporate strategy tool, which we will examine further in a later chapter on strategy and organisation in the multi-business firm. In terms of business strategy, the matrix does identify market attractiveness and competitive strength as the two most important coordinates of strategic positioning. However, it uses very limited measures of both: Market growth is used as a surrogate for market attractiveness, and relative market share for competitive strength. The first does not explain why the mature stage in some markets can be more profitable than the growth phase in others (e.g. the US soft drink versus personal computer markets in the 1990s), while the second does not explain why some lower-share companies can also earn above-average profits, not just the market leaders (e.g. BMW in the automobile industry).

The positioning view of strategy

Over the last twenty-five years, two perspectives have come to dominate the field of competitive analysis, one that stresses market position and the other core competence. While the two primary coordinates of the market-led or positioning view: market attractiveness and competitive strength, had been anticipated in the G-S matrix, the positioning perspective only began to come to full fruition in the work of Michael Porter (1980, 1985). Porter's main analytical tools, the Five Forces Model for industry analysis, the three Generic Strategies and the Value Chain are all now considered to be strategy staples in both teaching and practice.

Industry attractiveness and market power

Strategic analysis within the positioning view starts with the structure of the market, or industry, and how it might be shaped to advantage. It is often referred to as the market power approach to strategy, or the 'outside-in' approach. The aim is to establish a privileged or powerful, hard-to-replicate position in an industry that is difficult to enter and is secure from substitution.

The first major tool in the positioning perspective is the Five Forces model.[11] This emerged from sustained empirical research by Porter and colleagues at Harvard Business School over the 1970s into the question: Why are some industries inherently more profitable than others? For Porter, market growth rate alone did not provide the answer. He identifies five 'competitive forces' that shape the longer run profitability of any industry and determine its structural attractiveness. These are ease of entry, threat of substitution, power of buyers, power of suppliers and competitive rivalry. Each has the potential to drive profitability out of the industry, and together they constitute an expanded view of competition. For example, firms are seen to compete for profit margin not only with their rivals, but also with their buyers and suppliers.

A major contribution of Porter's Five Forces model is that it has given strategists a very powerful tool for identifying and analysing the most significant threats facing their business. It also helps those seeking to diversify to assess which new markets offer the most attractive opportunities. Most advanced students of strategy are very familiar with the model and it is not our purpose to provide a full treatment of it here. However, the following potential pitfalls should be noted when trying to apply it in practice. One is the tendency to slip between industry and firm levels of analysis, without distinguishing between them and end up drawing the wrong conclusions. For example, it might be seen that if Ryanair is doing well in the airline industry, then the industry must be attractive, at least to Ryanair, but this is to confuse industry attractiveness with competitive strength. It should be possible to make an assessment of the overall structural attractiveness of the industry independent of the fortunes of any particular player.

There is also a danger of confusing rivalry and substitutes. In everyday language, we might talk about Pepsi being a substitute for Coke, but in terms of the Five Forces model, these should be seen as rivals rather than substitutes. A substitute is a product that will satisfy the same user need, but based on different materials or technology. The threat of substitutes is a threat to the industry as a whole, not just to particular players (e.g., the threat of plastic as a substitute for aluminium in the packaging industry, or coffee for cola in the beverage industry). Moreover, it is often useful to distinguish between barriers to entry into the industry and barriers to mobility or repositioning within it. For example, the soft drink industry has low barriers to entry, otherwise how can we explain the proliferation of small local brands. The real barriers of significance in this industry are the barriers to mobility (or strategic repositioning) from a minor to a leading player. These are the barriers that help explain why Coke and Pepsi between them still dominate the industry internationally, and why even a company as resourceful as Philip Morris, owner of the Marlboro and Miller brands, was unable to propel itself into the same league, following its acquisition of Seven-Up many years ago.

Finally, over the years, Porter has often been asked whether he had ever considered adding a 'sixth' force to his famous framework. However, as he put in a recent interview: 'I didn't come to the conclusion that there were five forces until I had looked at hundreds of industries'.[12] Two nominees that have often been mooted by others as the potential sixth force are government and organisations with complementary products and services. While both indeed can have a major influence on industry profitability, their influence is not monotonic. So you cannot say in the case of either of these, as you can with each of the other five, that where their influence is strong, they always tend to drive profitability out of the industry. For example, when the power of suppliers increases, the impact on industry profitability tends to be negative. When the power of government increases, the impact on industry profitability can turn out to be negative in one case, positive in another. It is not always in the one direction. Strong government influence might lead to the lowering of barriers to entry in one situation, and to the raising of them in another. The impact of organisations with complementary products and services on the profitability of any given industry is similarly non-monotonic. Again the influence can be one way or the other, depending on how some or all of the five main forces are affected. So, according to Porter (2008), variables such as government and complementary products and services are to be viewed more accurately as *factors* to be taken into account in any given situation and assessed in terms of how they impact on the five main forces, rather than as generic independent *forces* to be added to the basic model.

Competitive positioning

In addition to the Five Forces model for assessing industry attractiveness, Porter (1985: 2) also addressed the question of competitive positioning: 'A firm in a very attractive industry may still not earn attractive profits if it has chosen a poor competitive position'. So how do we go about developing a strong competitive position? Porter identified low cost and differentiation as the two main dimensions of competitive strength. He also added the third dimension of broad (industry-wide) versus narrow (niche) competitive scope, to offer three viable positioning choices: low cost, differentiation and focus. In trying to help strategists with the further question of how to implement any given positioning choice, he recognised that 'Competitive advantage cannot be understood by looking at a firm as a whole. It stems from the many discrete activities a firm performs in designing, producing, marketing, delivering, and supporting its product'. So he offered the Value Chain as an analytical tool for breaking the firm down 'into its strategically relevant activities in order to understand the behaviour of costs and the existing and potential sources of differentiation' (1985: 33).

As a further insight into how to put these basic ideas into practice, Porter (1996, 2001) has more recently reorganised them into what he calls the six principles of strategic positioning. These are:

(1) The right goals (focus on long-run profitability);
(2) A clear value proposition (Offering unique value for particular uses/to particular customers);
(3) A distinctive value chain (performing different activities than the competition, or the same activities in a different way);
(4) Accepting the necessity of trade-offs (not trying to be all things to all customers);

(5) Activity system fit/alignment (internally consistent and mutually reinforcing value chain activities); and

(6) Continuity of direction (keeping to the discipline of the strategy).

Porter (1996) offers South West Airlines (SWA) as a good example of the power of these six principles of competitive positioning in action. SWA has a clear 'no frills' value proposition, underpinned by a distinct value chain or activity system of highly aligned and mutually reinforcing elements, like secondary airports, point-to-point flight routes, standardised aircraft and so on, focused on the most price-sensitive end of the market. As part of its strategy SWA accepts the inherent trade-offs involved and is careful to forgo any temptation to compromise its clear competitive positioning in the search for short-term gain. Failure to make the appropriate trade-off in the value proposition between cost and differentiation, or between broad and narrow scope, is a recipe for ending up with an unclear 'stuck-in-the-middle' strategic position, underpinned by an activity system with poor and inconsistent internal alignment and sub-optimum economic impact.

The notion of a distinctive activity system, with a high level of internal fit is central to the potency of competitive strategy based on this market power or positioning perspective. In his model, Porter outlines three levels of fit: from the lowest one of simple consistency among the elements, through a higher one where some of the elements reinforce others, to the highest one of activity system optimisation where all of them reinforce each other. The higher the degree of fit, the more difficult the positioning is for others to imitate and the more sustainable the competitive advantage that flows from it. Again, Dell provides a good example. This is illustrated in the following explanation by former CEO Kevin Rollins of Dell's positioning advantage in the PC industry in the late 1990s and early 2000s, and the difficulties competitors had in trying to replicate it:

> " It's not as simple as just having a direct sales force. It's not as simple as having mass customization in the plant or manufacturing methodology. It's a whole series of things in the value chain from the way we procure, the way we develop product, the way we order and have inventory levels, and manufacturer and service support. The entire value chain has to work together to make it efficient and effective.[13]

Clear competitive positioning is the fundamental tenet of this view of strategy, and the most basic choice is the one between cost and differentiation. However, to maintain its power in the market, the cost leader can never afford to allow its value proposition to become too far out of line on functionality and service, while the differentiator can rarely afford to allow its own value proposition to become too far out of line on costs. Significant shifts in the price/performance relationship at either the price or the performance end can transform a market and result in a major change in relative market power. The classic example is the Ford Model T. 'Any colour as long as it's black' was an effective proposition for almost a decade while the Model T was priced much lower than the competition. Once gap in pricing began to erode to the point where the mass market became willing to pay a bit extra for some choice, the strategy quickly lost its effectiveness. In short, within this view of strategy, companies, to sustain their competitiveness, need to ensure that they have clear advantage (cost or differentiation) on at least some activities in their value chain, while trying to stay close to parity on the others.

The competency view of strategy

The second major perspective in competitive analysis to emerge since 1980 is the competency-led, resource-based view of strategy. The Resource-Based View (RBV) has its early roots in Edith Penrose's (1959) book *The Theory of the Growth of the Firm*, while the seminal article in its development as a theoretical perspective is generally acknowledged to be Wernerfelt's (1984) 'A resource-based view of the firm'. Today, in both theory and practice, the most influential concept in this resource-based perspective continues to be the Prahalad and Hamel (1990) notion of core competency, first developed in their classic article 'The core competence of the corporation'. So while we recognise that the RBV is concerned with a spectrum of company-specific assets and resource endowments, our analysis here will concentrate mainly on core competencies as the resource of widest interest in competitive analysis and strategy development.

Core competency

Interest in this alternative view of strategy came to prominence in the early 1990s at a time when many companies were facing radically new, more dynamic and volatile competitive environments. It was a context in which strong enduring market positions were becoming more difficult to establish and secure in many industries, particularly those where industry boundaries were becoming increasingly fluid and continually being redefined by technological convergence. For example, up to the early 1990s, the personal computer, mobile phone and home entertainment industries were still largely separate competitive domains. This is no longer the case today, as companies like Sony, Nokia and Microsoft continue to invade each others' patches and the boundaries between these once-distinct markets continue to become more volatile and defuse over time.

The competence-led perspective differs from the market-led approach by tending to work from a different starting point and by laying its strategic bets in a different place. The positioning perspective starts by assessing what industry we want to be in and the competitive position we want to take within it, and follows by considering the resources and skills that we will need to compete (an 'outside-in' approach to competitive analysis and strategy development). The competence-led approach, on the other hand, begins by assessing which distinctive competencies we want to build, and then follows by looking for the market opportunities that might exploit them best (an 'inside-out' approach).

Two ideas are central to the core competence perspective on competitive analysis. The first is the concept of core competence itself. In practice, many strategists still tend to use the term 'core competence' as if it was simply synonymous with 'strength' (in the SWOT sense). However, this association is too loose to be really useful. For example, a company like Canon might see itself as having a particular strength in lens production, but so too might its competitors like Kodak or Xerox. For a competence to be considered strategic, or 'core' in the Prahalad and Hamel sense, it must fulfill a number of key conditions: it must be rare, difficult to imitate or substitute and valuable to customers across a range of product–market opportunities, present and future.[14] A core competence typically has a technology dimension, but it also has organisational and collective learning dimensions that integrate it into the social fabric of the company.[15] It is not just about the know-how itself, but also about the ability to mobilise it, and it is this multi-dimensional and organisational character that makes it so difficult to replicate. The second idea is rooted in the relationship between core competency, core product and end product. It invites us to take a multi-level look at competitiveness and market influence, and we will examine this in more detail later.

Canon provides one of the best examples of the power of this perspective. Over the last thirty years the company has become a significant and highly profitable player in the camera, office-copier and desktop printer markets, yet its strategy has rarely been position-based, except, perhaps, when it first set out to 'beat Leica' in the camera market in the early years. Over most of its history since then, Canon's strategy has been competence-led. The company has laid its main strategic bets on the development of deep expertise in fine optics, precision mechanics, fine chemicals and semiconductors. It is a strategy that combines depth of learning with breadth of imagination in the search for market opportunities to apply its expertise, and it is one that has served Canon well in allowing it to migrate relatively easily across a number of product-market categories over its history to date.

Core product

Canon's competence-led strategy has allowed it to punch above its apparent weight in market after market, and here is where the distinctions between core competency, core product and end product are seen to be at their most significant. In office printers, for example, Canon's market share is small compared with rivals like Hewlett-Packard and Olivetti. Yet to fully understand the market influence of Canon in the printer market, we also need to look at relative share at the core product level. In the laser printer market, for example, a core product is the laser engine that embodies most of a laser printer's key technologies. As Prahalad et al. (2001: 247) have recently reminded us, most managers still 'tend to underestimate the power of core product dominance'. Not so those at Canon. For well over a decade, Canon has commanded an eighty per cent-plus manufacturing share of laser engines, much of which it supplied to the market leaders. By choosing to supply its laser engines to Olivetti and

Hewlett-Packard, rather than using its proprietary technology solely to distinguish itself in terms of market position, Canon has been, in effect, borrowing the market shares of major competitors to help accelerate its investment in competency leadership and increase its influence over the ongoing evolution of the technologies critical to the industry's future.

In industries such as desktop printers, where the most strategic technologies or platforms are embedded in key components and subsystems (i.e. core products), end-product market share alone is no longer an adequate measure of market power. One of the major contributions of the competency-led perspective is that it invites us to look at competitiveness at three levels: end product, core product and core competency, in order to more fully understand where the most influence is being wielded over an industry's further evolution. It also provides a strategic rationale for collaborating with competitors. Every product development cycle produces two main outputs, the new product itself and the learning that is generated during its development. Only the first becomes accessible to the market when a firm decides to license its technology to competitors, so that the impact of potential technology 'leakage' can be quite minimal, particularly where the cycle between each successive generation of the product is relatively short. Furthermore, not only can the decision to supply market rivals with core products enable a company like Canon to recoup its R&D investment in any given cycle faster than if it had to rely solely on its own end products, it also reduces the incentive for its rivals to make their own investments. This helps Canon to retain the investment initiative, while capturing the lion's share of the learning opportunities that are key to ongoing competency leadership.

Positioning versus competency – where it matters[16]

It might be argued that these perspectives are largely two sides of the same coin and that the difference between them is of much more interest to academics than to practitioners. After all, any company with a strong market position is likely to have distinctive competencies to underpin it, while a competency is only truly 'core' if it has strong value in the marketplace. Does it matter whether you build your strategy based on positioning rather than competency, or vice versa?

To answer this we need to examine a little more closely the nature of the competitive advantage reflected in each of the two perspectives. The first emphasises 'privileged' pre-emptive market positioning; the second, distinctive know how. No doubt, over time, South West Airlines (SWA) has developed special expertise in the execution of its no-frills strategy in the airline industry. However, SWA's most sustainable advantage seems to be rooted more in privileged market position than in proprietary knowledge. While followers into the low-cost carrier segment of the US industry have found it very difficult to match SWA, the ability of Ryanair to replicate this strategy and recreate the SWA business model in the European airline industry, with similar spectacular results, and then use its market position to ward off other would-be imitators, suggests as much. Competitive advantage based on a privileged market position usually tends to reflect significant pre-emptive advantages in market-specific investments, skills and infrastructure (aircraft, location-routes, landing rights etc. in the case of SWA and Ryanair), which later movers will find more expensive to replicate. In the early 2000s, Michael O'Leary, the CEO of Ryanair, seemed to reflect this point when he dismissed the prospects of newer entrants into the same competitive space with the warning that there were 'huge barriers to entry now, and none of these new airlines is going to find a price point below Ryanair'.[17]

In contrast to either SWA or Ryanair, Canon's strategy over most of its history has been based on difficult-to-replicate know-how rather than pre-emptive market dominance. Canon's strategy has been relatively 'product-market agnostic', to use a phrase of Gary Hamel's. Is it a camera company, an office products company or a printer company? Where else might Canon's competencies play? The company has laid its bets primarily on its expertise in precision optics, fine chemicals, precision mechanics and semiconductors, and seems willing to enter any market where this combination of know-how can be leveraged to full advantage. Canon has focused its branding strategy on the company and its corporate identity, rather than allow itself to become too strongly identified with any particular product or market. In sum, the primary source of sustainable competitive advantage in each of the SWA and Canon cases is seen to be located in a different place. In the first, it is rooted in industry structure and pre-emptive positioning, and in the second, in organisation-wide expertise and competency leadership.

There are several areas in strategic analysis where it matters which perspective you take. Two, in particular, will be highlighted here. The first is corporate strategy in the multi-business firm and the second, strategic renewal. While both topics will be examined more fully later in the book, what is of most immediate interest to us here is how the positioning and competency perspectives provide their own insight into these important strategic challenges.

Two questions are central to strategic analysis in the multi-business context: which businesses to be in, and how can corporate strategy add value over and above that which the businesses themselves can generate collectively as stand-alone entities? The two perspectives approach these questions using different logic and they tend to address different paths to growth.

The positioning perspective follows the logic that corporate strategy develops from business strategy, because as Porter (1987:46) sees it, 'diversified companies do not compete, only their business units do'. Furthermore, since his research has shown that new businesses were added to corporate portfolios through acquisition in more than seventy per cent of all cases, Porter directs his main strategic advice towards this mode of growth. He suggests that corporate strategists should apply three tests to any potential target: (1) the attractiveness test (is the acquisition target's industry structurally attractive or can it be made so?); (2) the cost of entry test (will the entry cost outweigh all future profits?); and (3) the better-off test (will the new business gain competitive advantage from its link with existing businesses, or vice versa?). The potential gains from the last test are expected to come largely through the sharing of product or market related assets (economies of scope).

In contrast, the core competence perspective offers more help to strategists pursuing corporate development through organic growth. To begin with, it differs from the positioning perspective by stressing that effective business strategies can also be grown out of a coherent corporate strategy focused on the development of core corporate know-how. Indeed, for Prahalad and Hamel (1990:83), any perspective that fails to bring out 'the crucial distinction between competitive strategy at the level of a business and competitive strategy at the level of an entire company' is myopic, and a recipe for resource fragmentation and missed opportunity.

The concept of core competence, as a strategy for corporate growth, looks to combine depth of expertise with breadth of application in ways that transcend individual business units and readily extend to new market creation. It also tends to lead to very different decisions about the direction of diversification. For example, no traditional positioning logic would have directed a corporate development pattern for Canon that would have seen it go from cameras to calculators to photocopiers to printers. Yet this diversification pattern makes quite a lot of sense when viewed through the logic of core competency (i.e. where can we find the most attractive opportunities to leverage our existing core expertise in fine chemicals, precision mechanics and fine optics, and where might the addition of new expertise to the pool, such as a competency in semiconductors, help to widen our opportunities further?). We see a similar type of competency logic reflected in Honda's diversification pattern, which leverages depth of learning in small engines and power trains into product-market opportunities as diverse as motorcycles, automobiles (a market which MITI, the powerful Japanese industrial development agency, actually tried to discourage Honda from entering), snow blowers and lawn mowers. We can also see it even more dramatically illustrated in the case of 3M, a company with over 60,000 products and more than thirty key technology platforms, where as Prahalad and Hamel (1990: 82) point out, 'what seems like an extremely diversified portfolio of businesses belies a few shared core competencies', built around deep know-how in adhesives, substrates and advanced materials.

A second key area that illustrates the difference between the positioning and competency perspectives is strategic renewal. One of the key strengths of the positioning perspective is the guidance that it gives on how to finesse a successful strategy in order to fully exploit a unique market position, once established. As noted earlier, central to this view of strategy is the notion of the activity system underpinning any clear competitive position, and the degree of fit within it. As Porter (1996: 70) likes to emphasise, 'fit is a far more central component of competitive advantage than most realize'. Michael O'Leary of Ryanair seems to agree. When asked what he saw as the biggest threat to his company's successful strategy his answer was the temptation to move away from the discipline of the model.[18]

However, where do you turn for insight and guidance when your market collapses and your strategy is no longer effective? How do you set about strategic renewal? How do you go about looking for what Zook (2007) refers to as those 'hidden assets' on which a new foundation for growth can be most reliably established? Do you start with competence or positioning? This was the dilemma that faced Nokia in the early 1990s following the break-up of the USSR, when the company was a mini-conglomerate with interests in the paper, rubber and electronics sectors, and at a time when its telecommunications business was still a relatively minor element in its overall corporate portfolio. In facing this renewal challenge, Nokia found little help in the positioning approach and turned to the competence-led ideas of Prahalad and Hamel for inspiration in regaining charge of its destiny. Under the leadership of Jorma Olilla, Nokia decided to bet its future on its budding expertise in digital telecommunications, and sold off its other activities, including many that were still profitable, to allow it to refocus on this area. It was a strategy based firmly on the concepts of strategic intent, capability leverage and market creation, ideas all central to the competence perspective, and Gary Hamel was a frequent visitor to the company's headquarters during the early stages of its renewal process.[19] Nokia's competence-led renewal strategy eventually saw it seize the initiative in the fastest-growing segment of the mobile telecommunications market, and become the global leader in the mobile handset market in less than a decade.

As Markides (1999) points out, firms in today's increasingly competitive environment need a more dynamic approach to strategy development that can focus concurrently on two different processes, exploiting a current market position while exploring for a new one. A major lesson from the Nokia example is that while the positioning approach remains crucial to the first, the competence-led perspective may hold the key to the second.

Beyond competitiveness to value innovation

While the positioning and competency approaches have dominated the strategy field since the early 1980s, the last decade or so has seen a shift in emphasis away from the field's traditional focus on competition to a newer strategic logic of value innovation. Driving this shift has been the

growing recognition that traditional routes to marking out and defend-
ing competitive space are becoming less and less effective as entry and
mobility barriers are relentlessly assailed in market after market, switching
costs are all but disappearing in many instances, and competencies tend
to lose their market relevance more rapidly than before. Obsession with
competition, particularly in 'mature' markets is fast becoming a recipe for
'strategy convergence', as the major players rapidly imitate each other and
well-informed consumers increasingly pick up most of the value.[20] Value
innovation, on the other hand, shifts the focus from the competition to the
customer, and offers firms a way to break free from the 'tunnel vision' of the
product life cycle, and the perceived constraints of market maturity.[21] As
Kim and Mauborgne (1999a: 43) put it, would-be value innovators tend to
ask: 'How can we offer buyers greater value that will result in soaring profits
irrespective of industry or competitive conditions?' – and they go on to
explain how this perspective differs from traditional competitive analysis:

> To achieve sustained profitable growth, companies must break
> out of the competitive and imitative trap. Rather than striving
> to match or outperform the competition, companies must culti-
> vate value innovation. Emphasis on value places the buyer, not
> the competition, at the center of strategic thinking; emphasis on
> innovation pushes managers to go beyond incremental improve-
> ments to totally new ways of doing things.

The value innovation perspective is still a developing one, embracing a
variety of related ideas that have been emerging over the last decade, all
variations on the theme of how to generate price/functionality breakthroughs for customers through innovation in the way in which value
is currently conceived and configured within any given industry. The
following sections will examine three of the more prominent of these
approaches to date, 'blue ocean strategy,' 'disruptive innovation' and
'experience innovation' in some more detail.

Value innovation – variations on a theme

W. Chan Kim and Reneé Mauborgne have been in the vanguard of the
value innovation wave since it began to take hold in the late 1990s.[22]
They have recently drawn their ideas together into the concept of 'blue

ocean strategy.' Central to this concept is the notion of value pioneering, perhaps the most general representation of the value innovation approach, and one that can apply at any level in the market pyramid.

Value pioneering and 'blue ocean strategy'

In their variation on value innovation, Kim and Mauborgne (2004, 2005) invite us to imagine the market universe composed of two sorts of oceans, red and blue. Red oceans are known or established market spaces, where the trend today is towards increasing competitive intensity, and the water is getting more and more bloody. In contrast, blue oceans are those market spaces that are still waiting to be discovered, and value innovation strategy is aimed at creating such spaces and dominating their growth. A prime example is the Montreal-based enterprise Cirque du Soleil, started by a group of street performers in 1984 and now one of Canada's largest cultural exports. This company created a whole new market opportunity by reinventing the circus as a theatrical experience, propelling it beyond the intensifying competition among the likes of Barnum & Bailey and Ringling Brothers vying with more conventional strategies in a declining industry. The lesson Kim and Mauborgne draw from this and similar cases is that often the best way to beat the competition is to stop trying to beat it and rather set out to make it irrelevant by developing a compelling new value proposition capable of creating a fresh uncontested market opportunity.[23]

Such value pioneering need not involve a leading edge technology. What is required is a compelling new way to reconfigure value that represents a quantum leap beyond the current value/cost frontier. This usually involves some innovation at the business model level. By pushing out the value/cost frontier, the value pioneer will be able to escape the traditional cost/differentiation trade-off until others learn to replicate the new business model and follow its lead. Such value innovation is not a new phenomenon. Value pioneers have been creating such opportunities since the days of Henry Ford and the Model T, and any company that has risen to prominence over the years based on the reconfiguration of value in an existing market, such as Wal-Mart in discount retailing, IKEA in the furniture industry and Dell in personal computing can all be considered to fit into this category. What is new is the way in which the concept of value innovation has been coming to the fore as a strategic logic in its own right, along with the emergence of more systematic ways to go about using it. One of the primary aims of blue ocean strategy is to reverse the process of finer and finer segmentation that usually accompanies the transition to industry maturity in PLC-based strategy through the creation of new aggregations of demand that span existing market boundaries like the circus and the theatre.

One very powerful notion linking several approaches to value innovation is a focus on the latent opportunities in current non-consumption. When Cassella Wines, a relatively recent Australian entrant into the California wine market, arrived on the scene some years ago, it focused less on how to join in the battle for existing wine drinkers than on how to create a new market opportunity among non-wine consumers, a value innovation that saw it expand the overall wine market and become the number one imported wine in the California region within a two-year period.

Disruptive innovation

The focus on non-consumers is also one of the central elements in disruptive innovation theory, the second of the value innovation perspectives to be discussed here, and the most rigorous to have emerged to date. The non-consumers normally targeted by 'disruptive' innovators are those below the bottom of the current market, still priced out of access to even the most basic version of the product or service. Nearly two decades ago, Richard Foster (1986: 116) in his book *Innovation: The Attacker's Advantage*, had noted how industry leadership 'changes hands in about seven out of ten cases when discontinuities strike', and this finding still seems to hold true to the present day.[24] The reasons why continue to confound us. Do industry leaders lose their capacity for innovation as they get bigger, or do they lose their motivation? The answer may be a combination of both. In a later chapter, we will look more closely at why the large business organisation too often tends to become 'a nearly perfect idea-killing machine', and how this might be avoided as firms grow.[25] The theory of disruptive innovation was developed by Clayton Christensen[26] to address the motivation issue.

For Christensen, the problem is not so much that the leading incumbents lose their motivation to be the innovators in their industries as they mature, but rather that they become motivated to innovate in ways that are ultimately self-defeating. The issue for them lies more in the dynamics of innovation at the industry level than in the pathologies of the large bureaucratic organisation. The theory of disruptive innovation has three basic elements: (1) the relentless short-term pressure on industry leaders from the financial markets for further growth; (2) the distinction between sustaining and disruptive innovation; and (3) the change in market context over time from underserved to overserved in terms of product features.

In disruption innovation theory, industry leaders are not seen to stop innovating as they grow. Rather, what happens is that the kind of innovation that they tend to concentrate on is very different from that of disruptive new entrants. The relentless pressure from the capital markets for further growth draws the incumbents towards sustaining innovation, which they define as innovation targeted at their most attractive high-margin customers at the higher end of the market pyramid. New entrants that try to compete with them at this end of the market typically pose little threat. The fortunes of the incumbents are much more at risk from disruptive innovators at the lowest end. As in value innovation more generally, disruptive innovation need not involve a breakthrough in technology. The most common form combines existing technology with a business model designed to be profitable at price points near the base of the market pyramid or better still at points that are 50% or more, below it. This is typically done by reconfiguring the business model to provide the basic functionality at very low price points, while still being as profitable as the conventional model, through combining lower margins with higher asset productivity. A good example is the new low-cost carrier segment in the airline industry. Using just such a strategy, Ryanair has been able to drive fresh expansion in the 'mature' European airline market by converting more and more non-fliers into customers and then dominating this new segment as it continues to grow. This is classic disruptive innovation.

According to the traditional Porter view of strategy, industry leaders should be in pole position to further consolidate their industry leadership as a market matures, unless they fall asleep at the switch. They have the advantages of scale, experience and privileged market position, which late entrants should find very difficult to overcome. The theory of disruptive innovation presents a more dynamic view of incumbent versus late entrant competition that reveals the increasing vulnerability of industry leaders as the market evolves. The process typically takes the following pattern. Most new markets begin with product offerings that are 'not yet good enough' in terms of features to fully serve the unmet needs of the market. Over time, sustaining innovation continues to add functionality until a crossover stage is reached where the product becomes 'more than good enough' to serve the needs of the majority of existing and/or potential consumers. By then the market is ripe for disruptive innovation. Disruptors enter with a stripped-down version of the product and a business model designed to be profitable at low margin. Because of their higher overheads, the leading incumbents find themselves with little short-term incentive to fight it out with the disruptors and intensify their sustaining innovation efforts aimed at generating even more profits from their most attractive customers at the top of the pyramid. However, this is a strategy that will eventually leave them increasingly vulnerable to upwards migration by the disruptors, once the latter become more firmly established in the marketplace, since it is always easier to move a lower overhead business model higher up the market, than it is to move a higher overhead model down.

The process of disruptive innovation is endemic and leaves all innovators with a difficult dilemma, since even the disruptors eventually tend to turn into sustainers as they migrate up-market and then become themselves vulnerable to the next wave of disruption.[27] In many respects, this is just the Schumpeterian process of creative destruction playing itself out, and while it may be very difficult for the firms concerned at any given time, it may be good for the industry and the economy as a whole over the longer run. However, leading incumbents are never without potential responses, once they have a better understanding of the disruptive innovation process and how it might assail them. These can range from stepping up the price/functionality attractiveness of the current offering, as Gillette did with its Sensor product line in response to the threat of the low-price disposables, disrupting the disruption by radically redefining the basic value proposition, as Swatch did in electronic watches or even by embracing the disruption and being the first to scale it up, as Schwab did in online broking.[28] The best way of all might be to learn how to become a serial disruptor and develop a core capability in disruptive innovation.[29] Regardless of the option chosen, however, one classic piece of advice will still tend to apply to any such defensive strategy. It will require investment, and the ability to withstand the relentless stock market pressure for earnings in the short term, in order to protect the company's future prospects.[30]

Experience innovation and the co-creation of value

The third approach that we examine here is experience innovation. One of the most influential strategy books of the 1990s was Hamel and Prahalad's (1994) *Competing for the Future*, in which they brought together in one place the main set of ideas informing their core competency perspective. Since then, both have also been to the fore in advancing the value innovation idea: Hamel with the development of an analytical and prescriptive framework for 'business concept innovation' in *Leading the Revolution* (2000a) and for 'management innovation, in *The Future of Management* (2007), and Prahalad in providing his own peek into the changing competitive landscape and the growing influence of what he and his co-authors call 'experience innovation' in shaping it, in *The Future of Competition*[31] and *The New Age of Innovation*.[32]

In the business world of tomorrow, as Prahalad and his recent co-authors see it, value will be increasingly co-created by companies and their customers interactively rather than merely exchanged between them, and the emergence of more connected, informed and active consumers is already transforming the company–customer relationship and the value creation process. We are already moving from a world in which our view of value innovation is company centric and product/service focused to one that will become increasingly consumer centric and experience focused, where products become more in the nature of value platforms or portals rather than repositories. Take the example of a cardiac pacemaker. Traditionally the value has been mainly embodied in the device itself, and in its implantation. The value to the patient becomes greatly enhanced, however, if the pacemaker has a built-in capability for remote monitoring and diagnosis, using new mobile communications technologies. Now the main unit of value changes from the product to the experience of the consumer in any particular context. Not only can the patient's personal physician be alerted of any serious heart rhythm deviations in a more timely fashion, but when the patient is away from home, he can be directed to the nearest hospital and the medical team on the spot given access to the full relevant medical history. In such a scenario, most of the value is to be found in the interaction of the patient with other elements of his wider value network, including the communications service providers and the medical support staff. The level of value created on any particular occasion is very specific to the given individual, event and context, as the 'close-to-home' versus 'away-from-home' scenarios in the example given above illustrate. Value becomes less a function of the product alone and more a function of the experience in context.

The two main building blocks of this emerging perspective are experience environments, which become the locus of value innovation, and experience networks, which become the locus of all the relevant competencies. It is a view of value innovation that stresses the rising importance of networks, not just firms, in the future competitive landscape. Firms will be rewarded in this new environment for the contribution that they make towards the creation and management of these experience environments and networks, and as their roles converge, the traditional distinction between consumers and producers will become increasingly blurred. The market becomes more of an interactive forum than a basic mechanism for business-to-consumer exchange, and cost becomes a weaker determinant of value. While products and markets, as we have come to know them, do not disappear under this new perspective, their functions are set to change considerably. The shifting locus of innovation and competencies implicit in this emerging experience innovation paradigm implies that firms will have to go beyond traditional ways of thinking in trying to determine how best to go about differentiating themselves and building strategic capital in this new network-oriented competitive landscape.[33]

In what Prahalad and Krishnan (2008) call this new 'N = 1, R = G' competitive space, every company will have to develop its own approach to the interactive co-creation of personalised value with each of its customers (N = 1), using access to resources from multiple sources on a global scale (R = G or Resources = Global). The current 'MySpace and Facebook generation' of Internet-savvy consumers 'will grow up expecting to be treated as unique individuals, and they will have the skills and the propensity to engage in a marketplace defined by $N = 1$' (p. 40). The pioneers are already in evidence, and they are not all high-technology companies like Apple, eBay, Amazon and Google (firms like Starbucks in coffee retailing, Goodyear in tyres, Nike in shoes, ING in Financial Services and ICICI Prudential in health insurance, are also experimenting their way rapidly into this $N = 1$, $R = G$ environment). In a world in which 'the confluence of connectivity, digitization, and the convergence of industry and technology boundaries are creating a new dynamic between consumers and the firm', few industries will be unaffected, and few firms will be able to compete in this environment on their own (p. 3).

From 'firm-to-firm' to 'network-to-network' competition

The glimpse that Prahalad and his co-authors give us into the emerging competitive landscape not only underlines the growing significance of value innovation in all its various guises, but also of strategic networks. Back in the mid-1990s, James F. Moore (1996: 78) proclaimed the 'end of industry as a useful concept in contemplating business' and urged us to adopt the concept of the business ecosystem as a more insightful alternative. Industry remains a robust concept in strategic analysis, but the network view of strategy continues to grow in importance with each passing day.

Over a decade ago, in what now seems a very prescient article, Normann and Ramirez (1993: 65–6), anticipated the fundamental reorientation in strategic mindset needed to thrive in this still evolving environment:

> Increasingly, successful companies do not just add value, they reinvent it. Their focus of strategic analysis is not the company or even the industry but the value-creating system itself, within which different economic actors –suppliers, business partners, allies, customers – work together to co-produce value. Their key strategic task is the reconfiguration of roles and relationships among this constellation of actors, in order to mobilize the creation of value in new forms and by new players. And their underlying strategic goal is to create an ever-improving fit between competencies and customers. To put it another way, successful companies conceive of strategy as systematic social innovation: the continuous design and redesign of complex business systems.

Strategic outsourcing – opportunities and risks[34]

For most companies, the move from firm-to-firm to network-to-network competition begins with strategic outsourcing. This is a good place to start in looking at the potential advantages and risks associated with collective approaches to strategy and the search for an 'ever-improving fit between competencies and customers'.

Interest in the potential of strategic outsourcing has been on the increase over the last two decades. The earliest outsourcing strategies were mainly driven by the desire to lower costs in the face of intensifying global competition, typically by moving low-skilled, labour-intensive activities to Southeast Asia and other low-cost locations. Recent times have seen a growing awareness of the potential of outsourcing to support a range of strategies beyond just that of lower costs, with further variations arising all the time. Four of the most striking are highlighted here.

The first of these is *focus*. In today's intensely competitive environment, many companies turn to outsourcing as a way of hiring 'best in class' partners to perform routine business functions and allow them to focus internally on those key activities in their value chains where the impact will be most felt by their customers. A good example is Nike. From the start, the company decided to concentrate on product development and marketing, and outsource most of its production and much of its sales and distribution. This is the strategy that allowed Nike to keep its focus and grow so quickly during the 1970s. Closely related to focus is the strategy of using outsourcing in order to be able to *scale without mass and complexity*. This is clearly one of the benefits that companies, like Nike, opting for a focus strategy with extensive outsourcing tend to enjoy from the outset. For example, over the 1978–82 period, during the steepest phase in Nike's early growth, the company saw its revenues scale up nearly ten-fold from $71M to $690M, while the employee population grew at only half of that rate from 720 to 3600.[35] In fact, Nike continued to retain many of the characteristics of the smaller entrepreneurial firm until it came close to reaching $1B in turnover before the lack of more formal management systems began to become a serious impediment to its further development. However, the prospect of being able to scale up without a pro rata increase in bureaucratic bulk and complexity can be an attractive reason to consider outsourcing at any stage in a company's development, not just at start-up. For example, in early 2000, when employee numbers at Nokia were increasing at the rate of 1000 per month, and fast approaching the 60,000 mark, CEO Jorma Ollila decided to outsource a significant portion of production in both the mobile handset and network equipment businesses, in order to slow down expansion in organisational mass without impeding the company's momentum in the marketplace.[36] At the time, Nokia was already widely recognised to be one of the least bureaucratic of global companies, and Ollila looked to a strategy of outsourcing to help him keep it that way.

Outsourcing has also been a key element in many of the most impressive examples of *disruptive innovation* to date. IKEA is a classic example. As we have noted earlier, the primary aim of most disruptive innovation is to create a whole new segment at a price point well below the base of the current market pyramid and then to dominate this segment as it grows. A key requirement is the development of an innovative business model capable of producing returns at least as good as those of the leading incumbents, but doing it at significantly lower cost through much higher asset productivity. Outsourcing often plays a key role in such innovative business models, and certainly did so in the case of IKEA. At the time of the company's founding in the early 1950s, the European furniture industry was highly fragmented geographically. National department stores established exclusive relationships with leading manufacturers locally to allow them to offer their own distinctive product lines, reflective of local tastes and traditions. This resulted in most quality new furniture being a luxury that few could afford, least of all the young setting out to furnish their first homes. IKEA revolutionised this industry by developing a line of simple, elegant, 'modern' designs with wide appeal and prices far below prevailing norms. Key to this revolution was the company's novel 'production-oriented retailing' business model, with outsourcing at its heart, not only of production but also of the final assembly and delivery activities to the customers themselves.[37]

A fourth area where outsourcing is making its mark is in *strategic repositioning*, and a classic example of the potential of outsourcing in this regard is IBM. One of the biggest judgement calls that Lou Gerstner (2003) made in his leadership of IBM's transformation in the mid-1990s was that services, not technology, would be the major growth opportunity for the company in the years ahead, particularly in the corporate computing market. IBM had always prided itself on its reputation for service, but this was service tied to products. What Gerstner had in mind was consultancy and solutions integration services as a major business driver in its own right. In 1992, Services generated $9.2 billion in revenue for IBM. Within ten years IBM Global Services had grown into a $30 billion business, involving half the corporation's human resources, and was on its way to becoming of even greater significance under the e-business 'on-demand' vision of Sam Palmisano, Gerstner's successor.[38] Outsourcing has been central to IBM's new strategic direction, both as a driver and as an enabler. Under this new strategy IBM has become an extensive provider of outsourcing services to others as part of its own repositioning as a solutions integrator in the IT operations area, while at the same time becoming a more extensive user of outsourcing services itself, primarily in product manufacturing. The company views the latter as allowing it to 'leverage the skills of the industry where it makes sense' and 'focus our own investments on areas that deliver the highest value to our customers'.[39]

In spite of its increasing attractiveness, strategic outsourcing is not without risks. One of the most important is the risk of losing key skills and capabilities that will ultimately lock the company out of untold future opportunities.[40] A dramatic example can be seen in the evolution of the General Electric-Samsung outsourcing relationship in the early history of the microwave oven industry.[41] In the early 1980s, GE was still investing heavily in its own manufacturing capability in the US, when it decided to outsource the production of some of its models at the small-to-medium end of the range to Samsung, which at that time was little known outside of Korea. While the initial contract was for just 15,000 units, GE quickly found itself on a steep dependence spiral that ultimately saw it ceding most of the investment and skills initiative in microwave production to its outsourcing partner within just two years. For Samsung, the arrangement allowed it to scale up its production and engineering at a rate that would not have been possible without the access it was given to GE's consumers, and this one small outsourcing contract set the stage for the later emergence of the Asian partner as a global powerhouse in consumer appliances.

Companies may also risk turning to outsourcing at the wrong stage in a market's evolution. Christensen (1997), in his theory of disruptive innovation, argues that the critical transition in this regard is when a market changes from being underserved to overserved with features.[42] After this transition, the product rapidly becomes a commodity and the primary basis for competition shifts to other aspects of the value proposition beyond the functionality, such as price, delivery, convenience and customisation. In the PC market, for example, it is now widely recognised that IBM outsourced too early in its anxiety to slow down the progress of Apple Computer, and in doing so allowed the initiative at the features-driven stage of the market's evolution to flow mainly to Intel and Microsoft. When the personal computer later became a commodity, the market began to favour the business model of Dell, with extensive outsourcing at its heart, and Dell used this insight again and again in the timing of its entry into adjacent markets in the early 2000s.[43] As former CEO Kevin Rollins explained it at the time, 'the beauty of our model is that commodities fall right into our sweet spot', so Dell just needed to 'continue to catch products as they move into the commodity phase and apply our low-cost direct model'.[44]

From strategic outsourcing to business networks and 'ecosystems'

The growing use of strategic outsourcing has been a major feature in the ongoing transformation in the global business environment from 'firm-to-firm' to 'network-to-network' competition, a transformation that reflects a number of significant developments over the last thirty years, including the liberalisation in world trade, the globalisation of market demand and competency access, the increasing convergence in product/service categories, the growing sophistication of intermediate markets, the mobility of capital, talent and know-how and the rapid increase in worldwide connectivity through the ever-increasing power and availability of new information and communications technologies.

Giving this trend away from the dominance of the vertically integrated firm, it is sometimes hard to imagine why high levels of vertical integration ever made commercial or strategic sense. A major part of the explanation is historical, as can be seen, for example, in the recent evolution of the IT industry. Up to the early 1980s, the IT industry was dominated by a small number of highly integrated manufacturers, like IBM and Digital, which controlled the key technologies in both hardware and software. These companies sold very high margin products to a relatively small base of industrial and commercial customers. Manufacturing was very labour intensive, with little automation, few economies of scale and little incentive to buy in anything other than very basic components and raw materials. The whole independent sub-supply sector remained underdeveloped in terms of range, scale, quality and efficiency. It was a period during which companies found it more advantageous to produce their own printed circuit boards, manufacture their own semiconductors, processors and peripherals, integrate and distribute their own systems, write their own software and support their installed base with their own service operations.

The IT industry has since experienced rapid growth through the convergence of computing and telecommunications and the emergence of a whole new mass-market segment following the arrival of the personal computer. Rapid expansion in the primary market, and the rapid diffusion of technical know-how, had enabled the emergence of new intermediate markets in the sub-supply area on a scale capable of supporting levels of specialisation and investment intensity that would have been unthinkable in the late 1970s. All the time that this was happening, many of the strategic technologies were migrating backwards into the printed circuit board and microprocessor areas, while increasingly sophisticated customers pressed for more and more compatibility across hardware and software platforms to allow them greater freedom to mix and match. By the mid-to-late 1980s, it was already becoming clear that the range of value-adding activities in the IT value chain was becoming too wide and complex for any single company to be able to excel in across the board. The traditional, highly integrated, business models of IBM and Digital were already starting to creak under their own weight, and the initiative was passing on to newer arrivals such as Dell, Sun Microsystems and Cisco, with much more specialised, flexible and scalable business models based on extensive outsourcing.

Developments such as these, that have driven the transformation to less integrated forms of business organisations and more extensive use of strategic partnerships, continue apace. Increasingly, we are seeing the emergence of more complex, multilateral strategic relationships across the value chain, giving rise to the growing importance of the network or ecosystem perspective in strategic analysis.

According to Hagel and Seely Brown (2005), radical reductions in the coordination costs across firm boundaries, due to Internet connectivity and other advances in multimedia technologies, are spurring a further wave of specialisation in the competitive landscape reaching right into core operating processes that were once seen as integral to any firm. The traditional model, as they see it, is really a composite of three more fundamental and distinct business types: infrastructure management, product innovation and commercialisation and customer relationship management, each requiring 'very different economics, skills and even cultures to be successful'. Firms that continue to keep them tightly bundled are likely to become 'increasingly vulnerable to more focused competitors' collaborating with best-in-class specialists in complimentary areas. This is already evident in industries such as financial services, pharmaceuticals and IT, and is placing an increasing premium on the ability of any firm to orchestrate the process of collaborative capability-building across an extensive business network.

As these two authors see it, coming decades will also attach a further premium to the ability of firms in developed economies to orchestrate collaborative networks that are able to tap into the value to be found in rapidly developing regions of the world such as India and China, not only for cost advantages, based on wage or salary arbitrage, but also for access to an increasing array of unique and valuable skill sets such as semiconductor fabrication in Korea or plasma TV competencies in China. Access to such location-specific skills will be not only crucial to competing successfully within these emerging markets – the kinds of innovations currently driving growth in the mobile telephony arena in India and China today are quite unique to those markets and the know-how is not directly available to the likes of Nokia or Ericcson – but for many Western firms they are also likely to prove significant further down the road when many of the business solutions developed for Indian and Chinese consumers migrate to more advanced economies in the form of disruptive innovations.[45]

Among the earliest exemplars of the new type of business network likely to thrive in the emerging competitive landscape is the firm of Li

& Fung, while the high technology cluster that has grown around Bangalore provides a good example of the type of specialised local business ecosystem likely to be a crucial source of unique location-specific skills and capabilities in the future. Li & Fung is a one hundred-year-old company in the apparel industry, based in Hong Kong. Key to its recent emergence as a global company was the reinvention of its business model in the mid-1970s that placed it at the hub of an international network involving more than 8000 firms, spanning 40 countries and linking well-known retailers like The Limited and The Gap with the assets and capabilities of yarn weavers in China, dyers in Thailand, cutters in Bangladesh and final assemblers in South Korea. This has seen Li & Fung grow to $5B in revenue, with 30–50% returns on equity and a sustained record of double-digit growth for more than two decades. Over a similar timeframe, the local economy around Bangalore in India has grown into a commercial community with world-class capabilities in software and business process outsourcing services, strong ties to Silicon Valley, a growing influx of Western venture capital and the emergence of a number of indigenous world-class companies such as Infosys and Wipro.

What will be the main implications for strategy at firm level in this evolving commercial landscape where 'the crucial battle' is no longer between individual firms 'but between networks of firms', and where strategy is increasingly becoming 'the art of managing assets that one does not own'?[46] The typical business ecosystem comprises one or a few leading participants, or hubs, with the majority of the participants being smaller, more specialised players. According to Iansiti and Levien, hub firms tend to adopt one of two alternative leadership strategies, 'keystone' and 'dominator', each with very different implications for the longer-term viability of the network, while the rest can be considered as niche players. As they see it, business ecosystems tend to be built around an interactive platform that attracts a diverse set of specialised players with a wide range of capabilities, willing to make their own specific investments in the even-widening functionality of the network to further enhance its value. Collectively, the niche players provide most of the functionality, but the contribution of the hub is crucial to the overall health of the network.

Keystone leaders typically play a system-wide role, while remaining a relatively small part of their ecosystem's mass. They are generally more effective than dominators in the creation and sharing of value across the network. The contrast between eBay and Enron provides a telling illustration. During the late 1990s, both succeeded in harnessing the power of the Internet in leveraging the assets of others to create new markets, but, as Iansiti and Levien point out, the one that 'shared the wealth ended up making so much more money' (p. 61). The primary challenge for a keystone leader, such as eBay, is to ensure that the marginal value of its platform over the marginal cost of creating, maintaining and sharing it, continues to rise rapidly with the number of players using it. Value dominators, such as Enron, tend to use their position to extract too much value from the network, while physical dominators, such as IBM in the 1970s, tend to take too large a direct role in their ecosystem's activities. Either of these approaches tends to diminish the attractiveness of the network for existing and new niche players, undermining the health of the ecosystem and increasing its vulnerability to rapid collapse.

According to Iansiti and Levien, Microsoft has shown itself to be an effective keystone in the software industry over the years, contrary to the perception in many quarters, including government regulators. The company's market capitalisation in this domain has never risen above 40% (compared with 80% for IBM in the computer domain of the late 1970s), and its influence greatly exceeds its relative share of its network's aggregate value. Microsoft's own software specialists represent just a fraction of the 5 million or more that currently programme using the Windows platform, and the company supports its wider developer network with the efforts of 2000 employees and a budget of some $600m per annum. However, network leadership strategies are always dynamic and the company could easily fall into the dominator mode in its videogame ecosystem, as any network leader will always be under temptation to do, unless it takes care to avoid it. Nvidia, the microchip graphics technology specialist is a good example of a highly successful niche player within the videogame and multimedia domains. Such players need to be able to assess whether the networks of interest to them are keystone or dominator led, and the strategic imperative for a niche player is to keep pushing out the boundaries of innovation in its own specialised domain, in order to enhance its capacity for value creation and bolster its influence within the wider ecosystem. Niche players always need to recognise that the network leaders share the wealth because it makes good economic sense to do so, and they must continue to earn the right to stay in the network. They also need to be careful not to become too tightly coupled to the specialised assets of others in the network, and thereby limit unduly their future business ecosystem options.

Finally, the issue of how to share the wealth within any particular business ecosystem takes on particular significance in the case of two-sided networks or two-sided markets. These are networks that potentially generate revenues and costs for platform providers from groups of users on both sides of the network, the demand and supply sides. A good example is the online auction industry, where companies like eBay generate revenues and costs from servicing the needs of both the buyers and the sellers. Videogames is another, where platform companies like Sony and Microsoft generate costs and revenues by servicing the needs of both consumers and producers of electronics games. In these, and many other such industries, like 'software, portals, media, payment systems and the Internet', platform providers must find a way to 'get both sides of the market on board'.[47]

According to Eisenmann et al. (2006), platform companies in two-sided markets face three main strategic challenges: (1) establishing the right pricing strategy on both sides of the network; (2) deciding when to compete and when to cooperate with other potential platform providers in what are often potentially 'increasing returns/winner-takes-all' competitive contexts[48] and (3) protecting themselves from being 'enveloped' by other platform providers in adjacent industries with the potential to develop attractive multi-platform bundles of functionalities that single platform specialists simply can't match. In the case of the pricing challenge, in particular, platform providers like Google typically make most of their revenues from one side of the network, not always the consumer side, and often end up subsidising the other side. Getting the pricing balance between the two sides right can be the difference between success and failure, as Apple discovered in its competition with Microsoft some years ago, when the two companies took opposite approaches to their pricing of software developments kits to third-party developers – Apple charging $10K per Mac kit,

Microsoft giving Windows kits away for free, and in the process attracting a much greater number of applications to the Windows platform. Up to recently, as Eisenmann et al. (2006: 101) have noted, 'the strategic implications of two-sided markets have gone largely unexplored'. This is set to change, and 'strategies for two-sided markets' are likely to be a topic of growing importance in competitive analysis for quite some time to come.

Summary

In this chapter we examined the key concepts at the heart of competitive analysis, one of the most central concerns in strategic management. We began by identifying the 1980 publication of Porter's landmark book *Competitive Strategy* as a widely recognised watershed in the development of the strategy field, and the rest of the chapter was organised around the main concepts and developments that preceded this watershed and followed on from it. We first reviewed three major concepts that had already made their mark on the strategy field before the advent of Porter's ideas: the product life cycle, the experience curve and the growth-share matrix. All three concepts were to influence much of what was to come later, as well as continuing to provide insights in their own right, and they remain staples in strategic analysis right through to the present day. The product life cycle concept was one of the first to demonstrate the need to think strategically about market evolution and the timing of new product investments and returns, while the experience curve was one of the first to make the link between learning and competitiveness. The growth-share matrix drew both of these together into an early framework for strategic positioning, a perspective on strategic analysis that was to come to much fuller development in the work of Michael Porter.

We then went on to examine the two perspectives that have dominated the area of competitive analysis since 1980, the positioning view and the competency view, the first rooted in market power and the second in firm-specific assets and resource endowments, and we focused on each of these in turn. In our examination of the positioning view of strategy we looked briefly at the concepts of Michael Porter, the dominant influence within this perspective over the last twenty-five years, including the Five

Forces model, the generic strategies and the value chain, and at his more recent distillation of these ideas into six principles of competitive positioning. When we came to the competence view of strategy, we looked first at the basic concept itself, and then examined how it differs from the positioning view and where the difference matters most and why, from a practical point of view. We ended the chapter with a look at two of the most recent developments making their mark in the area of strategic analysis: value innovation and network-to-network competition, and how, together, they look set to redefine the nature of the competitive landscape in the coming decade.

In this chapter, we concentrated mainly on strategy and competitive analysis at the level of the single business firm or individual strategic business unit. A whole set of additional considerations come into play when we shift the focus of our strategic analysis to the multi-business firm, and we turn to consider these in the next chapter.

Notes

1 Porter (1980).
2 Hamel and Prahalad (1994).
3 Christensen and Raynor (2003); Kim and Mauborgne (2005).
4 Hamel (2000a).
5 Prahalad and Ramaswamy (2004).
6 Utterback and Abernathy (1975); Tushman and Anderson (1986); Utterback (1994); Moore (2005).
7 Markides and Geroski (2003a).
8 Galbraith (1956: 47).
9 Henderson (1973).
10 For an expanded discussion of the role of learning in the strategy field, see Leavy (1998).
11 Porter (1979, 2008).
12 Argyres and McGahon (2002: 46).
13 Fishburne (1999).
14 See also Barney (1995).
15 Prahalad et al. (2001).
16 The overall discussion of the positioning versus competency view in this chapter draws freely from Leavy (2003c).
17 Capell (2003: 19).
18 O'Higgins (1999).
19 Steinbock (2001).
20 Hamel (2000a: 48).
21 Moon (2005).
22 Kim and Mauborgne (1997a, 1999b, 2000, 2002).
23 Leavy (2005a).
24 Foster and Kaplan (2001).
25 Hirshberg (1999: 16).
26 Christensen (1997), Christensen and Raynor (2003).
27 See Leavy (2004a)

[28] Charitou and Markides (2003).

[29] Christensen and Raynor (2003).

[30] Porter (1985).

[31] Prahalad and Ramaswamy (2004).

[32] Prahalad and Krishnan (2008).

[33] Leavy and Moitra (2006).

[34] The following discussion draws freely from Leavy (2004b).

[35] Rikert and Christensen (1993).

[36] Doornik and Roberts (2001).

[37] Grol et al. (1998).

[38] Hemp and Stewart (2004).

[39] IBM (2002).

[40] Lei and Slocum (1992).

[41] Magaziner and Patinkin (1989).

[42] See also Christensen et al. (2001).

[43] Zook and Allen (2003).

[44] Rangan and Bell (2002: 3).

[45] Khanna and Palepu (2006), Gadiesh et al. (2007).

[46] Iansiti and Levien (2004: 11, 1).

[47] Rochet and Tirole (2003: 990).

[48] Arthur (1996).

INTRODUCING 'STRATEGIC LEADERSHIP, GOVERNANCE AND RENEWAL'
• STRATEGY, LEADERSHIP AND THE NEW AGENDA • THE CONTEXT OF
BUSINESS IN SOCIETY • COMPETITIVE ANALYSIS AND VALUE INNOVATION
• STRATEGY AND ORGANISATION IN THE MULTI-BUSINESS FIRM •
STRATEGIC PROCESSES – INNOVATION • STRATEGIC PROCESSES – TRANSFORMATION
AND RENEWAL • SOME FINAL THOUGHTS AND REFLECTIONS

5   strategy and organisation in the multi-business firm

Introduction

The strategic management of the Multi-Business Firm (MBF) is one of the oldest topics in the strategy field, and it is in this context that the distinction between business strategy and corporate strategy becomes really meaningful. The central challenge for corporate management is how to create more value overall than the businesses could generate as stand-alone entities with direct access to the capital markets in their own right. As Foss (1997: 314) has put it: What is it that the MBF can do 'that cannot be done by the financial markets or the business units, acting as independent market contractors'? Are there any generic corporate strategies that can help to create the additional value? Or is the added value to be found primarily in the corporate management model – in the way that MBFs are organised and managed?

While the topic is one of the oldest in the strategy field, it also remains one of the most controversial. Over the last four decades, the MBF experience has been far from impressive, with more value destroyed than created,[1] and the belief still prevails in many quarters that, at best, 'most multi-business companies are the sum of their parts and nothing more'.[2] Yet, there have been many notable exceptions, companies like General Electric (GE), United Technologies, 3M, Canon, Virgin and ISS, which have managed to make it work over extended periods of time. In this chapter we will try to find out why.

We begin with an examination of how, over the years, the field has tried to find the answer to this central challenge facing the MBF through

167

'corporate strategy'. We revisit the BCG growth-share matrix, one of the earliest tools developed to help in this regard, and briefly look at some of the strengths and limitations of such strategy matrices more generally. Over the years, research has generally supported the view that related diversification tends to be more successful than unrelated, and we look at how our perspective on the key dimensions of relatedness has been evolving over time, extending the range of options on which coherent corporate strategies can be developed. In the later part of the chapter we shift our focus onto the MBF organisational model and examine how this has been evolving over time to become a source of corporate advantage in its own right. We highlight four new directions in which we see this link between organisation and competitiveness continuing to evolve in the MBF, and use the transformation at GE since 1980 by way of illustration. We close the chapter with a brief consideration of the particular issues involved in managing the HQ-subsidiary relationship in the globalising firm, and finish by reviewing some of the most recent attempts to create a more effective balance between centralisation and decentralisation, which remains the primary and perennial organisational challenge in the MBF.

Corporate strategy in the MBF

Since its earliest days, the corporate strategy literature has been preoccupied with the related themes of diversification and decentralisation.[3] The post-war decades, from the early 1950s to the late 1970s, saw a rapid expansion in multi-business activity as leading companies looked to take full advantage of economic recovery by expanding beyond their traditional areas. At the same time, the widespread adoption of the multi-divisional form of organisation, pioneered in companies like DuPont and General Motors, appeared to offer just the kind of structural innovation to accommodate such diversity with a single corporate entity. Rapid growth through acquisition became the rage and many companies developed into industrial conglomerates, the likes of Textron, with activities spanning military helicopters, gold bracelets, chain saws, stationery, polyurethane foam and fine china, to mention just part of the range.[4] This rapid rise of the MBF brought with it the need to make a distinction between corporate and business strategies, and the major innovations in the strategy field during the 1970s were developed to help companies deal with the relationship between the two.

The BCG growth-share and other strategy matrices

The growth-share, or business portfolio, matrix, discussed in some detail in the previous chapter, was developed by the Boston Consulting Group (BCG) in the early 1970s to help diversifying companies to address two fundamental issues in corporate strategy: What businesses should a company be in? And how should corporate resources be allocated among them?[5] The BCG matrix provided a framework for managing the corporation as a portfolio of businesses, balancing corporate cash flow, risk and opportunity, so that management, rather than the capital markets, could retain primary sway over future strategy. The original two-by-two version of the growth-share matrix was found to be too simplistic in practice, but the portfolio idea that underpinned it caught on, and a later, more sophisticated, three-by-three GE/McKinsey version was developed, which became quite widely used by the end of the decade.

Associated with the portfolio approach was the requirement to organise the diversified corporation into Strategic Business Units (SBUs) for planning purposes, based on product–market focus. Each SBU was seen to have a distinct strategic thrust in terms of both cash flow (net user or net generator) and development (grow/hold/harvest/divest). While there was much initial enthusiasm for the concepts of corporate strategy matrices and SBUs, they were rarely straightforward to operate in practice. In a contemporary study of ten firms with varying levels of experience, Bettis and Hall (1983: 97) found that 'none of them had been successful in using the basic model'. Among the most difficult challenges were trying to constitute SBUs unambiguously as discrete businesses, limiting their number and dealing with relatedness among them. Should a company manufacturing washing machines, microwave ovens and fridge freezers consider each a separate SBU, or should it lump them together under appliances? Should it break them down further into consumer and commercial markets? Too many distinctions tended to lead to an unwieldy number of SBUs, potentially running into hundreds in the case of some of the largest companies. On the other hand, too much aggregation tended to give rise to less-than-optimum business strategies that were too broadly targeted. For example, treating the entire commercial appliances division as a cash cow, say, might not be the wisest option if the market prospects and competitive strengths of the different appliance types were quite diverse.

There were also other limitations. In the original BCG matrix, market growth was used as a surrogate for industry attractiveness, and market share for relative competitive strength. Porter's (1980, 1985, 1996, 2001) frameworks for industry analysis (Five Forces) and competitive positioning (Generic Strategies – Value Chain – Six Principles) have since helped to provide a sounder, more comprehensive basis for assessing any business on each of these dimensions, as we saw in Chapter 4. The BCG and other such matrices were further limited by their inability to deal with the issue of relatedness among different business units and how this might be leveraged for corporate advantage.

Is relatedness the key?[6]

So where is corporate advantage to be found in the MBF beyond the balancing of cash flows among the businesses? How can corporate strategy add value? The classic rationale for multi-business strategy emphasises the significance of economies of scale and scope.[7] Over the last two-and-a-half decades, companies like Canon, Cisco, Honda and Nike have shown how to build global market presence through strategic partnering and flexible manufacturing, so that scale, in the traditional sense of high levels of capital intensity, no longer seems to be so decisive an advantage in many industries.[8] On the other hand, the potential synergies from economies of scope are still seen as significant, and the link between relatedness and performance in the MBF remains a central theme in corporate strategy research.

One of the current wisdoms in the area of corporate strategy is that related diversification tends to create more value for shareholders over the longer term than unrelated (conglomerate) diversification.[9] This finding emerged in a pioneering study by Richard Rumelt (1974), and subsequent research has tended broadly to support it. Empirical experiences like the dramatic collapse of the conglomerate wave in the late 1970s and early 1980s, and the major redeployment of corporate assets that accompanied it, also seem to bear it out. As a *Business Week* editorial of the time described it: 'Unlike other manias in the past, particularly the conglom-erate craze of the 1960s, the present surge of acquisitions and divesti-tures includes a trend that should be encouraged', namely 'a swing back towards simplifying the corporation into an enterprise of related business activities' (1981: 74). However, exactly where the advantage of related diversification lies has proven to be more difficult to pin down. To begin with, follow-on studies questioned whether the superior performance of related diversification was due to economies of relatedness at firm level or mainly reflected industry effects due to overall differences in market selec-tion patterns and prowess.[10] Porter (1987) later underlined the importance of both elements when he argued that the essential tests for adding any new business to a diversifying MBF should include the structural attrac-tiveness of industry and the competitive advantage that the new business will gain through its linkages with others in the corporate portfolio.

Even if we accept that economies of relatedness are important, this still begs the question as to what types of relatedness are likely to be most significant. Traditionally, we have tended to think about relatedness in terms of markets and products, as reflected in Ansoff's (1965) well-known directional-growth matrix. For some, like Theodore Levitt, market relatedness clearly took precedence. In his classic article Marketing Myopia, he argued that the railroads missed out on the most attractive opportuni-ties to grow and diversify because they defined their market too narrowly: 'The reason they defined their industry wrong was because they were railroad-oriented instead of transportation-oriented; they were product-oriented instead of customer-oriented'.[11] Over the years, there have been many examples of successful diversification based on market relatedness, such as Nike's entry into leisure apparel, and Gilette's into personal care products. However, there have also been some notable failures such as Satchi and Satchi's unsuccessful move into consulting and Coca Cola's into wine, and these suggest caution. As Zook and Allen (2003) point out, expanding into adjacent markets is often much tougher that it appears, and three-quarters of the time the effort fails. In fact, an all too common mistake that companies make is to diversify too soon and underestimate the growth potential that still remains in the core business.[12]

While market relatedness can often be a good basis for generating corporate advantage in the MBF, the logic, in itself, is not compelling.

An extensive study by Nathanson and Cassano (1982), pointed elsewhere. Coming at the issue from a different direction, they found that corporate management in MBFs tended to have much greater difficulty managing product diversity than market diversity, implying that product relatedness might be the more important consideration. Again, however, the overall experience with product-related diversification has been very mixed. Levi-Strauss has struggled for decades to diversify within the apparel category, ICI eventually hived off its pharmaceuticals business, having found it to be incompatible with its core industrial chemicals activity, and there are few examples to date of companies that have migrated successfully from consumer to industrial electronics or from light to heavy power tools. In short, as Goold and Campbell (1998) point out, many of the hoped-for economies from product or market relatedness have proved difficult to realise in practice, because too many synergy initiatives tend to generate unintended 'knock-on effects' from poor alignment between parenting skills at the corporate level and the key success factors at business level. Porter (1987:46) also emphasises that 'diversification inevitably adds cost and constraints to business units', so that if the hoped-for synergies fail to fully materialise, then more value may be destroyed than created.

The early emphasis on market and product relatedness in the literature on corporate strategy in the MBF reflected the traditional dominance of the market power or positioning approach to strategy development. As noted in the previous chapter, one of the basic premises of this perspective on the MBF is that 'diversified companies do not compete, only their businesses do', so that overall corporate strategy is seen to 'grow out of and reinforce business strategy'.[13] Indeed, Jack Welch seemed to reflect this view when he once explained early in his leadership tenure that 'there is no single plan for a company with as many businesses and markets as GE' and that his strategic aim was to 'evolve into a company that's either number 1 or number 2' in each of its diverse arenas.[14] However, we have also seen how the Resource-Based View (RBV) of strategy, which has come to prominence in more recent times, takes issue with this assertion by stressing that effective business strategies can also be seen to grow out of a coherent corporate strategy, and how for some of its most prominent proponents any perspective that fails to bring out 'the crucial distinction between competitive strategy at the level of the business and competitive strategy at the level of the entire corporation' is myopic, and a recipe for resource fragmentation and missed opportunity.[15] In essence, the RBV invites us to look at corporate strategy from a different angle, one rooted primarily in firm resources.[16] Resource relatedness is emphasised over product or market relatedness, with business strategies seen to flower out of core corporate know-how.

There is, however, a range of views as to how resource-relatedness is linked to successful corporate strategy. One of the most influential is the core competency perspective, which we discussed at some length in the previous chapter, and review again more briefly here. For Prahalad and Hamel (1990), the distinguishing feature of companies, like Honda and Canon, with sustained records of successful diversification is the way that they manage their companies as portfolios of competencies as well as portfolios of businesses. The kind of diversification pattern that emerges in the RBV perspective is one based on depth of know-how and breadth of application. We see this reflected in Honda's deep firm-wide expertise in small engines and power trains applied to products and markets as diverse as motorcycles, automobiles, snow blowers and lawnmower. We also see it in Canon's depth of expertise in fine optics, precision mechanics, fine chemicals and semiconductors, applied to such diverse businesses as cameras, calculators, office copiers and computer printers. One of the most striking examples is 3M, with over 60,000 products and more than 30 key technology platforms. As Prahalad and Hamel (1990: 19) have highlighted, 'what seems to be an extremely diversified portfolio of businesses belies a few shared core competencies', built around deep know-how in adhesives, substrates and advanced materials. Such resource-related diversification is not confined to manufacturing. It is also to be seen in Wal-Mart's application of its core logistical expertise across a diverse range of retailing and wholesaling formats.

While conceptually appealing, the notion of core competency has proven to be difficult enough to apply in practice. Core competencies involve both tangible dimensions like technologies, and less tangible ones such as organisation-wide learning and the kind of culture that supports it. As defined by Prahalad and Hamel (1990: 19), core competencies are 'the collective learning in the organization, especially how to coordinate diverse production skills and integrate multiple streams of technology'.

Such competencies are of strategic significance only if they provide potential access to a wide variety of market opportunities, make a significant contribution to benefits perceived as important to customers, and are difficult to substitute for or imitate. Many feel that such a definition gives more guidance on how to recognise an existing core competence than on how to create a new one. It should also be acknowledged that the resource-related diversification strategies of companies like Honda are open to a variety of interpretations. Stalk and his colleagues see the main building blocks of corporate strategy as business processes rather than competencies, and the key to successful diversification as the ability to transform key processes into strategic capabilities that are 'so flexible and robust' that they can be applied to many businesses.[17] In their view, the secret to Honda's successful diversification lies less in the kind of core competencies highlighted by Prahalad and Hamel than in its unique 'dealer management' and 'product realization' capabilities. As they see it, rivals like General Motors have always had comparable competencies in engines and power trains, but what they really lacked were the business process capabilities to leverage them into new markets as quickly or effectively as Honda.

Furthermore, there are others for whom the linking of such resource-based relatedness back to market power is far more important than trying to distinguish competencies from capabilities or arbitrate between them.[18] As they see it, the relatedness that really counts is among strategic assets, which are market specific. Honda's ability to transfer its know-how on dealer relations from motorcycles to lawnmowers will only be significant in corporate strategy terms if dealer relations is also a strategic asset or key success factor in the lawnmower market and/or if what Honda learns from the lawnmower market can be used to improve its competitive advantage in one or more of its original businesses. Oil companies like BP learned this lesson the hard way when they tried to transfer their exploration and extraction capabilities to mining and found they could not exploit them to advantage. The key success factors in the mining business turned out to be very different, placing a premium on quite different corporate 'parenting' skills and value propositions.[19]

While such debates remain unresolved, and reflect the relative immaturity of the RBV,[20] what is clear is that this perspective has widened considerably the range of product–market diversity within which a rationale for economies of relatedness might be found. Indeed, the link between relatedness and successful corporate strategy does not end with products, markets and competencies or capabilities. C.K. Prahalad and Richard Bettis, in their seminal contribution to the cognitive perspective on strategy, have widened the scope for relatedness still further by suggesting that much of the explanation linking diversification with performance might actually reside in the shared cognitive schemata or 'dominant logic' of corporate management.[21] In this view, strategic variety, rather than business variety, may often be the most limiting factor in determining how much diversity any given corporate executive team can cope with successfully. The bottom line, as they have put it, is that 'each management team at any given point in time has an in-built limit to the extent of diversity that it can manage', and relatedness 'may be as much a cognitive concept as it is an economic or technical one'.[22]

No doubt, product, market or competency relatedness can all be effective ways of keeping business variety to manageable proportions. However, the concept of dominant logic invites us to consider a still wider range of viable diversification patterns based on an even more expanded set of relatedness dimensions. A corporate 'dominant logic' might be built around a particular generic strategy, as Emerson Electric and Tyco have been able to do through a consistent low-cost emphasis across their diverse business sets. It might also be built around a particular type of business activity, such as manufacturing. For example, US conglomerate United Technologies and British conglomerate BTR were able to develop corporate management models that have been effective in managing a diverse range of manufacturing businesses. BTR later found their model wanting when they tried to migrate it to the distribution sector, a temptation that United Technologies has so far been very careful to avoid.[23] It might be also be built around a particular type of business model, such as the one that Dell developed for the personal computer industry and later extended, with considerable success, to other activities such as the server, storage and printer segments. It might even be possible to build an effective dominant logic around a type of process, such as mass production, as BIC has been able to do in disposable ballpoint pens, razors and lighters, or a repeatable strategic formula – first footwear, then apparel, then equipment, then global – as Nike has done in one adjacent sports market after another.[24] However, what is most clear is that there are dimensions of relatedness beyond those of product and market alone that are capable of providing coherence to a much wider degree of corporate diversity than has hitherto been supposed.

Organisation and competitiveness in the MBF

Does corporate management in the MBF add value primarily through strategy or through organisation? Is relatedness the only route to creating value in the multi-business company? While the weight of the literature to date seems to suggest as much, yet there are still some highly diversified companies like GE, with seemingly little relatedness across their many business activities, which continue to generate value way beyond the sum of the parts. Cases like these invite us to look beyond the realm of strategy alone, to examine in some detail the relationship between corporate organisation and competitiveness in the MBF and how this has been changing over time.

For most of the last four and a half decades, the relationship between internal organisation and firm performance has been considered primarily in terms of structure. In fact, as we noted in our opening chapter, the relationship between strategy and structure is one of the oldest themes in the strategy field, and Alfred Chandler's (1962) thesis that 'structure follows strategy' is one of the seminal propositions. It later became one of the cornerstones of the Harvard Business School business policy model, which has been so influential in strategic management teaching and research over the years.[25]

Does structure follow strategy – can structure Be strategic?

Chandler's classic study showed how desired changes in strategy, in pursuit of new opportunities, arising from changes in technology and market structure, tended to press companies into new structural arrangements. Historically, new strategies of diversification seemed to require new decentralised, divisional, forms of organisation to make them effective. His structure-follows-strategy proposition was subsequently supported by French,

German and British studies.[26] In related work, Wrigley (1970) classified large firms into single-product, dominant-product, related-product and unrelated-product categories, and Rumelt (1974) then extended this work to examine how the match between diversification strategy and structure influenced economic performance. While the Wrigley–Rumelt research focused on the horizontal dimension of the strategy–structure relationship, Williamson (1975) later took the lead in examining the vertical dimension, and developed the transaction-cost approach to the study of economic organisation, which has since become one of the most influential in the literature.

The Chandler–Wrigley–Rumelt studies of the 1970s were primarily concerned with corporate strategy, and this was almost totally equated with diversification. Their central concern was how best to integrate diverse related and unrelated business activities within a single corporate structure, and the dominant strategy paradigms of the time, like the BCG growth-share matrix and its variants, reflected this orientation. However, as Miller (1986: 233) was later to argue, the seminal Chandler–Wrigley–Rumelt studies had 'merely scratched the surface', and there was 'clearly more to the concepts of both strategy and structure' than the link between product–market diversification and corporate divisionalisation. For example, Waterman and his McKinsey colleagues[27] argued that economic performance was dependent on the appropriate alignment of strategy with organisation in a much wider sense than structure (proposing a '7-S' framework – strategy, structure, systems, staff, style, shared values and skills). Peters (1984: 111) further argued that 'distinctive organizational performance' was 'almost entirely a function of deeply engrained repertoires' (anticipating the emergence of the RBV), and Burgleman (1983a) showed that many of the mechanisms developed by corporate-level management to control the execution of current strategy also tended to pre-condition the emergence of future strategy.[28] In sum, the seeds of future strategy are already deeply embedded in the current organisational context, so that strategy can be seen also to follow structure.

The 1980s brought a shift in emphasis from corporate to business strategy, as more and more companies looked to protect their core businesses from intensifying competition, and interest in the strategy–structure relationship was extended to the business level. At the start of the decade, Porter (1980) introduced concept of generic strategies (low cost, differentiation and focus). Around the same time Mintzberg (1981) developed a typology of structure that went beyond the U-form (Unitary form – functionally centralised) and M-form (Multi-divisional) categories at the heart of the Chandler–Wrigley–Rumelt perspective. In it, he identified five distinct configurations – the simple form, the machine bureaucracy, the professional bureaucracy, the divisional form and the adhocracy. Organisations, he argued, function at their most effective when they achieve internal coherence and harmony across many different organisational and administrative dimensions (reporting relationships, job specifications, spans of control, liaison devices, etc.). As Miller (1986: 237) was quick to spot, there was a 'considerable' and 'heartening' overlap between the Porter and Mintzberg typologies. For example, the machine bureaucracy configuration was closely matched to the requirements of a low cost generic strategy, while the adhocracy was more consistent with differentiation based on innovation, and the simple form with focus. Seen in this way, we could truly say that strategy is structure and structure is strategy. Choose a low cost strategy and you will need a machine bureaucracy configuration to make it effective; choose a machine bureaucracy as your structural configuration and, at its most effective, you will be competing on cost (and efficiency). Porter's generic strategies are characterised by high degrees of internal alignment and complimentarity, as are Mintzberg's structural configurations. Both are seen as highly stable, honed to purpose and not to be readily departed from without cost or consequence. Hybrid structures and 'stuck-in-the-middle' strategies are seen to be relatively ineffective and unsustainable over time.

Building 'organisational advantage' – new directions[29]

One of the most important developments in more recent times is the growing tendency to look at organisation as a strategic variable in its own right – and building organisational capability as the primary route to creating corporate-wide competitiveness in the MBF.

Traditionally, as we have already seen, the tendency was to view organisation in the very narrow sense of structure, and to see its impact on competitiveness as subordinate to strategy. Nowadays, the limitations of this view are becoming more and more exposed with every passing year. The period since the early 1990s has been marked by increasing dynamism in the environment of business organisations, as markets have become more volatile, industry boundaries more diffuse and firm structures more fluid, all under the influence of unprecedented changes in technology and competition. This new dynamism has been underpinned by a fundamental shift in the primary driver of wealth creation from material to knowledge capital. In this new context more and more researchers and practitioners have been drawn towards the resource-based notion that distinctive organisational capabilities provide a more durable basis on which to build sustainable competitive advantage than relying too heavily on defensible market positions alone.[30]

Against this background, it is not surprising that we are already moving towards a new perspective on the relationship between organisation and competitiveness that promises to take us well beyond the restricted horizons and static character of the traditional strategy–structure framework. The concept of organisational capability that lies at the heart of most resource-based theories embraces much more than structural form. It also extends to organisational functioning and culture, and in doing so involves a more direct and dynamic conceptual link with competitiveness, which is no longer seen as subordinate to strategy, but as part of its very essence. Indeed, as Ghoshal and Bartlett (1998) have pointed out, structure in the narrow anatomical sense of the typical organisational chart may now be one of the least significant considerations. Organisations with similar structures now enjoy very different levels of organisational advantage. Traditionally, under the old strategy–structure linkage, structure took precedence over talent – people were selected to fit the corporate model. Today, as they see it, the challenge is to build 'an organisation flexible enough to exploit the idiosyncratic knowledge and unique skills of every individual employee', where creating the right 'behavioural context' takes precedence over structure.[31]

One of the most striking aspects in the MBF landscape over the last two decades is the growing awareness that we are leaving behind something very familiar in terms of the corporate management model, and heading towards something very new, whether it be the 'learning organisation',[32] the 'visionary company',[33] the 'living company',[34] the 'individualised corporation',[35] the 'horizontal organisation',[36] the 'capability-creating organisation',[37] the 'resilient company',[38] a 'company of citizens'[39] or some reflection of all of these; and whether it be one that 'brings the market inside',[40] finds new ways of building 'the collaborative advantage'[41] or best combines the two. To date the transformation has been largely practice-led, as leading companies experiment with more productive ways to build organisational capability and harness all the talent and ideas at their disposal. It has also been progressing at somewhat different rates across the globe.[42]

It is still not fully clear where these ongoing innovations in the organisation of the MBF are going to take us, or what the new MBF corporate organisation and management model will eventually look like.[43] However, we believe that the outlines of where we are heading are already quite discernable in the following four distinct and related shifts in emphasis that have been taking place in recent times in both theory and practice, all of them revolving around the growing importance of organising for learning, innovation and engagement, not just for control, efficiency and predictability.

Vertical and horizontal scope – beyond minimising cost to maximising value

The strategy–structure literature from its earliest days has been concerned with the question of vertical integration and the expansion of vertical scope, one of the major growth options available to any MBF. Up to recently, most explanations for vertical integration centred on the analysis of transaction costs, and under what kind of structure such costs would be minimised.[44] In the Transaction Cost Economics (TCE) view, where markets and hierarchies are seen as alternative forms of organisation for economic activity, the presence of vertically integrated hierarchies is seen to reflect vertical market failure, where an in-house alternative appears more attractive. Vertical markets typically fail when (1) there are only a small number of buyers and sellers (small numbers); (2) supplying the product or service requires specialised investments in facilities, equipment or skills (high asset specificity); and (3) there are frequent transactions between the parties. According to the TCE perspective, these conditions tend to limit the options open to both parties, and make the relationship more vulnerable to opportunistic behaviour. Where present, they tend to result in higher transaction costs in the marketplace and provide the incentive to bring the relevant transactions in-house.

The TCE perspective remains one of the most influential frameworks for the strategic analysis of vertical integration. However, as a basis for understanding the organisation-competitiveness relationship, it can be found wanting on a number of grounds. It is based on a very 'under-socialised' view of human behaviour in market transactions that fails to recognise the influence of the wider system of social norms and values within which such transactions take place.[45] 'Self-interest with guile' is the model of motivation underpinning TCE,[46] and lack of trust is seen as 'the quintessential cause of transaction costs'.[47] Moreover, TCE analysis tends to be static. One of its major strengths is its ability to provide a framework for analysing the relative efficiency of different structural arrangements under equilibrium conditions. In the dynamic conditions that most organisations face today, the notion that cost-minimisation is the primary measure of the effectiveness of any structural arrangement is debatable. Maximising value may be the more appropriate criterion, and one that subsumes cost minimisation while putting the emphasis on what many now refer to as 'dynamic' rather than static efficiency. The concept of 'dynamic efficiency' is one more associated with innovation and adaptability, and is focused more on the challenge of trying to extend the current productivity frontier rather than simply trying to optimise within it.[48] It is also more in tune with the RBV of the firm, in which 'the primary task of management' is seen to be 'to maximize value through the optimum deployment of existing resources and capabilities, while developing the firm's resource base for the future'.[49]

Shifting our perspective from minimising costs to maximising value also turns our attention to the role of trust in organisational effectiveness, and there is growing interest in the impact of trust in economic and organisational analysis. As Fukuyama (1996: 7) has argued, a nation's welfare and ability to compete are 'conditioned by a single, pervasive cultural characteristic: the level of trust inherent in the society'. When we restore the concept of trust back into organisational economics, we underline the significance of a new type of wealth-creating asset, 'social capital', within and across organisational boundaries. New types of structural alternatives to markets and hierarchies then become viable, in both theory and reality. Among the most notable of these are supplier partnerships and alliance networks, the strategic significance of which we have discussed already in the previous chapter. There is no doubt that the growing prevalence of such networks can be understood to some extent in terms of cost minimisation, albeit with some modifications to basic TCE theory. However, according to Powell (1990) in only a small percentage of cases are such relationships driven by this concern. In a dynamic environment, such networks present a company with opportunities to harness the complementary competencies of other firms in the creation of value and deepen its own competencies through the wider access to learning and new ideas that such relationships can provide. The main benefit offered by the network structure is the enhancement of intangible assets, both social and intellectual, rather than the minimisation of transaction costs.

The newer emphasis on maximising value rather than just minimising cost in the organisation of the MBF increasingly applies to synergies being sought through economies of scope in horizontal as well as vertical integration. What the diverse business units in the MBF can learn from each other, and also from each other's strategic partners, is playing an increasingly significant role in the generation of added value beyond any cost savings to be realised through the sharing of more material assets or common 'factors of production' alone.[50]

Structural design – beyond fit and alignment to stretch and creative tension

One of the strongest themes in the strategy–structure literature to date has been the idea that effectiveness depends on a high degree of internal alignment among an array of organisational elements, elevating it almost to the status of central structural design principle in the strategy domain. In recent times, however, the heavy emphasis on fit and alignment is being re-examined, particularly for the dynamic conditions that are prevalent today.

Fit and alignment work particularly well in conditions of equilibrium. Miller (1986), one of the early advocates for the potency of alignment, argued that the harmonious configuration of strategy, structure, systems and culture was a far more powerful determinant of organisational effectiveness than the optimisation of any one of these elements alone. Moreover, such alignment could be finessed and strengthened over time, making it a very potent source of competitiveness where market structures were relatively stable. It is because of this that the notions of configuration and alignment, as popularised in the McKinsey 7-S framework and in Porter's principles of competitive positioning, have proved to be so insightful in explaining the long run effectiveness of companies such as Wal-Mart or Southwest Airlines, and why their success has been so hard for others to imitate. As Miller (1987: 697) has pointed out, such configurations 'have an internal logic, integrity, and evolutionary momentum of their own, as well as a central enduring theme that unifies and organises them' which gives them great durability.

However, in more dynamic conditions, the case becomes less convincing. As Pascale (1991: 49) has pointed out, 'fit contributes to coherence – but too much of it risks over-adaptation.' Miller (1996: 510) also warns that any organisation will risk losing its 'resilience and relevance' if 'the orchestrating theme of a configuration becomes too obsessive a preoccupation'. Dynamic environments put a premium on inventive strategies, and one of the primary sources of creativity is 'divine discontent', as the late psychologist Anthony Storr (1991: 205) liked to term it. Hamel and Prahalad (1993) have argued that the most creative strategies are born in the gap between an organisation's resources and its aspirations, shifting the focus from fit to stretch, and from resource endowment to resourcefulness. Likewise, Nonaka (1988a) and Senge (1990) have argued that the capacity of organisations to learn and renew themselves depends on their ability to generate creative tension through aspirational crisis. Canon's plunge into the personal photocopier market, Ted Turner's into twenty-four-hour televised newscasting and Richard Branson's into the airline industry are among the most impressive illustrations of the power behind this idea. In fact, as Pascale (1991: 107) has put it, 'inherent tension within organisations is the primary, if not the only, vehicle for self-regeneration'.

The importance of some degree of tension and creative disalignment is becoming increasingly recognised in practice, though some of the most enduring companies have long benefited from this basic insight. The decision by Proctor & Gamble during the 1930s to promote interbrand competition within the company was one of the earliest attempts to develop a deliberate 'mechanism of discontent' within a corporate organisation.[51] So also was the maxim, enshrined by Robert Woodruff and Paul Austin into the culture at Coca Cola: 'The world belongs to the discontented'.[52] The relentless effort by Andy Grove and his successors to create and maintain a culture of 'constructive conflict' and creative 'paranoia' at Intel, and the various 'innovate-or-die' self-disciplines imposed within companies like Merck, Motorola and 3M, all illustrate the variety of ways in which these companies and their strategists have been trying over the years to sustain creative tension within their organisations and encourage their people to embrace it.[53]

Organisational effectiveness – beyond structure to process and culture

Alongside this awareness of the role of creative tension, there has been growing recognition of some other basic paradoxes that lie at the heart of the organisation-competitiveness relationship within the MBF.

The diversification wave made possible by the spread of the multi-divisional form of organisation was also fed on the twin beliefs that the good manager could manage any business and that any diverse set of businesses could be managed effectively with the right strategic planning framework and the right organisational design. The main strategy tool of the time, the business portfolio matrix lacked the ability to deal will potential relatedness across the business units, as noted already, so many companies turned to the concept of the matrix organisation in an attempt to address this issue through structure.[54] One of the first diversified companies to make the transition from the basic divisional structure to the matrix form was Dow Corning, which 'made this revolutionary and novel move' with 'fingers crossed'.[55] The basic idea involved overlaying firm-wide coordination of functions across business-based divisions, or of businesses across country-based divisions, in an attempt to design or 'hard wire' synergy directly into the corporate structure. By the mid-1970s, the number of well-known companies adopting the matrix structure, the likes of GE, Shell and Citibank, was impressive and growing rapidly. While there were some teething problems, contemporary researchers like Davis and Lawrence (1978: 142) believed that the matrix organisation was destined to 'become almost commonplace' and that managers would soon come to 'speak less of the difficulties and pathologies of the matrix and more of its advantages and benefits'.

By the early 1980s, however, much of the early optimism was already evaporating. An influential study by Kotter (1982) cast major doubt over the notion that the talented manager is equally effective in any industry context. Furthermore, Bartlett and Ghoshal (1990: 139) concluded that after decades of experimentation the ideal structure for the diversified firm had yet to emerge, and that the matrix structure, from which so much had been expected, had proved to be 'all but unmanageable – especially in an international context'. Before long, even the early exemplars, like Dow Corning, were retreating towards more conventional, geography-based, structures. It became increasingly clear by the early 1990s that the effective management of the diversified firm involved a number of underlying tensions or paradoxes that could not be resolved through static structural solutions alone. In fact, as Doz and Prahalad (1991: 146) came to see it, the matrix form itself reflected the 'structural indeterminacy' inherent in these tensions, and they emphasised the need to focus more on 'underlying processes', rather than just structure, in the search for their resolution. In a similar vein, Ghoshal and Mintzberg (1994: 8) noted that most MBFs 'swing like a pendulum' between centralising and decentralising 'and never seem to get it right', and they suggested that more of the energy of these companies 'should be invested into sustaining a dynamic balance' among these basic tensions, rather than trying to eliminate them.

It was management legend, Alfred Sloan, in his classic book *My Years with General Motors*, who first articulated the most basic organisational challenge facing the MBF in terms of what he called the principle of decentralisation with co-ordinated control. As Sloan (1963: 429) explained:

> From decentralisation we get initiative, responsibility, development of personnel, decisions close to the facts – in short, all the qualities necessary for an organisation to adapt to new conditions. From centralisation we get efficiencies and economies. It must be apparent that co-ordinated decentralisation is not an easy concept to apply.

Likewise, Percy Barnevik, during his tenure as CEO of ABB, viewed the organisational challenge at the heart of the MBF as trying to grapple with 'three internal contradictions', aiming to be 'global and local', 'big and small' and 'radically decentralised with central reporting and control'.[56] For Jack Welch at GE, it was how to get 'that small company soul – and small company speed – inside our big company body'.[57]

As Day and Wendler (1998) have pointed out, any form of economic organisation, market or hierarchy, must concern itself with two main functions: how to motivate the creation of value and how to coordinate it. In their purest forms, markets tend to be better at the first, hierarchies at the second. The MBFs of the 1970s and early 1980s had become top-heavy with coordination, and over the last two and a half decades, more and more of them have been moving beyond structural solutions alone in their attempts to manage this central paradox. An increasing number have been drawn towards the concept of federalism, which involves attention to underlying processes and values in addition to structure. This is a significant development both in theory and practice. According to Handy (1992), the basic principles of federalism, that autonomy releases energy; that people need to be well-informed, well-intentioned and well-educated to interpret the common interest; that individuals prefer being 'led' to being 'managed', all now seem in tune with the needs, demands and paradoxes of modern corporate life. Conceiving the MBF as a federation does not eliminate the tensions and paradoxes inherent in the matrix approach. Rather, it internalises them in the roles of key managers, so that matrix management becomes less a structure and more a frame of mind.[58] For companies that have successfully adopted it, the federal perspective, with its strong leaning towards decentralisation, offers a more effective way to balance the motivating and coordinating functions of the MBF than the more traditional matrix structure.

Overall, the key insight seems to be that federalism must be embraced as a philosophy, not just a structure. As the experiences of companies like GE show, successful transformation to a more federal approach requires holistic attention to management skills and culture, not just structure, and it cannot be successful without mutually reinforcing changes in all of these areas. For as Handy (1992: 60) has pointed out, the federalist approach is not just an organisational form but also a 'way of life' that has to reach right into the 'soul' of the corporation to be fully effective. However, the principle of radical decentralisation at the heart of the federal model may not be the best option in all circumstances. IBM in the early 1990s was also seen to be suffering from 'top-heavy syndrome,' and the CEO of the time, John Akers, decided to move towards a more federal model, involving the radical decentralisation of 'Big Blue' into thirteen 'Baby Blues' to try to reinvigorate the company.[59] Reversing that direction and keeping IBM together as a more integrated entity was, Lou Gerstner (2003: 61), the architect of the company's successful turnaround in the mid-nineties, later recalled, 'the most important decision I ever made – not just at IBM, but in my entire business career'.

The main point to note in all of this is that regardless of the relative merits of any particular structural form in any particular circumstance, the secret to organisational effectiveness in the MBF is no longer to be found mainly in structure, but rather in process and values. Authors like Ghoshal and Bartlett (1998) now argue that the MBF should be conceived increasingly as a 'portfolio of processes' as well as a portfolio of businesses and competencies. In their recent study, similar companies with similar structures were found to differ widely in effectiveness, as did similar companies with different structures. For them, what makes the likes of Canon, 3M and GE so effective as MBFs is the way they organise themselves around three key processes: the entrepreneurial process, the integration process and the renewal process, with business level managers primarily responsible for the first, the corporate executive team for the second and the CEO for the third.

Guiding metaphor – beyond the 'machine' to the 'living system'

The new emphasis on value-maximisation, creative tension and process rather than structure, are all largely inconsistent with the traditional mechanistic perspective through which the organisation-competitiveness relationship has tended to be seen up to now. The original concepts of structure following strategy, the TCE framework, and the notions of alignment and fit were firmly grounded within this mindset. In the main, it is rooted in a Newtonian–Cartesian view of the world in which any complex system is best understood through breaking it down into its more elemental components and analysing how they fit together.

As Morgan (1986: 13) has pointed out, the 'mechanistic mode of thought has shaped our conception of what organisation is all about', while Senge (1997: viii) believes that 'almost all of us adopt the machine assumption without ever thinking about it'. While this mode of thinking has served us reasonably well in conditions of stability and equilibrium, it is increasingly inappropriate as a perspective for understanding the organisation-competitiveness relationship in conditions of dis-equilibrium and volatility, where knowledge has become the primary driver of wealth creation. The current emphasis on devolving responsibility for strategy, innovation and entrepreneurship more widely throughout the organisation is inconsistent with the mechanistic model.[60] So too is the perspective that sees the creation of the learning organisation as the major key to competitiveness.[61]

More and more, the strategy field is being drawn away from the mechanistic model towards more organic metaphors in the search for a more fruitful perspective within which to try to understand the organisation-competitiveness relationship in more dynamic contexts.[62] Nowadays, interest is growing in the concept of the MBF as a living, complex adaptive system.

The living system perspective differs from the mechanistic model in a number of important respects. In living systems, the relationship between the overall system and its component parts is seen to be more loosely coupled than in the machine model, and overall system coherence is seen to be more a process of interactive mutual adjustment, or co-evolution, than one of master–slave mechanical transmission.[63] The components of an organic system are seen as systems within systems, with some scope for self-directed and autonomous action, and at every level 'there is a dynamic balance between self-assertive and integrative tendencies'.[64] Leaders are seen to be integral, interdependent, organic elements of the system, operating within it rather than on it, and the exercise of leadership is a more widely distributed process.[65] Perhaps the most distinguishing feature of any living system is that the whole is more than the sum of the parts, a feature that flows directly from the semi-autonomous interactivity among the constituent elements, horizontally as well as vertically. The main emphasis in analytically trying to understand such a system, therefore, is on integration and synthesis, which contrasts sharply with the reductionist orientation of the mechanistic perspective. As Capra (1982: 286–7) has put it:

> " The systems view looks at the world in terms of relationships and integration ... Systemic properties are destroyed when the system is dissected, either physically or theoretically, into isolated elements. Although we can discern individual parts, these parts are not isolated, and the nature of the whole is always different from the sum of the parts.

Viewing the MBF through a living systems perspective adds to our insight in a number of important ways. To begin with, it draws attention to the way that organisations learn and evolve. For example, as a living system grows, new properties emerge that do not exist at lower levels of elaboration, which gives the concept of emergent strategy and strategic coherence a whole new meaning. One of the most notable features of living systems is their capacity for social or collective learning. As Capra (1982: 300) has noted, bees and ants in great numbers 'act almost like cells of a complex organism with a collective intelligence and capabilities for adaptation far superior to those of the individual members', while de Geus (1997b: 57) has argued that just as 'birds that flock learn faster', so too do organisations 'that encourage flocking behaviour'. Flocking encourages two key criteria for institutional learning – individual mobility and social propagation.[66] It is no surprise, then, that organisations like Kao, Canon and 3M, well known for their capacities for learning, innovation and self-renewal, tend to view themselves in living systems terms.[67]

Two features of the shift from the mechanistic to living systems perspective of particular interest to current thinking on strategy and organisation in the MBF are the corresponding shifts in emphasis from hierarchy to network (from vertical to horizontal) relationships, and from structure to context and process.

In its emphasis on network, context and process, the living systems perspective is very much more in line with the kind of thinking on social systems reflected in the federalist philosophy. Both are similar in the 'dual-citizenship' view they take of the relationship between the parts and the whole, and in recognising the importance of paradox, diversity and internal dialectical tension in organisational learning and renewal. As Bartlett and Ghoshal (1993: 40) have noted, for some time now, managers in the MBF have been recognising that companies are complex social institutions, not just economic instruments, and are increasingly 'replacing the hard-edged strategy-structure-system paradigm of the M-form with a softer, more organic model built around purpose, process and people', reflecting this transition from a mechanistic to living systems mindset.

Finally, the living systems model, with its emphasis on contextual thinking, lends itself to a more inductive role for leadership in the corporate strategy process, which has led to the emergence of an intra-ecological perspective on organisational learning and renewal, combining competitive, or market-like, and collaborative, or hierarchy-like, dimensions. One of the main ways in which a living system regenerates itself is through the birth, death and rebirth of its subsystems, and the 'living company' is not immune from this reality, particularly in the face of ever-increasing disruptive change, prompting Bower and Christensen (1995: 53) to argue that 'for the corporation to live it must be willing to see business units die'. Within such a perspective, the growing interest in organisational innovations like the federalist approach and 'bringing the market inside' can be interpreted as the search for greater intra-ecological efficiency than that offered in the more traditional multi-divisional management model. The ecological efficiency of any system, and hence its capacity for adaptation, learning and self-renewal, depends on the competition for survival at subsystems level and on the stochastic processes of variation, selection and retention that characterise it. In this respect, the modern, radically decentralised, MBF, can be distinguished from the more traditional form in the scale, diversity and population dynamics of its individual business units, and in the ease with which the ecologically weaker subsystems can be isolated and winnowed.

Towards a new management model: the case of GE 1981–2001[68]

Perhaps, nowhere is the changing perspective on strategy and organisation in the MBF to be seen more clearly than in the transformation that took place in GE under the leadership of Jack Welch.

The case of GE is worth examining here in some detail because for the last forty years and more it has been the benchmark for best practice in the MBF context. In the 1960s, the company initiated the now well-known Profit Impact of Marketing Strategy (PIMS) project to help it with the task of finding a more strategic way to allocate capital across the business units in the diversified MBF. It was also one of the first to introduce the SBU concept to help give more coherence to the strategic planning process. During the 1970s, the GE/McKinsey version of the business portfolio matrix became the most popular planning tool of its era. Over the 1973 to 1981 period, the company had been divided into 43 SBUs for planning purposes, with a sophisticated corporate planning process that required so much detail on each of these units, the then CEO, Reginald Jones, introduced a further layer of corporate management, at the sector level, to help him manage it.

In 1981, when Welch took over, GE was still regarded as the exemplar of its time, and Jones as a management legend. Yet, Welch, who had led a number of GE's businesses under this system, recognised that while it had helped to strengthen GE's overall discipline and financial performance during the Jones era, it had also drained much of the entrepreneurial spirit out of the business units, undermining their readiness to compete in the more difficult trading conditions he foresaw lying ahead. As Welch later described it:

> " We had constructed over the years a management apparatus that was right for its time, the toast of the business schools. Divisions, SBU, groups, sectors, all were designed to make meticulous, calculated decisions and move them smoothly forwards and upwards. The system produced highly polished work. It was right for the 1970s, a growing handicap in the early 1980s and would have been a ticket to the bone-yard in the 1990s.[69]

Over the following twenty years, Welch set about transforming the GE corporate management model, a process that continues to evolve under his successor, Jeffrey Immelt. Along the way, according to leadership guru, Noel Tichy, Welch 'set a new contemporary paradigm for the corporation that is the model for the 21st century'.[70] This new model is a modern exemplar of strategy and organisation in the MBF, and reflects many of the developments discussed in this chapter.

Perhaps the most striking change in the new GE corporate model is the orientation towards people and ideas. Over the last two decades, GE has come to see its people as the primary source of its productivity and the transfer of learning as the most significant source of corporate advantage. The implications for the traditional MBF model have been revolutionary. On the one hand, the new GE approach pushes full accountability for business performance much further down the organisation than ever before. In addition, it now seeks the primary benefits of corporate coordination in a different place, in organisational learning and the transfer of best practice rather than in more traditional economies of scale or scope. The overall effect is a different kind of MBF, which has changed the way that the corporate function relates to the businesses and the way the businesses relate to each other.

Welch began his transformation of the GE corporate management model by simplifying the corporate strategy process, and eliminating much of the bureaucracy that had been introduced to support it. As noted earlier, in his view there could be 'no single plan for a company with as many businesses and markets as GE', so the strategic aim was 'to evolve into a company that's either Number 1 or Number 2 in its arenas'.[71] Welch had learned from first-hand experience 'the insecurities that result from hanging on to businesses that are weak in their marketplaces',[72] and he was determined to have only strong businesses in the GE portfolio. Businesses outside the number one or two positions were to be fixed, sold or closed. In a typical example, Welch exchanged GE's consumer electronics business for Thomson Electronics' medical systems business in a transaction that strengthened the global position of each in its retained activity. On the other hand, every business that could rise to the challenge was to be given a chance to flourish, even those in mature, 100-year old, industries like GE lighting. To facilitate this change in approach, Welch eliminated the sector layer, and reorganised the company into thirteen major businesses reporting directly to the CEO. Out went the detailed, SBU-based, planning books, to be replaced by a five-page 'playbook' for each of the major businesses, focused on the global dynamics of their markets and how they were being changed, or could be changed, by the actions of GE and its competitors.

Removing the top management layer alone saved the company $40M in annual overhead. However, as Welch later explained, that was just a bonus that paled in importance when compared 'to the sudden release of talent and energy that poured out after all the dampers, valves and barriers had been removed'.[73] The overall effect of taking out the corporate overseers and pushing responsibility way down into the businesses was to turn more and more functionaries into businesspeople. Welch was also prepared to reward them accordingly, with steeply differentiated incentives closely related to commercial performance, producing hundreds of GE millionaires and rewarding thousands more in ways that was 'changing their game and their lives'.[74] In short, this process of radical decentralisation helped to rekindle the fires of entrepreneurship deep within GE, and bring more of the features of the marketplace right into the heart of the company and its operations.

Not everyone was found to flourish under this new model. When the layers were removed, 'many managers were suddenly exposed who weren't leaders at all',[75] and the new management model has helped to provide GE with the basis for a leadership development system that many now see as one of its main corporate advantages. Welch extended his number 1 and number 2 thinking to his executive talent in an approach to leadership development, more familiar in sport or in the performing arts than in the traditional managerial hierarchy, that 'finds the best and culls the rest'.[76] Everyone already on board was given the chance to 'try out' for a place in the new GE set-up, but for a company determined to be the global standard bearer, Welch believed that GE had to be strong enough to select and retain only 'A' players in its leadership cadre.

The right leadership in the right businesses was just the first part of the Welch formula for transforming the MBF management model. During the second half of his tenure, Welch concentrated on boosting people productivity right across the corporation. He began by further strengthening the competitiveness of the individual businesses through developing a revolutionary process, called 'Work-Out', for tapping into the hidden value of his people right down to the level of the individual operative. Up to this stage, he saw himself concentrating primarily on strengthening the main components of GE's diversity, its individual businesses.

The success of 'Work-Out' helped to point the way to a whole new source of added value that hitherto had been largely neglected by MBFs. Over the remainder of his tenure as CEO, Welch concentrated on finding new ways to leverage the scale of GE by harnessing its intellectual capital through the rapid transfer of learning. Knowledge-based programmes like 'Best Practices', 'Boundary-less' and 'Six Sigma' were introduced to encourage GE executives to look beyond their businesses, and even beyond the corporation itself, in the search for more productive ideas and practices. In Jack Welch's own words it was 'all about moving intellectual capital – taking ideas and moving them around faster and faster'.[77] The ongoing impact of this effort, in the words of one Merrill Lynch analyst, has been to transform GE from a collection of businesses to a 'repository of information and expertise that can be leveraged over a huge installed base'.[78] To ease the circulation of ideas, GE strove to break down barriers to communication both vertically and horizontally. No formal synergy programmes were forced upon the businesses, but a lot of corporate effort was invested into providing the opportunity and incentive to share ideas.

The new corporate management model, as illustrated in the GE case, also has implications for the role of the CEO. As in the case of Jack Welch, corporate leaders that are pioneering new approaches to the corporate management of the MBF no longer seek to make their most distinctive contributions through strategy and structure in the more traditional sense. Rather, they concentrate on shaping the behavioural context or 'social architecture' of the corporation, to use Jack Welch's term, and defining its identity and values. In GE's case, the company took three years to develop a statement of core values, built around the themes of 'facing up to reality', 'being open and candid', 'changing before you have to change', 'striving for simplicity' and 'respecting individual dignity'. At GE these were treated as more than simply inspirational aphorisms. Welch saw them as central to the process of maximising intellectual capital, and business leaders who were able to deliver their numbers but not prepared to live these values did not survive. As he once explained, GE had to know if its people were open, candid and believed in quick action, because he could see 'how essential' it was 'for a multi-business company to become an open, learning organisation'.[79]

Learning and entrepreneurship – the key dimensions in the new MBF model

The transformation at GE is ongoing, with similar transformations happening in other major corporations, the likes of BP (British Petroleum) and Siemens to mention just two of the many.[80] At its heart is an effort to reshape the corporate management model in the MBF around two main value-adding processes: learning and entrepreneurship, dimensions also becoming increasingly prominent in much of the thought-leadership literature on strategy and organisation in the MBF in recent times.[81] Today, there are few MBFs where the 'fires of entrepreneurship' continue to burn as intensely as they do at Virgin.[82] Yet, it is only relatively recently that Richard Branson and his firm have begun to think seriously about the potential benefits of sharing learning across its businesses.[83] One the other hand, few are the companies that have developed the ability to share learning and ideas across diverse businesses, and leverage their intellectual capital, as effectively as 3M. In many ways the new corporate model that pioneers like GE and others have been reaching for is one that will combine the entrepreneurial drive of a Virgin with the organisational learning capability of a 3M. Few to date have come closer to realising this than GE, which is why its twenty-year effort and beyond to redefine the corporate management model for the MBF is so significant for theory and practice alike.

Traditionally, as we have seen, the search for synergy in the MBF has tended to be 'hardwired' into the company strategy and structure through the sharing of tangible assets and through dual-reporting matrix organisations. At the heart of this traditional approach lies an awkward compromise – the advantages to be gained in sharing of assets and accountability tended to conflict to some degree with the ability to drive the responsibility for full P&L and balance sheet performance as far down into the business units as possible in order to sharpen the focus and maximise the entrepreneurial drive at that level. Knowledge as an asset does not have to be 'divided' and 'allocated' in the same somewhat arbitrary way that is unavoidable when sharing a manufacturing plant, distribution system or sales force (The experience of Gillette Asia in trying to generate synergies from shared distribution and sales activities among different business units, as described in Kanter and Dretler [1998], provides a good illustration of some of these difficulties). Rather, by its nature, knowledge is a different kind of asset that can not only be more readily shared with little loss of focus or control over the key levers of performance at the business level, but that can also appreciate in value with use.

In fact, it can now be argued that what the recent experience of companies like GE, BP and many others have shown over the last two decades and more is that there are still at least two important ways in which the corporate management model can be more effective than the market in maximising the value to be generated from any given collection of businesses, both of which are learning oriented – the first is knowledge transfer and the second is leadership development.[84] As Foss (1997: 317) puts it, because such capabilities are hard to 'trade', and 'because learning processes have to be coordinated', together they help to provide 'a positive rationale' for the MBF. The premium that GE has clearly gained out of transforming its management model in order to tap more fully into its intellectual capital is eloquent testimony to the first, while the premium that the wider corporate market continues to put on GE leadership alumni, the likes of Larry Bossidy (by Allied Signal/Honeywell) and James McNerney (by 3M and Boeing), is eloquent testimony to the second.

The HQ-subsidiary relationship in the globalising firm

Finally, lying at heart of the organisational challenge facing all MBFs is the question not just of how much influence headquarters should seek to exercise over the subsidiary businesses but also how this might need to vary over time and situation. This is particularly pertinent to companies diversifying internationally.

The appropriate relationship between corporate headquarters (HQ) and the business units or subsidiaries seems to depend on the type of corporation and the nature of its development. For example, in the late 1980s, Goold and Campbell (1987) identified three distinct styles of HQ-Subsidiary relationship typically operating across the domain of British MBFs, which they classified as Strategic Planning, Strategic Control and Financial Control. Chandler (1991: 36) later compared the British with the US experience and concluded that these three different styles tended to 'result from different paths to growth, and therefore, from different patterns of investment and from different sets of organizational capabilities'. In Financial Control companies, corporate control and influence was exercised primarily through the annual budget, with responsibility for business strategy almost totally devolved to the units. This has been typified by such highly diversified companies as Hanson Trust in Britain and Tyco in the United States. The Strategic Planning and Strategic Control styles tend to be characterised by much greater degrees of involvement by headquarters in the development and coordination of business unit strategies. However, even here, Goold (1991: 76) found that informal strategic control seemed to predominate, especially where there were 'strong linkages between businesses in the corporate portfolio, high levels of uncertainty, and multiple, complex, hard-to-measure sources of competitive advantage'.

The appropriate level of control between HQ and the businesses may vary over time, and across the company, with a unit's stage of development. This seems particularly apt in the case of many globalising service industries. Take a company such as Kentucky Fried Chicken in the fast food industry or IKEA in furniture retailing. The initial priority on entering a new national or regional market is to test the basic service concept in the new territory. Later, if the concept is found to be viable, the priority then shifts to expanding the branch network to stake out the territory and get good market coverage before competitors with similar service concepts have a chance to entrench themselves. Finally, when the rate of expansion in the number of outlets begins to slow, the commercial priority shifts to operating performance for cash and profit generation. In the first stage the emphasis at HQ should be primarily on financial control, giving the local unit seed capital and allowing it the strategic and operational freedom to experiment and learn about the local market. In the expansion stage the funding requirements of the subsidiary should be assessed in terms of overall corporate and business priorities and imperatives, and some degree of strategic control may seem appropriate – should the subsidiary manage its own growth or should HQ continue to support it with additional capital and skills? It is at the third stage that subsidiary performance can be most greatly leveraged by tighter strategic and operational integration with the rest of the network, exploiting to the full the kind of economies of scale, scope and experience typically available to such services companies.[85]

The recent swing in emphasis back towards integration

While the globalising firm presents its own particular issues for the HQ-Subsidiary relationship, these are largely variations on the central organisational challenge facing all MBF, the paradoxical challenge of decentralisation with coordinated control, as Alfred Sloan famously characterised it. Today, we tend to use a slightly different version of the same principle to describe this organisational challenge, 'autonomy with collaboration', and look for the solution to balancing the inherent tension involved in a different way.

The restructuring wave of the 1990s, characterised by radical decentralisation, sought to rekindle the flames of entrepreneurship within the MBF, by restoring as much autonomy as possible to the individual business units. By the early 2000s it had become apparent that this approach had gone too far, leading to serious deficiencies in corporate integration in many cases. Radical decentralisation had undermined the capacity of many MBFs to mobilise their organisation-wide core competencies to full effect, to compete based on their ability to provide solutions not just discrete products and to present a more coherent face to corporate customers.

The ability to foster collaboration across the business units remains central to the organisational advantage in the MBF. Today, however, we tend to look to less hierarchical forms of integration, laying greater emphasis on the integrating power of processes and values and less on that of structure.[86] The knowledge management movement of the last decade in the corporate world, and the growing interest in 'knowledge-based' theories of the firm,[87] both reflect the ever-widening recognition that the sharing of intellectual capital is the new key to realising the organisational advantage in the MBF. At the same time, the difficulties that many companies have experienced in trying to implement effective knowledge management strategies point to the futility of seeking to create the 'learning organisation' advantage through attention to just structure and systems alone.[88]

New advances in information and communications technologies, and the development of knowledge management infrastructure, are key enablers in any effort to maximise the value of intellectual capital on a corporate-wide basis. However, the ability to reap the full benefits of such advances also depends heavily on softer issues like motivation, shared values, trust and intercultural sensitivity, and these are ultimately issues of leadership and culture.[89] In fact, as Kanter (2008: 45) discovered in a recent in-depth study of global giants like IBM, Cisco, CEMEX and P&G, shared values turn out to be 'the key ingredients' in enabling the 'most vibrant and successful of today's multinationals' to move 'as rapidly and creatively as much smaller enterprises' while maintaining high degrees of corporate coherence and global integration. 'How are companies putting it all together again without destroying the vitality of the parts?', ask Ghoshal and Gratton (2002: 33). The answer they have found lies in a combination of four distinct and interrelated non-hierarchical types of integration: operational, intellectual, social and emotional. All are central to where the new organisational advantage is most likely to be found in the MBF in the years ahead.

Summary

In this chapter, we focused on the additional considerations that come into play in the strategic management of the MBF. We highlighted how in the single business firm, business and corporate strategy are more or less synonymous, but that the distinction becomes more meaningful in the multi-business context. In the MBF, business strategy continues to be concerned with the competitiveness of each business in its own market. Beyond this, however, the MBF is challenged with the additional question of how the corporate function can add value over and above what the businesses can generate collectively as stand-alone entities.

In our examination of this challenge, we highlighted how the search for answers is increasingly taking us beyond strategy into considerations and leadership and organisation, and we looked at all of these dimensions. We started by looking at the main frameworks that have emerged to date to guide the development of corporate strategy, beginning with the BCG and the other strategy matrices that were the dominant perspectives in the 1970s and early 1980s, and we examined their strengths and shortcomings. One major shortcoming of the BCG matrix, and of its various derivatives, was an inability to deal with the question of relatedness among the business units. In this regard, we also saw how, since the early 1970s, it has become one of the common wisdoms in the MBF literature that related diversification tends to create more value for shareholders over the longer run than unrelated (or conglomerate) diversification. This led us into a discussion of what kinds of relatedness corporate strategy might seek to exploit. We noted how the early literature tended to focus primarily on relatedness at the product–market level, and highlighted how our perspective on the nature of relatedness has since been expanded to include several other dimensions, including core competency, dominant logic and generic strategy, and we examined the core competence perspective on relatedness in some detail. Taking in the round this expanded list of relatedness variables extends the range of diversification patterns open to any given MBF under the rubric of related diversification.

We moved on in the second part of the chapter to focus more intensely on the variables of leadership and organisation. We began this section by asking if corporate management primarily adds value through strategy or organisation. For much of its forty-year history, the strategy field's clear answer to this question was strategy. Organisation as a variable tended to be seen mainly in terms of structure and was considered it subservient to strategy – in line with the 'structure-follows-strategy' principle first laid down by Alfred Chandler. We examined why, in more recent times, the recognition is growing, among scholars and practitioners alike, that organisation, in its wider sense, is a potential strategic variable in its own right. In line with this development, we noted that the corporate management model for the MBF has been in transition since the early 1980s. We also highlighted four of the most significant trends, or shifts of emphasis, in the organisation literature reflecting this development. The kind of corporate management model that companies at the leading edge of this transformation are reaching for is one that combines the entrepreneurial prowess of a Virgin, with the organisational learning capability of a 3M. GE continues to be at the forefront of this effort, and we examined in some detail the evolution of the company's corporate management model over the last twenty-five years and its implications for how perspectives are changing on the relationship between leadership, strategy and organisation in the MBF.

In the final part of the chapter we turned to examine briefly the headquarters-subsidiary relationship in the globalising firm, and we ended the chapter by highlighting the renewed interest being taken in processes of integration within the MBF, after a prolonged period in which the major emphasis had been on radical decentralisation. Today's leading companies have also renewed their interest in organic paths to growth, in the wake of the difficulties and disappointments experienced by many during the recent waves of mergers and acquisitions. The challenge that the larger company faces in trying to reignite and sustain its capacity for innovation as it grows will be the main focus of our next chapter.

Notes

[1] Porter (1987).
[2] Collis and Montgomery (1998).
[3] Chandler (1962), Sloan (1963), Ansoff (1965).
[4] Bettis and Hall (1983).
[5] Henderson (1973).
[6] This discussion draws freely from Leavy (2001).
[7] Chandler (1962, 1990).
[8] Hansen and Nohria (2004).
[9] Tanriverdi and Venkatraman (2005).
[10] Christensen and Montgomery (1981), Rumelt (1982).
[11] Levitt (1960: 45).
[12] Zook (2004).
[13] Porter (1987: 46).
[14] Lowe (1998: 116).
[15] Prahalad and Hamel (1990: 20).
[16] Chatterjee and Wernerfelt (1991); Markides and Williamson (1994); Collis and Montgomery (1998); Piscitello (2004); Tanriverdi and Venkatraman (2005).
[17] Stalk et al. (1992: 67).
[18] Markides and Williamson (1994), Markides (1997).
[19] Campbell et al. (1995), Goold and Campbell (2002).
[20] See the recent debate between Priem and Butler (2001), and Barney (2001).
[21] Prahalad and Bettis (1986), Bettis and Prahalad (1995).
[22] Prahalad and Bettis (1986: 497).
[23] Campbell et al. (1995); Heisler (2004).
[24] Zook and Allen (2003).
[25] Andrews (1971), Mintzberg et al. (1998).
[26] Pooley-Dias (1972), Thanheiser (1972), Channon (1973).
[27] Waterman et al. (1980), Pascale and Athos (1981).
[28] See also Bower (1970).
[29] This discussion draws freely from Leavy (1999).
[30] Grant (1996); Teece et al. (1997), Ghoshal and Bartlett (1998).
[31] Ghoshal and Bartlett (1998: 8).
[32] Senge (1990).
[33] Collins and Porras (1996).
[34] de Geus (1997a, 1997b).
[35] Ghoshal and Bartlett (1998).
[36] Ostroff (1999).
[37] Miller et al. (2002).
[38] Hamel and Valikangas (2003).
[39] Manville and Ober (2003).

40 Halal (1994), Hamel (1999), Malone (2004).
41 Hansen and Norhia (2004).
42 Pettigrew et al. (2000).
43 Hamel (2007).
44 Williamson (1975).
45 Granovetter (1985).
46 Hill (1990: 500).
47 Jarillo (1988: 36).
48 Ghemawat and Ricart I Costa (1993).
49 Grant (1996: 110).
50 Tanriverdi and Venkatraman (2005).
51 Collins and Porras (1996).
52 Pendergrast (1994).
53 Grove (1996), Collins and Porras (1996).
54 Galbraith (1971).
55 Goggin (1974: 54).
56 Taylor (1991: 95).
57 Byrne (1993: 51).
58 Bartlett and Ghoshal (1990).
59 Kirkpatrick (1992).
60 de Geus (1997a), Senge (1997).
61 Stata (1989); Senge (1990), Hamel and Prahalad (1994), Ghoshal and Bartlett (1998).
62 Farjoun (2002).
63 Eisenhardt and Galunic (2000).
64 Capra (1982: 304–5).
65 Lewin and Regine (2000).
66 de Geus (1997b), Bonabeau and Meyer (2001), Gladwell (2002).
67 Ghoshal and Butler (1992), Ghoshal and Ackenhusen (1992), Bartlett and Mohammed (1995).
68 This discussion draws freely from Leavy (2001).
69 Welch (1989).
70 Byrne (1998: 43).
71 Lowe (1998: 116).
72 Lowe (1998: 118).
73 Welch (1988).
74 Byrne (1998: 49).
75 Lowe (1998: 122).
76 Stewart (1999: 75).
77 Stewart (1999: 74).
78 Stewart (1999: 69).
79 Lowe (1998: 84).
80 Prokesch (1997), Voelpel et al. (2005).
81 Day and Wendler (1998); Ghoshal and Bartlett (1998); Hansen and Nohria (2004).
82 Hamel (1999: 78).
83 Dick and Kets de Vries (2000).
84 Ghoshal and Bartlett (1998), Tichy and Cohen (2002).
85 Quinn and Paquette (1990).
86 Ghoshal and Gratton (2002), Kanter (2008).
87 Grant (1996), Nonaka et al. (2000).
88 Paik and Choi (2005), Voelpel et al. (2005).
89 Nahapiet and Ghoshal (1998), Kim and Mauborgne (1997b).

INTRODUCING 'STRATEGIC LEADERSHIP, GOVERNANCE AND RENEWAL'
• STRATEGY, LEADERSHIP AND THE NEW AGENDA • THE CONTEXT OF
BUSINESS IN SOCIETY • COMPETITIVE ANALYSIS AND VALUE INNOVATION
• STRATEGY AND ORGANISATION IN THE MULTI-BUSINESS FIRM •
STRATEGIC PROCESSES – INNOVATION • STRATEGIC PROCESSES – TRANSFORMATION
AND RENEWAL • SOME FINAL THOUGHTS AND REFLECTIONS

6 strategic processes – innovation

Introduction

'We now stand on the threshold of a new age – the age of revolution', according to Gary Hamel (2000a: 4). While Hamel has rarely been known for understatement, most would now agree that the strategic premium on innovation and renewal has never been so high. As Leonard and Straus (1997: 111) starkly put it: 'Innovate or fall behind: the competitive imperative for virtually every business today is that simple', while others argue that the only way for companies to stay ahead in this 'age of discontinuity' is to learn to outpace the market in their rate of internal creative destruction and renewal.[1] In this chapter and the next, we will examine the strategic processes of innovation and renewal, and how they interrelate.

In this, the first of these two chapters, we concentrate on innovation. Within the corporate world, the early years of the twenty-first century have been marked by a definite shift away from over-reliance on mergers and acquisitions in propelling corporate growth, towards 'a return to the power of ideas'.[2] Throughout this chapter, we look at some of the main implications involved in trying to put innovation back at the top of the corporate agenda. In the early part, we focus on the relationship between creativity and innovation in organisational settings. We begin by trying to develop a deeper understanding of the nature of the creative process and individual creativity. We then proceed to look at some of the key considerations involved in trying to foster creativity and innovation in organisational contexts, including how to go about building a corporate culture for creativity, nurturing and leading the creative process and maintaining an effective balance between creativity and efficiency. We then go on to examine the growing interest in the concept of 'open innovation' and the impact that this perspective is already having on R&D strategy and the competitive landscape of many industries. We also look at the impetus that the open innovation approach is giving to the emergence and development of more efficient markets for trading in Intellectual Property (IP). We end the chapter with a focus on the organisational challenges involved in Internal Corporate Venturing (ICV) and with a look at the nature of the 'growth imperative' driving such activity, asking just how 'imperative' companies should really take it to be when thinking about the kind of approach to corporate development that might be in their best longer term interest.

Innovation and creativity[3]

In a recent Accenture survey, over 80 per cent of executives worldwide expressed the belief that their companies 'will become more dependent on innovation', and innovation is now one of the most common themes in the annual messages of CEOs to their shareholders.[4] As Kao (1997: 1) has put it, the business world 'is already launched on a new quest' for 'the creativity advantage'. Unfortunately, the track record to date has not been impressive, particularly in the larger organisation. History shows that the 'most discouraging fact of big corporate life is the loss of what got them big in the first place: innovation'.[5] So how do we go about looking for the creativity advantage?

The key to the innovation advantage – is it talent or organisation?

One of the central debates in the innovation literature is the issue of whether the creativity advantage is primarily rooted in talent or organisation. Peter Drucker (1985: 40) puts the main emphasis on the latter: 'Innovation is organised, systematic, rational work'. So do many others. For Hargadon and Sutton (2000: 157), innovation has 'everything to do with organisation and attitude and very little to do with nurturing solitary genius'. However, there are also many who believe that exceptional talent provides the crucial edge, especially in knowledge-intensive industries: 'High-end knowledge workers are a lot like artists' and 'perform the work that is most critical to an organisation's strategy or mission'.[6] A company like Microsoft hires only the brightest of software graduates, and it recognises the most gifted as strategically significant. As Bill Gates once put it: 'Take our 20 best people away, and I will tell you that Microsoft will become an unimportant company'.[7] Thomas Edison is often invoked as an example that supports the organisation view,[8] but he is actually a good illustration of the partial truths inherent in both sides of the argument – Edison was remarkably systematic in his approach to invention, but then Edison was also a remarkable talent.

Much of this talent-versus-organisation debate tends to spring from the tendency to focus on different aspects of innovation. In this regard, the distinction made by March (1991) between exploring for new knowledge and exploiting existing knowledge is particularly insightful and increasingly influential. The first requires a higher-order of creativity than the second. The first emphasises the role of talent, the second of organisation. The first looks to build its innovation advantage primarily on the frame-breaking idea, the second on the cumulative power of a myriad of small refinements. Industry context is important. The first takes prominence in industries like pharmaceuticals and microprocessors, the second in industries like mass retailing. For example, Wal-Mart is an excellent example of a company that generates significant competitive advantage from the cumulative power of small ideas. High technology companies like Intel typically look to benefit from the power of big and small ideas alike.

The talent-versus-organisation debate is further clouded by the kind of caricatures of the 'creative personality', frequently to be found in the more popular innovation literature. The following by Ziegler (2002: 54) is not untypical: If you embrace innovation, does that mean hiring more 'oddly dressed people who will spice up your meetings with catchy "icebreakers" and transform the next board meeting into something reminiscent of California in the late 1960s?' While mostly done in the best of good of humour, such stereotyping tends to reveal a general insecurity within the business world about the nature of the unusual in the creative personality, and to deflect our attention from trying to understand it more fully.

In our view talent and organisation are both important to being able to compete on innovation. In the following sections of this chapter, we will look at how business organisations and their leaders can make themselves more attractive to creative talent and how this can also help them to better harness the creativity of the people already at their disposal. We will also highlight the balance to be struck between creativity and efficiency, two organisational goals that tend to pull in different directions, and look at how far companies can, and should, go in seeking to reorganise themselves around the creative priority.

Understanding the unusual person with unusual ideas

Innovation depends on ideas, and the primary source of ideas is talented individuals. Yet, up to recently, the business world in general has tended neither to seek, nor attract, creative talent in any numbers, and many organisations still have much to learn about how to become a lot more 'hospitable to the unusual person and unusual ideas'.[9] Increasingly, as the strategic resource becomes talent rather than capital in this new economic era,[10] learning how to find and foster creative talent will have to become the norm, not the exception.

Cognitive ability – divergent thinking

Such learning begins with trying to deepen our understanding of individual creativity and the creative personality. Serious efforts to develop valid and reliable measures of creativity go back to the 1950s, and focused initially on the link between creative potential and general intelligence. It soon became apparent that the relationship was fairly weak beyond a minimum threshold.[11] We have long since come to recognise that there are many exceptionally intelligent people who are only moderately creative (according to one unkind soul, our universities are full of them), and vice versa. Jan Smuts, the former South African Prime Minister, speaking of Churchill at the height of the Second World War, valued his particular genius over that of more appraising, measuring minds: 'That is why Winston is indispensable. He has ideas'.[12] In sum, creativity involves a range of cognitive abilities that are different from those measured by IQ.

Early on, one major insight was the distinction drawn by J.P Guilford (1956) between divergent and convergent thinking ability. The creative personality is marked by its capacity for divergent thinking, characterised by originality, fluency of ideas, flexibility and the ability to elaborate and redefine. This concept of divergent thinking remains 'the key idea in the psychologist's conception of creativity'.[13] In contrast, most traditional measures of cognitive ability, like IQ tests, have tended to emphasise a propensity for convergent thinking towards a single solution. To date, most scholastic accolades and recruiting norms still tend to favour the convergent thinker.

The psychodynamics of creativity

We have also learned over time that cognitive ability alone is not a sufficient predictor of creative output. Emotional factors are also crucial.

Creative production often springs from the attempt to fashion external symbolic order (whether in the form of words, mathematics, music or art, for example) out of internal psychological chaos of one sort or another. Indeed, there is a long tradition associating creative output with various types of inner struggle, including neuroses. History shows that some of the most creative talents the world has known, such as Michelangelo, Byron, Tolstoy and Steinbeck, struggled with emotional turbulence throughout most of their productive lives, while others like Newton, Descartes and Einstein had strong tendencies of a schizoid nature. The fact that such tendencies often provide the motive force for creative output is rarely easy for us to acknowledge, particularly in the highly ordered world of business organisations. While few imaginative people exhibit such pathologies in the extreme, nevertheless, 'some split between the inner world and the outer world is common to all human beings' and 'the need to bridge the gap is the source of creative endeavour'.[14]

Also difficult for the highly rational world of business to come to terms with is the role of the unconscious mind. Yet among creative individuals its importance is widely recognised.[15] How does the unconscious influence creativity? Much of the current literature on creativity looks to Jung for the explanation, particularly to his concept of the shadow.[16] We all have two personalities, the one we show to the world and the one we tend to keep within ourselves. The one we hide, our shadow personality, holds the key to understanding the unconscious. Beneath the polished surface of our 'civilised' personas lies, what Jung often referred to as 'the two-million-year-old man that is in all of us', our more elemental, intuitive selves, still 'hardwired' for evolutionary survival.[17] Human development in the modern world is a process of multiple adaptations to the expectations of parents, teachers, pastors, peers, employers and so on. Along the way, a lot of primal instincts and desires, not just those of libido or aggression, get consigned to our shadow, hidden but far from inactive. As poet David Whyte (1997: 4) reminds us, 'the field of human creativity has long been a constant battleground between the upper world we inhabit every day and the deeper untrammelled energies alive in every element of life'.

The Jungian concept of the shadow can help us to understand why the creative personality at maturity may not be as fully adapted as the rest of us, and why, in moderation, this may be one of its virtues. It is a personality that never fully 'grows up', in terms of society's expectations. Such people tend to put less of themselves 'into-the-box' over the course of their development. As a result, the creative personality tends to retain more of the curiosity of the preschool child, and be more influenced by its own intrinsic standards than those of domain or profession. It is also more willing and able than most of us to draw upon the contradictions embedded in the two sides of the personality, whatever the emotional consequences. Federico Fellini (1997: 32), the famous film director, exemplified this when he said of himself: 'I have an easy-going nature, but in order to get an artistic result I am capable of being harsh and cruel'. This 'negative capability' to live within 'uncertainties, mysteries, doubts, without any irritable reaching after fact and reason', Keats believed to be central to literary achievement and was a quality that Shakespeare had in abundance.[18] It is also something that Andy Law tended to look out for in recruiting creative talent during his heyday at St Luke's, the award winning advertising agency:

> " I want to feel that people have really reached something danger-
> ous in the themselves – that they have been to amazing places
> and been quite frightened ... It is terrifying to have no pretences
> about yourself, yet that's what gives you the psychological
> resources to question all the rules.[19]

Creative individuals are usually marked by total absorption in their work and 'all love what they do'.[20] They also tend to be marked by their insatiable curiosity, a burning need to explore that is emotional as much as intellectual. As Nobel laureate, Arthur Schawlow (1982: 42), one explained:

'The most successful scientists often are not the most talented. But they are the ones who are impelled by curiosity. They have to know what the answer is'. Curiosity and dedication both seem to be crucial to creative production at the highest level, because it is now widely recognised that it takes about ten thousand hours (about ten years) of intense effort to develop the mastery needed to make a truly original contribution in most major walks of life.[21] Consequently, as Harvard psychologist, Howard Gardner has pointed out, the creative personality often makes a Faustian bargain that 'chooses perfection of the work over perfection of the life', and major work–life imbalance is not uncommon.[22] The age at which impact seems to peak varies across both individuals and domains, and, in this context, aging tends to be more meaningful when seen in terms of 'mileage' rather than chronology. Research suggests that the creative personality is least likely to be a first-born, and more likely to be forged at either end of the socioeconomic spectrum than from within the secure comfort of the middle ground. Precollege education seems to have remarkably little impact, threatening curiosity rather than stimulating it, and performance at high school is often a poor predictor of creative potential. In contrast, many seem to finally find their voices at college, often with the help of inspiring mentors and intellectual soul mates. Few creative people tend to remember themselves as popular growing up, and marginality is a common theme.

In sum, the creative personality seems to be marked out by deep internal divisions and by the strength of ego to live within them productively. It is intensely driven, yet relaxed enough to coax and wait on inspiration. It is smart, yet naïve, sceptical yet credulous, playful yet disciplined, passionate yet objective, a confusion of opposites defying ready classification.[23] It is often 'the tension between these opposites, and the need to resolve this tension, which provides the motive force for creation'.[24]

Fostering creativity and innovation in organisational settings

While the foundation for building the 'creative advantage' in any organisation lies in a deeper understanding of personal creativity, it also extends to developing a greater understanding of the creative process itself and how it can be fostered in institutional settings. As Mumford and Simonton (1997: 2) have put it: 'If there is anything we have learned in more than a century of research, it is that creative achievement is a complex phenomenon which flowers only under the right conditions'. Historically, business organisations have tended to emphasise efficiency over innovation, and action over ideas. They have been 'too often prisons for the human soul', offering little, if any, attraction for highly creative talent and rarely going near to harnessing the creativity of the people already at their disposal.[25] As Jerry Hirshberg (1999: 16), the founding CEO of Nissan Design International, once put it:

> " No one in a corporation deliberately sets out to stifle creative thought. Yet, a traditional bureaucratic structure, with its need for predictability, linear logic, conformance to accepted norms, and the dictates of the most recent 'long-range' vision statement is a nearly perfect idea-killing machine.

Building a corporate culture and context for creativity

So what kind of overall organisational context is most supportive of creative production? From what we know to date the answer seems to be one that makes creativity central to its overall mission and the project its primary organising principle; one that designs its motivation and reward systems around talent and contribution rather than title and status, and encourages risk-taking and experimentation, while celebrating well-intentioned failure as a necessary step on the road to success; and one that values diversity in expertise, personality and background and looks to unity of purpose rather than uniformity of outlook in aligning its energies.[26] It is a context built on intrinsically challenging and emotionally engaging work,[27] and one in which creativity features prominently in the company's overall value system. It is the kind of overall context most readily to be found in organisations whose primary business is creativity, relatively small companies like IDEO, Nissan Design International and ideation firm BrightHouse, where they talk about 'heart-storming', not just brainstorming, as they seek to tap into passions as well as intellects in the search for new ideas.[28]

Can such a context be replicated and sustained in the larger organisation? For many observers, the benchmark has long been 3M. Consistently ranked among the world's most respected companies, the company was once described by Fortune magazine as a kind of 'corporate Petri dish' that fosters a culture of innovation. According to Ghoshal and Bartlett (1998: 43): 'At the foundation of everything in 3M is a deep, genuine, and unshakeable belief in the ability of the individual' and 'surrounding it are a series of organizational policies and management practices that build on and leverage that basic belief'. The context for creativity at 3M has also been supported by key phrases constantly repeated over the years that served as guiding principles from the main architect of the company's founding culture, William McKnight: phrases like: 'Listen to anyone with an original idea, no matter how absurd it might sound at first'; 'Encourage, don't nitpick. Let people run with an idea'; 'Hire good people, and leave them alone'; 'If you put fences around people you get sheep – Give people the room they need' and 'Give it a try – and quick'.[29] The company reinforced these values with its well-known thirty per cent goal (30% of sales to be generated from products less than three years old), and with organisational structures, policies and practices that rewarded creativity, like its 'dual ladder' career system designed to allow creative individuals promotional opportunities outside the managerial hierarchy, its prestigious Carlton Society to acknowledge outstanding originality and its various technical councils and forums designed to encourage the free movement and uptake of ideas, to mention just a few of the better known examples.[30]

In more recent times, Google has emerged to rival 3M as the most cited exemplar of how to nurture and preserve a culture of innovation with scale.[31] While 3M and Google evolved their innovative culture almost since their foundations, the recent histories of companies like General Electric, Nokia, Oticon and Whirlpool have shown how long-established, more traditional companies have also been able to transform themselves from management-driven to ideas-driven organisations. As a result, they have found themselves able to tap into considerable reservoirs of creativity already within their organisations. Building the right corporate context for creativity not only makes an organisation more attractive to highly creative talent, but it also helps to unleash the creativity of the people already on board, because as Mumford and Simonton (1997: 6) have put it:

> " In the workplace creativity and innovation may hide in many overlooked corners – in the sales force, among entrepreneurs, among engineers desperately trying to bring new products on line, and with managers trying to find ways to marshal the necessary resources. If we can identify the most favourable environments, we should discover that behind the 'dark grey suits' of the organization man or woman dwells an individual whose creativity still remains to be fully realised.

Nurturing and leading the creative process

Fostering creativity in institutional settings is not just a matter of having a supportive corporate culture. It also requires a deeper understanding of the creative process itself.

One of the most fundamental aspects of the creative process is its probabilistic nature. Success is never guaranteed, and it remains at root a process of 'controlled chaos', as James Brian Quinn (1985) likes to describe it. When Nobel Laureate, Linus Pauling was once asked how he went about generating good ideas, his answer was, 'you have a lot of ideas and throw away the bad ones'.[32] Creativity seems to thrive on multiple, diverse, independent and rapid experimentation. It also thrives in a failure-tolerant environment, where success and failure are viewed 'more like the siblings they actually are'.[33] Over a century ago, Thomas Edison believed that creative production was a function of the number of experiments that could be carried out within any given timeframe, and experience since has offered us little reason to revise this view.[34] When it comes to innovation, as Thomas Watson Sr. of IBM once put it: 'The fastest way to succeed is to double your failure rate'.[35]

When creativity is pursued through group activity, additional considerations of leadership and team dynamics come into play. The creativity of any group is built on individual talent, and the leaders of highly creative groups typically 'love talent and know where to find it'.[36] Group harmony and cohesion are rarely the primary concerns, and the fountainhead of innovation is often to be found in the 'creative abrasion' that inevitably arises from the uninhibited interaction of diverse personalities, backgrounds and thinking styles.[37] To generate new insight, as Bill

Gates of Microsoft sees it: 'You have to listen carefully to all the smart people in the company. That's why a company like ours has to attract a lot of people who think in different ways, it has to allow a lot of dissent and then it has to recognise the right ideas and put some real energy behind them'.[38] Likewise, at Disney, they have long believed that 'ideas come out of an environment of supportive conflict'.[39] Discomfort helps people to 'break out of mindless action',[40] and the struggle inherent in all creation 'strengthens the end result'.[41] According to Fischer and Boynton (2005: 119), too often 'from a polite team comes a polite result', so what is important is that people can work together and stimulate each other productively. Shared obsession tends to provide the main cohesion rather than good fellowship.

The leadership of creative groups requires special qualities, and is often 'much more an art, a belief, a condition of the heart, than a set of things to do'.[42] Creative groups tend to look to each individual to contribute where they can be most effective and do not allow status and labels to get in the way. One of the most popular metaphors for the creative group is the jazz combo, particularly at the idea-generation stage, where leadership often moves around dynamically as different players drive the performance forward at different times.[43] Different players also tend to excel at different roles, some as original thinkers, others more as promoters and brokers.[44] Some will have a special talent for product innovation, others for innovation in the business or management models.[45] All of these roles need to be recognised and valued.

At companies like IDEO, the central value driving the innovation process is a 'democracy of ideas'. According to Bennis and Biederman (1997), creative groups do need strong leadership, but in the sense of emotional strength not highly directive behaviour. Such leaders need to be able to cope with responsibility for a process that is typified by 'confusion, incomplete information, paradox, irony and fun for its own sake', as they like to describe it at IDEO, and the central feature of the process is order eventually emerging from chaos.[46] As Andy Grove (1996: 160) once put it, when a leader is 'able to alternatively let chaos reign then rein in chaos'; this dialectic can be very productive, and over the years at Intel they have become very effective at knowing when to leave hierarchy out of the process and when to bring it back in again. Finding the right balance between play and discipline is also essential to ensure that much of the learning generated through the trial-and-failure nature of the creative process does not get lost. According to CEO, David Kelley, one of the reasons why they are so effective at innovating at IDEO is because ' we've done thousands of products, and we've been mindful'.[47] Most successful innovations tend to emerge 'not at the centre of a company's field of focus but at its periphery', and most true breakthroughs are surprises.[48] The invention of the 'post-it' note at 3M is one of the most widely known examples.

Balancing creativity and efficiency

Effective innovation in organisational settings involves a delicate balancing act between play and discipline, practice and process, creativity and efficiency, where organisations need to 'learn to walk the fine line between rigidity – which smothers creativity – and chaos – where creativity runs amok and nothing ever gets to market'.[49] How is such a balancing act to be effected and can most organisations pull it off?

It starts with trying to find the right balance of people. This is how they see it at Intel, for example, as former CEO Andy Grove once explained:

> Being a manufacturer of high-technology 'jelly beans', Intel needed a special blend of two types of people. The wild-eyed, bushy-haired boy geniuses that dominate laboratories could never have taken the technology to the mass-production, 'jelly beans', stage. But the straight -laced, crew-cut manufacturing operators of conventional industry would never have generated the technology in the first place.[50]

It also involves trying to strike the right balance between play and procedure in the innovation process itself. At IDEO, they have evolved a four-phase methodology that has helped them to produce a steady stream of highly innovative products. Yet they remain wary of too much formalisation because they would never expect much innovation to emerge from any process where you 'crank the handle and you know exactly what is going to come out the other end'.[51]

The balancing act also extends to the level of the organisation itself, particularly in the rapidly growing company, when the limits of informal coordination sooner or later become exceeded. Microsoft, a company well known for its ability to attract and retain creative talent, first came to recognise this reality in 1994, when headcount had risen rapidly to reach the 15,000 mark. Robert Herbold was hired from the more process-driven Proctor & Gamble to become Microsoft's first-ever chief operating officer, with a brief to improve overall profitability by 'balancing centralised discipline and individual innovation'.[52] Likewise, Nokia, another of the world's most talent-rich companies came to recognise by 1998 a pressing need to rebalance its ideas-driven culture, developed during its 1992–6 entrepreneurial growth phase, with more 'fact-based management'.[53] Getting the timing right is often key. Many years ago, Xerox 'screwed down the clamps of process' too early following the development of the 914 copier,[54] while more recently Netscape was too late in introducing business discipline and lost valuable ground in its competition with Microsoft as a result.[55] During the dot.com crash, many youthful and exuberant companies paid the ultimate price for putting too much faith in creativity and too little value on traditional business discipline and experience.

Open innovation

For companies looking to raise their innovation game to a new level, the opportunities and challenges extend beyond the internal issues of developing a corporate culture that is more hospitable to creative individuals and more conducive to the generation and sharing of ideas. It also extends to other key elements of the innovation process and how these might be more fully leveraged across, as well as within firm boundaries.

Innovation – absorption and integration, not just invention

For a long time, the tradition in the West had been to associate innovation almost exclusively with the lone inventor and technological breakthrough, a perspective that puts a particularly high premium on individual genius and the 'megawatt' idea. It was a tendency that 'historically cast entrepreneurs and mavericks as virtual folk-heroes',[56] and undervalued the role played by teamwork and the cumulative power of numerous ideas for incremental improvement, or what some call the 'thousand flowers' approach to innovation.[57] The innovative genius of companies like Matsushita and other Japanese companies in being able to seize the technological initiative in markets like video recorders, photocopiers and random access memory chips, had more to with 'creative imitation' and downstream development than it had with invention, and Cohen and Levinthal (1990: 131) have defined this facility to innovate through the acquisition and exploitation of externally generated knowledge as a firm's 'absorptive capacity'. The ability to compete on innovation does not stop at invention or absorption. It also extends to the ability to integrate across functions in the design and production of products or services. As Hamel and Prahalad (1994) have stressed, absorption and integration are just as central to innovation as invention, and often more decisive in industries with fairly predictable technological trajectories. The balance between creativity and structure tends to change as the emphasis shifts from invention to absorption and integration.

From 'closed' to 'open' innovation

The recognition that innovation involves absorption and integration as well as invention opens up the possibility that companies with different skills might pool their competencies and/or share technology to improve the overall productivity of their innovation efforts. Over the last decade and more, we have seen this reflected in the increase in technology alliances and partnerships, 'pre-competitive' R&D consortia, and the rise in interest in the overall perspective and strategy of 'open innovation'.

The concept of 'open innovation' has been popularised by Henry Chesbrough (2003a) to highlight the opportunities presented to companies by technology sharing, both inbound and outbound, through importing ideas generated outside the firm for internal product development and/or exporting ideas generated inside the firm to allow others to bring them to market. Cisco is one of the prime examples of the newer age companies that have embraced the concept of open innovation as an inherent element of their business models, and the company built one of its core skills around this principle, its distinctive 'innovation by acquisition' capability.[58] In comparing his organisation's strategy of outsourcing its R&D with the more traditional approach of its main rival, Don Listwin of Cisco Systems once explained: 'Lucent wants the smartest group of people in Bell Labs. But if we are not good at something, we've got Silicon Valley. It's our Lab'.[59]

While Cisco embraced the open innovation mindset early on in its development, two high profile examples that have made the transition to a more open approach to innovation much later in their histories, with impressive effect, are IBM and P&G (Procter & Gamble).

When Lou Gerstner became CEO of IBM in 1993, he recognised that he had inherited 'one of the most prolific and important scientific research laboratories in the world', with 'more Nobel laureates' than all but a few countries. However, one of the things that puzzled him most was why the company was unable to 'bring its scientific discoveries into the marketplace effectively'.[60] The main impediment, he discovered, was not a lack of sufficient commercial orientation in the R&D function, but rather the unwillingness of IBM product strategists to risk any cannibalisation of existing products, particularly in the core mainframe business, or to work with others in the industry in bringing IBM technology to market. The first step that he took in 'opening the company store' was to increase the licensing of IBM technology, both product and process, to third parties. Over the 1994 to 2001 period, annual revenues from this strategy alone increased from $500M to $1.5B. As he later reflected:[61] 'If our technology team had been a business unto itself, this level of income would have represented one of the largest and most profitable companies in the industry'!

Licensing was just a start. Gerstner expanded the open innovation strategy further by moving on to selling technology components to others, starting with commodity chips in the Dynamic Random Access Memory (DRAM) memory business. While this was not so profitable in itself, it allowed the company to establish itself quite quickly as a reliable supplier–partner in the semiconductor area. The major reward followed later when IBM entered the custom-designed microchip business, enabling it to participate in the growth of exciting new markets in access devices and digital appliances, as well as networking and communications gear. Over the following decade, the company's efforts to become a leading player in the microchip business were not to be without their challenges. However, one of the biggest payoffs was to come in the videogame industry, where IBM's new processors came to be chosen over those of Intel and AMD to power the third generation of Sony, Microsoft and Nintendo game consoles.[62]

As a result of this decision in the mid-1990s to open out its approach to innovation, 'for the first time in its history' IBM was positioned to 'benefit from the growth of businesses outside of the computer industry', extending its core skills 'to entirely new markets'.[63]

If IBM's recent history provides a good illustration of the power of open innovation to leverage external pathways to market, that of P&G is an equally striking illustration of the potential of using externally generated ideas to power internal product innovation. When A.G. Lafley took over as CEO of P&G in 2000, one of his primary concerns was the declining productivity of the company's traditional innovation model. For most of the previous decade, P&G had found itself, along with many other 'mature' companies of its type, spending more and more on R&D with less and less impact on its top line growth. The innovation model that had delivered organic growth rates of 4 per cent to 6 per cent, when the company was a $25B business, could no longer sustain this kind of growth rate when P&G had reached $70B. Inspired by the pioneering moves of companies like IBM and Eli Lilly, then experimenting with the emerging concept of open innovation, the new CEO set P&G on a multi-year mission to acquire 50 per cent of its innovation outside the company. As two of his senior executives most closely associated with this new 'Connect & Develop' (C&D) strategy recalled:

> We needed to move the company's attitude from resistance to innovations 'not invented here' to enthusiasm for those 'proudly found elsewhere'. And we needed to change how we defined, and perceived, our R&D organization – from 7500 people inside to 7500 plus 1.5million outside, with a permeable boundary between them. It was against this backdrop that we developed our connect and develop innovation model.[64]

In the late 1980s P&G had moved from a centralised to a globally networked internal innovation model, and the company had already learned that most of its best innovations tended to come from 'connecting ideas across internal businesses'. The C&D strategy built on this insight, extending it to collaborative networking beyond the company's boundaries. Key organisational elements of the new strategy included the development of both proprietary and open networks. One organisational innovation was the creation of a new role, the 'technology entrepreneur'. By 2006, P&G

had seventy of these in position, all senior executives, operating out of six 'connect and develop' hubs in China, India, Japan, Western Europe, Latin America and the United States, and scouting the world for products, product ideas and promising technologies. The company has also developed a proprietary innovation network with its top fifteen suppliers – in effect, a network with a combined R&D staff of 50,000 – with whom it has been developing 'co-creation' innovation activities,[65] which go well beyond the more traditional joint development efforts in terms of closeness and depth of collaboration.

As part of its connect and develop strategy, P&G has also been active in promoting the expansion of new open innovation networks, the likes of InnoCentive, NineSigma, YourEncore and Yet2.com. This is another new phenomenon associated with growing impact of the open innovation philosophy. InnoCentive is a good example. This initiative was launched by Eli Lilly in 2001 to 'open out the traditionally closed loop of defining and solving a scientific research problem' through the creation of an electronic marketplace that connects problem 'seekers' and 'solvers' across a web-based network. This was done in order to increase the likelihood of problem–solution serendipity.[66] By 2005, InnoCentive's network of solvers had already expanded to more than 80,000 scientists ranging across 173 countries worldwide, including many retired technologists happy to keep their hand in. As the CEO of the new venture, Darren Carroll,[67] described the rationale:

> It's the broadest possible approach. What we were looking for when we founded InnoCentive was a way to exponentially expand our clients' share of mind. A CEO of a research innovation company today first looks for solutions to scientific questions from employees or from a relatively small group of outside contractors. When most companies try to open up to the outside world they are only opening the door a crack. To work exponentially smarter, companies have to open up to people who they don't normally go to who might have new answers ... We're helping senior management to convince their scientists that their greatest value to the company is not being problem solvers (but, rather) solution finders. That's a tough idea for some scientists to accept. But it is absolutely critical for the survival of research facilities in the US, particularly given the cost issues that US and Western European companies are facing today.

Five years on from its inception, it was already clear that the C&D strategy was working – open innovation at P&G had led to a major leap in innovation productivity. By early 2006 the company had already reached a level of 35 per cent of innovations fully or partly based on externally sourced ideas, up from about 15 per cent at the beginning of new strategy. R&D productivity had increased by 60 per cent, with the success rate on innovation more than doubled, while R&D investment as a percentage of sales had actually fallen from 4.8 to 3.4. Most significantly, the company had found a way to reignite organic growth.

What we are seeing in examples like those of Cisco, IBM and P&G, represents little less than a paradigm shift, according to Henry Chesbrough (2003a, 2003c). In research-intensive industries, such as electronics and pharmaceuticals, the 'closed' or fully integrated model of innovation has tended to predominate up to recently, and for good reason. It has its roots in what Gary Hamel (2006: 74) has described as Thomas Edison's 'most notable invention', the establishment in the early 1900s of the industrial research laboratory, which first 'brought management discipline to the chaotic process of scientific discovery'. This 'institution of the central research laboratory and internal product development' became 'a critical element in the rise of the modern industrial corporation'.[68] For much of the twentieth century, the closed innovation model was very effective in many industries, which explains why it prevailed for so long. In effect:

> " Corporate R&D organizations were working at the cutting edge of scientific research. Inside their four walls, they featured the best equipment, staffed by the best people focused on long-term R&D programmes that were funded at significant levels. There seemed to be strong economies of scale in R&D as well: The largest companies in the industry were able to fund the most research and generally enjoyed the most advanced technologies as a result. These companies' lead in research and development helped them achieve the largest profits of all the firms in the industry. And this commitment to R&D was viewed as a barrier to entry for their competitors. Any company that wanted to enter the industry would have to make similarly large, long-term investments in order to compete.[69]

For the companies that benefited most from this virtuous cycle, it was great while it lasted. Xerox is a classic example. During its heyday in the

1950s and 1960s, the company created the closest thing to a commercial monopoly from its technological leadership in the plain paper photo-copying industry, and for more than a decade, as demand grew rapidly, the company continued to control over 90 per cent of the market using this approach to innovation. For much of this time its annual investment in R&D dwarfed those of any of its rivals and exceeded the total annual revenues of most of them. Following a similar approach to innovation, IBM's lead in the mainframe computing market, at its zenith, was almost as commanding.

According to Chesbrough (2003a, 2003b, 2003c), at least five major factors have since served to erode many of the advantages of the closed innovation model and tip the balance towards the more open approach. These are the dramatic rise in the availability and mobility of knowledge workers, the increasing availability of venture capital, the growth in options for ideas sitting on the shelf, the increasing capability of external suppliers and the shortening of product life cycles. Again Xerox provides a classic example of the impact of this transition. From the late 1970s the company had the painful experience of watching the impact of its R&D weakened as many of the great ideas coming out of its leading edge PARC laboratory were left unused. Even worse, many of them were eventually exploited by others, with no return to Xerox, because its innovation model was too internally focused. Under the open innovation approach, this is much less likely to happen, which is one of its most striking advantages (see Table 6.1 for a comparison between the principles of closed and open innovation).

In the early decades of the twenty-first century, the trend towards open innovation looks set to continue apace. Does this mean that there is no longer a role for the more traditional model? According to Chesbrough (2003b), the closed-open choice is one degree more than dichotomy, and most companies and their industries lie on a continuum. In some, like the nuclear power industry, where technological advance still depends largely on internal ideas, the mobility of technologists is low, and venture capital continues to play a negligible role, rapid uptake of the open philosophy remains unlikely. At the other end of the continuum lie industries like the movies, where the innovation model has long been very open. Most companies and their industries are likely to lie somewhere in between.

Table 6.1 **Contrasting principles of closed and open innovation**

Closed innovation principles	Open innovation principles
The smart people in the field work for us	Not all the smart people in the field work for us
To profit from R&D, we must discover, develop and ship it ourselves	External R&D can create significant value; Internal R&D is needed to claim some portion of that value
If we discover it ourselves, we will get to market first	We don't have to originate the research in order to profit from it
If we are first to commercialise an innovation, we will win	Building a better business model is better than getting to market first
If we create the most and best ideas in the industry, we will win	If we make the best use of internal *and* external ideas, we will win
We should control our IP so that our competitors don't profit from our ideas	We should profit from others' use of our IP, and we should buy others' IP whenever it advances our own business model

Source: Chesbrough, H. 'The era of open innovation, MIT Sloan Management Review, Spring 2003

From its early experiences with a more externally oriented approach to innovation, P&G is also learning 'never to assume that "ready to go" ideas found outside are truly ready to go', nor to 'underestimate the internal resources required'.[70] For its part, IBM continues to struggle to 'straddle a philosophical chasm' in trying to make the optimum choice about how far it should go in sharing its innovations, particularly in the strategic open source software battleground.[71]

Up to now, the marketplace for trade in IP has remained quite inefficient and underdeveloped, but this is quickly changing.[72] As it does, the momentum for more open innovation is only likely to get stronger. In the years ahead, the challenge for many firms will be to find the right balance between closed and open innovation, rather than have to choose between them, and to develop the dynamic capability to adjust this balance 'on the fly' as the global context for innovation continues to rapidly evolve.

New business venturing in the established corporation

As we have seen already, one of the most notable features of the early years of the twenty-first century is the renewed interest in innovation as the primary strategy for driving top-line growth. As Jeffrey Sonnenfeld (2004: 30), president of Yale University's Chief Executive Institute, noted, for the most recent generation of corporate CEOs, 'the art of the deal is fading, and the value of the idea is once again on the rise'. In these early years of the new millennium, we can already see this broadly based trend reflected in the IBM of Sam Palmisano, the GE of Jeffrey Immelt, the P&G of A.G. Laffley and the Pfizer of Henry 'Hank' McKinnell, just to mention a few of the most prominent examples. Furthermore, this 'return to the power of ideas' is riding on a wave of new concepts on how to harness innovation for corporate growth. These not only include product and process innovation, but also 'disruptive' innovation, 'blue ocean' market innovation, business model innovation, experience innovation and several other forms of value innovation, already examined in an earlier chapter.

In this chapter, we have been looking at the strategic challenge facing the larger organisation in trying to preserve and enhance its capacity for creativity and innovation as it grows. We have also looked at the impact that the rise in open innovation is promising to have on R&D effectiveness. Over the last ten years or so, many companies have been making significant strides in meeting such challenges and taking advantage of such trends. To date, however, the impact has been mainly on the productivity of product and process innovation closely linked to the mainstream business. When it comes to the related challenge of how to build a new growth business within the established corporation, the track record across the corporate world remains unconvincing. So even where companies have no shortage of ideas, why are too many of them still so poor at turning them into successful new business ventures?

Why is the pattern of ICV activity so cyclical?

Up to the now, interest in ICV seems to come in cycles,[73] and there is little sign that this is likely to change any time soon. As Burgelman and Valikangas (2005: 26) have noted, over several decades the pattern seems to be that 'periods of intense ICV activity are followed by periods when such programmes are shut down, only to be followed by new ICV activities a few years later'. Interest in the topic within the strategic management literature has also tended to follow suit, peaking in the late 1960s,[74] the early to mid-1980s[75] and on the rise again in the mid to late

2000s, while declining in-between times. Perhaps, nowhere are the vicissitudes associated with this pattern more poignantly illustrated than in the following insight offered by John Steen of Courtalds, the UK fibres company, to Campbell and Park (2005: 26) in one of the more recent studies in the new business venturing area:

> " You decide the core is not growing fast enough. You invest in new businesses. They under-perform; and seven years later you are worse off than when you started, having sold or closed the last of the new initiatives. I have seen my company do this three times.

What Steen observed at Courtalds is far from unique. Philips first introduced a corporate venturing activity in the 1960s, pared it back in the mid-1970s, rebooted it and then pared it back again in the 1980s, only to revive it yet again in the late 1990s.[76] Likewise, over the last decade and a half, we have seen any number of promising initiatives, like the New Ventures Group at Lucent or the GameChanger programme at Shell, wound up, pared back or sold off, and others like the Xerox Technology Ventures replaced by Xerox New Enterprise and then the latter terminated.[77] Over a similar period, we have also seen companies as diverse as Intel and McDonald's invest countless millions in their own new venture efforts with mixed results at best.[78] The reasons for such a stop-start pattern are both strategic and organisational. Whether it is by acquisition or organic growth, as we have already seen in the previous chapter, companies tend to do better when their efforts to diversify are into areas closely related to their core businesses.[79] As they run out of such opportunities and seek to push the boat out further, the odds become more steeply stacked against them. As Roberts (1980: 134) noted many years ago, 'entering unfamiliar markets, employing unfamiliar technology, and implementing an unfamiliar organization structure', each in its own way represents a formidable challenge, so put all three together in a new business venture and 'it is no wonder that their joint probability of success is rather small'.

With the odds against success so high, and the experience to date quite bruising for many, why do companies keep coming back for more? According to Garvin (2004: 18), the answer is that 'ultimately growth means starting new businesses', and 'most firms have no alternative' because 'sectors decline' (as they did for Pulman railroad carriages and Singer sewing machines), 'technology renders products and services obsolete' (as electronic imaging has done in the photographic industry) and 'markets saturate' (as Dell, Intel and Microsoft are all still struggling to come to grips with in the personal computer sector). Again, the insight of another of the respondents in the recent Campbell and Park (2005: 13) study, Mats Lederhausen, the senior executive responsible for new growth initiatives at McDonald's in the late 1990s, is revealing:

> " All we know is that we have to try to keep growing. We know that the misery of uncertainty is far better than the certainty of misery. If we don't try to grow we will fail, and at least if we try we have a chance of sustained growth.

Estimates in the literature about the length of the cycle vary, from ten-year intervals downwards,[80] and one possible explanation for the cyclical pattern is that ICV activity simply follows the general business cycle. A related explanation is that it follows the ebb and flow of the independent venture capital market.[81] Vibrancy here tends to transmit an onward pressure to the corporate sector to make itself more adventurous, if it is not to risk losing both investment and talent to go-it-alone start-ups. However, many view these macroeconomic explanations as partial at best, and believe that corporate strategic and administrative factors are more decisive. From a strategic point of view, for authors like Burgelman and Valikangas (2005: 27), the single biggest factor is likely to be the 'interplay between the prospects of a company's mainstream businesses and the availability of uncommitted financial resources'. Quite simply, since ICV activity is difficult and risky, company strategists tend not to prioritise it when they have other options. All-out corporate ICV drives tend to be launched only when the company has plenty of finance available and the opportunities for growth in the mainstream businesses are limited. Even then, ICV initiatives can be ultimately undermined by lack of synchronisation with key elements of corporate administrative systems, such as planning/budgeting cycles not being attuned to the special needs of start-up ventures and being too impatient for growth, or a corporate development process that tends to move 'fast-track' managers on too quickly, depriving ICVs of continuity of commitment and consistency of purpose.

According to Campbell et al. (2003), a major reason why ICV programmes often fail to deliver is due to companies setting up venture units with 'mixed objectives' and 'mixed up' business models. From their analysis of nearly 100 venturing units, they identify five main types of ICV: ecosystem venturing, innovation venturing, harvest venturing, private equity venturing and 'new legs' venturing. The purpose of ecosystem venturing is to enhance the development of a company's network of complimentary businesses, innovation venturing seeks to invoke the methods of the venture capital industry to improve the productivity of the corporate R&D activity, harvest venturing is used to turn IP into cash through new business spin-out and private equity venturing is pursued purely for financial returns. Viable business models exist for four of these five types, typically resting on some identifiable advantage over the independent VC. This might be deeper knowledge of key technologies in the case of ecosystem venturing or privileged access to particular deal flows in the case of private equity venturing. Where such advantages are absent, corporate venturing units rarely match the skills and acumen of the independent venture capital companies.

Intel Capital, the venturing arm of Intel Corporation, provides an interesting example of ICV variety in a single company setting.[82] Some of Intel's individual businesses had been involved in various venturing activities over many years when the company first launched a corporate activity in 1991. It did this 'with the goal of investing in technologies that were both strategic to Intel and financially viable'. In the mid-1990s, it extended this to investing in companies 'that complimented Intel's offerings' in order to make 'the whole market work better'. This broader vision saw the company's corporate venturing activities evolve into four main areas: ecosystem development, typified by the Intel Capital's investment in a number of complementary companies to promote the adoption of the Itanium processor; market development investments like those in Ru-Net Holdings in Russia and Internet Technologies China; 'gap-filling' investments in companies like Micron Technology to promote the development of complementary technologies; and 'eyes-and-ears' investments, typically the smallest financial commitment of the four, just to allow Intel to 'keep abreast of new trends and technologies outside its current area of competence'.

Corporate entrepreneurship – a top-down or bottom-up phenomenon?

Is the entrepreneurship process in the larger organisational context primarily a top-down or bottom-up phenomenon? This remains a hotly contested issue, as is evident in the recent direct exchange between Robert Burgelman, a long-standing proponent of the bottom-up view, and Andrew Campbell, a prominent advocate of the top-down perspective.[83] Should top management be driving new business venturing directly as a strategic planning process, identifying the opportunities and then picking the best managers to head up these ventures? Or should they concentrate on trying to create the kind internal environment that will best liberate the more commercially adventurous talent and entrepreneurial impulses already existing deep within their organisations and give them the chance to come to the fore and flourish?

This top-down/bottom-up debate is one that stretches back to the time when strategy first emerged as a field of study in its own right in the early 1960s. Certainly many of the earliest advocates of formalised corporate planning initially looked to it as a way of trying to institutionalise the entrepreneurial function within the well-established firm.[84] Steiner (1979: 10) reflected this when he argued that 'in a fundamental sense' formal strategic planning was 'an effort to duplicate what goes on in the mind of a brilliant, intuitive planner'. Other advocates of the top-down strategic planning perspective were more circumspect. Argenti (1980: 30), for example, believed that corporate planning in the hands of a team of professional managers could never hope to 'compete with the entrepreneur' in terms of innovative flair or capacity, but that it should at least help to 'protect a managed company from failure'.

On the bottom-up side there have been many notable advocates over the years, including Peters and Waterman (1982), Kanter (1983, 1989) and Hamel (1999, 2000a), popularising the notions of 'skunk works', 'empowerment' and 'bringing the market inside', respectively. One of the first to highlight the significance of bottom-up entrepreneurship in the larger organisation was Bower (1970) in his classic study of the resource allocation process. The picture that emerged from his data was not one of top-down identification of investment opportunities. Rather the opportunities were more typically identified at the business unit level and advocated upwards, with corporate management acting more in the role of shapers of context, backers of initiatives and definers of the rules of the game. Burgelman's (1983b) empirical study of ICV later identified two major strategic processes typically operating in the larger complex organisation: 'induced strategic behaviour' and 'autonomous strategic behaviour'. The first of these is integral to traditional planning. However, the second originates outside of it, yet is key to strategy innovation. How this works is that any given corporate strategy establishes a 'structural context', which induces the alignment of structures, systems and behaviours around it. However, this is also a powerful, self-reinforcing dynamic that can only be radically realigned through autonomous strategic behaviour (internal entrepreneurial initiatives not induced by the existing strategy) bubbling up from below. In sum, the bottom-up perspective on corporate venturing could be characterised as a 'Schumpeter inside' perspective in which 'the internal entrepreneur, like the external entrepreneur, enacts new opportunities and drives the development of new resource combinations or re-combinations', and it is 'precisely these efforts – to extend the firm's domain of competence, to elaborate and recombine the current capabilities, and define new, unanticipated opportunities – which makes internal entrepreneurial activity a vital part of the strategy process in large, established firms'.[85]

While the debate between the top-down and bottom-up approaches to corporate entrepreneurship is likely to energise the strategy field for many years to come, future research is likely to move away from the either-or dichotomy and try to establish the circumstances in which the one or the other perspective is likely to be the more effective, and even how they might interplay to best effect. As Amo and Kolvereid (2005: 12) recently summarised it, the top-down perspective takes the view that 'having employees with intrapreneurial personalities is pointless or even counterproductive unless a deliberate corporate entrepreneurship strategy is in place', while the bottom-up perspective tends to suggest the reverse. This has led them to conclude that 'there is reason to expect that a model that incorporates both approaches will perform better than any model based on only one of them', and they have found some empirical evidence to support this contention. We see a similar view reflected in the Dess and Lumpkin (2005) notion of 'Entrepreneurial Orientation' (EO) as a measure of the level of company-wide dedication to entrepreneurship. We also see it reflected in the 'opportunity-based organization' blueprint of Eisenstat et al. (2001: 56–7), aimed at giving organisations the flexibility to 'bring the most useful resources to bear on the most promising opportunities', and 'emulate the market responsiveness of start-ups without sacrificing the advantages of scale and scope'.

Organising and managing a new corporate venture

One of the most difficult organisational challenges facing any corporate management is how much autonomy to give a new business venture, regardless of whether the venturing process has been initiated from the top or below. This is also a long-standing debate in the ICV literature, with little sign of resolution any time soon.

How much autonomy should the new venture be given?

One of the most influential contributions informing this debate is the distinction, noted earlier, between exploration and exploitation, where: 'Exploration includes things captured by terms such as search, variation, risk taking, experimentation, play, flexibility, discovery, innovation', while 'exploitation includes such things as refinement, choice, production, efficiency, selection, implementation, execution'.[86] Organisations as they grow and adapt are continually challenged to maintain the most effective balance between these two orientations, the one promoting efficiency (exploitation) and the other entrepreneurship (exploration). In the context of ICV, an organisation needs to be able to explore for new venture possibilities while continuing to exploit to the full, the potential of its core business. The problem is that these two goals tend to pull in different directions, and they have the potential to undermine each other if not carefully managed. Maintaining the most effective balance between them is what lies at the heart of the organisational challenge facing ICV activity in the established firm.

Even companies that have been successful in creating a better internal climate for creativity and idea generation will see their efforts come to little fruition if they fail to meet this structural challenge successfully. Conventional wisdom suggests that new ICVs need 'their own space', and the proposition that 'new businesses prosper best when separated from their corporate parents has become a commonplace'.[87] Indeed, the potentially overpowering effect of a strong core business has been likened to that of the creosote tree: little can grow in its shadow. New business ventures that are natural outgrowths of the core business are, of course, the major exception. But where a new business venture is a true strategic innovation or breakthrough business for an organisation – characterised by Govindarajan and Trimble (2004: 69) as a 'creative and significant departure' from traditional company practice in at least one of three areas: (1) design of the end-to-end value chain architecture, (2) conceptualisation of delivered customer value, (3) identification of potential customers – some level of independence from the mainstream business is widely seen to be desirable by many leading authors.[88]

So how much autonomy should a new business venture have and why? Over the years, a number of authors have offered their own contingency perspectives, most of them variations on a theme.[89] More than two decades ago, for example, Burgelman (1983c) identified the key contingencies as (i) the strategic importance of the new venture; and (ii) its operational relatedness to the core – the higher the two, the greater the pull towards integration with the core business; the lower the two the greater the push for autonomy, even spin-out. In more recent times, Christensen and Raynor (2003: 184) have suggested that the key considerations are the degree of fit with the parent organisation's processes (by which they mean the patterns of interaction, coordination, communication and decision-making by which inputs get transformed into things of greater value) and values (by which they mean the standards by which employees make prioritisation decisions). Those processes likely to be of most significance are 'the enabling or background processes that support investment decisions', such as the customary approach to conducting market research, translating analysis into financial projections, negotiating plans and budgets, and so forth, while the most relevant values revolve around acceptable gross margins and how big a business opportunity has to appear before it becomes interesting (often referred to as the 'materiality' question). For Markides and Charitou (2004) the most important variables are the degree of conflict between the two business models and how strategically related the new market is to the mainstream business.

Many now argue that to compete successfully with dual business models, you need a dual-purpose organisation, capable of balancing the need to explore with the need to exploit, and the need for autonomy with the need for integration – too much integration and the ICV may run the risk of being smothered by the mainstream business, but too much autonomy and the ICV stands to lose any potential advantage that its association with the corporate parent might offer over independent competitors in the same marketplace. As Day et al. (2001: 21.) put it: 'Although new ventures do need space to develop, strict separation can prevent them from obtaining valuable resources and rob their parents of the vitality they can generate'.

In the search for organisational solutions, O'Reilly and Tushman (2004: 76) examined thirty-five new business venturing initiatives and found that the most successful firms tended to 'separate their new exploratory units from their traditional, exploitative ones, allowing for different processes, structures, and cultures', while 'maintaining tight links across units at the senior management level'. They invoked the notion of the 'ambidextrous organization' to characterise this structural form, and offered USA Today and Ciba Vision as two of their prime examples. Taking this perspective a step further, Birkinshaw and Gibson (2004) have argued that 'structural' ambidexterity must be complemented by 'contextual' ambidexterity (by which they mean an ambidextrous orientation, weaved deeply into the behavioural fabric of the firm, that enables individual employees to become more adept at making choices between alignment-oriented and adaptation-oriented activities), if full mastery of adaptability and alignment is to be realised. They offer Renault and Oracle as current exemplars and link their notion of the ambidextrous orientation quite closely to Ghoshal and Bartlett's (1998) concept of the 'individualized corporation' and Tichy's 'leadership culture'.[90]

Coming from a different angle, Govindarajan and Trimble (2005b) argue that any company trying to achieve breakaway growth with a high potential new business venture typically faces a *forgetting* challenge and a *borrowing* challenge; the first concerns how far the new business needs to depart from the traditional business model, and the second concerns what key linkages to the mainstream business need to be retained for the venture to make its full impact. Corning and the New York Times are companies that struggled with these two challenges and almost fumbled them completely before coming good in the end. In the case of Corning, the company initially tried to keep its new CMT (Corning Microarray Technologies) venture too close to its traditional way of operating and failed to recognise that all four major elements of a new venture's organisational code (structure, systems, skills and culture) typically need to differ from those of the mainstream business. CMT almost failed to take off until it was allowed to 'forget' most of the traditional Corning way of doing things and given more autonomy. Likewise, when it first set up its NYTD (New York Times Digital) venture, the Times made the same mistake as Corning, keeping the new business too closely integrated with its core operation, and ending up with little more than a newspaper online. After it corrected this error, an 'explosion in creativity' followed. In giving NYTD a lot more independence, however, the company went to the opposite extreme, leaving the new venture cut-off from access to some of the most important complementary assets of the core business, including the newspaper's prize-winning 'branded' content and its existing base of advertisers. Not until a better balance was established between the need to 'forget' and the need to 'borrow' was the new venture primed to reach its full potential.

Finally, views not only differ on where the balance between independence and integration should be struck, but also on the level at which the integration should take place as well as on the timing. Some, like O'Reilly and Tushman (2004), suggest that the new and existing businesses should be operationally independent, with tighter links at the strategic level, while others, like Govindarajan and Trimble (2005a, 2005b), argue for a small number of carefully selected operational links with a high degree of strategic autonomy. Others still, suggest that the most effective independence-integration balance may vary over the development of the new venture,[91] and even vary in the direction of separation-to-phased integration or integration-to-phased separation, dependent on the circumstances.[92] The current challenges facing IBM in the corporate management of its EBO (Emerging Business Opportunities) programme have as much to do with the problems of effective reintegration as they have with the launching of successful business ventures in the first place.[93]

New venture leadership, planning and accountability

The organisation and management challenges presented to the well-established company by ICV activity do not end with structure. They also encompass such issues as leadership, planning and accountability. Among the most crucial is leadership. As Campbell and Park (2005: 31) have noted: 'The venture capital industry has a saying that there are only three things to think about when selecting projects to support: management, management, and management. The same applies to new businesses inside larger companies'.

Over the years companies have struggled to get this right. Ineffective leadership was one of the main contributors to the difficulties that Corning experienced in its first attempt to get its CMT venture successfully off the ground.[94] It was also a major contributor to the spectacular failure of the 'Pandesic' joint-venture between Intel and SAP,[95] which ended up accumulating more than $100M in start-up costs before being finally wound up. In looking back at this disaster, Christensen and Raynor (2003: 181) reflected that the 'truly interesting question' was not what the management team in charge of the venture got wrong, but 'how such capable, experienced, and respected managers – among the best that Intel and SAP had to offer – could have made these mistakes' to begin with.

In the large company context, corporate management often pick a talented executive from the core business and reassign him/her to the ICV. One of the difficulties with this is that such a manager may lack the entrepreneurial passion to build a new-growth business. Even if they have the passion, they may still lack sufficient personal and organisational clout to secure the footing of the new venture as it grows, especially when the leaders of the core business begin to see it competing for attention and resources.[96] Most of all, they may lack the most vital experience and skills. According to Christensen and Raynor (2003), corporate leaders often tend to focus too much on the question of who has the 'right stuff' and not enough on whether their management skills have been honed through the most appropriate 'school of experience'. Having a track record as a high-flying talent within the core business is generally not enough in itself. As Campbell and Park (2005: 31) point out: 'Within an existing business there are many managers who understand the products, the markets, and the essence of the business model needed to make a profit' but in new business ventures 'all three of these areas of knowledge may be absent'. Given all of the uncertainties associated with a new business venture, then, some exposure to project failure, along with a demonstrated capacity to learn from it and the resilience to bounce back quickly, may be among the most valuable formative experiences for the would-be leader of an ICV.

Ineffective corporate management of ICVs can also result from inappropriate approaches to planning and accountability. This again was evident in CMT, Pandesic and many other cases. For example, the corporate culture at Corning, like that of many established companies, tended to emphasise strict accountability to plans, where projections were considered to be commitments, and delivering on them a key measure of managerial effectiveness. This is a valuable discipline when applied to fully exploiting the profit opportunities in the mainstream business but it turned out to have dysfunctional consequences when it was extended to an exploratory venture like CMT. In most new business ventures, setting projections is bound to be a speculative exercise until most of the key uncertainties surrounding the product, market and business model have been resolved. Yet, when CMT initially failed to meet its projections, the corporate system treated this as failure to execute rather than a necessary part of the experiment-and-learn process for new venture success. As Govindarajan and Trimble (2004: 70) have put it: 'When the future is unknowable, the foremost planning objective must be learning, not accountability'. Pressure on the venture's leaders to get the numbers back on track only served to misdirect their efforts, setting in train a self-defeating cycle which almost killed the project during its first two years of operation.

History shows that in the vast majority of cases, the initial strategy and business model developed for new ventures are rarely the same as those that ultimately bring success,[97] so the only thing that can be predicted with any certainty about the earliest projections is that they are likely to be very inaccurate. As Garvin (2004: 19) points out: 'Starting a new venture is essentially an experiment' and a new ICV 'simply has to prototype its initial concept, get it into the hands of users, assess their reactions, and then repeat the process until it comes up with an acceptable version'. New ventures are typically undertaken 'with a high ratio of assumption to knowledge', as McGrath and MacMillan (1995: 44) put it, and one of the main priorities early on is to reduce this ratio as quickly as possible by systematically converting assumptions into knowledge. Traditional planning and control systems are not the most suited to this task because they are 'designed to implement a proven strategy' rather than for rapid learning (Govindarajan and Trimble 2004: 70). Two of the most interesting alternatives on offer in the new venture literature, 'discovery-driven planning'[98] and 'theory-focused planning',[99] are variations on the idea that for new ventures early assumptions and predictions are best viewed as hypotheses to be tested, or theories to be verified or rejected, en route to discovering the right strategy and business model. Both are aimed at speeding up the predict-and-learn cycle within the planning process, and companies pursuing ICV activities need to think about how to build in learning transfer mechanisms when designing their venture divisions.[100]

It follows from above that in the early stage of a new business venture, managers should be judged on how quickly they are able to experiment their way to the most viable strategy and business model, rather than on how close they come to meeting their early projections, or even how quickly they can grow the business. According to Christensen and Raynor (2003), one of the mistakes that many established companies made in their rush to develop new online ventures during the dot.com bubble was that they were 'impatient-for-growth' and 'patient-for-profit', when the other way around might have been wiser. As a result, too many of them tried to scale up these ventures too rapidly before a commercially viable business model had been developed.[101] 'Patient-for-growth' but 'impatient-for-profit' is the advice that could be applied to most new business ventures.

One of the thorniest issues that corporate management have to face in their ICV activities is how to determine the most appropriate incentives. How steeply rewarded should the leaders of a new ICV be, and to what extent should they be rewarded more like entrepreneurs than professional managers? How far should a corporate venturing process go to replicate the practices of the venture capital market internally? Here again, there are few clear answers. Perhaps the biggest fear that companies have in not employing strong enough incentives is that venture managers will leave and set up on their own. Some years ago, a venture capitalist captured this concern most sharply when he pointed out to Block and Ornati (1987: 44) that the 'only reason for our existence is the inability of corporations to provide the financial incentives which can be achieved in an independent start-up'. At the same time, incentives that deviate too widely from the corporate norm are likely to create resentment and undermine the ability of the new venture to leverage the complimentary corporate assets and competencies most needed to give it the edge over independent competitors in the marketplace. The prevailing pattern to date lies somewhere in-between, and the intensity of the incentives in corporate venturing tends to be weaker than those that typically operate in the independent venture capital sector.[102]

ICV and the growth imperative – how imperative?

We began this chapter by highlighting the intensifying pressure on companies to become more innovative. Furthermore, as firms get larger, and the opportunities for further growth in the core business appear to be diminishing, they feel under increasing pressure to develop new businesses and create new markets. As Mackey and Valikangas (2004: 89) have observed, the reality is that the financial markets 'expect growth' and there is 'a deeply held assumption that neither a company nor its management is viable unless it is able to grow'.

'Stewardship versus entrepreneurship: that's the fundamental distinction between the mediocre mass and the revolutionary wealth creators', according to Gary Hamel (1999: 71). While new business venturing is adventurous and exciting, the strategic and organisational challenges that it presents to the established firm are both formidable and daunting, and up to the present too much corporate value continues to be destroyed by well-intentioned internal venturing activities that are misguided or mismanaged. So before we draw the chapter to a close, it behoves us to examine the question of just how 'imperative' this growth imperative really is, and how sensible it is for companies to allow themselves to become so caught up in it.

The challenge to keep the growth momentum going just gets bigger, as companies themselves get bigger. Estimates vary, but somewhere in the $30B–$70B range, the nature of the growth challenge for most companies seems to become different in kind, not just in degree. According to research by the Corporate Strategy Board (1998), when many companies get to such a size their growth often stalls, and very few have been able to reignite it to sustainable levels above the general rate of economic growth. Rather than try to be too adventurous and risk destroying value, many such companies might be wiser to readjust their ambitions and focus on maximising their returns within a lower growth scenario? 'No tree grows to the sky', as Nuala Beck (1992: 91–2) has pointed out, and 'hard as it is to accept', most companies may eventually need to come to terms with the fact that 'nothing goes on forever, even for the brightest and the best'. As Campbell and Park (2004: 28) put it, 'some companies must face up to a future of lower growth'.

So what is the larger company to do? Mackey and Valikangas (2004) have identified at least three viable options. The first of these is breaking up the company and spinning out some of its major business units, as IBM did with Lexmark, HP with Agilent and 3M with Imation. Such spin-outs often lead to the generation of additional value, both in the spin-out itself and also in the refocused core. Companies can also experiment with new corporate forms, as GE has done during the second phase of the Jack Welch era and since, and turn themselves more into network, or 'boundaryless', companies, leveraging the assets of their ecosystems to generate greater market dynamism with less internal bureaucratic mass and complexity. The third option is to make the transition from 'growth' to 'value' stocks, content to reward shareholders in a different way through larger dividends and lower P/E ratios. This is rarely an easy option for shareholders to embrace, but often it may prove to be in their best interests over the longer term.

Companies can also recognise where their true assets and skills lie, and can build their strategies for growth accordingly. For example, Zook (2004) argues that companies too often turn to diversification prematurely, long before the potential of their mainstream business has been fully exploited. Campbell and Park (2004: 28) tend to agree: 'Most mature businesses have more mileage in them than their managers presume'. A classic example is the European airline industry, and the fresh expansion in the air passenger business following the entry of the low-cost carriers, at a time when many of the established players were diversifying unsuccessfully into hotels and other non-core activities. Furthermore, in their recent study of new business venturing, Campbell and Park (2004: 27) found that 'the real problem' was 'a shortage of opportunities rather than a shortage of courage or venturing skills'. They concluded: 'We believe that the numbers game is a losing game' and the 'alternative is to be selective: to invest in opportunities only when the company has a significant advantage'.[103] For these authors at least, there is a 'time to fish and a time to cut bait' in the corporate venturing area. So, instead of trying to push 'water uphill with new business initiatives, companies may have to learn a harder skill – patience', where the 'art is to return as much money to the financial markets as possible while still keeping a watchful eye out for other unique propositions'.[104]

For researchers like Campbell and Park (2005: 40) there are 'so few examples of companies that succeed in achieving the combination of continuous new business creation and dedication to the core, that this is, for most, an unrealistic objective'. Others like Markides and Geroski (2003a, 2003b) agree, but see, in this, a way forward for the established firm. In their own analysis of twenty markets created in the last 100 years, the authors found that the companies that pioneered the creation of new markets, or 'colonized' them, were rarely the same as those that ended up scaling them up to mass market potential, or 'consolidating' them, and dominating their growth. Why? Their research pointed to 'a simple reason for this phenomenon: the skills, mind-sets, and competencies needed for discovery and invention not only are different from those needed for commercialisation; they conflict with the needed characteristics', which means that 'firms good at invention are unlikely to be good at commer-cialisation, and vice versa'.[105] Trying to be effective at both exploration and exploitation might be a highly desirable ambition, but it can often be misguided, and there are very few truly ambidextrous organisations to be found as yet. A more realistic approach for most established com-panies might be to specialise on consolidation and leave the pioneering to others, the kind of strategy favoured by those who make the case for outsourcing innovation.[106] 'Scaling up a market is an important activity that requires as much creativity and innovation as the discovery of a new market', and for Markides and Geroski (2003b: 53), at least, this should be 'how big companies innovate'.

Summary

In this chapter we examined in some detail the first of two major strategic processes – innovation. We saw how companies today are coming under greater pressure than ever to be innovative in everything that they do in order to survive and thrive. We began our analysis by asking whether the key to the innovation advantage rests in individual talent or in systematic process and organisation, and highlighted the importance of both of these elements. We then went on to examine how business leaders might go about making their organisations more creative, which is particularly challenging for the larger, well-established firm. This begins with trying to develop a deeper understanding of creativity at the personal level – of how creativity relates to general intelligence and of the psychodynamics of the creative process. While highlighting that the foundation for building the 'creative advantage' resides in personal creativity, we also recognised that organisational and cultural factors are key to bringing it to the fore and harnessing it more productively. With this in view, we looked at how creativity and innovation can best be fostered in organisational settings; the elements involved in building a culture and context for creativity, the dynamics involved in leading creative groups and the need at all levels, individual, group and organisational, to establish and maintain the right balance between innovation and efficiency.

We later went on to highlight how innovation in organisational settings involves more than invention, and how processes of absorption and integration are also important to the effectiveness of the overall effort. This led us directly into an examination of the emerging perspective of 'open innovation' and the way in which this new approach is being drawn upon by many leading companies, like IBM and P&G, to boost the productivity of their research and development and wider innovation activities. In the final part of the chapter we turned to look at the process of ICV and the particular challenges involved in trying to build a totally new growth business within the well-established firm. This is as much about execution as ideas. We looked at why, to date, the pattern of internal venturing has been so cyclical and also why, more often than not, the venturing activities of the larger corporation often end up destroying more value than they create. We examined the current debates about whether the process of corporate venturing is better driven from the top-down or from the bottom-up, how much autonomy a new corporate venture should be given and how its leaders should be chosen, measured and rewarded. We drew the chapter to a close with a brief examination of how real the growth 'imperative' is for the well-established company, and how in their response to it, rather than feel pressured into premature corporate venturing, many might be wiser to consider other options.

If one of the reasons that companies look to ICV is to identify new pathways to growth, another is to stimulate the process of corporate renewal. In many ways we can think of corporate transformation as an innovation process involving the reinvention of the company as a whole. It is to this major strategic challenge than we turn to in our next, and penultimate, chapter.

Notes

1 Foster and Kaplan (2001), Hamel and Valikangas (2003).
2 Sonnenfeld (2004: 30).
3 This discussion draws freely from Leavy (2002) and Leavy (2005b).
4 Ziegler (2002: 52).
5 Peters and Waterman (1982: 200).
6 Davenport et al. (2002: 43 and 45).
7 Stross (1996: 44).
8 Hargadon and Sutton (2000), Ziegler (2002).
9 de Pree (1994: 28).
10 Bartlett and Ghoshal (2002).
11 Barron (1969).
12 Moran (1967: 196).
13 Gardner (1993: 20).
14 Storr (1991: 222).
15 Barron et al. (1997).
16 Zweig and Abrams (1991), O'Neil (1993).
17 Stevens (2001: 82). E.O. Wilson (2007: 62), the well-known biologist, offers a similar insight in *The Creation: An Appeal to Save Life on Earth*:

> Our relationship with nature is primal. The emotions it evokes arose during the forgotten prehistory of mankind, and hence are deep and shadowed. Like childhood experiences lost from conscious memory, they are commonly felt but rarely articulated. Poets, at the highest human level of expression, try. They know that something fundamental moves beneath the surface of our conscious minds, something worth saving.

The reader is also referred back to the quote from Senge & Carsted (2001: 26) on page 61.

18 Storr (1991: 239).
19 Coutu (2000: 145).
20 Csikszentmihalyi (1996: 107).
21 Chase and Simon (1973), Gardner (1993), Csikszentmihalyi (1996).
22 Gardner (1993: 362).
23 Csikszentmihalyi (1996).

24 Storr (1991: 268).

25 Handy (1997: xiii).

26 Hirshberg (1999), Tesluk et al. (1997), Mumford and Simonton (1997).

27 Amabile (1997).

28 Sutton (2002).

29 Collins and Porras (1996: 152).

30 Collins and Porras (1996), Ghoshal and Bartlett (1998).

31 Schmidt and Varian (2005), Hamel (2007).

32 Csikszentmihalyi (1996: 116).

33 Farson and Keyes (2002: 66).

34 Thomke (2001).

35 Farson and Keyes (2002: 64).

36 Bennis and Biederman (1997: 201).

37 Leonard and Strauss (1997).

38 Schlender (1998: 44).

39 Wetlaufer (2000: 116).

40 Sutton (2002: 185).

41 Kao (1997: 81).

42 De Pree (1989: 148).

43 Kao (1997).

44 Sinetar (1985), Ziegler (2002).

45 Davenport et al. (2003).

46 Thomke and Nimgade (2000: 5).

47 Thomke and Nimgade (2000: 3).

48 Hillis (2002: 152).

49 Brown and Duguid (2000: 73).

50 Nanda and Bartlett (1994: 6).

51 Thomke and Nimgade (2000: 8).

52 Herbold (2002: 75).

53 Doornik and Roberts (2001).

54 Brown and Duguid (2001: 94).

55 Cusumano and Yoffie (1998).

56 Bolton (1993: 30).

57 Kanter (1988).

58 Southwick (2000).

59 Killick et al. (2001: 17).

60 Gerstner (2003: 148).

61 Gerstner (2003: 149).

62 Nuttall (2005), Hamm and Elgin (2005).

63 Gerstner (2003: 151).

64 Huston and Sakkab (2006: 61).

65 Prahalad and Ramaswamy (2004).

66 Raynor and Panetta (2005: 4).

67 Allio (2004: 8–9).

68 Chesbrough (2003a: 24).

69 Chesbrough (2003a: 29).

70 Huston and Sakkab (2006: 66).

71 Miller (2006).

72 Chesbrough (2006).

73 Fast (1978), Chesbrough (2000).

74 Peterson (1967).

75 Roberts (1980), Sykes (1986).

76 Van Basten Battenberg and Birkinshaw (2002).

[77] Burgelman and Valikangas (2005).

[78] Campbell and Park (2005).

[79] Rumelt (1974), Zook and Allen (2003).

[80] Fast (1978), Block and MacMillan (1993).

[81] Chesbrough (2000).

[82] For more see Yoffie (2005) from which the quotes to follow are drawn.

[83] See Campbell (2003), Burgelman (2003).

[84] Ansoff (1965).

[85] Burgelman (1983c: 164 and 158).

[86] March (1991: 71).

[87] Day et al. (2001: 21).

[88] Burgelman (1983c), Drucker (1985), Kanter (1989), Christensen (1997), O'Reilly and Tushman (2004), Govindarajan and Trimble (2005a).

[89] Burgelman (1983c), Christensen and Raynor (2003), Markides and Charitou (2004).

[90] Tichy and Cohen (2002).

[91] Iansiti et al. (2003).

[92] Markides and Charitou (2004).

[93] Garvin and Levesque (2004).

[94] Govindarajan and Trimble (2005a).

[95] Bower and Gilbert (2005).

[96] Campbell and Park (2005).

[97] Bhide (2000).

[98] McGrath and MacMillan (1995).

[99] Govindarajan and Trimble (2004).

[100] McGrath et al. (2006).

[101] See also McGrath et al. (2006) on the lessons to be distilled from Nokia's recent experiences with ICV.

[102] Chesbrough (2000).

[103] Campbell and Park (2005: 28).

[104] Campbell and Park (2004: 28).

[105] Markides and Geroski (2003a: 3).

[106] Quinn (2000).

INTRODUCING 'STRATEGIC LEADERSHIP, GOVERNANCE AND RENEWAL'
STRATEGY, LEADERSHIP AND THE NEW AGENDA • THE CONTEXT OF
BUSINESS IN SOCIETY • COMPETITIVE ANALYSIS AND VALUE INNOVATION
• STRATEGY AND ORGANISATION IN THE MULTI-BUSINESS FIRM •
STRATEGIC PROCESSES – INNOVATION • STRATEGIC PROCESSES – TRANSFORMATION
AND RENEWAL • SOME FINAL THOUGHTS AND REFLECTIONS

7 strategic processes – transformation and renewal

Introduction

In this, the second of our two chapters on strategic processes, we turn our attention to the strategic process of transformation and renewal. Sooner or later, all organisations come to face the need to reinvent themselves, when the strategic and organisational recipes that brought them their initial success are no longer able to sustain it. If most large companies still find it exceedingly difficult to incubate radically new businesses to help them maintain their dynamism as they grow, most find it even more difficult to renew their core business, when this becomes the pressing need. According to Ari de Geus (1997a: 1), we still have much to learn about how to keep our leading corporations healthy over the longer term: 'Human beings have learned to survive, on average, 75 years or more, but there are very few companies that are that old and flourishing'. What happens when companies go into decline? Why are they often so slow at taking the required action? Why is it so difficult for companies to renew themselves? Why is crisis and new leadership often needed to bring about successful renewal? How do the dynamics of strategic transformation and renewal usually play out and how can the process best be analysed and managed? These are the kinds of questions that will concern us throughout this chapter.

Transformation and renewal are strong terms that have mixed connotations in the literature with some using the terms interchangeably and others identifying the components of each. For example, transformation has been divided into substrategies like regeneration and reinvention

243

while renewal has been underpinned by aspects of organisational learning. The former comprise change strategies that yield short-run impacts on systems and financial results aimed at value chain efficiencies. Normally, transformation goes beyond efficiency gain to focus on effectiveness with multi-level changes in strategy, resources and mental acuity. Renewal is a step further. It involves the fostering of processes that positively avoid mental ossification and senility, promote paradigmatic change, trigger continual innovation and value ambition and direction. This 'second-order' change has been summed up as:

> a process of dissolving an existing organisational order and creating a new one. Order in an organisation refers to the structural and cognitive order, which affects the pattern of ... resource deployment, organisational structure, systems, processes and cultures. There can be no self-renewal without the dissolution and creation of order.[1]

Such transformation and renewal implies a persistent commitment over time to an integration of short-term tactics with long-term change strategies. Grinyer and McKiernan (1990) found that organisations that had negotiated major recovery strategies successfully used two sets of actions. The first contained actions targeted at survival and initial recovery (e.g. cost cutting, product market pruning). Once revived, a second set of actions (e.g. acquisition of new capabilities, new product markets) helped sustain the recovery into the long term. These latter 'renewal' actions embodied organisational learning routines so the memory would not forget, or dare to repeat, the trauma of the past.

This combination of short-term tactics integrated with longer term changes is typified in many of the most prominent renewal stories of the last few decades from the transformations at Harley-Davidson and General Electric in the early 1980s, to the turnarounds at IBM and Nissan in more recent years.[2] Together, the two sets represent the balance between preservation, a control-dominated activity, and progress, a creative and experimental process, that is at the heart of sustainable development. So, we can think about transformation and renewal as sustained change on a grand scale that evokes, and inspires, learning.

Corporate transformation and renewal is a complex, multifaceted strategic management challenge, and we will examine it from two angles,

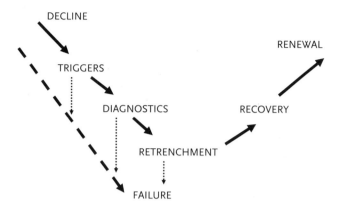

Figure 7.1 **Six stages of organisational decline and renewal.**

which we hope will combine both breadth and depth of perspective. In the early sections to follow, we will highlight the more generic features of this strategic challenge by framing them within a six-stage model of organisational decline and renewal. The six stages involved are: (1) organisational decline; (2) triggers for action; (3) diagnostics; (4) retrenchment; (5) recovery; (6) renewal, and we will analyse the most typical features of each of these stages in turn (see Figure 7.1). Later in the chapter we will focus more closely on the dynamics of the transformation and renewal process and how these typically play out over time in particular cases.

Typical stage-by-stage characteristics

A good starting point in trying to deepen our understanding of the strategic challenge involved in transformation and renewal is to look at its spectral opposite, the process of decline and failure. What happens when an organisation goes into decline?

Stage one: organisational decline

Decline can be viewed as an unintentional contraction of managerial strategic discretion over external and internal factors. This depends on the extent to which an organisation owns, uses and controls the resources at its disposal. These resources can be grouped into physical, human and organisational capital. Discretion varies over each resource and over time. In positive growth phases, executives will have an increasing say in the way things should be. In decline, discretion contracts, as control is lost, first over common elements and then over crucial ones. When control has gone, the organisation is broken up or allowed to die. We can observe the process of decline by examining its symptoms and causes.

Symptoms of decline

Poor performance happens to most organisations. For some, it is a temporary hitch and the strength of their underlying resources and strategy will eventually return them to prosperity. For others, it can represent the early symptoms of a deeper malaise to follow. Some will receive the messages, take action early and probably recover well. Others will hesitate, ignore the symptoms and continue into a downward spiral. The deeper and more severe this spiral becomes, then the more incisive the treatment required. If resources are not strong enough to endure the treatment then failure becomes inevitable. So the longer the symptoms are misread or ignored the greater the probability of ultimate demise.

The symptoms of decline are different from its causes. Because both are numerous and because their complexity increases as the spiral develops, this distinction is not always obvious. Symptoms are a sign or indication of the existence of a problem; they may accompany it and serve as evidence of it. They indicate source problems and should be a good guide to effective treatments. The best analogy is in medicine where high blood pressures and temperatures are symptoms of an illness and accompany it. However, doctors who treat the symptoms alone will not get long lasting results.

Common symptoms of decline are presented in Table 7.1. These are grouped by managerial discretion over the resource category and so signal a potential decrease in discretion over the resources concerned. They are not exhaustive but representative. Note, however, that healthy companies which have strong, counter-balancing growth features can display the same symptoms. A comprehensive diagnostic process will help managers to discriminate between the two.

Symptoms are either public or private. The former relate mainly to financial resources and are easy to measure and observe in the public domain.

Table 7.1 **Symptoms of corporate decline**

Physical	Managerial	Behavioural	Financial
• Old plant & equipment	• Managerial paralysis	• Culture of cynicism & fatalism	• Decreasing: profit, sales, liquidity & dividends etc.
• Problematic access to raw materials	• High turnover of good employees	• Increase in red-tape	• Window dressing of accounting information
• Repeated failure of product launches	• High absenteeism	• Retreat internally	• Increase debts
• Obsolete or hopeless products	• Employees withdraw from communal activities	• Distorted language & existence of taboo words	• Deteriorating gearing, shareholder value
• Lack of investment in new technology	• High levels of managerial stress	• Problems ignored	• Public re-financing
• Worsening terms of trade	• Embarrassing loss of CEO	• Reason for problems blamed on others	• Raising new funds to fund losses
• Major disaster	• Emergency board meetings; board conflict • Lack of leadership • Loss of credibility of senior staff	• Key executives economical with the truth in public • No sense of urgency • Lack of strategy • Declining levels of service • Fear	• Financial restructuring Plans • Breach of banking covenants • Post-acquisition integration poor • Worsening terms of trade • Litigation

Source: Developed from Grinyer, Mayes, McKiernan (1988), Slatter and Lovett (1999) and Neumair (1998)

External stakeholders may only see such symptoms on a selective basis. A cautious management, opaque financial reporting and clever advisors can deliberately obscure the severity of the underlying problems. Cautioned to protect their share price or external credibility, executives craft their explanations with care and deliver them with confidence. This behaviour effectively creates a division between those who know the full story and those who do not. The latter could be both external stakeholders and/or other executives. Even at the most senior level, the dominant managerial coalition may keep key managers out of the information circle for political reasons. Slatter and Lovett (1999) refer to this as the 'reality gap'; the difference between the reported performance and the actual performance.

Private symptoms of decline pertain mainly to the other two resource categories in Table 7.1, 'human' and 'organisational' capital. They are more difficult to measure and are more likely to be part of internal reporting systems thus giving top management some discretion on their dissemination. They will not be easy to identify or confirm by external observers. Moreover, as each organisation has a unique culture, they will tend to be specific. This makes them more difficult for an external observer to generalise from or to compare with indicators from other organisations. There is an irony here, as these difficult-to-measure, externally unobservable symptoms are likely to be more closely related to actual causes of decline than the public symptoms.

Causes of decline

Causes are antecedents that are followed by a certain phenomenon. They may be the root of a problem singly or in multiples and can exacerbate an existing problem. Turnaround research has identified the main popular causes of decline (e.g. poor management, poor financial control). These can be termed secondary causes and distinguished from their underlying primary causes, which are due to dysfunctions in the corporate learning system. The two sets are illustrated in the model depicted in Figure 7.2 below. First, this shows the direction of a good diagnostic process from the trace of observable symptoms to the learning dysfunctions. Second, it shows the causal direction from primary, through secondary causes to the public and private symptoms.

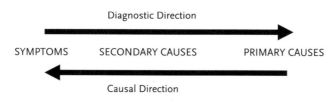

Figure 7.2 **Decline chain factors.**
(*Source:* Developed by the authors from Neumair (1998))

Secondary causes of decline

The majority of secondary causes are internal to the organisation but they occur frequently as multiple causes along with external ones, complicating the diagnosis. Moreover, there is a tendency to see all such causes as the fault of incumbent management. Management is the ultimate arbiter of an organisation's market position and resource base, and accusations of poor decision-making, inaction and inadequate antennae can be levelled easily. But this may just be a convenient reaction. It rarely provides analysts with sufficient data to make a proper diagnosis. If they were to believe it, their instinctive solution would be to replace the existing management team. This runs the risk of throwing out innocent parties who may be needed in any attempted turnaround. Moreover, it could enable the main problem to go unnoticed elsewhere.

The main secondary causes of decline are outlined in Table 7.2. They are broken down into Financial, Demand and Managerial. Some of the elements listed could be incorporated into others, for example, excess plant capacity and R&D overspend into high cost structure.

Primary causes of decline

Organisational learning plays a central role in distinguishing failing from surviving companies and underpins superior performance. The level of organisational knowledge shapes the way that companies perform. This knowledge may have been accumulated through years of learning in the sector and, more broadly, influences the behaviour of the top management team. It can focus it in a certain direction:

> a relatively permanent change in behaviour that results from reinforced practice or experience.[3]

Table 7.2 **Main secondary causes of decline**

Financial	Demand	Managerial
• Poor financial control	• Adverse shifts in commodity prices	• Poor management
• Acquisitions	• Changes in market demand	• Management unresponsive to change
• Poor financial policy	• Increased competition	• Management problems
• Big projects fail	• Marketing problems	• Poor strategy formulation
• Overtrading	• Depressed prices	• Poor strategy implementation
• Poor accounting information	• Recessions	• Strategic oscillation
• Poor gearing	• Aggressive market share building	• Strike activity
• High cost structure	• Import penetration	
• Excess plant capacity	• Technological innovation	
• R&D overspend	• Bad luck	
• Poor working capital management	• Government policy	

Source: Grinyer, Mayes, McKiernan (1988), Slatter and Lovett (1999), Argenti (1976), Pearce & Robbins (1994)

Primary causes of decline are the result of defects in the corporate learning process. Learning becomes important when conditions begin to change. Hence, companies with good learning routines will be expected to survive, and some to prosper. Companies with defective routines are more likely to drift down the spiral of decline. The reasons will be different for each and are likely to interact in powerful combinations. The main ones are:

- *The rigidity of mindsets*

Past experiences can lead management to encode learning into powerful routines that then influence future behaviour patterns. Belief systems evolve slowly over time[4] and, once formed, can be changed only by strong external pressures (e.g. failure of a main market) or by the autocratic directions of a new CEO. These strong paradigms can turn organisations into closed systems that store their learning about the world in a system of 'rules and routines'. Such a view can represent the construction of the 'only possible world':

> The whole transaction has a tendency to become self-fulfilling. [...] The particular is made general and becomes accepted to the extent that the access to the totality of the larger world, in the shape of possible alternative views, is blocked. Perspectives tend to become ossified.[5]

Parameters of the world that do not fit are ignored, so environmental adaptation is severely limited. As the mindset becomes more rigid, learning can become an obsolete activity thereby preparing the organisation for ossification.

- *The inadequacies of youth*

Many companies fail young. Stinchcombe (1965) offers four reasons for this 'liability of newness'. First, a new business, whose capacity is limited, has to learn much from its environment to configure its learning routines successfully. Second, new businesses must develop trusting relationships among strangers in its competitive domain to survive. The learning capacity of the firm will be influenced by the template formed by the particular characteristics and ideologies of the founding entrepreneur and by environmental factors and cultural norms dominant at the time, e.g. location, technology. Neumair (1998) has referred to these as 'congenital defects' that are imprinted permanently on the learning routines from the start. The organisation can easily 'lock-in' to a faulty recipe unknowingly at an early stage in its life. Third, necessary professional protocols often lag behind the non-routine, emergent thrusts of the entrepreneur. Gaps can be narrowed only by the careful application of reliable planning and control frameworks but this takes up valuable time. Fourth, time is also needed to form strong stakeholder networks in its immediate environment. Such pressures can make managers jump between activities in a random manner, paying scant attention to each, so leading to flawed routines.

- *The overconfidence of middle age*

Middle-aged companies can suffer from two distinct but associated problems. First, success breeds confidence and this reinforces existing routines as the best way of doing things. These 'super routines' become organisationally legalised and can lock a firm into a predictable direction of development. However, they remain susceptible to sudden environmental impacts that demand new routines. Miller (1990) has called this the Icarus Paradox, where the seeds of destruction lie in past recipes for success. Existing assets are locked in and any search for new rules will be within the already strong paradigm of the dominant coalition, so aggravating the position. Managerial discretion wanes and if the company does not unlearn, it will eventually fail.

Second, corporate development can follow a process of punctuated equilibrium where a period of relative stability is followed by one of dysfunctional change. During stability, rules and routines are developed and reinforced in an incremental way. During revolutionary times, the existing framework is broken and strategy, structure, power and control change discontinuously. The phase of stability produces a consistency of rules and routines through minor adjustment (e.g. Kaizen). With this process, a whole rule and routine set can converge over time to a much-reduced set based upon what works best. Such fine-tuning can have disastrous consequences. For example, in the run up to the Challenger disaster in 1986, NASA had rendered their supplier system so cost efficient that parts were reduced in size and weight continuously, including the O-rings in the solid rocket booster that caused Challenger to disintegrate:

> Success breeds confidence and fantasy ... managers usually attribute success to themselves and not to luck ... (they) grow more confident of their own abilities ... and skills, and of their organisation's existing programmes and procedures. The most important lesson to learn from the Challenger disaster is not that some managers made the wrong decisions or that some engineers did not understand adequately how O-rings worked; the most important lesson is that fine tuning makes failures likely.[6]

This convergence process can be accompanied by groupthink where managerial thinking goes unchallenged[7] as managers reinforce each other's prejudices, emphasise the positives, play down criticism and engage in hubris, a dangerous managerial cocktail that seduces them to take on big projects with which the system is not capable of coping, as evident, for example, in cases like Enron and Vivendi.

- *The docility of old age*

Companies fail due to lethargic inactivity related to environmental myopia and processing inertia. The former occurs when the organisation fails to see the soft signals of threats and opportunities through poor scanning systems that view the world selectively. This can be compounded by older executives who often choose risk-averse behaviour so investments

7

INTRODUCING 'STRATEGIC LEADERSHIP, GOVERNANCE AND RENEWAL' • STRATEGY, LEADERSHIP AND THE NEW AGENDA • THE CONTEXT OF BUSINESS IN SOCIETY • COMPETITIVE ANALYSIS AND VALUE INNOVATION •

in new products and processes fail to materialise. The latter occurs when signals have been detected and action demanded but the existing set of routines is so cumbersome as to delay the effectiveness of the action.

Hence, primary causes of decline can be seen as problems associated with the organisation's learning routines. What distinguishes surviving from failing companies is the ability to process signals profitably, i.e. the ability to continuously learn. We return to this issue in the final stage of turnaround-renewal.

Stage two: triggers for action

In decline, powerful routines that control behaviour can prevent early action taking place. Such inertia contributes to crisis:

> " What we loosely term fact consists of powerful forces that obscure management's ability to discern looming threats and so to implement needed changes. These inertial forces derive from crystallized features of firms and the business communities in which they operate.[8]

When crisis looms, managers naturally hold onto what is familiar. Their existing routines act as a comfort zone, artificially and temporarily protecting them from change.

Triggers

To achieve change against a strongly held belief system frequently requires significant external or internal jolts. Externally, outside stakeholders can exert influential pressure. Internally, we argue that change is triggered in companies because actual or anticipated performance falls below a level that is regarded as acceptable. In declining companies, managers adjust their expectations of what constitutes acceptable performance downward, thus postponing the point at which they decide to take action. So, counter to much of the turnaround literature, companies do not take action automatically during decline. Something happens that triggers the action. This triggering could be because the continuous decline in actual or relative performance passes through or falls significantly below an existing level of aspiration. This is illustrated in Figure 7.3[9], below.

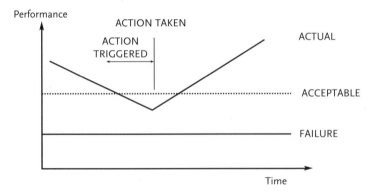

Figure 7.3 **Triggering action.**

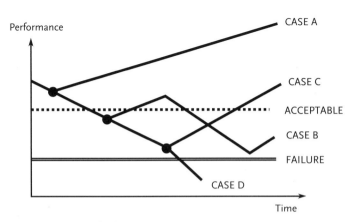

Figure 7.4 **Responses to decline.**

This aspiration level is an acceptable level of performance influenced by members of the dominant coalition, the performances of peer organisations or the perceptions of external stakeholders, such as the investment analysts of financial institutions.

The aspiration level can have a strong psychological effect. Companies respond to its presence differently so it is important to see turnaround as unique to each organisation and not as a generic process. We illustrate such responses in Figure 7.4.[10]

For the organisations in Case A (we can call them *Visionaries*), the very threat of approaching the aspiration level is enough to trigger recovery action. These tend to be smaller companies, who can take quick decisions, especially in the reorientation of their product markets. Where inertia is stronger in Case B organisations (we can call them *Laggards*), these have to pass through their aspiration level and lie below it before action is triggered. These companies have slower decision-making and poorer information systems that mean a delayed reaction to current predicaments. They usually suffer major declines in primary markets, hence cost cutting and rationalisation strategies are used to engineer recovery. Both Visionaries and Laggards have internal management teams who see the need to change. Where very strong inertia is present in Case C organisations (we can call them *Sleepers*), these may have to lie significantly below the aspiration level before action is taken. Here, management can pass through a period of denial of the problem, to blaming it on other sources (such as cheap imports), to window dressing the evidence (like the accounting information), to witnessing the departure of many good managers whose morale and active standpoint had reached frustration levels and who, ironically, would normally be crucial to any successful recovery, to the final intervention of external agencies like the banks who no longer see any future in prolonging the ineffectiveness of the existing senior management team. Organisations at this late stage tend to be faced with very sharp declines in performance. Unfortunately, high exit barriers typically prevent immediate divestment and high levels of industry concentration tend to induce competitor infighting for market share as the industry contracts. *Sleepers* face multiple and major structural problems, to a much greater degree than the visionaries or laggards, and adopt multiple solutions to match, such as retrenchment, closure, heavy cost cutting. Their trigger is the threat of extinction, often greatly amplified by the presence of predators.

Finally, in Case D organisations (we can call them *Dodos*), the inertia is so great that no amount of triggering can correct the imbalances in product markets or internal processes and here, performance falls so far below a break-even level, as indicated by the Failure line, that recovery is impossible.

Managerial behaviour in decline

Much of the literature on organisational decision-making and adaptation stems from the classic work by Cyert and March (1963) that emphasises the behavioural and cognitive approaches of managers. Their original model can be incorporated into a sequential search process with higher-level learning rules. In the process of decline, organisations are faced with a search for solutions, once signals have been spotted and action deemed necessary. First, the search for solutions is sought at the operating level via cost cutting, moves to the administrative level via tighter controls and then to the strategic level via product market changes. This widening search process accords with the natural inclinations of managers to stay within their normal operating patterns, beliefs and rules (templates) as long as possible. *Visionaries* have the space and time to enact a full sequence of searches until an adequate solution is found. *Laggards* jump quickly to cost cutting and tighter controls and then may proceed to strategic switching within the same Operations, Beliefs and Rules (OBRs). *Sleepers*, however, decline to a more dangerous point whereby their recovery is not possible within the current template. This template has to be dismantled by either external intervention (usually involving the replacement of the CEO, MD and some functional directors who preach within the existing template) or by an internal reorganisation.

Within each type, an individual's response to crisis varies. Stress rises in each case as performance fails. At first, some stress is good; it heightens the senses and can galvanise managers into creative thought and action. However, as the stress mounts beyond a certain point, anxiety can set in with its own deleterious effect on performance. Research[11] suggests crisis is characterised by information overload and selective information searches, a focus on short-term operations rather than longer-term strategy, a tendency towards autocratic management, fragmented decision-making, an impaired judgement, a focus on simple rather than complex solutions and the collapse of formal structures. Managers alter their behaviour, or have their behaviour altered by, crises. It is not always easy to predict how individuals might respond in any particular situation, unless some pre-planning has been rehearsed that involves collective sense making, grounded in communication and trust. But, this has to be built up over a considerable period of time. The actions that will determine the success of later action occur long before decisions need to be made. Starkey (2000), appraising the work of Weick (1996), points out:

> " Successful decisions ... depend upon the presence of adequate sense-making processes that can be activated appropriately. It is essential that this sense-making preparation takes place and that what is learnt is resilient under later pressure.
> (p. 15)

Unfortunately, the corporate world lags behind the military and the emergency services in taking time out for such preparation.

Stage three: diagnostics

Action has to be triggered in declining companies due to different degrees of inertia. The first action triggered should be a careful diagnostic routine that explores the complex relationship between symptoms, secondary causes and primary causes of decline. Symptoms present problems for the diagnostic process because of manipulative window-dressing practices, especially when trouble may be brewing. Secondary causes present corporate doctors with a quandary because of the complicated interaction between symptoms and causes, and the isolation of the key problem(s) from the complex interplay between the causal variables is often quite a challenge. The direction of cause and effect between them is not always obvious:

> One might identify intense price competition ... as a causal factor of decline ... but is this the real cause or is it the firm's inferior cost position relative to its competitors that is the cause? If this is the cause, is it due to lack of market share, or to the firm's conservative financial policy of not investing in modern plant and equipment, or to both? If financial policy is to blame, what causes management to adopt such a policy? ... . In practice, a chain of inter-related causal factors and multiple causes can be identified in most situations.[12]

Clearly, a sound environmental scanning system (such as scenario planning), and management information and control systems (like a 'balanced scorecard'), will guide a good diagnostic procedure. But turnaround executives could learn much from their medical colleagues who emphasise the avoidance of hasty decisions, the adoption of multiple perspectives and broad information searches, the consideration of ambiguous symptoms and the generation of multiple hypotheses. Clearly such principles will be tailored to the particular situation as they guide internal teams towards a better diagnosis early so that the real secondary causes can get the treatment they need before crisis occurs. A simple framework may bring some reduction of stress and anxiety to the process and so help ensure a considered response.

Stage four: retrenchment

As witnessed in the Sleepers case, companies have a natural tendency to retreat to what they know best when crisis hits. Autocratic management, tighter control, cost cutting, rationalisation and other retrenchment policies seem to be automatic first options for organisations in travail. At root, such strategic change is central to any turnaround process, especially if the sector is growing and organisational decline is steep. However, change is notoriously difficult to achieve, especially if there is a new CEO and the organisation is large, highly diversified and has little financial slack. The trick is to treat each situation with a customised rather than a generic toolkit, paying attention to perceptions of externalities and internal cultural dimensions, before leaping into retrenchment wholeheartedly. Typical retrenchment strategies are depicted in Table 7.3.

Despite the powerful forces constraining strategic change in the routines of the business, logic alone dictates that troubled companies should look to survival and the achievement of a positive cash flow. Once safety is reached, management decides how to progress[13] either through a slimmed down form of some version of their previous strategy (efficiency response) or the pursuance of growth and development with a new strategy (entrepreneurial response). This process suggests the notion of stages in turnaround action with retrenchment preceding any consideration of strategic reorientation.

Robbins and Pearce, (1992)[14] suggest that retrenchment is strongly related to turnaround success, that cost tactics are mandatory but both cost and asset rationalisations are used as the decline gets steeper, that external sources of decline lead to entrepreneurial response and that internal sources lead to efficiency responses. Small firms, too, respond as dramatically to downturns with retrenchment as large ones,[15] but they make more strategic responses and have an equal liking for entrepreneurial and efficiency responses, with the latter showing greater returns.

Despite laying the seeds of recovery, retrenchment has been accused of sapping employee morale through too much cost rationalisation causing some with special skills (e.g. marketing) to leave and others to resist. Moreover, some organisations in retrenchment (usually smaller, with low liquidity or with new CEOs) tend to alter structures from organic to mechanistic increasing their rigidity and restricting innovative and entrepreneurial recovery responses.[16] Hence retrenchment, though a key stage in the turnaround process, is not without its pitfalls.

Table 7.3 **Retrenchment strategies**

Strategy	Types of action	Suitable conditions
RETRENCHMENT		
• Cost reduction	• Reduce expenses	• Internal causes
	• Stronger financial controls	• Rigid templates
	• Intensive efforts to reduce production costs	• Sales 60–80% of break-even
		• Late stage of decline
• Asset redeployment	• Sell assets	• Overexpansion/low capacity use
	• Shutdown or relocate units	
	• Debt reduction	• Sales 30–60% of break-even
	• Rights issues	• Rapid technological change
		• Entry of new competitors
		• Decline steep
		• Late stage of decline
		• Cost reduction not enough

Source: adapted from Slatter (1984), Grinyer, Mayes and McKiernan (1988) and Hoffman (1989)

Stage five: recovery

Recovery follows a successful retrenchment by way of an efficiency or an entrepreneurial pathway. Typical recovery strategies are depicted in Table 7.4. The former is important when the main secondary causes of decline are internal and usually consists of liquidation, divestment, product elimination and labour rationalisation. The latter is important when the main causes of decline are external and usually consist of market penetration, segmentation, entry to new markets, acquisitions and new product development. The choice depends on two drivers. First, change is governed by the rigidity of the existing template. The evidence suggests that dramatic change away from a dominant template is rare. Hence many recovery routes, governed by the old ways, are minor adaptations on what is already known. Any larger strategic response tends to be internal efficiency gains around the core business. Hence, the recovery strategies of many organisations are within their existing belief and rule systems rather than determined by a fundamental change in ideology. Entrepreneurial recovery strategies are rare and may be delayed by the enduring presence of strong templates. When they do occur, it is usually through acquisition or a change in CEO. Acquisitions bring new frameworks from outside and allow the current template to exist in a much reduced form within a division of the organisation, helping to pacify powerful stakeholders and to facilitate change through longer-term coalescence. New CEOs are associated with a complete abolition of the old templates, as incumbent managers exit and new ones enter. They make entrepreneurial approaches more likely.

Second, recovery strategies are influenced by several contingent factors. For instance, the steep declines will sap financial resources and limit the amount of enterprise that occurs; powerful stakeholders (e.g. banks, major creditors) will dictate policy to their own ends; the growth or decline in general sector trading conditions can dictate enterprise or efficiency; the number and type of causes of decline will dictate the number and type of strategy responses. Again, each recovery situation is different and its solution demands customisation. But there are two elements that are common to the design, the restructuring of both leadership and management and the quirky issue of 'windfall gains'.

Leadership is one of the critical elements of recovery. Not all turnarounds require a new CEO, but fresh CEOs bring new vision, energy and ways of doing things. Symbolically, they signal an unfreezing of the old templates internally and a renewed stakeholder confidence externally. The CEO's style is significant.

Leadership traits differ at different stages of the business cycle and it is common to witness a more autocratic style during crisis and recovery, as the conditions require direct control, short lines of command and clear vision. Appropriate abilities include strong motivational and communication skills, flexibility, excellent diagnostics and analysis, hard work and timely action.

Recovery situations require CEOs to be 'hard and soft' at the same time. Hard, because change will be resisted and unpopular decisions will have to be made, such as labour rationalisation. Soft because staff that remain need to be motivated and encouraged to play a part in a recovery effort. This is frequently when they are at their lowest ebb, having endured cutbacks under previous leadership regimes for months as the firm declined. Such CEOs are rare. Research[17] shows how the chances of obtaining a successful turnaround are greater when the CEO also chairs the Board, so increasing power to a virtual monopoly. Clearly, a time will come when staff grow tired of this style, of its lack of inclusiveness and the rule of fear. In addition, CEOs with such styles have a sell-by date. They tend to lose interest when the organisation is safe and trading conditions

Table 7.4 **Recovery strategies**

Strategy	Types of action	Suitable conditions
RECOVERY		
• Selective Product-market	DEFENSIVE	
	• Decrease marketing efforts	• Overexpansion
	• Divest products	• High capacity use
	OFFENSIVE	
	• Increase marketing efforts	• External causes
	• Increase prices	• Operating & strategic
	• Improve quality/service	weaknesses
	• Invest in new technology	• Early stage of decline
• Repositioning	DEFENSIVE	
	• Niche	• Overexpansion
	• Market penetration	• Improved short-run profits
	• Decrease price	• External causes
	• Divest products	• Rigid OBRs
	OFFENSIVE	
	• Diversification into new	• Major decline in market share
	products	• External causes face non-diversified firms

Source: adapted from Slatter (1984), Grinyer, Mayes and McKiernan (1988) and Hoffman (1989)

prosper. As necessary control systems lag behind market enterprise, the pressure for change increases. A return to a more democratic style during a subsequent renewal phase is likely.

With or without a change in CEO, organisations can benefit from broader thinking among senior management. If it is necessary to break the rigidity of the old template, some members of the dominant coalition will need to be replaced, often in areas like marketing and finance. A new team at the top with a committed, positive 'bias for action' and one that stimulates innovative behaviour will boost staff and stakeholder confidence. If no breaking of the template is necessary, then internal management teams have to show a considerable and sustained bias for action to overcome natural accusations of inaction during the early decline phases. Such approaches mean credible changes in practice, styles and systems.

Windfall gains can be defined as independent, external changes in circumstances that help boost the recovery actions. The main windfalls are cyclical upturns in demand, government action, exit of competitors, favourable exchange rate movements and pure luck. These events can significantly alter the revenue–cost equation and help stimulate recovery.

As most of them tend to have a general impact across all organisations in the sector, they cannot alone lead to recovery. But they can help by easing the pressure on the financing of the recovery efforts. However, some are down to good fortune, such as, for example, the fortuitous historical location of plant in an area later earmarked for new industrial development. The trick to understanding luck is the new positive posture that the recovery team adopts. Luck occurs often but is frequently not taken advantage of by the existing management team due to its diminished perception resulting from templates that are too rigid or from stress in crisis situations. A new team, with new perceptions, can turn yesterday's ignored opportunities into tomorrow's successful projects.

Stage six: renewal

The recovery phase does not contain a one-off set of measures that guarantee improved performance indefinitely. Further measures have to be taken continuously through the medium of a new 'learning culture' that will invigorate and renew the organisation's strategic posture.

Continuing characteristics involve careful harnessing of the functional competencies of the organisation by a management team that carries its action-orientated style and energy across from the renewal phase. The team will balance the building of strong, inner corporate values with market acuity, staying close to customers. It acts through a slim head office and a shallow organisation structure with decentralised power. Direction and operations are conducted through systematic strategic management with comprehensive information scanning and systems. Active product portfolio balance is achieved through a wide search for opportunities, an investment in growth markets where the organisation is competitively strong, the maintenance of entry barriers in core markets and active divestments. Strong marketing practice is a necessary accompaniment supported by tight financial control and the continuous attention to quality across the value chain activities.

The painstaking development of a learning culture takes the organisation to new levels. Learning draws upon experience, memories and past actions. This knowledge is then processed by individuals or groups and compared with current action through a feedback mechanism. If the feedback is positive and the stimuli strong enough, it may then transfer into a modification of current templates that govern behaviour. However, as environments become more dynamic and complex, the need for continuous learning necessitates acceleration in the change of organisational routines to ensure successful adaptation.

Organisational learning

Recent work in open systems theory, cybernetics and complexity science explains the process of organisational learning by viewing organisations as self-organising systems, characterised by:

> the ability to continuously renew and recycle their components, while maintaining the integrity of their overall structure and [...] to reach out creatively beyond physical and mental boundaries in the processes of learning, development and evolution.[18]

Any change in external or internal conditions can be addressed within the system's vast range of possible configurations. Their inherent mechanisms help prevent many of the primary causes of decline. Agents within the system learn to anticipate some of the results of their actions over time through a set of decision rules that form the organisation's memory bank.[19] The organisation learns through:

- *Exploitation:* This involves the development of existing, strong rules, at the expense of those that do not work well. It includes benchmarking, flexibility in the harmony between strategy and structure, enhancement of radical innovation through loose-coupling, importation of new learning routines from alliances and acquisitions, adoption of efficiency gaining techniques, such as Business Process Reengineering (BPR), quality enhancement via zero-defects policies and achievement of faster times to market.
- *Exploration:* This involves the search for new rules to improve existing ones through refinement, scanning and continuous improvement. It includes scenario planning, the challenging of existing rules through creative tension, new visions and the institutionalisation of doubt, the embracing of risk, uncertainty and conflict, experimentation and the design of control systems to maximise the acquisition of knowledge.
- *Mutation:* A random mutation element operates that can change or modify rules independently of the normal routines. It is present to 'think the unthinkable' and to avoid ossification. It includes learning from a

continuous flow of new blood, ensuring that Boards are creative and challenging, and the instigating of 'skunk works'.

Clearly, an organisation that solely relied on exploitation for rule development would be closed from new rules and eventually converge on the best of what it already had. A reliance solely on exploration would yield too many rules for the classifier system to test and implement. The system would become unstable. Any system with low rates of mutation tends to conservatism, while one where the rates are too high could tend towards chaos. A balance is sought between the learning elements.

Such rule-based decision-making is consistent with much of the traditional organisational learning literature:

> " By rules we mean the routines, procedures, conventions, roles, strategies, organisational forms and technologies around which political activity is structured. We also mean the beliefs, paradigms, codes, cultures, and knowledge that surround, support, elaborate, and contradict those roles and routines.[20]

Because organisational cultures are different, each rule set is unique, as is the learning process and routines associated with it:

> " It is the routines themselves, and the ability of management to call upon the organisation to perform them, that represents the firms' business capability ... because routines involve a strong tacit dimension, they may not be easy to imitate. To the extent that this is so, routines contribute to a firm's distinctive competencies and capabilities.[21]

Learning to learn

Such classifier learning mechanisms mean that organisations have to maintain a balance among the individual elements (exploitation, exploration and mutation) and constantly maintain and develop the routines within each. Practically, this translates into the careful design of the planning and control systems. This is what De Geus (1988: 70) was talking about when he referred to 'planning as learning' and 'corporate planning as institutional learning'. Corporate learning should be a natural process, one given the same time, attention and investment as any other process in the business. It should become endemic in the culture. It should be the biggest investment.

The process dynamics of transformation and renewal

Before concluding our examination of transformation and renewal strategies, we turn to focus more closely on the dynamics of process. As we have seen, strategic renewal is ultimately a process of deep learning and cultural transformation. It requires insight not only into what kind of strategic change will be required and the typical stages involved but also requires process insight into how to manage the dynamics of change successfully.

Incremental and punctuated models of the change process

One of the most influential process models of strategic change to date is James Brian Quinn's (1980, 1982) model of logical incrementalism. Quinn developed his model to deal with two major issues that beset the early efforts of formal strategic planning to sustain an optimum fit between any organisation and its changing environment over time. The first is the finite information processing capabilities of individuals and organisations or the 'bounds to rationality'[22] that tend to constrain firms and lead them to adapting to their environments, as they perceive them, always with some degree of time-lag and lack of precision.[23] The second is the inherently political nature of all major change processes in organisations of any size and complexity. Quinn envisioned the skilful management of strategic change as an incremental 'continuous, evolving, political, consensus-building process with neither finite beginning nor end',[24] and offered the principle of logical incrementalism as a 'purposeful, powerful management technique for integrating the analytical, behavioural, political and timing aspects of strategy formulation' (p. 614).

However, few companies to date have ever managed to come close to the ideal of the continuously adaptive organisation in spite of the early hopes invested in formal corporate planning and logical incrementalism as models of process. As Miller and Friesen (1980: 591) have noted, 'the one theme that stands out in the literature is that organizations tend to demonstrate great sluggishness in adapting', even 'when their environments threaten them with extinction'. Since the early 1980s much of mainstream thinking has shifted towards a more punctuated perspective in which the process of organisational renewal is characterised by long phases of evolutionary change interspersed with short, sharp bursts of more revolutionary and disruptive transformation.[25] Such a punctuated perspective on the process of renewal in both nature and in human affairs enjoys strong support in many fields of study,[26] including the biological sciences,[27] economic development,[28] philosophy,[29] psychology,[30] history[31] and anthropology.[32]

The punctuated perspective is pervasive in any social system, including complex organisations, because of the many strong conservative tendencies operating within these systems at psychological, political and institutional levels, and the necessity for any process of strategic renewal to eventually confront and overcome them. These forces are not just the manifestations of bureaucratic rigidity and inertia. More often, they are the outgrowth of a once successful strategy and its overadaptation to passing circumstances, and too often they remain active long after they have lost their relevance and functionality. The organisation gets locked into a particular strategic mindset, political balance and set of attitudes and behaviours that become increasingly aligned with the requirements of an existing strategy, and eventually difficult to realign when circumstances require a new one. Within the strategy field, some tend to see this cyclical pattern in terms of fit and functionality while others see it as a historical pattern.

Tushman et al. (1986: 39) see the long evolutionary periods of alignment and convergence as 'profoundly functional', allowing a company to 'build on strengths' and finesse them through continuous incremental improvements and consolidations, and suggest that premature attempts at frame-breaking change can be 'quite dysfunctional' while the organisation remains successful. When such changes do become necessary, as a result of industry discontinuities or product life cycle shifts, 'the more rapidly they are implemented, the more quickly the organization can reap the benefits of the following convergent period'. In a similar vein, Miller (1982: 132) has argued that 'the functional aspects of resistance to change' have been generally ignored in organisational studies, and the desirability of piecemeal and incremental change overemphasised.

For him, the ideal fit among strategy, structure and environment could be seen to involve a consistent configuration, a belief reflected in the 7-S framework developed by McKinsey and popularised by Pascale and Athos (1981) and Peters and Waterman (1982). The advantages of such a configuration, according to Miller (1996: 510), include synergy, clarity of direction, difficulty of imitation, distinctive competence, commitment, speed and economy, and, as he sees it, configuration is 'likely to be a far greater source of competitive advantage than any single aspect of strategy'.[33] So while within-configuration adjustments are easily accommodated, between-configuration transitions will tend to be systemically resisted for sound functionality and fit reasons until the case for change becomes almost overwhelming.

While Tushman et al. (1986) and Miller (1982, 1986, 1996) tend to emphasise the potential functionality of the punctuated pattern of strategic renewal, others like Pettigrew (1985, 1987) and Johnson (1988, 1990) have tended to focus more on the political, cultural and historical nature of the process in their explanations for why the punctuated pattern persists. According to Johnson (1988), a strategy of logical incrementalism often fails to keep pace with the rate of environmental change, because of the political and cultural consolidation associated with a stable organisational paradigm. This eventually leads to significant 'strategic drift', which eventually necessitates a burst of radical readjustment to bring the organisation and its environment back into alignment. In this perspective, the pattern is not so much seen as functional, more as just historically inevitable.

Process dynamics[34]

Given that there are always strong forces for continuity in organisations, how do major transformations come about? What are the main dynamics of the process? One of the most popular perspectives is the classic Lewin (1951) 'unfreeze-change-refreeze' model. Many of the later models of process are variations on this multi-phase view.[35] Some stress the importance of 'unlearning', double-loop learning, and the renewal of shared mental models, in radical organisational change.[36] Others see the revolutionary change process mainly in terms of fundamental revisions in organisational ideologies or archetypes.[37] Most see the process of transformation involving destruction and reconstruction.[38] The entire process typically takes time, and represents a period of uncertainty, dissonance, heightened political tension and general organisational discomfort. How do such processes start, how do they play out, how can they be managed strategically?

There are as yet few definitive models beyond the basic unfreeze–change–refreeze framework, and different authors tend to focus on different aspects of the process. However, certain themes recur. Most agree on the emergent/learning nature of the process, and on the importance of momentum, critical mass, leadership and crisis as key elements in the determination of the direction, pace and ultimate success of the renewal process. To overcome the forces for continuity, a momentum for change must be developed. Momentum building often involves political and cultural action, not just logical persuasion, because of the multiple rationalities and special interests typically operating across hierarchical and functional boundaries in most organisations. As Pettigrew (1987: 659) aptly depicted it, transformation is 'ultimately a product of a legitimation process shaped by political/cultural considerations, though often expressed in rational/analytical terms'. If the transformation is to be ultimately successful, this momentum must eventually be brought to a critical mass, or 'tipping point',[39] beyond which a self-sustaining dynamic can begin to take hold.

Few have difficulty with the foregoing as an overall outline of the dynamics of process. Where views still tend to differ are on questions like: where does the initial momentum come from, and how does it typically build up? What role does an experimental/learning approach play? Can such a process be deliberately managed, and if so how? How important a stimulus is crisis and/or a change of leadership to the success of the transformation?

The emergent nature of the process

The seeds of transformation are often sown within organisations long before the process becomes highly visible and deliberately managed. This emergent nature has been a common feature of some of the most documented transformation processes over the last few decades, including those at Cadbury, ICI, Ford and IBM. At Cadbury the process 'passed through several stages', with no clear beginning or end,[40] while the transformation at Ford, which many contemporary observers described as 'the comeback of the 1980s', was seen to involve 'a confluence of initiatives undertaken at every level of the organization' without a definitive 'master plan'.[41] Nor was there a master plan involved in the case of ICI.[42] 'Innovation in emerging strategies' was seen as 'critical' to successful rejuvenation in the cases studied by Stopford and Baden-Fuller (1990: 399), as it also proved to be in the case of IBM.[43] As Kanter (1991: 8–9) put it, 'organizations seeking total transformation cannot avoid the messy, mistake-ridden muddling stage', and retrospective accounts often neglect to describe just 'how much trial and error was involved'. Some have argued that in many ways the process of transformation and renewal can be seen most usefully as an innovation process, and managed accordingly,[44] understanding that the old formula is no longer working, and that the new formula is unlikely to pop out fully formed. The key innovators are often those in the middle of the organisation, with much less vested in the status quo than many in the highest echelons.[45]

The reasons why such processes often tend to be more emergent than deliberate are partly cognitive, partly political and partly cultural. Even where visions for change were developed, they often remained necessarily vague and ambiguous in the early stages of transformation, and only became more fully developed, and widely accepted, after extended phases of experimentation and legitimisation.[46] As Child and Smith (1987: 590) have put it, the 'wide acceptance and cohesion' provided by 'the traditional and hitherto dominant ideology' often 'provided a clear position against which the case for change had to be developed'. For example, at Ford, during the Petersen–Poling era of the early to mid-1980s, successful transformation required the erosion of the traditional finance-dominated mindset and functional parochialism, before significant renewal could become a real possibility, while at AT&T, following deregulation, the traditional inward-looking engineering mindset had to be replaced with a more market-oriented ideology, and the organisation had to be convinced that 'Mother Bell' did not live here anymore.[47] Similar mindset changes were essential to successful renewal at both IBM and Nissan.[48]

Managing the process – building momentum

The strategic management of transformation often requires the 'patience' to persevere with the difficult 'conditioning' process of challenging the ideology that was 'nurtured' in an earlier era.[49] It requires the subtle ability to do this while recognising that renewal must be ultimately brought about through metamorphosis of the old ideology rather than through its total destruction, a challenge aptly captured by Carlos Ghosn (2002: 37), the architect of Nissan's recent transformation, as one of 'saving the business without losing the company'. The leadership of transformation demands an intellectual and intuitive understanding of the existing configuration among dominant mindsets, power balance, cultural norms and organisational routines that form the essence of any internally consistent paradigm or archetype.[50] Successful renewal also requires leadership with the courage to pursue bold new strategic initiatives, while trying to stimulate and harness emergent energies and opportunities.[51] For example, the willingness of the Petersen–Poling leadership to invest in the highly innovative, 'bet-the-company' Taurus project at Ford Motor Company during the 1980s, when the traditional ideology was pointing strongly to retrenchment, was a critical element in the success of the transformation process at the time. So was the willingness of Lou Gerstner to bet the future of IBM on remaining a unified enterprise and reversing the strategy already in place to break the company up into several 'mini-Blues'. The same kind of courage was also shown by Carlos Ghosn in his determination to make the reincarnation of the Z-car the signature of company renaissance during the Nissan revival of the late 1990s, and to invest in his conviction that 'there is no problem at a car company that good products can't solve', by pouring millions into new products and production facilities, while the company continued to struggle with massive debt obligations.[52]

In many, if not most cases it is not necessary for the leaders of transformation to instigate the key projects on which the strategy for renewal will be incubated and ultimately come to full fruition. A case in point was the initiative by the technical team to stake out a new architecture for the System/390 at IBM in advance of Lou Gerstner's arrival on the scene, which was soon to become a centrepiece of the renewal strategy at the company. As IBM's transformational leader later recalled: 'I have always been thankful (and lucky) that some insightful people had made that decision before I'd arrived. My job was to simply reaffirm it and to protect the billion dollars we would spend on it over the next four years'.[53] Other insightful people at IBM also helped to persuade him of the potential opportunities in the services area, and later on in e-business, in the overall effort to restore the company to industry leadership, not just commercial viability.[54] Autonomous initiatives of various kinds tend to arise in most organisations as part of ongoing activity. Skilled leadership of transformation often involves, among other things, the ability to identify and nurture those initiatives with renewal potential, which can help to subvert the old ideology and open the organisation up further to the potential and possibility of change. This was certainly the case with both the services and the network initiatives at IBM, where top-down imposition of change alone would not have been sufficient, and might even have been counterproductive.[55] It can also involve highly dramatic and symbolic acts, like the 1.5B Yen recall of the old product line at Asahi breweries, the 900-mile, four-day, mass 'Freedom Ride' at Harley Davidson or the relocation of headquarters at companies like AT&T, Oticon and IBM, all designed to impress the world, both inside and outside, that a new era was dawning.

As with reforming movements more generally, the renewal process in organisations can often be characterised as a contest between relatively small numbers of reforming activists on the one side and conservative activists on the other for the hearts and minds of the uncommitted majority. Once the forces for change reach critical breakthrough, the process tends to develop its own self-sustaining dynamic. This is the point at which the uncommitted, even those still not fully convinced of the merits of the new direction, finally accept its inevitability and no longer want to risk being left behind. Kim and Mauborgne (2003: 62) see the dynamic at work in terms of tipping point theory, which 'hinges on the insight that in any organization, once the beliefs and energies of a critical mass of people are engaged', and the initial cognitive, political, resource and motivational hurdles have been sufficiently overcome, support for a new direction or strategy can often 'spread like an epidemic, bringing about fundamental change very quickly'. A key challenge within this view of process is building the movement for change to critical mass or tipping point level.

Typically, most of the activists needed to get the movement for change underway already exist within the organisation, no matter how inert or stuck-in-the-past the situation might appear to be. As Gary Hamel (1996) has pointed out, there are revolutionaries in every company, even those that are successful, and a common feature of some of the most successful transformations in recent times, including those at Harley Davidson, IBM and Nissan, is that they were brought about largely on the back of the talent already on board within those organisations. For example, the team that led the turnaround at Harley Davidson, following the management buyout in 1981, was largely the same as it had been when the company was losing its way under the ownership of AMF, the leisure and industrial products conglomerate. In a similar vein, it is very striking that the transformational leaders at IBM and Nissan brought in with them only a handful of executives in carefully selected areas, and these were just drops in the ocean when viewed in the context of the thousands of people, and hundreds of managers and professionals, then working at each of these companies. At IBM, as Lou Gerstner (2003: 23) later recalled, it had been widely expected that he 'would have to bring in a lot of people from the outside', such was the level of 'rigor mortis' then besetting the company and its culture, but he recognised that the organisation had always had 'a rich talent pool – perhaps the best in the world' and he earnestly hoped that heavy reliance on outsiders was not going to be necessary. In time, this proved to be the case.

While the process of building the momentum for change to 'critical mass' or 'tipping point' does not necessitate the full conversion of the greater number, what is required is to unearth potential activists for change and find a way to empower them. You do not need many to begin with. As a former CEO at Whirlpool, Jack Sparks, once declared, 'Give me 40 people' and 'I can run this company'.[56] But, according to Mike Walsh, former CEO of Tenneco, you have to 'pick those with a burning desire for change', and they are often 'buried down the organization'.[57] As Gary Hamel (1996: 74) has argued provocatively:

> 'Where are you likely to find people with the least diversity of experience, the largest investment in the past, and the greatest reverence for industrial dogma? At the top' ... *But* 'if you go down and out into your organization – out into the ranks of much maligned middle managers, for instance – you will find people straining against the bit of industrial orthodoxy. All too often, however, there is no process that lets those revolutionaries be heard.'

Likewise, Pascale and Sternin (2005: 73), point out that 'somewhere in your organization, groups of people are already doing things differently and better', a phenomenon that Heifetz (1994:183) refers to as 'creative deviance on the front line'. One of the main secrets to generating a momentum for change is to 'find these areas of positive deviance and fan their flames'.[58]

How do you identify such potential activists and bypass the formal hierarchy to empower them. One of the first initiatives taken by Carlos Ghosn[59] during the transformation process at Nissan was to declare that he was 'not going in with any preconceived ideas' and to set up nine cross-functional teams, in key areas like purchasing, engineering and R&D. These he staffed with line managers in their thirties and forties from different departments, divisions and countries to help generate ideas for change, and he took a close personal interest in the selection of the team leaders. By cascading these efforts deeper into the organisation he not only managed to widen the constituency for change to more than 500 middle managers but he had also set in train a process that allowed the most able and committed of the change activists at all levels in the organisation to reveal themselves. During the transformation process he continued to meet with these activists on a regular basis even after the initial task of the cross-functional teams was completed, for as long as there remained within the company those who still clung to the view that 'this will blow over' (p. 8). The use of cross-functional task forces has proven to be just as effective in building momentum and widening the constituency for change in many other cases, as has the extensive use of executive education in challenging traditional mindsets, attitudes and behaviours.

Building a momentum for change frequently involves the patient management of every opportunity to move the change agenda forward, sometimes 'waiting for people to retire to exploit any policy vacuum created' or 'backing off and waiting or moving the pressure point for change', as required to keep the process moving forward.[60] Often it requires replacing some of the most prominent guardians of the old ideology, particularly those in senior management positions who, even after being allowed some reasonable time to adapt themselves to the requirements of the new situation, remain unwilling or unable to get on board.[61] However, ultimate success requires that the transformation process be as inclusive as possible and that any such decisions, if they eventually need to be taken, are done so in a fair, reasonable and humane way. For example, at IBM, Lou Gerstner (2003: 23) told his top fifty executives that 'everyone starts with a clean slate' regardless of past successes or failures, and all would get the chance to prove themselves, while Carlos Ghosn sent out the message at his first board meeting at Nissan that there was 'a place for every single person in this company who wants to give the company a chance for recovery, no matter what age, what gender, what citizenship'.[62]

The success of the momentum-building phase can often hinge on the outcome of certain key defining episodes or projects, and transformational leaders do not need to orchestrate the entire process with equal intensity, if they know how to recognise and leverage them. These are moments of truth when new ideas and values are tested in a very visible way, which amplifies or attenuates the momentum for change as a consequence. The most defining episode in the transformation of Ford during the 1980s was the Taurus project, which was widely recognised as pivotal to the financial and commercial turnaround of the company. It was a project in which the future face of Ford, whether fundamentally new or just incrementally adjusted, was always going to be clearly visible. In the event, the new processes (employee involvement, concurrent engineering, outward-looking benchmarking, cross-functional cooperation) and new values of the company were given very concrete expression in the Taurus project, which then became the engine for transformation throughout the rest of the company. By way of contrast, IBM's venture into the personal computer business can be seen in hindsight as an opportunity lost to begin the larger process of corporate renewal long before the need became so critical. To be fair, the company's leaders at the time did have the insight to set up the new venture at Boca Raton far away from corporate head-quarters in the early 1980s in order to allow it the space to develop the different kind of mindset, behaviours and attitudes needed to compete in a more market-oriented context, and their strategy was quite successful in this respect. What they failed to see, however, was the early opportunity that the Boca Raton project also presented to incubate a process of poten-tially much wider corporate transformation, in the manner of the Taurus project at Ford, and IBM came in time to pay a heavy price for this lack of foresight. It was a lesson not lost on Lou Gerstner when leading the transformation process at the company just over a decade later.

Is crisis a necessary trigger?

A recurring and enduring theme in the literature is the crucial part often played by crisis in triggering the transformation process.[63] For example, the 'crisis mentality', or 'shared sense of impending disaster', was cited as a major 'catalyst' in the transformation process at Ford, and helped a lot of people to get 'religion'.[64] Likewise, for Lou Gerstner (2003: 77) at IBM, 'the sine qua non of any successful corporate transformation is public acknowledgement of the existence of a crisis', while the growing recognition of a 'the burning platform' at Nissan helped to focus minds and prepare the organisation and its wider stakeholders for a programme of radical change.[65]

Discontinuities, like deregulation, technological breakthrough or for-eign competition, are common sources of externally induced crisis, and sooner or later such discontinuities or strategic inflection points, as they like to call them at Intel,[66] are bound to happen in most industries. How-ever, there is strong evidence to suggest that many, if not most, of the crises leading to turnaround and transformation result from internal errors of commission and omission.[67] At AT&T, for example, the company could have 'detected the shape of its future as early as 1968', and had several chances later to prepare in a more gradual way for the transformation that eventually took place during the 1980s. Likewise, in the late 1970s, the developments that led to the dramatic downturn in performance at Ford, and to one of the biggest losses in corporate history up to then, had been discernable well in advance of the eventual crisis. The same pattern was evident at IBM, where it quickly became clear to Lou Gerstner (2003: 27) that the previous leadership already 'understood most, if not all, of the business issues' that he and his team eventually came to tackle over the ensuing years; while at Nissan, there were several minor efforts at restructuring and several years proclaiming in successive annual reports that 'we've turned the corner', that we are 'back on track and shifting up a gear', and that 'strategic reform was the message at Nissan' before Carlos Ghosn's appearance on the scene in 1999.[68]

Shortly after his arrival at IBM, Lou Gerstner (2003: 42) was left to wonder at how 'such a truly talented people' could 'get themselves into such a morass' as others must have wondered in cases such as Ford and Nissan. Like 'the proverbial frog that dies when temperatures are gradually increased but immediately jumps out when tossed into a boiling pot of water', organisations too often adapt themselves to gradually declining performance and continue to deny its implications until shock therapy is administered.[69] Overall, as Pettigrew (1987: 665) has put it, transformation seems to require crisis, because in non-crisis situations, even the most senior advocates of change often 'do not have sufficient leverage to break through the pattern of inertia in their organizations'.

Is new leadership normally required?

Can current incumbents successfully lead the transformation of their companies, especially those in crisis? The evidence suggests it is unlikely, though there have been some exceptions over the years, like the painful and dramatic turnaround at Citibank in the early 1990s which was led by John Reed, after 'most of the damage' had 'occurred on his watch'.[70] Overall, however, Hoffman (1989) reports that leadership change is very common during the early stages of turnaround, and in such situations the top manager is almost twice as likely to be replaced by an outsider as an insider.[71] One of the first priorities of the turnaround leader is often to apply the shock therapy, to shake the company out of denial. This is a very difficult thing for any incumbent to do, a point well captured by Ryuzaburo Kaku – the transformational leader at Canon who was appointed to lead Canon out of crisis in the mid-1970s, after he had done something 'very unJapanese' and confronted denial in his own superiors on the board[72] – when he reflected later in his career:

> " In order for a company to survive forever, the company must have the courage to be able to deny at one point what it has been doing in the past; the biological concept of 'ecdysis' – casting off the skin to emerge in a new form. But it is difficult for human beings to deny and destruct what they have been building up. But if they cannot do that, it is certain that the firm cannot survive forever. Speaking about myself, it is difficult to deny what I've done in the past. So when such time comes that I may have to deny the past, I would inevitably have to stand down.[73]

The levels of denial at IBM and Nissan were stunning, given the scale of the crisis at each of these companies, particularly the erosion of competitive position. At Nissan, for example, Carlos Ghosn saw it as his duty 'to clarify the environment, to make sure that there is the maximum light in the company'. In line with this, he spent his first three months relentlessly pointing out to employees and the media at large that Nissan was 'in bad shape' and had been 'losing global market share continuously since 1991', with a drop in output of more than 600,000 units, equivalent to 'more than the total annual car sales of the Volvo brand'. He also saw that his status as an outsider allowed him to challenge 'in a very decent way what has been done without anybody's having a second thought about, "Hey, where were you when we were doing this?"' This is what also gave him the credibility to impose the rule that 'no sacred cows, no taboos, no constraints' would be permitted to stand in the way of returning the company to profitability as the top priority.[74]

Since the process of transformation is fundamentally one of changing peoples' mindsets, attitudes and behaviours, one of the key leadership skills is the productive management of anxiety. If there is too little anxiety, the organisation will have little impetus for change. So part of the skill of transformational leadership is to allow the people within the organisation to feel the anxiety of impending crisis, not shield them from it. Sometimes, a leader bent on renewal may even need to 'manufacture a crisis' as Jack Welch did at General Electric in the early 1980s, in order to inject a sufficient sense of urgency in cases where clear evidence of serious financial or commercial decline is not yet visible.[75] On the other hand, too much anxiety may lead to an organisation becoming paralysed by fear, so the leader of major change 'must have presence and poise', as Heifetz and Laurie (1997: 128) point out, because 'regulating distress is perhaps a leader's most difficult job', and one that requires considerable emotional strength as well as professional ability. The transformational leader must also have the emotional strength to maintain the pressure for change even after the initial crisis has passed, and avoid the temptation to declare victory too soon before the process of more enduring cultural change and deep organisational learning has been firmly secured.[76]

So transformational leadership requires not only the ability to make the organisation face reality, by revealing the nature of the situation facing the company in the starkest terms, but also the ability to inspire hope and revive morale. As Kanter (2003: 61) points out, companies in crisis are usually caught in the grip of a vicious cycle of 'secrecy, blame, isolation, avoidance, lack of respect, and feelings of helplessness' and the turnaround needed is one of psychology as much as finance or strategy. In such a situation, the symbolism associated with a change of leadership can play its own significant part in the transformation effort. The highly visible drama associated with the arrivals of Lou Gerstner at IBM, a foreigner to the technology industry, and Carlos Ghosn at Nissan, a foreigner, full-stop, helped to heighten the sense of crisis and of expectation in each of these organisations and condition them for radical change. A heightened sense of crisis is the kind of context most likely to give rise to charismatic devotion[77] and this is more likely to attach itself to a new leader already cast in the role of potential saviour, which may also prove to be very functional in the overall achievement of success.

Towards the 'resilient' organisation

While the punctuated pattern of strategic transformation and renewal has tended to predominate up to now, a cyclical process that alternates between benign evolutionary periods during which companies become overadapted to passing circumstances and aging recipes for strategic success, following by sharp, harsh bursts of a necessary 'creative destruction' corrective, is far from ideal.

To begin with, many firms just do not survive the corrective process. As Arie de Geus (1997a) points out in The Living Company, too many corporations die prematurely, with the average life expectancy still only a small fraction of what should be their maximum life potential. For example, the average life of the typical Fortune-500 company is forty to fifty years and has been declining over time, a finding that has been echoed in some of the most influential business books over the last few decades from Peters and Waterman's (1982) *In Search of Excellence* and Collins and Porras' (1996) *Built to Last,* to Gary Hamel's (2000a, 2007) *Leading The Revolution* and *The Future of Management.* This can be taken as an indictment of all of us with a professional interest in strategic management. It can also be viewed as one of our greatest challenges looking towards the future.

With all of the efforts that we made to date to improve the practice of strategic management, it can be reasonably argued that we are still not doing enough to help our leading companies to stay healthy for longer. Why should this matter, if the process of 'creative destruction' is how the economy overall renews itself?[78] This process is far from costless and, in terms of human dislocation, it can be very wasteful as well as distressing. So at the very least, we should be anxious to learn how to manage the process of strategic transformation in ways that will increase the likelihood of companies surviving the difficult corrective phase and help in mitigating the collateral damage.

However, in the current business environment, this may not be enough. As Gary Hamel (2000a: 5), colourfully put it: 'Today we live in a world that is all punctuation and no equilibrium'. While important voices caution against overhyping the call for revolution, and undervaluing the case for continuity,[79] few doubt that we are living at a time when the pace of change in the global business environment is rapidly accelerating. It is the kind of dynamic context for business that makes the question of organisational longevity, and how to improve it, a particularly pressing one across the board. Within the strategy field, this is reflected in the growing interest in the concept of corporate resilience. Of the seventeen companies acclaimed by Collins and Porras in 1996 as 'built to last', only six have continued to outperform their industrial average over the last decade. 'Call it the resilience gap', say Hamel and Valikangas (2003: 52), in a world 'becoming more turbulent than organizations are becoming resilient'.

Hamel and Valikangas (2003: 53) see resilience as the ability of a company 'to dynamically reinvent business models and strategies as circumstances change'. Foster and Kaplan (2001: 15) tend to portray it as the ability of companies to increase their rates of internal 'creative destruction to the level of the market itself, without losing control of present operations', de Geus (1997b: 53) contents himself with the characterisation of being 'very good "at management for change", as we say in modern lingo'. There is remarkable similarity in what all three of these sources highlight as the key requirements for improving organisational resilience. As Hamel and Valikangas (2003: 54), indicate, there is as yet 'no simple recipe for building the resilient organization', but they point to four main organisational imperatives as useful starting points: conquering denial, valuing variety, liberating resources and embracing paradox. De Geus (1997a), in his prescription for improving organisational longevity, identifies the common characteristics of long-lived companies in terms of valuing people before assets, providing failure-tolerant space for the development of ideas, organising for learning and developing the organisation as a human community built around shared values, not just as a money-making machine.

The main insight offered by Foster and Kaplan (2001: 15) is that companies can learn to 'make themselves more like the market' by opening up their decision-making processes to make full use of the collective talents of the corporation and its partners, stimulating a ten-fold increase in their levels of creativity through the promotion of more divergent thinking, and relaxing conventional notions of control to find a better balance between control and permission. Similar to the Foster and Kaplan view, resilience, as Lawler and Worley (2006) see it requires the ability to create organisations that are 'built to change', not just designed to 'cope' with it periodically. 'This means creating an organisation that encourages experimentation, learns about new practices and technologies, monitors the environment', is committed to 'continuously improving performance' and to a view of people as 'open and willing to learn and as eager to try new things'.[80]

All of these recipes, despite some differences in orientation and emphasis, present a fairly consistent picture of where the focus must be to improve the strategic resilience of organisations in the years ahead, and we will return to this challenge briefly in our concluding chapter.

Summary

In this, the second of our two chapters on strategic processes, we turned our attention to the challenge of corporate transformation and renewal. We addressed this challenge from two complementary angles, one that concentrated primarily on the generic strategic and structural character-istics of renewal and the other on the dynamics of process.

To help in the analysis of the generic characteristics, we offered a six-stage model of corporate decline and renewal, and provided a detailed examination of the features that tend to typify each stage. The stages were: organisational decline, triggers for action, diagnostics, retrenchment, recovery and renewal. In the organisational decline stage, we highlighted the importance of being able to distinguish between symptoms, second-ary causes and primary causes, and identified some of the most common primary causes. In the next stage, we identified three types of organisa-tions that typically differ in their responsiveness to the early warnings of impending decline: 'visionaries', 'laggards' and 'sleepers'. We explored the reasons for these differences and examined the triggers needed by each to spark the necessary response. This led us to consider in the third stage the kind of diagnostic and decision procedures needed to develop effective turnaround strategies in crisis situations, an area where we in the business world still have much to learn from the approaches used by the emergency services. In stages four and five we highlighted how the balance between efficiency and entrepreneurial responses tends to vary with the primary causes of decline, whether external or internal, and also as we move through retrenchment to recovery, we examined the question of whether, and in what kind of circumstances, these two stages might be pursued in parallel. We also looked at the changing skills sets, hard and soft, typically needed by CEOs for retrenchment and recovery, and explored the ques-tion of whether, and how, any given leader is likely to remain fully effec-tive over both of these stages. When it came to the sixth and final stage and the question of whether or not there is likely to be real and lasting renewal, we highlighted the importance of deep organisational learning and a radical change in learning routines as the key to such an outcome.

In the latter part of the chapter we focused more closely on the dynamics of the transformation and renewal process in particular cases.

We began by highlighting the ongoing debate within the strategy field about the nature of the process itself, and examined the two opposing traditions in the literature, one that sees the company as continuously adaptable and the other that views it as relatively inflexible. We saw how these two traditions have given rise to two different perspectives on the process of strategic change, logical incrementalism and punctuated equilibrium, and we looked briefly at the thinking behind each of them. We noted that the punctuated perspective continues to mirror more closely the reality of the experience to date, though the concept of the continuously renewable organisation still remains the goal. We also highlighted how most of the managerial models of the strategic renewal process, within this overall punctuated view, tend to be variations of the classic three-phase, unfreeze–change–refreeze, approach developed originally by Kurt Lewin. We then examined key aspects of the dynamics of transformation and renewal (emergent nature, momentum building, critical mass/tipping point, defining episodes), along with their implications for the successful management of the process. We returned again to the prevalence of crisis and new leadership in transformation and renewal, highlighted in the earlier part of the chapter, and examined more closely the roles they often play in helping to move the process forward.

We ended our examination of the transformation and renewal process by looking at the most recent efforts to take us further towards the goal of the continuously renewing organisation in both theory and practice, concentrating in particular on the growing interest in the notion of strategic and organisational 'resilience'. We will pick up the theme of resilience again briefly in the concluding chapter of our book, as we turn to offer some final thoughts and reflections.

Notes

[1] Nonaka (1988a: 57).
[2] Teerlink and Ozley (2000), Welch (2001), Gerstner (2003), Ghosn and Ries (2005).
[3] Luthans (1980: 205).
[4] Kuhn (1970).
[5] Golding (1980: 763).
[6] Starbuck and Milliken (1988).
[7] Janis (1972).
[8] Fombrun (1992: 48).

[9] Figures 7.3 and 7.4 are taken from 'Sharpbenders' by Grinyer, Mayes & McKiernan, (1988).

[10] These simple models can be enhanced by introducing the cost of actions and the variation in aspiration levels. A fuller treatment is given in Grinyer, Mayes, McKiernan (1988).

[11] Based on the work of Slatter (1984), Smock (1955), Milburn (1972), Weick (1996).

[12] Slatter (1984: 20).

[13] Bibeault (1982).

[14] These results have been questioned (Barker and Mone [1994]) who argue that retrenchment is a consequence of steep decline and not the cause of an increased performance and that there is no performance difference between those that retrench and those that do not. However, the original authors (Pearce and Robbins [1994]) have pointed to methodological problems in Barker and Mone's study that cast some doubt on their findings.

[15] Pearce and Robinson (1994).

[16] Barker and Mone (1998).

[17] Mueller and Barker (1997).

[18] Capra (1982).

[19] See Holland (1995), Neumair (1998).

[20] March and Olsen (1989: 22).

[21] Teece, Pisano and Shuen (1990: 20).

[22] Simon (1955, 1956).

[23] Smircich and Stubbert (1985).

[24] Quinn (1982: 623).

[25] Greiner (1972), Miller and Friesen (1980), Pettigrew (1985), Tushman et al. (1986), Mintzberg and Westley (1992), Foster and Kaplan (2001).

[26] Capra (1982), Gersick (1991).

[27] Gould and Eldredge (1993).

[28] Schumpeter (1934).

[29] Kuhn (1970), Tarnas (1996).

[30] Peck (1990), O'Neil (1993).

[31] Toynbee (1972), Schlesinger (1989).

[32] Benedict (1935).

[33] See also Porter (1996).

[34] This discussion draws freely from Leavy (1996a), chapter 6.

[35] Schein (1985), Goodstein and Burke (1991), Stopford and Baden-Fuller (1990), Johnson (1990), Antonioni (1994), Strebel (1994), Fiol et al. (1999).

[36] Argyris and Schon (1978), Starbuck (1982) Nystrom and Starbuck (1984), Barr et al. (1992).

[37] Pettigrew (1987), Johnson (1988), Stopford and Baden-Fuller (1990), Gersick (1991).

[38] Foster and Kaplan (2001).

[39] Gladwell (2002), Kim and Mauborgne (2003).

[40] Child and Smith (1987: 591).

[41] Schlesinger et al. (1990: 5–6).

[42] Pettigrew (1985).

[43] Hamel (2000b), Gerstner (2003).

[44] Nonaka (1988a), Chew et al. (1991), Hamel (2000a).

[45] Kanter (1982), Nonaka (1988b), Hamel (1996).

[46] Pettigrew (1987), Nonaka (1988a), Stopford and Baden-Fuller (1990).

[47] Kennedy (1989).

[48] Gerstner (2003), Ghosn and Ries (2005).

[49] Pettigrew (1987: 667).

[50] Greenwood and Hinings (1988), Johnson (1988).

[51] Hoffman (1989), Stopford and Baden-Fuller (1990), Robbins and Pearce (1992), Ghosn (2002).

[52] Hughes et al. (2003: 4).

[53] Gerstner (2003: 45).

[54] Hamel (2000b); Gerstner (2003).

[55] Hamel (2000b).

[56] Tichy and Devanna (1986: 193).
[57] Sherman (1993: 44).
[58] Pascale and Sternin (2005: 73).
[59] Hughes et al. (2003: 3).
[60] Pettigrew (1987: 667).
[61] Kotter (1995).
[62] Hughes et al. (2003: 2).
[63] Starbuck et al. (1978), Kanter (1983), Pettigrew (1987), Nonaka (1988a), Grinyer and McKiernan (1990, 1994).
[64] Schlesinger et al. (1990: 5).
[65] Hughes et al. (2003: 4).
[66] Grove (1996: 3).
[67] Hoffman (1989).
[68] Hughes et al. (2003: 4).
[69] George (2003:1).
[70] Loomis (1991: 64).
[71] O'Neill (1986).
[72] Sandoz (1997: 10).
[73] Ackenhusen and Ghoshal (1992: 17).
[74] Hughes et al. (2003: 4).
[75] Pascale (1991: 174).
[76] Heifetz (1994), Kotter (1995).
[77] Westley and Mintzberg (1989), Bryman (1993).
[78] Schumpeter (1934).
[79] Wetlaufer (2001), Abrahamson (2004).
[80] Lawler and Worley (2006: 21).

INTRODUCING 'STRATEGIC LEADERSHIP, GOVERNANCE AND RENEWAL'
STRATEGY, LEADERSHIP, AND THE NEW AGENDA • THE
CONTEXT OF BUSINESS IN SOCIETY • COMPETITIVE ANALYSIS AND VALUE
INNOVATION • STRATEGY AND ORGANISATION IN THE MULTI-BUSINESS FIRM •
STRATEGIC PROCESSES – INNOVATION • STRATEGIC PROCESSES – TRANSFORMATION
AND RENEWAL • SOME FINAL THOUGHTS AND REFLECTIONS

8   some final thoughts and reflections

We began this book by making a case for restoring a more generalist 'big picture' perspective to the teaching of strategy and leadership, particularly at the MBA and executive education levels, and by offering *Strategic Leadership: Governance & Renewal* as a resource to help support this process. We have built our offering around the broad thematic headings of Strategy, Leadership and the New Agenda, the Context of Business in Society, Competitive Analysis and Value Innovation, Strategy and Organisation in the Multi-Business Firm, and the two strategic processes of Innovation and Transformation/Renewal. We have done this in the belief that these are the major themes and topics in strategy, leadership, governance and renewal that any postgraduate or executive student of business will need to be most familiar with to be effective in general management positions today.

In this, our final chapter, we feel that it is appropriate to conclude with some reflections on where we see the strategy field at present, in both theory and practice, in terms of current position and future challenges. In our opening chapter, we reviewed how the strategy field has developed since its early beginnings as a self-conscious discipline back in the early 1960s and highlighted many of the major frameworks, tools and perspectives that have been added to the arsenal of the strategist over the years. We also highlighted how perspectives on the influence of organisational variables (such as leadership, structure, culture, process) on sustained competitiveness and growth have evolved from where they had once been seen as largely subsidiary to strategy, to where they are now increasingly recognised as of potential strategic significance in their own right.

Strategic management at a crossroads?

> " Strategic management should have grown up by now. Yet, its protracted history, through the planning, learning, positioning and resource base paradigms ... has, after four decades, left it groping out of adolescence for direction, role, respect and contribution.[1]

As academic disciplines go, strategy is still a relatively young domain, and characteristic of a field that is still maturing; it continues to have periodic crises of identity and 'dark nights of the soul'. In the world of practice, for example, for most of the 1960s and 1970s, when the strategy field was still in the very early stages of its evolution, business in the Western world had become totally enthralled with its latest poster child, and looked to corporate planning as a systematic way to institutionalise the entrepreneurial function with the larger corporation. In the early 1980s, these hopes had begun to fade, and by late 1982, according to a feature in *Fortune Magazine* 'the concept of strategy' had become 'positively bedraggled'.[2] Then, in the early 1990s, not long after Henry Mintzberg (1994), in *The Rise and Fall of Strategy Planning*, had seemed to have delivered the final obituary, and Prahalad and Hamel (1994) had begun the search for 'a new paradigm', *Business Week* was happily announcing that after a decade of downsizing, strategic planning was making a comeback, and 'big thinkers' were 'back in vogue'.[3]

Similar cycles of doubt and optimism have also been a feature on the research front over the years. At the turn of the new millennium, strategic management seemed to be at another crossroads here also, as some prominent academics had begun to describe the then state of strategy studies as a spectre of irrelevance and stagnation.[4] For many, this was seen to be the result of the grip that industrial economics, with its strong positivist orientation, had taken over research in the domain. The dominance of the notion that market structure determined the conduct of firms and, thereby, their performance, spawned numerous quantitative studies. Such studies were typically designed to explore the relationships between structure, conduct and performance in a deterministic manner, so that structural equation modelling with large-scale samples at the industry level came to dominate much of the research in strategy from the early 1980s onwards. This legacy was to grip the field for more than two decades thereafter.

An emerging strategy-as-practice perspective

The main argument of the critics was that research carried out using the dominant worldview and methods of the industrial economics tradition tended to reveal very little about what it is to be a strategist or indeed about the praxis of strategy. For others, these methodological approaches to strategy research, borrowed from the natural sciences (portrayed by some critics as 'physics envy') had little to offer in explaining the human condition. More importantly, the relationships between people, their embedded leadership and how they managed, or were managed, were left unexplored. In recent years, a new 'strategy-as-practice' research theme has been emerging from this milieu.[5] Its underlying assumption is that, in order to understand strategy, it is necessary to understand how it is put together, by whom and with what ramifications. The 'strategy-as-practice' perspective aims to bridge the gap between organisational strategy and the work of managers, especially top managers. In particular, it places top managers at the centre of a group's relationships within the distributed activity of the strategy process, and helps explain how those relationships are constructed and how they operate at a technical and task level.

A 'strategy-as-practice' orientation is strongly reflected in the approach that we have taken in this book, where 'putting leadership back into strategy', to use Montgomery's (2008) expression, must be a central concern. First, we avoid the overly deterministic worldview of the more traditional structure–conduct–performance perspective, and tend to see strategy as rooted within the organisation's context and culture. Second, we focus around the CEO as the responsible practising strategist, as well as the top management team, and this is reflected in the emphasis that we place on leadership. Third, we approach strategy in the messy manner in which strategy occurs in practice. Rarely is strategy *designed* 'ab initio' and painted as if from a blank canvas. Strategy issues occur in a tangle of context and culture and are often wrapped up in the flesh of other factors. Hence, we adopt a thematic approach throughout the book in which this complex web is ever present. Finally, we place the human condition at the heart of our offering. We ask questions about what affects that condition, about its perception, about how it should cope under uncertainty and about its cognitive flexibility and adaptation. More so, we ask how humans can build resilient organisations that will endure the slings and arrows of challenging future contexts.

Building strategic resilience and endurance

The picture emerging at the end of the previous chapter of what will be required to meet the challenge of building resilience provides us with a useful way to draw together many of the major themes that we have covered in this book.

To begin with, it is recognised widely that organisations looking to survive and thrive in the new economic context, are unlikely to be able to do so within a traditional command-and-control approach to management and organisation. This is too inflexible for anticipated future contexts. What is most probably going to be required is greater emphasis on leadership, not just at the strategic level but throughout the organisation. There will be growing interest in how to develop a 'leadership culture' as a strategic capability. Strategic leaders need a much greater awareness of the wider business context, along with a deeper appreciation of corporate responsibility consistent with the growing impact of business institutions on the full realisation of human potential and the sustainability of the economic development process. The ability to engage major stakeholders fully, and retain their trust, will demand no less.[6]

Companies determined to meet the resilience challenge will almost certainly have to concern themselves increasingly with value innovation and wealth creation, not just wealth appropriation. Indeed, strategists are likely to take an increasing interest in the potential of business partnerships and networks in their efforts to generate better, more innovative and more closely tailored matches between customer needs and best-in-class competencies. They will have little option in a future competitive landscape that is expected to morph rapidly, with the rise of internet-savvy Generation Y, beyond the best that any kind of mass-customisation has to offer, to what C.K. Prahalad, in his most recent book, envisages as an 'N = 1, R = G world'.[7] This is a world in which value will be 'co-created' with consumers, one personalised, interactive experience at a time (N=1), through the orchestration of access to resources from multiple sources on a global scale (R=G). In such a world, the ability to deconstruct and reconfigure, in real-time, business models and the business processes that underpin them, is likely to become the dynamic capability most central to value innovation, competitive differentiation and strategic resilience at the business strategy level.

At the corporate level, in the multi-business company, the key to resilience may lie in an overhaul of the corporate management model itself.[8] Where the traditional model was designed for efficiency, the new model will have to prioritise adaptability and innovation. Where the traditional model sought to centralise the entrepreneurial function through formal corporate planning, the new model will try to devolve the entrepreneurial function as deeply into the businesses as possible. Where the traditional model emphasised hierarchical coordination to ensure coherence across the business units, the new model will emphasise more 'horizontal' and adaptable modes of coordination, through integrative processes and shared values.[9] Where the traditional model sought to 'hardwire' synergy into the organisation structure through shared activities (economies of scale) and assets (economies of scope), the new model will look to create additional value at the corporate level through the softer, more dynamic, processes of shared learning and cross-business innovation. The trick in generating this added value on an ongoing basis will be the ability to institutionalise the capacity for innovation at scale, and to develop a corporate capability for incubating new business ventures more effectively. Where the central metaphor at the heart of the traditional model was the machine, the central metaphor at the heart of the new model will be the 'living system', with the evolutionary process of variation, selection and retention operating to promote regenerative processes not only at the level of the business unit, but also in the allocation of resources such as capital, talent and ideas. Finally, improving the corporate capacity for learning and innovation, and organising for greater internal mobility of resources, should help a corporation to manage more effectively the process of corporate transformation and renewal itself, initiating the process earlier and mitigating much of its more deleterious effects.

Having said all that, we need to recognise, as the late John Gardner argued in his classic book *On Leadership*, that the problems of the aging organisation are systemic:

> " I once believed that it might be possible to design an ever-renewing organization, one that would never run down, never lose its vitality. It would provide for dissent, it would institutionalise the devil's advocate, it would provide the seedbeds for new ideas and solutions. It would never cease learning and developing. But after many years, I concluded that human beings are much too firmly wedded to the status quo to let anyone get away with such a scheme.[10]

So we should never underestimate the size of the challenge inherent in the aspiration for continuous self-renewal. However, the one consideration we should always keep in mind is that 'the key to renewal is the release of human energy and talent'.[11] The route to building more resilient organisations would seem lie in finding ever-better ways to institutionalise this principle.

Once again, a study of history helps drive the point home. Success is volatile. Few companies occupy stable positions in the Financial Times or Wall Street 500 league tables from year to year. The average life expectancy of Fortune 500 companies from birth to death is between forty and fifty years. Over a five-year period, we see the leadership rankings typically change as energy companies vie with pharmaceutical companies and cell phone operators for the fastest growing, largest market value or largest asset base. In ten years' time, we now expect the occupants of the top ten positions to be different again. Today's winners are often tomorrow's losers. Why does no one stay on top of the table? Why do leading companies fall from grace? The reasons are many, most typically: corporate arrogance and hubris, lack of vision and risk taking, insufficient attention to weak signals, constraints arising from the business models of yesterday, biases inherent in internal decision-making processes and a failure to see and grasp opportunities emerging in other sectors. Put simply, they focus internally and sharp changes in their external ecosystems make it difficult for the old internal processes to adapt quickly enough. They break the law of requisite variety by preserving internal processes and cultures that may have been appropriate for an earlier context and fail to develop the entrepreneurial lifeblood needed to respond to contemporary and future terrains.

So how then, can we help our organisations to avoid these traps and become more resilient? According to Gary Hamel (2007) in *The Future of Management*, the traditional command-and-control approach to management that served us well for most of the last century was based on a 'small nucleus of core principles': standardisation, specialisation, hierarchy, goal alignment, planning and control, and the use of extrinsic rewards to shape human behaviour. These principles were developed to solve the problem of 'how to maximise organisational efficiency and reliability in large scale organisations'. However, these same principles are likely to be 'inefficient and often toxic', when it comes to the challenge of how to create organisations that are highly adaptable and engaging. So we now need to look for new ones. Hamel, himself, suggests looking well beyond the traditional literature on strategy and management for inspiration. He points to five quite diverse domains that might be most fruitful: the literatures on Life, Markets, Democracy, Faith and Cities. From Life he distils the principle of 'variety'; and from Markets, 'flexibility'; while Democracy yields up 'activism'; Faith, 'meaning'; and Cities, 'serendipity'.

The most surprising of these to business leaders will almost certainly be the last. Few of us would ever think of looking to the literature on Cities for inspiration into how to make our organisations more enduring. 'Cities are resilient', Hamel argues, and he has often wondered why street life seems 'so much more interesting and energising than corporate life'. He goes on to suggest that business leaders could learn a lot from the writings of new urban theorists like Richard Florida and Jane Jacobs. Experts like these have much to reveal about how great cities contribute to the generation of 'new pools of economic use' through enabling diverse people to interact and discover opportunities to trade information, goods and ideas, and how, at least in part, cities are 'able to reinvent themselves because they make it easy for individuals to reinvent themselves'. Great cities also show how 'you can organise for serendipity'.[12]

Before concluding with this focus on the question of how we can help our organisations to become more resilient, let us return once more to the work of Arie de Geus (1997a), mentioned briefly in the previous chapter.

De Geus, an experienced senior planner, studied organisations that were larger than his own company, Shell, and had lived longer (Shell was founded in the 1890s). In asking the question – what determines corporate longevity – his research team identified four key factors:

Resilient companies were sensitive to their context

They were alert to soft signals, had developed peripheral vision and made good sense of the context that ebbed and flowed around them. This was done at a time when data flows and information were not widely available and emphasised the need for companies to be able to harness the sixth sense of the entrepreneur to gauge the potential happenings around them. (How companies can improve their sensitivity to context is something we reflected on at length in one of our early chapters).

Resilient companies were tolerant

The corporate centre was gentle over experimentation at the fringes. Outliers, eccentricities and experiments were encouraged, so the internal culture did not get trapped around a dominant logic and remained flexible and readied for opportunity.

Resilient companies were conservative in their financing

The Enron scandal has sparked off a renewal of interest in governance processes and served to warn companies against the potential excesses of fanciful financing. Resilient companies were frugal, controlled the use of capital and maintained a healthy reserve in readiness for the seizing of opportunity when it arose.

Resilient companies were cohesive with a strong sense of identity

They embraced the notion of a corporate 'community' with the human spirit at its core, where deeply embedded and shared values served as reliable guides to action. There was a sense that continuity would stem from within, and that each generation of leaders was simply the custodian for the next.

Such organisations pay great attention to generating the right internal culture and behaviours. They place people and their development at the heart of their concerns, and their employees, in turn, reciprocate with high levels of flexibility, awareness, engagement, and commitment.

In many ways, the overall picture that emerges from our thematic examination of strategy, leadership, governance and renewal in this book mirrors closely the insights from de Geus's findings. Strategy offerings, like top companies, come and go. SWOTs (1960s), portfolio approaches (1960–70s), experience curves (1970s), shareholder value (1980–90s), positioning techniques (1980s), core competencies (early 1990s), value disciplines (late 1990s), disruptive technologies (late 1990s) and blue ocean strategy (late 1990s–2000s) compete for the attention of CEOs and strategists through powerful publicity and convenient outlets. A manager's appetite for these goods seems insatiable and so there will be plenty more techniques and technologies arriving in the airport bookshops as the decades roll on. But beneath the surface of this unending wave of next 'big ideas', the basic tenets underpinning strategic and organisational resilience have remained the same. Close attention to the external context (the demand side) and close attention to the internal culture (the supply side) remain essential so the two can move swiftly in harmony when the need arises. For the strategy field and its ongoing development, there is an irony here. While economists may have started the problem of over aggregation and excessive measurement that threw the study of strategy off on a particular trajectory, leaving the human element languishing on the sidelines, within their basic toolbox of 'demand' and 'supply', the same economists had the most basic analytical ingredients to better inform the strategy field, but failed to use them to full advantage! We can all learn from this mistake.

Our own belief, reflected in the overall approach that we have taken in *Strategic Leadership, Governance & Renewal*, is that the ongoing challenge of how to build strategic and organisational resilience will best be served through perspectives on the field of strategic management theory and practice that continue to view it as a humanity as well as a science, a domain that must encompass the human spirit as well as the 'laws of the marketplace'. This is the perspective that we have tried to maintain and foster throughout this book.

Notes

1 McKiernan and Carter (2004: 3).
2 Kiechel (1982: 34).
3 Byrne (1996: 46).
4 Whittington et al. (2003).
5 See Jarzabkowski (2005).

[6] Senge et al. (2008).

[7] Prahalad and Krishnan (2008).

[8] Ghoshal and Bartlett (1998), Lawler and Worley (2006), Hamel (2007), Kanter (2008).

[9] Ghoshal and Gratton (2002), Kanter (2008).

[10] Gardner (1993: 130).

[11] Gardner (1993: 136).

[12] See Leavy 2008, for an expanded summary of Hamel's *The Future of Management*.

references

Abrahamson, E. (2004), 'Avoiding repetitive change syndrome', *MIT Sloan Management Review*, Winter: 93–5.

Ackenhusen, M. and Ghoshal, S. (1992), 'Canon: Competing on capabilities', Case No. 392-031-1, INSEAD.

Albert-Roulhac, C. and Breen, P. (2005), 'Corporate governance in Europe: current status and future trends', *Journal of Business Strategy* 26 (6): 19–29.

Allio, R.J. (2004), 'CEO Interview: the InnoCentive model of open innovation', *Strategy & Leadership* 32, 4: 4–9.

Amabile, T.M. (1997), 'Motivating creativity in organizations: on doing what you love and loving what you do', *California Management Review*, Fall: 39–58.

Amo, B.W. and Kolvereid, L. (2005), 'Organizational strategy, individual personality and innovation behaviour', *Journal of Enterprising Culture*, March: 7–19.

Andrews, K.R. (1971), *The Concept of Corporate Strategy*, Homewood Illinois: Irwin.

Ansoff, H.I. (1965), *Corporate Strategy*, New York: McGraw-Hill.

Ansoff, H.I. (1979), 'The changing shape of the strategy problem', *Journal of General Management* 4 (4): 42–58.

Antonioni, D. (1994), 'A new model of organizational change', *Organization Development Journal* 12 (3): 17–28.

Argenti, J. (1968), *Corporate Planning: A Practical Guide*, London: Allen & Unwin.

Argenti, J. (1976), *Corporate Collapse: The Causes and Symptoms*, New York: McGraw-Hill.

Argenti, J. (1980), *Practical Corporate Planning*, London: George, Allen & Unwin.

Argyres, N. and McGahan, A.M. (2002). 'An interview with Michael Porter', *Academy of Management Executive* 16, 2, 43–52.

Argyris, C. and Schon, D.A. (1978), *Organizational Learning: A Theory of Action Perspective*, Reading MA: Addison-Wesley.

Arthur, W.B. (1996), 'Increasing returns and the new world of business', *Harvard Business Review* July–August: 100–9.

Badaracco, J.L (2001), 'We don't need another hero', *Harvard Business Review*, September: 121–6.

Barker, V. and Mone, M. (1994), 'Retrenchment: cause of turnaround or consequence of decline', *Strategic Management Journal* 15: 395–405.

Barker, V. and Mone, M. (1998), 'The mechanistic structure shift and strategic reorientation in declining firms attempting turnaround', *Human Relations* 51: 1227–58.

Barney, J.B. (1986), 'Organizational culture: can it be a source of sustainable competitive advantage?', *Academy of Management Review*, 11 (3): 99–120.

Barney, J. (1995), 'Looking inside for competitive advantage', *Academy of Management Executive* 9 (4): 49–61.

Barney, J.B. (2001), 'Is the resource-based "view" a useful perspective for strategic management research? Yes', *Academy of Management Review* 26 (1): 41–56.

Barr, P.S., Stimpert, J.L. and Huff, A.S. (1992), 'Cognitive change, strategic action, and organizational renewal', *Strategic Management Journal* 13S: 15–36.

Barron, F. (1969), *Creative Person and Creative Process*, New York: Holt, Rinehart & Winston.

Barron, F., Montouri, A. and Barron, A. (1997), *Creators on Creating*, New York: Tharcher Putnam.

Bartlett, C.A. and Ghoshal, S. (1990), 'Matrix management: not a structure, a frame of mind', *Harvard Business Review*, July–August: 138–45.

Bartlett, C.A. and Ghoshal, S. (1993), 'Beyond the M-form: towards a managerial theory of the firm', *Strategic Management Journal* 14: 23–46.

Bartlett, C.A. and Ghoshal, S. (2002), 'Building competitive advantage through people', *MIT Sloan Management Review*, Winter: 34–41.

Bartlett, C.A. and Mohammed, A. (1995), '3M: Profile of an Innovating Company', Case No. 9-395-016, Harvard Business School.

Bartlett, C.A. and Nanda, A. (1995), 'Ingvar Kamprad and IKEA', Case No. 9-390-132 (Revised), Harvard Business School.

Bartlett, C.A., Elderkin, K. and McQuade, K. (1995), 'The Body Shop International', Case No. 9-392-032 (Revised), Harvard Business School.

Basu, S. and Schroeder, R.G. (1977), 'Incorporating judgements in sales forecasts: application of the Delphi Method at American Hoist and Derrick', *Interfaces* 7 (3): 18–27.

Beck, N. (1992), *Shifting Gears: Thriving in the New Economy*, Toronto: Harper Collins.

Bell, D. and Graubard, S.R. (1997), *Towards the Year 2000: Work in Progress*, Cambridge MA: MIT Press.

Benedict, R. (1935), *Patterns of Culture*, London: Routledge & Kegan Paul.

Bennis, W. and Biederman, P. (1997), *Organizing Genius: The Secrets of Creative Collaboration*, London: Nicholas Brealey.

Bennis, W. and Nanus, B. (1985), *Leaders: The Strategies for Taking Charge*, New York: Harper & Row.

Berman, P. (1998), 'Throwing away the book', *Forbes*, 2 November: 174–81.

Bettis, R.A. and Hall, W.K. (1983), 'The business portfolio approach – where it falls down in practice', *Long Range Planning* 16 (2): 95–104.

Bettis, R.A. and Prahalad, C.K. (1995), 'The dominant logic: retrospective and extension', *Strategic Management Journal* 16: 5–14.

Bhide, A. (2000), *The Origin and Evolution of New Businesses*, New York: Oxford University Press.

Bibb, P. (1996), *It Ain't as Easy as it Looks*, London: Virgin.

Bibeault, D. (1982), *Corporate Turnaround – How Managers Turn Losers into Winners*, New York: McGraw-Hill.

Biggert, N.W. and Hamilton, G.G. (1987), 'An institutional theory of leadership', *Journal of Applied Behavioural Science*, 23 (4): 429–41.

Birkinshaw, J. and Gibson, C. (2004), 'Building ambidexterity into an organization', *MIT Sloan Management Review*, Summer: 47–55.

Block, Z. and MacMillan, I.C. (1993), *Corporate Venturing: Creating New Businesses Within the Firm*, Boston: Harvard Business School Press.

Block, Z. and Ornati, O. (1987), 'Compensating corporate venture managers', *Journal of Business Venturing* 2: 41–51.

Bobbit, P. (2002), *The Shield of Achilles: War, Peace and the Course of History*, New York: Knopf, Borzoi Books, Random House.

Bolton, M.K. (1993), 'Imitation versus innovation: lessons to be learned from the Japanese', *Organizational Dynamics* 22: 30–45.

Bonabeau, E. and Meyer, C. (2001), 'Swarm intelligence: a whole new way to think about business', *Harvard Business Review*, May: 107–14.

Bower, J.L. (1970), *Managing the Resource Allocation Process*, Homewood, Illinois: Irwin.

Bower, J.L., Bartlett, C.A., Christensen, C.R., Pearson, A.E. and Andrews, K.R. (1991), *Business Policy: Text and Cases*, 7th Edition, Homewood Illinois: Irwin.

Bower, J.L. and Christensen, C.M. (1995), 'Disruptive technologies: catching the wave', *Harvard Business Review*, January–February: 43–53.

Bower, J.L. and Gilbert, C. (2005), 'Pandesic – The Challenges of a New Business Venture (A)', Case No. 9-399-129, Harvard Business School.

Bower, J.L. and Matthews, J. (1996), 'Marks & Spencer: Sir Richard Greenbury's Quiet Revolution', Case No. 9-395-054, Harvard Business School.

Branson, R. (1998), *Losing My Virginity: The Autobiography*, London: Virgin.

Brockhoff, K. (1975), 'The reference of forecasting groups in computer dialogue and face to face discussions', in H. Linstone and M. Turoff (Eds), *The Delphi Method: Technique and Applications*, London: Addison-Wesley.

Brown, J.S. and Duguid, P. (2000), 'Balancing act: how to capture knowledge without killing it', *Harvard Business Review*, May–June: 73–80.

Brown, J.S. and Duguid, P. (2001), 'Creativity versus structure: a useful tension', *MIT Sloan Management Review*, Summer: 93–4.

Bryman, A. (1993), 'Charismatic leadership in business organizations: some neglected issues', *Leadership Quarterly* 4 (3/4): 289–304.

Burgelman, R.A. (1983a), 'A model of the interaction of strategic behaviour, corporate context and the concept of strategy', *Academy of Management Review* 8: 61–70.

Burgelman, R.A. (1983b), 'Corporate entrepreneurship and strategic management: insights from a process study', *Management Science* 29 (12): 1349–64.

Burgelman, R.A. (1983c), 'Designs for corporate entrepreneurship in established firms', *California Management Review*, Spring: 154–66.

Burgelman, R.A. (2003), 'Corporate venturing: Practice and you get luckier', *EBF*, Winter: 38–39.

Burgelman, R.A. and Valikangas, L. (2005), 'Managing internal corporate venturing cycles, *MIT Sloan Management Review*, Summer: 26–34.

Burns, J.M. (1978), *Leadership*, New York: Harper & Row.

Burt, T. (2001), 'Jac the Knife falls foul of family pressures', *Financial Times*, 29 November.

Business Roundtable (2006), *Business Roundtable Corporate Governance Survey Key Findings*, Washington: Business Roundtable.

Business Week Editorial (1981), 'Deconglomerating business', *Business Week*, 24 August: 74–4.

Buzzel, R. and Gale, B. (1987), *The PIMS Principles*, New York: Free Press.

Byrne, J.A. (1993), 'Enterprise: how entrepreneurs are shaping the world and what big companies can learn', *Business Week*, 6 December: 40–51.

Byrne, J.A. (1996), 'Strategic planning: After a decade of U.S. downsizing, big thinkers are back in vogue', *Business Week*, 2 September: 46–9.

Byrne, J.A. (1998), 'Jack: a close-up look at how America's #1 manager runs GE', *Business Week*, 8 June: 40–51.

Cadbury, A. (1992), *The Committee on Financial Aspects of Corporate Governance*, London: Gee and Company.

Cadbury, A. (2002), *Corporate Governance and Chairmanship: A Personal View*, Oxford: Oxford University Press.

Campbell, A. (1994), 'The Body Shop International – the most honest cosmetic company in the world', case reproduced in B. De Wit and R. Meyer, *Strategy – Process, Content, Context: An International Perspective*, Minneapolis/St.Paul: West Publishing Company.

Campbell, A. (2003), 'Corporate venturing: wait and watch', *EBF*, Winter: 36–7.

Campbell, A. and Park, R. (2004), 'Stop kissing frogs', *Harvard Business Review*, July–August: 27–8.

Campbell, A. and Park, R. (2005), *The Growth Gamble*, London: Nicholas Brealey.

Campbell, A., Birkinshaw, J., Morrison, A. and van Basten Battenberg, R. (2003), 'The future of corporate venturing', *MIT Sloan Management Review*, Fall: 30–7.

Campbell, A., Goold, M. and Alexander, M. (1995), 'Corporate strategy: the quest for parenting advantage', *Harvard Business Review*, March–April: 120–32.

Capell, K. (2003), 'Ryanair rising: Ireland's discount carrier is defying gravity as the industry struggles', *Business Week*, 2 June: 18–20.

Capra, F. (1982), *The Turning Point*, New York: Simon & Schuster.

Carter, C. and McKiernan, P. (2004), 'The millennium nexus: strategic management at the cross-roads', *European Management Review* 1 (1): 3–13.

Chandler, A.D. (1962), *Strategy and Structure: Chapters in the History of American Industrial Enterprise*, Cambridge MA: Harvard University Press.

Chandler, A.D. (1990), 'The enduring logic of industrial success', *Harvard Business Review*, March–April: 130–40.

Chandler, A.D. (1991), 'The functions of the HQ unit in the multi-business firm', *Strategic Management Journal* 12: 31–50.

Channon, D. (1973), 'Strategy and structure in British Enterprise', Doctoral dissertation, Graduate School of Business Administration, Harvard University.

Charitou, C.D. and Markides, C.C. (2003), 'Responses to disruptive innovation, *MIT Sloan Management Review*, Winter: 55–63.

Chase, W.G. and Simon, H.A. (1973), 'Perception in chess', *Cognitive Psychology* 4: 55–81.

Chatterjee, S. and Wernerfelt, B. (1991), 'The link between resources and type of diversification: theory and evidence', *Strategic Management Journal* 12 (1): 33–48.

Chesbrough, H. (2000), 'Designing corporate ventures in the shadow of private venture capital', *California Management Review*, Spring: 31–49.

Chesbrough, H. (2003a), *Open Innovation: The New Imperative for Creating and Profiting from Technology*, Boston: Harvard Business School Press.

Chesbrough, H. (2003b), 'The era of open innovation', *MIT Sloan Management Review*, Spring: 35–41.

Chesbrough, H. (2003c), 'The logic of open innovation', *California Management Review*, Spring: 33–58.

Chesbrough, H. (2006), *Open Business Models: How to Thrive in the New Innovation Landscape*, Boston: Harvard Business School Press.

Chew, W.B., Leonard-Barton, D. and Bohn, R.E. (1991), 'Beating Murphy's Law', *Sloan Management Review*, Spring: 5–16.

Child, J. and Smith, C. (1987), 'The context and process of organizational transformation – Cadbury Limited in its sector', *Journal of Management Studies* 24 (6): 565–93.

Christensen, C.M. (1997), *The Innovator's Dilemma*, Boston: Harvard Business School Press.

Christensen, C.M. and Raynor, M.E. (2003), *The Innovator's Solution*, Boston: Harvard Business School Press.

Christensen, C.M., Raynor, M.E. and Verlinden, M. (2001), 'Skate to where the money will be', *Harvard Business Review*, November: 73–81.

Christensen, H.K. and Montgomery, C.A. (1981), 'Corporate economic performance: diversification strategy versus market structure', *Strategic Management Journal* 2: 327–43.

Clegg, S.R. (1990), *Modern Organizations: Organization Studies in the Post-Modern World*, London: Sage.

Clements, M.P. and Hendry, D.F (1995), Macro-economic forecasting and modelling', *Economic Journal* 105 (431): 1001–13.

Coates, J.F. (2000), 'Scenario planning', *Technological Forecasting & Social Change* 65 (1): 115–23.

Cohen, W.M. and Levinthal, D.A. (1990), 'Absorptive capacity: a new perspective on learning and innovation', *Administrative Science Quarterly* 35: 128–52.

Collins, J. (2001), 'Level 5 leadership: the triumph of humility and fierce resolve', *Harvard Business Review*, January: 67–76.

Collins, J.C. and Porras, J.I. (1996), *Built to Last: Successful Habits of Visionary Companies*, London: Century.

Collis, D.J. and Montgomery, C.A. (1998), 'Creating corporate advantage', *Harvard Business Review*, May–June: 71–83.

Colvin, G. (1999), 'The ultimate manager', *Fortune*, 22 November: 95–7.

Corporate Strategy Board (1998), *Stall Points: Barriers to Growth for the Large Corporate Enterprise*, Washington DC: Corporate Executive Board.

Cousens, R., Steinberg, T., White, B. and Walton, S. (2002), Generic Scenarios: A Strategy Futures Paper, London: UK Cabinet Office, Strategy Unit.

Coutu, D. (2000), 'Creating the most frightening company on earth: an interview with Andy Law of St. Luke's', *Harvard Business Review*, September–October: 143–50.

Coyle, R.G. and Yong, Y.C. (1996), 'A scenario projection for the South China Sea: further experiences with field anomaly relaxation', *Futures* 28 (3): 269–83.

Csikszentmihalyi, M. (1996), *Creativity*, New York: Harper Perennial.

Cusumano, M.A. and Yoffie, D.B. (1998), *Competing on Internet Time: Lessons from Netscape and its Battle with Microsoft*, New York: Free Press.

Cyert, R. and March, J.G. (1963), *A Behavioural Theory of the Firm*, Englewood Cliffs, NJ: Prentice Hall.

Czarniawska, B. (1997), *Narrating the Organization*, Chicago: University of Chicago Press.

Dalkey, N.C. (1968), *Experiment in Group Production*, Santa Monica CA: Rand Corporation.

Dalton, C.M. and Dalton, D.R. (2005), 'In defense of the individual: the CEO as board chairperson', *Journal of Business Strategy* 26 (6): 8–9.

Davenport, T.H., Cantrell, S. and Thomas, R.J. (2002), 'The art of work', *Outlook*, Number 1: 43–9.

Davenport, T.H. Prusak, L. and Wilson, H.J. (2003), 'Who's bringing you hot ideas and how are you responding?', *Harvard Business Review*, February: 58–64.

Davis, S.M. and Lawrence, P.R. (1978), 'Problems of matrix organizations', *Harvard Business Review*, May–June: 83–94.

Day, J.D., Mang, P.Y., Richter, A. and Roberts, J. (2001), 'The innovative organization: why new ventures need more than a room of their own', *The McKinsey Quarterly*, Number 2: 21–31.

Day, J.D. and Wendler, J.C. (1998), 'The new economics of organization', *The McKinsey Quarterly*, Number 1: 4–18.

Dearlove, D. (2003), 'John Kay: The thought leader interview', *Strategy + Business*, Fall: 1–7.

De Geus, A. (1988), 'Planning as learning', *Harvard Business Review*, March–April: 70–4.

De Geus, A. (1997a), *The Living Company*, Boston: Harvard Business School Press.

De Geus, A. (1997b), 'The living company', *Harvard Business Review*, March–April: 51–9.

De Jouvenal, B. (1967), *The Art of Conjecture*, New York: Basic Books.

Demsetz, H. and Lehn, K. (1985), 'The structure of corporate ownership: causes and consequences', *Journal of Political Economy* 93: 1155–77.

De Pree, M. (1994), *Leadership is an Art*, London: Arrow.

Desai, M. (2003), 'India and China: an essay in comparative political theory', Paper presented at the IMF Conference on India/China, Delhi, November.

Dess, G.G. and Lumpkin, G.T. (2005), 'The role of entrepreneurial orientation in stimulating effective corporate entrepreneurship', *Academy of Management Executive* 19 (1): 147–56.

Dick, R. and Kets de Vries, M.F.R. (1995), Branson's Virgin: The Coming of Age of a Counter-Cultural Enterprise, Case No. 495-014-1, INSEAD.

Dick, R. and Kets de Vries, M.F.R. (2000), 'The house that Branson built: virgin's entry into the new millenium', Case No. 400-002-1 (Original version), INSEAD.

Dick, R. and Kets de Vries, M.F.R. (2007), The House That Branson Built: From Counter-culture to Corporate Culture, Case No. 400-002-1 (Revised version), INSEAD.

Doornik, K. and Roberts, J. (2001), Nokia Corporation: Innovation and Efficiency in a High-Growth Global Firm, Case No. S-IB-23, Graduate School of Business, Stanford University.

Doz, Y.L. and Prahalad, C.K. (1991), 'Managing DMNCs: a search for a new paradigm', *Strategic Management Journal* 12: 145–64.

DTI (2002), *Foresight Futures 2020: Revised Scenarios and Guidance*, London: Department of Trade and Industry, HMSO, UK.

Drucker, P.F. (1985), *Innovation and Entrepreneurship*, London: William Heinemann.

Dumaine, B. (1993), 'America's toughest bosses', *Fortune*, 18 October: 44–51.

Dunn, D. and Yamashita, K. (2003), 'Microcapitalism and the megacorporation', *Harvard Business Review*, August: 46–54.

Ebers, M. (1985), 'Understanding organizations: the poetic mode', *Journal of Management* 11 (2): 51–62.

Ehrlich, S.P., Pearson, A.E. and Sorensen, R. (1991), Honda Motor Company and Honda of America, Case No. 9-390-111 (Revised): Harvard Business School.

Eisenhardt, K.M. and Galunic, D.C. (2000), 'Coevolving: at last a way to make synergies work', *Harvard Business Review*, January–February: 91–101.

Eisenmann, T., Parker, G. and Van Alstyne, M.W. (2006), Strategies for two-sided markets', *Harvard Business Review*, October: 92–101.

Eisenstat, R., Foote, N. Galbraith, J. and Miller, D. (2001), 'Beyond the business unit', *McKinsey Quarterly*, Number 1: 54–63.

Eitzen, D.S. and Yetman, N.R. (1972), 'Managerial change, longevity and organizational effectiveness', *Administrative Science Quarterly* 17: 110–16.

Esler, P. (2003), *Conflict and Identity in Romans: The Social Setting of Paul's Letter*, Minneapolis MN: Augsburg Fortress Publishers.

Fahey, L. and Randall, R.M. (1998), *Learning from the Future: Competitive Foresight Scenarios*, New York: John Wiley.

Farjoun, M. (2002), 'Towards an organic perspective on strategy', *Strategic Management Journal* 23: 561–94.

Farson, R. and Keyes, R. (2002), 'The failure-tolerant leader', *Harvard Business Review*, August: 64–73.

Fast, N.D. (1978) *The Rise and Fall of Corporate New Venture Divisions*, Ann Arbor, Michigan: UMI Research Press.

Fellini, F. (1997), 'Miscellany', in F.Barron, A. Montuori, and A. Barron (eds), *Creators on Creating*, New York: Tarcher Putnam.

Fiedler, E.R. (1977), 'The three Rs of economic forecasting – irrational, irrelevant and irreverent', *Across the Board*, June: 62–3.

Fiedler, F.E. (1965), 'Engineer the job to fit the manager', *Harvard Business Review*, September–October: 115–22.

Fiedler, F.E. (1967), *A Theory of Leadership Effectiveness*, New York: McGraw-Hill.

Fiol, C.M., Harris, D. and House, R. (1999), 'Charismatic leadership: strategies for effecting social change', *Leadership Quarterly* 10 (3): 449–82.

Fischer, B. and Boynton, A. (2005), 'Virtuoso teams', *Harvard Business Review*, July–August: 117–23.

Fishburne, R. (1999), 'ASAP dynamic 100', *Forbes ASAP*, 5 April.

Fombrun, C. (1992), *Turning Points: Creating Strategic Change in Corporations*, New York: McGraw-Hill.

Foss, N.J. (1997), 'On the rationales of corporate headquarters', *Industrial and Corporate Change* 6 (2): 313–38.

Foster, R.N. (1986), *Innovation: The Attacker's Advantage*, New York: Summit Books.

Foster, R. and Kaplan, S. (2001), *Creative Destruction: From Built-to-Last to Built-to-Perform*, London: FT Prentice Hall.

Fowles, J. and Fowles, R.B. (1978), *Handbook of Futures Research*, Connecticut: Greenwood Press.

Friedman, M. (1970), 'The social responsibility of business is to increase its profits', *The New York Times Magazine*, 13 September: 32–3, 122–4.

Fryer, B. (2003), 'Storytelling that moves people: A conversation with screenwriting coach Robert McKee', *Harvard Business Review*, June: 51–5.

Fukuyama, F. (1996), *Trust: The Social Virtues and the Creation of Prosperity*, Middlesex: Penguin.

Gabel, M. and Bruner, H. (2003), *Global Inc.: An Atlas of the Multinational Corporation*, New York: The New Press.

Gadiesh, O., Leung, P. and Vesting, T. (2007), 'The battle for China's good-enough market', *Harvard Business Review*, September: 81–9.

Galbraith, J.K. (1956), *American Capitalism: The Concept of Countervailing Power* (2nd Edition), Boston: Houghton Mifflin.

Galbraith, J.R. (1971), 'Matrix organizational designs', *Business Horizons* 15 (1): 29–40.

Gardner, H. (1993), *Creating Minds*, New York: Basic Books.

Gardner, H. (1997), *Leading Minds*, London: Harper Collins.

Gardner, J.W. (1993), *On Leadership*, New York: Free Press (Paperback Edition).

Garten, J. (2002a), *The Mind of the CEO*, London: Penguin.

Garten, J. (2002b), *The Politics of Fortune: A New Agenda for Business Leaders*, Boston: Harvard Business School Press.

Garter, J. (2000c), 'Don't let the CEO run the Board, too', *Business Week* 11 November: 13.

Garvin, D.A. (2004), 'What every CEO should know about creating new businesses', *Harvard Business Review*, July–August: 18–21.

Garvin, D.A. and Levesque, L.C. (2004), Emerging Business Opportunities at IBM (A), Case No. 9-304-075, Harvard Business School.

Gemmill, G. and Oakley, J. (1992), 'Leadership: an alienating social myth', *Human Relations*, 45 (2): 113–29.

George, B. (2003), *Authentic Leadership: Rediscovering the Secrets to Creating Lasting Value*, San Francisco: Jossey-Bass.

George, B., Sims, P., McLean, A.N. and Mayer, D. (2007). 'Discovering your authentic leadership', *Harvard Business Review*, February, 129–38.

Gersick, C.J.G. (1991), 'Revolutionary change theories: a multilevel exploration of the punctuated equilibrium paradigm', *Academy of Management Review* 16 (1): 10–36.

Gerstner, L.V. (2003), *Who Says Elephants Can't Dance?*, New York: Harper Business.

Ghemawat, P. (1985), 'Building strategy on the experience curve', *Harvard Business Review*, March–April: 143–9.

Ghemawat, P. and Ricart I Costa, J.E. (1993), 'The organizational tension between static and dynamic efficiency', *Strategic Management Journal* 14: 59–73.

Ghoshal, S. and Ackenhusen, M. (1992), Canon: Competing on Capabilities, Case No. 392-031-1, INSEAD.

Ghoshal, S. and Bartlett, C.A. (1998), *The Individualized Corporation*, London: Heinemann.

Ghoshal, S. and Butler, C. (1992), Kao Corporation, Case No. 392-049-1, INSEAD.

Ghoshal, S. and Gratton, L. (2002), 'Integrating the enterprise', *MIT Sloan Management Review*, Fall: 31–8.

Ghoshal, S. and Mintzberg, H. (1994), 'Diversifiction and diversifact', *California Management Review*, Fall: 8–27.

Ghoshal, S., Bartlett, C.A. and Moran, P. (1999), 'A new manifesto for management', *Sloan Management Review*, Spring: 9–20.

Ghosn, C. (2002), 'Saving the business without losing the company', *Harvard Business Review*, January: 37–45.

Ghosn, C. and Ries, P. (2005), *Shift: Inside Nissan's Historic Revival*, New York: Doubleday.

Gladwell, M. (2002), *The Tipping Point*, New York: Bay Back Books.

Godet, M. (2001), *Creating Futures: Scenario Planning as a Strategic Management Tool*, London: Economica.

Goffee, R. and Jones, G. (2005). 'Managing authenticity', *Harvard Business Review*, December: 87–94.

Goggin, W.C. (1974), 'How the multidimensional structure works at Dow Corning', *Harvard Business Review*, May–June: 83–94.

Golding, D. (1980), 'Establishing blissful clarity in life: managers', *Sociological Review* 28: 763–82.

Goleman, D. (1998), 'What makes a leader?', *Harvard Business Review*, November–December: 93–102.

Gompers, P., Ishii, J., and Metrick, A. (2003), Corporate Governance and Equity Prices', *Quarterly Journal of Economics*, 118, 107–55

Goodstein, L.D. and Burke, W.W. (1991), 'Creating successful organizational change', *Organizational Dynamics* 19 (4): 5–17.

Goold, M. (1991), 'Strategic control in the decentralized firm', *Sloan Management Review*, Winter: 69–81.

Goold, M. and Campbell, A. (1987), *Strategies and Styles: The Role of the Centre in Diversified Companies*, Oxford: Basil Blackwell.

Goold, M. and Campbell, A. (1998), 'Desperately seeking synergy', *Harvard Business Review*, September–October: 131–43.

Goold, M. and Campbell, A. (2002), 'Do you have a well-designed organization?', *Harvard Business Review*, March: 117–124.

Gordon, T.J. (1994), *Cross Impact Method*, Futures Research Methodologies, AC/UNU Millennium Project.

Gordon, T.J. and Helmer, O. (1964), *Report on a Long-Range Forecasting Study*, Santa Monica CA: Rand Corporation.

Gould, S.J. and Eldredge, N. (1993), 'Punctuated equilibrium comes of age', *Nature*, 18 November: 223–7.

Govindarajan, V. and Trimble, C. (2004), 'Strategic innovation and the science of learning, *MIT Sloan Management Review*, Winter: 67–75.

Govindarajan, V. and Trimble, C. (2005a), *10 Rules for Strategic Innovators: From Ideas to Execution*, Boston: Harvard Business School Press.

Govindarajan, V. and Trimble, C. (2005b), 'Organizational DNA for strategic innovation, *California Management Review*, Spring: 47–76.

Granovetter, M. (1985), 'Economic action and social structure: the problem of embeddedness, *American Journal of Sociology* 91 (3): 481–510.

Grant, R.M. (1996), 'Toward a knowledge-based theory of the firm', *Strategic Management Journal* 17S: 109–22.

Graves, J. (1992), 'Leaders of corporate change', *Fortune*, 14 December: 90–4.

Greenwood, R. and Hinings, C.R. (1988), 'Organizational design types, tracks and the dynamics of change', *Organization Studies* 9 (3): 293–316.

Greiner, L.E. (1972), 'Evolution and revolution as organizations grow', *Harvard Business Review*, July–August: 37–46.

Grinyer, P. and McKiernan, P. (1990), 'Generating major change in stagnating companies', *Strategic Management Journal* 11: 131–46.

Grinyer, P. and McKiernan, P. (1994), 'Triggering major and sustained change in stagnating companies', in H. Daems and H. Thomas (eds), *Strategic Groups, Strategic Moves and Performance*, London: Pergamon.

Grinyer, P., Mayes, D. and McKiernan, P. (1988), *Sharpbenders: The Secrets of Unleashing Corporate Potential*, Oxford: Basil Blackwell.

Grol, P., Schoch, C. and Roger, M. (1998), Ikea: Culture as Competitive Advantage, Case No. 398-173-1, Paris: Groupe ICPA.

Grove, A. S. (1996), *Only the Paranoid Survive*, London: Harper Collins.

Guber, P. (2007), The four truths of the storyteller, *Harvard Business Review*, December: 53–9.

Guilford, J.P. (1956), 'The structure of the intellect', *Psychological Bulletin*, 53: 267–93.

Hagel, J. and Brown, J.S. (2005), *The Only Sustainable Edge*, Boston: Harvard Business School Press.

Halal, W.E. (1994), 'From hierarchy to enterprise: internal markets are the new foundation of management', *Academy of Management Executive*, November: 69–83.

Hambrick, D.C. (1989), 'Strategic leadership', *Strategic Management Journal* (Special Issue) 10S: 5–15.

Hambrick, D.C. and Fukutomi, G.D.S. (1991), 'The seasons of a CEO's tenure', *Academy of Management Review* 16 (4): 719–42.

Hamel, G. (1996), 'Strategy as revolution', *Harvard Business Review*, July–August: 69–82.

Hamel, G. (1998), 'Strategy and the quest for value', *MIT Sloan Management Review*, Winter: 7–14.

Hamel, G. (1999), 'Bringing Silicon Valley inside', *Harvard Business Review*, September–October: 71–84.

Hamel, G. (2000a), *Leading the Revolution*, Boston: Harvard Business School Press.

Hamel, G. (2000b), 'Waking up IBM: how a gang of unlikely rebels transformed Big Blue', *Harvard Business Review*, July–August: 137–46.

Hamel, G. (2006), 'The what, why and how of management innovation', *Harvard Business Review*, February: 72–84.

Hamel, G. (2007), *The Future of Management*, Boston: Harvard Business School Press (with B. Breen).

Hamel, G. and Prahalad, C.K. (1993), 'Strategy as stretch and leverage', *Harvard Business Review*, March–April: 75–84.

Hamel, G. and Prahalad, C.K. (1994), *Competing for the Future*, Boston: Harvard Business School Press.

Hamel, G. and Valikangas, L. (2003), 'The quest for resilience', *Harvard Business Review*, September, 52–63.

Hamm, S. and Elgin, B. (2005), 'IBM discovers the power of one', *Business Week*, February 14th, 54–55.

Handy, C. (1992), 'Balancing corporate power: a new federalist paper', *Harvard Business Review*, November–December: 59–72.

Handy, C. (1997), 'Foreword' in W. Bennis and P.W. Biederman, *Organizing Genius: The Secrets of Creative Collaboration*, London: Nicholas Brealey.

Hansen, M.T. and Nohria, N. (2004), 'How to build collaborative advantage', *MIT Sloan Management Review*, Fall: 22–30.

Hargadon, A. and Sutton, R.I. (2000), 'Building an innovation factory', *Harvard Business Review*, May–June: 157–66.

Hart, S.L. and Christensen, C.M. (2002), 'The great leap: driving innovation from the base of the pyramid', *MIT Sloan Management Review*, Fall: 51–6.

Hatch, M.J. (1997), *Organization Theory: Modern Symbolic and Postmodern Perspectives*, Oxford: Oxford University Press.

Heifetz, R.A. (1994), *Leadership Without Easy Answers*, Cambridge MA: Belknap.

Heifetz, R.A. and Laurie, D.L. (1997), 'The work of leadership', *Harvard Business Review*, January–February: 124–34.

Heisler, G. (2004), 'The unsung CEO', *Business Week*, 1 November: 60–5.

Helmer, O. and Rescher, N. (1959), 'On the epistemology of the inexact sciences', *Management Science* 6 (1): 25–52.

Hemp, P. and Stewart, T.A. (2004), 'The HBR Interview – Samuel J. Palmisano: Leading change when business is good', *Harvard Business Review*, December: 60–70.

Henderson, B. (1973), 'The experience curve revisited: the growth share matrix of the product portfolio', *Perspectives*, Boston Consulting Group.

Herbold, R. (2002), 'Inside Microsoft: balancing creativity and discipline', *Harvard Business Review*, January: 72–9.

Hill, C.W.L. (1990), 'Cooperation, opportunism and the invisible hand: implications for transaction cost theory', *Academy of Management Review* 15 (3): 500–13.

Hillis, D. (2002), 'Stumbling into brilliance', *Harvard Business Review*, August: 152–2.

Hirshberg, J. (1999), *The Creative Priority*, London: Penguin.

Hoffman, R.C. (1989), 'Strategies for corporate turnarounds: what do we know about them?', *Journal of General Management*, Spring: 46–66.

Holland, J. (1995), *Hidden Order: How Adaptation Builds Complexity*, Reading MA: Addison-Wesley.

Hopfl, H. (1992), 'The making of a corporate acolyte: some thoughts on charismatic leadership and the reality of organizational commitment', *Journal of Management Studies*, 29 (1): 23–33.

Huff, A.S. (2000), 'Citigroup's John Reed and Stanford's James March on management research and practice', *Academy of Management Executive* 14 (1): 52–64.

Hughes, K., Barsoux, J.L. and Manzoni, J.F. (2003), Nissan's U-Turn: 1999–2001, Case No. 303-046-1, INSEAD.

Huntington, S.P. (1997), *The Clash of Civilizations and the Remaking of World Order*, New York: Touchstone.

Huston, L. and Sakkab, N. (2006), 'Connect and develop: Inside Procter & Gamble's new model for innovation', *Harvard Business Review*, March: 58–66.

Iansiti, M. and Levien, R. (2004), *The Keystone Advantage*, Harvard Business School Press.

Iansiti, M., McFarlan, F.W. and Westerman, G. (2003), 'Leveraging the incumbent's advantage', *MIT Sloan Management Review*, Summer: 58–64.

IBM (2002), 'IBM signs agreement with Sanmina-SCI to manufacture its NetVista desktop PCs in US and Europe', IBM Press Release, 8 January.

Janis, I. (1972), *Victims of Group Think*, Boston: Houghton Mifflin.

Jarillo, J.C. (1988), 'On strategic networks', *Strategic Management Journal* 9: 31–41.

Jarzabkowski, P. (2005), *Strategy as Practice: An Activity-based Approach*, London: Sage.

Jensen, M. and Mecklin, W. (1976), 'Theory of the firm: managerial behaviour, agency costs and ownership structure', *Journal of Financial Economics*, 4: 305–60.

Johnson, G. (1988), 'Rethinking incrementalism', *Strategic Management Journal* 9: 75–91.

Johnson, G. (1990), 'Managing strategic change: the role of symbolic action', *British Journal of Management* 1: 183–200.

Kanter, R.M. (1982), 'The middle manager as innovator', *Harvard Business Review*, July–August: 95–105.

Kanter, R.M. (1983), *The Change Masters*, New York: Simon & Schuster.

Kanter, R.M. (1988), 'When a thousand flowers bloom: structural, collective and social conditions for innovation in organizations', *Research in Organizational Behaviour* 10: 169–211.

Kanter, R.M. (1989), *When Giants Learn to Dance*, New York: Simon & Schuster.

Kanter, R.M. (1991), 'Change: where to begin', *Harvard Business Review*, July–August: 8–9.

Kanter, R.M. (2003), 'Leadership and the psychology of turnarounds', *Harvard Business Review*, June: 58–67.

Kanter, R.M. (2008), 'Transforming giants', *Harvard Business Review*, January: 43–52.

Kanter, R.M. and Dretler, T.D. (1998), '"Global strategy" and its impact on local operations: Lessons from Gillette Singapore', *Academy of Management Executive* 12 (4): 60–8.

Kao, J. (1997), *Jamming: The Art and Discipline of Business Creativity*, London: Harper Collins Business.

Kellerman, B. (1999), *Reinventing Leadership*, New York: State University of New York Press.

Kennedy, C. (1989), 'The transformation of AT&T', *Long Range Planning* 22 (3): 10–17.

Kets de Vries, M.F.R. (1990), 'The organizational fool: balancing a leader's hubris', *Human Relations*, 43 (8): 751–70.

Kets de Vries, M.F.R. and Miller, D. (1985), 'Narcissism and leadership: an object relations perspective', *Human Relations*, 38 (6): 583–601.

Khanna, T. and Palepu, K.G. (2006), 'Emerging giants: building world-class companies in developing countries', *Harvard Business Review*, October: 60–80.

Kiechel III, W. (1982), 'Corporate strategists under fire', *Fortune*, 27 December: 34–9.

Killick, M., Rawoot, I. and Stockport, G.J. (2001), Cisco Systems Inc. – Growth Through Acquisitions, Case No. 301-018-1, Graduate School of Management, University of Western Australia.

Kim, W.C. and Mauborgne, R. (1997a), 'Value innovation: the strategic logic of high growth', *Harvard Business Review*, January–February: 103–12.

Kim, W.C. and Mauborgne, R. (1997b), 'Fair process: managing in the knowledge economy', *Harvard Business Review*, July–August: 65–75.

Kim, W.C. and Mauborgne, R. (1999a), 'Strategy, value innovation, and the knowledge economy', *Sloan Management Review*, Spring: 41–54.

Kim, W.C. and Mauborgne, R. (1999b), 'Creating new market space', *Harvard Business Review*, January–February: 83–93.

Kim, W.C. and Mauborgne, R. (2000), 'Know a winning business idea when you see one', *Harvard Business Review*, September–October: 129–38.

Kim, W.C. and Mauborgne, R. (2002), 'Charting your company's future, *Harvard Business Review*, June: 77–83.

Kim, W.C. and Mauborgne, R. (2003), 'Tipping point leadership', *Harvard Business Review*, April: 60–9.

Kim, W.C. and Mauborgne, R. (2004), Blue ocean strategy, *Harvard Business Review*, October: 76–84.

Kim, W.C. and Mauborgne, R. (2005), *Blue Ocean Strategy*, Boston: Harvard Business School Press.

Kirkpatrick, D. (1992), 'Breaking up IBM', *Fortune*, 27 July: 112–21.

Kling, K. and Goteman, I. (2003), 'IKEA CEO Anders Dahlvig on international growth and IKEA's unique corporate culture and brand identity', *Academy of Management Executive*, 17 (1): 31–7.

Knights, D. and Morgan, G. (1992), 'Leadership and corporate strategy: towards a critical analysis', *The Leadership Quarterly*, 3 (3): 171–90.

Kotter, J.P. (1982), *The General Managers*, New York: Free Press.

Kotter, J.P. (1990), 'What leaders really do', *Harvard Business Review*, May–June: 103–11.

Kotter, J.P. (1995), 'Leading change: why transformation efforts fail', *Harvard Business Review*, March–April: 59–67.

Kuhn, T. (1970), *The Structure of Scientific Revolutions* (2nd Edition), Chicago: University of Chicago Press.

Kuhnert, K.W. and Lewis, P. (1987), 'Transactional and transformative leadership: a constructive/developmental analysis', *Academy of Management Review*, 12 (4): 648–57.

Kurtzman, J. and Rifkin, G. (2001), *From GE to Enron: Lessons on How to Rule the Web*, New York: Wiley.

Lackney, G. (1998), 'Changing patterns in educational facilities', paper presented at the CEFPI Conference, Vancouver, 1998 (from www.designshare.com).

Lane, B. (1989), 'Liberating GE's energy', *Monogram*, Fall: 3.

Lawler III, E.E. and Worley, C.G. (2006), *Built to Change: How to Achieve Sustained Organizational Effectiveness*, San Francisco: Jossey Bass.

Leavy, B. (1995), 'Strategy – but not as we know it', *World Link*, July–August: 30–5.

Leavy, B. (1996a), *Key Processes in Strategy*, London: Thomson Learning.

Leavy, B. (1996b), 'On studying leadership in the strategy field', *The Leadership Quarterly* 7 (4): 435–54.

Leavy, B. (1998), 'The concept of learning in the strategy field: review and outlook', *Management Learning* 29 (4): 447–66.

Leavy, B. (1999), 'Organisation and competitiveness – towards a new perspective', *Journal of General Management* 24 (3): 33–52.

Leavy, B. (2001), 'Creating value in the multi-business firm', *Journal of General Management* 27 (2): 51–66.

Leavy, B. (2002), 'Creativity – the new imperative', *Journal of General Management* 28 (1): 70–85.

Leavy, B. (2003a), 'Understanding the triad of great leadership: context, conviction and credibility', *Strategy & Leadership* 31 (1): 56–60.

Leavy, B. (2003b), 'A more creative organisation and a better breeding ground for leaders', *Irish Marketing Review* 16 (2): 51–6.

Leavy, B. (2003c), 'Assessing your strategic alternatives from both a market position and core competence perspective', *Strategy & Leadership* 31 (6) 29–35.

Leavy, B. (2004a), 'Practising disruptive innovation', a review of C.M. Christensen and M.E. Raynor, *The Innovator's Solution in Strategy & Leadership* 32 (2): 54–5.

Leavy, B. (2004b), 'Outsourcing strategies: opportunities and risks', *Strategy & Leadership* 32 (6): 20–5.

Leavy, B. (2005a), 'Value pioneering – how to discover your own "blue ocean": interview with W. Chan Kim and Renee Mauborgne', *Strategy & Leadership* 33 (6): 13–20.

Leavy, B. (2005b), 'A leader's guide to creating an innovation culture', *Strategy & Leadership* 33 (4): 38–45.

Leavy, B. (2008), 'Gary Hamel's clarion call to radically rethink management', a review of G. Hamel, *The Future of Management* in *Strategy & Leadership* 36 (3): 46–9.

Leavy, B. and Gannon, M. (1998), 'Competing for hearts and minds: a corporate cultural perspective on marketing', *Irish Marketing Review* 11 (1): 39–48.

Leavy, B. and Moitra, D. (2006), 'The practice of co-creating unique value with customers: an interview with C.K. Prahalad', *Strategy & Leadership* 34 (2): 4–9.

Leavy, B. and Wilson, D.C. (1994), *Strategy and Leadership*, London: Routledge.

Lei, D. and Slocum, J.W. (1992), 'Global strategy, competence-building and strategic alliances', *California Management Review*, Fall: 81–97.

Leonard, D. and Strauss, S. (1997), 'Putting your company's whole brain to work', *Harvard Business Review*, July–August: 111–21.

Levitt, T. (1960), 'Marketing myopia', *Harvard Business Review*, July–August: 45–56.

Levitt, T. (1965), 'Exploit the product life cycle', *Harvard Business Review*, November–December: 81–94.

Lewin, K. (1951), *Field Theory in Social Science*, New York: Harper & Row.

Lewin, R. and Regine, B. (2000), *The Soul at Work: Embracing Complexity Science for Business Success*, New York: Simon & Schuster.

Lieberson, S. and O'Connor, J.F. (1972), 'Leadership and organizational performance: a study of large corporations', *American Sociological Review* 37: 117–30.

Loomis, C.J. (1991), 'How does Reed hang on at Citi?', *Fortune*, November 18th : 63–8.

Lowe, J. (1998), *Jack Welch Speaks: Wisdom from the World's Greatest Business Leader*, New York: Wiley.

Lukes, S. (1974), *Power: A Radical View*, London: Macmillan.

Luthans, F. (1980), 'The learning process', in L. Cummings and R. Dunham (eds), *Introduction to Organization Behaviour*, Homewood Illinois: Irwin.

MacKay, R.B. and McKiernan, P. (2004), 'The role of hindsight in foresight: refining strategic reasoning', *Futures* 36: 161–79.

Mackey, J. and Valikangas, L. (2004), 'The myth of unbounded growth', *MIT Sloan Management Review*, Winter: 89–92.

Maccoby, M. (2000), 'Narcissistic leaders: the incredible pros, the inevitable cons', *Harvard Business Review*, January–February: 69–77.

Magaziner, I.C. and Patinkin, M. (1989), 'Fast heat: how Korea won the microwave war', *Harvard Business Review*, January–February: 83–91.

Malone, T.W. (2004), 'Bringing the market inside', *Harvard Business Review*, April: 107–114.

Manville, B. and Ober, J. (2003), *A Company of Citizens*, Boston: Harvard Business School Press.

March, J.G. (1991), 'Exploration and exploitation in organizational learning', *Organization Science* 2 (1): 71–87.

March, J.G. and Olsen, J. (1989), *Rediscovering Institutions: The Organizational Basis of Politics*, New York: Free Press.

Markides, C.C. (1997), 'To diversify, or not to diversify', *Harvard Business Review*, November–December: 93–9.

Markides, C.C. (1999), 'A dynamic view of strategy', *Sloan Management Review*, Spring: 55–63.

Markides, C. and Charitou, C.D. (2004), 'Competing with dual business models: a contingency approach', *Academy of Management Executive* 18 (3): 22–36.

Markides, C. and Geroski, P. (2003a), 'The two cultures of corporate strategy', *Strategy + Business*, Fall: 1–10.

Markides, C. and Geroski, P. (2003b), 'Teaching elephants to dance and other silly ideas', *Business Strategy Review*, Autumn: 49–53.

Markides, C.C. and Williamson, P.J. (1994), 'Related diversification, core competencies and corporate performance', *Strategic Management Journal* 15: 148–65.

Martelli, A. (1996), 'Scenarios and business strategy: some recent developments', *CEMS Business Review* 1: 279–97.

Mayo, A.J. and Nohria, N. (2005), 'Zeitgeist leadership', *Harvard Business Review*, October: 45–60.

McClean, B. (2001), 'Why Enron went bust', *Fortune*, 24 December, 53–8.

McGrath, R.G. and MacMillan, I.C. (1995), 'Discovery-driven planning', *Harvard Business Review*, July–August: 44–54.

McGrath, R.G., Keil, T. and Tukiainen, T. (2006), 'Extracting value from corporate venturing', *MIT Sloan Management Review*, Fall: 50–6.

McKiernan, P. and Carter, C. (2004), 'The millennium nexus: Strategic management at the cross roads', *European Management Review* 1: 3–14

McKinsey (2002), McKinsey Global Investor Opinion Survey on Corporate Governance, New York: McKinsey.

Michaels, E., Handfield-Jones, H. and Axelrod, B. (2001), *The War for Talent*, Boston: Harvard Business School Press.

Milburn, T. (1972), 'The management of crisis', in C. Hermann (ed.), *International Crises: Insights from Behavioural Research*, New York: Free Press.

Miller, D. (1982), 'Evolution and revolution: a quantum view of structural change in organizations', *Journal of Management Studies* 19 (2): 131–51.

Miller, D. (1986), ' Configurations of strategy and structure: towards a synthesis', *Strategic Management Journal* 7: 233–49.

Miller, D. (1987), 'The genesis of configuration', *Academy of Management Review* 12 (4): 686–701.

Miller, D. (1990), *The Icarus Paradox*, New York: Harper Business.

Miller, D. (1991), 'Stale in the saddle: CEO tenure and the match between organization and environment', *Management Science* 17 (1): 34–52.

Miller, D. (1996), 'Configurations revisited', *Strategic Management Journal* 17: 505–12.

Miller, D. and Friesen, P.H. (1980), 'Momentum and revolution in organizational adaptation', *Academy of Management Journal* 23 (4): 591–614.

Miller, D., Eisenstat, R. and Foote, N. (2002), 'Strategy from the inside out: building capability-creating organizations', *California Management Review*, Spring: 37–54.

Miller, K.L. (2006), 'The big blue yonder', *Newsweek*, Special Issue – Issues 2006: 60–4.

Mintzberg, H. (1981), 'Organization design: fashion or fit', *Harvard Business Review*, January–February: 103–16.

Mintzberg, H. (1987), 'Crafting strategy', *Harvard Business Review*, July–August: 66–75.

Mintzberg, H. (1994), *The Rise and Fall of Strategy Planning*, Englewood Cliffs, NJ: Prentice-Hall.

Mintzberg, H. and Waters, J.A. (1985), 'Of strategies, deliberate and emergent', *Strategic Management Journal* 6: 257–72.

Mintzberg, H. and Westley, F. (1992), 'Cycles of organizational change', *Strategic Management Journal* 13: 39–59.

Mintzberg, H., Ahlstrand, B. and Lampel, J. (1998), *Strategy Safari: A Guided Tour Through the Wilds of Strategic Management*, New York: Free Press.

Mito, S. (1990), *The Honda Book of Management*, London: Athlone Press.

Montgomery, C.A. (2008), 'Putting leadership back into strategy', *Harvard Business Review*, January: 54–60.

Moon, Y. (2005), 'Break free from the product life cycle' *Harvard Business Review*, May: 87–94.

Moore, G.A. (1991), *Crossing the Chasm*, New York: Harper Collins.

Moore, G.A. (2004), 'Darwin and the demon', *Harvard Business Review*, July–August: 86–92.

Moore, G.A. (2005), *Dealing with Darwin: How Great Companies Innovate at Every Stage of their Evolution*, New York: Portfolio.

Moore, J.F. (1996), 'The death of competition', *Fortune*, 15 April: 78–80.

Moran, Lord, (1967), *Winston Churchill: The Struggle for Survival 1940–1965*, London: Reader's Digest Association (Originally published by Constable, London).

Morgan, G. (1986), *Images of Organization*, Beverley-Hills, CA: Sage.

Mueller, G. and Barker, V. (1997), 'Upper echelons and board characteristics of turnaround and nonturnaround declining firms', *Journal of Business Research* 39: 119–34.

Mumford, M.D. and Simonton, D.K. (1997), 'Creativity in the workplace: people, problems and structures', *Journal of Creative Behaviour* 31 (1): 1–6.

Nahapiet, J. and Ghoshal, S. (1998), 'Social capital, intellectual capital and the organizational advantage', *Academy of Management Review* 23 (2): 242–66.

Nanda, A. and Bartlett, C.A. (1994), Intel Corporation – Leveraging Capabilities for Strategic Renewal, Case No. 9-394-141, Harvard Business School.

Nathan, J. (1999), *Sony: The Private Life*, Boston: Houghton Mifflin.

Nathanson, D. and Cassano, J. (1982), 'Organization, diversity and performance', *Wharton Magazine*, Summer: 19–26.

Neumair, U. (1998), 'A General Model of Corporate Failure, Survival and Evolution: A Complexity Theory Approach', Unpublished dissertation, University of St. Gallen.

Neustadt, R.E. (1990), *Presidential Power and the Modern Presidents*, New York: Free Press.

Nixon, R.M. (1982), *Leaders*, London: Sidgwick & Jackson.

Nonaka, I. (1988a), 'Creating organizational order out of chaos: self-renewal in Japanese firms', *California Management Review*, Spring: 57–73.

Nonaka, I. (1988b), 'Towards middle-up-down management: accelerating information creation', *Sloan Management Review*, Spring: 9–18.

Nonaka, I., Toyama, R. and Nagata, A. (2000), 'A firm as a knowledge-creating entity: a new perspective on the theory of the firm', *Industrial and Corporate Change* 9 (1): 1–20.

Normann, R. and Ramirez, R. (1993), 'From value chain to value constellation: designing interactive strategy', *Harvard Business Review*, July–August: 65–77.

Nuttall, C. (2005), 'IBM is the only certain victor in new console wars', *Financial Times*, May 16th.

Nystrom, P.C. and Starbuck, W.H. (1984), 'To avoid organizational crises, unlearn', *Organizational Dynamics* 12: 53–65.

OECD (1999), *Principles of Corporate Governance*, Paris: OECD.

O'Higgins, E. (1999), Ryanair: The Low Fares Airline, Video Case No. 399-122-3, University College Dublin.

O'Neil, J.R. (1993), *The Paradox of Success: When Winning at Work Means Losing at Life*, New York: McGraw-Hill.

O'Neill, H.M. (1986), 'Turnaround and recovery: what strategy do you need?', *Long Range Planning* 19 (1): 80–6.

O'Reilly, C. (1986), 'Corporations, culture and commitment: motivation and social control in organizations', *California Management Review*, Summer: 9–41.

O'Reilly, C.A. and Pfeffer, J. (2000), *Hidden Value: How Great Companies Achieve Extraordinary Results from Ordinary People*, Boston: Harvard Business School Press.

O'Reilly, C.A. and Tushman, M.L. (2004), 'The ambidextrous organization', *Harvard Business Review*, April: 74–81.

Ostroff, F. (1999), *The Horizontal Organization: What the Organization of the Future Looks Like and How it Delivers Value to Customers*, New York: Oxford University Press.

Paik, Y. and Choi, D.Y. (2005), 'The shortcomings of a standardized global knowledge management system: the case of Accenture', *Academy of Management Executive* 19 (2): 81–4.

Pascale, T.T. (1991), *Managing on the Edge*, Middlesex: Penguin.

Pascale, R.T. and Athos, A.G. (1981), *The Art of Japanese Management*, New York: Simon & Schuster.

Pascale, R.T. and Sternin, J. (2005), 'Your company's secret change agents', *Harvard Business Review*, May: 73–81.

Pass, C. (2006), 'The Revised Combined Code and Corporate Governance: An Empirical Survey of 50 Large UK Companies', *Managerial Law*, 48 (5): 467–78

Pearce, J. and Robbins, K. (1994), 'Retrenchment remains the foundation of business turnaround', *Strategic Management Journal* 15: 407–17.

Pearce, J. and Robinson, R.J. (1994), *Strategic Management: Formulation, Implementation and Control*, Burr Ridge: Irwin.

Peck, M.S. (1990), *The Road Less Traveled*, London: Arrow.

Pendergrast, M. (1994), *For God, Country and Coca Cola*, London: Phoenix.

Penrose, E.T. (1959), *The Theory of the Growth of the Firm*, New York: John Wiley.

Peters, T. (1984), 'Strategy follows structure: developing distinctive skills', *California Management Review*, Spring: 111–25.

Peters, T.J. and Waterman, R.A. (1982), *In Search of Excellence*, New York: Harper & Row.

Peterson, R.W. (1967), 'New venture management in a large company', *Harvard Business Review*, May–June: 68–76.

Pettigrew, A.M. (1985), *The Awakening Giant*, Oxford: Basil Blackwell.

Pettigrew, A.M. (1987), 'Context and action in the transformation of the firm', *Journal of Management Studies* 24 (6): 649–70.

Pettigrew, A.M., Massini, S. and Numagami, T. (2000), 'Innovative forms of organizing in Europe and Japan', *European Management Journal* 18 (3): 259–73.

Pfeffer, J. (1992), 'Understanding power in organizations', *California Management Review*, Winter: 29–50.

Piscitello, L. (2004), 'Corporate diversification, coherence and economic performance', *Industrial and Corporate Change* 13 (5): 757–87.

Pitcher, P. (1997), *The Drama of Leadership*, New York: Wiley.

Pooley-Dias, G. (1972), 'The strategy and structure of French industrial enterprise', Doctoral dissertation, Harvard Business School.

Porter, M.E. (1979), 'How competitive forces shape strategy', *Harvard Business Review*, March–April: 137–45.

Porter, M.E. (1980), *Competitive Strategy*, New York: Free Press.

Porter, M.E. (1985), *Competitive Advantage*, New York: Free Press.

Porter, M.E. (1987), 'From competitive advantage to corporate strategy', *Harvard Business Review*, May–June: 43–59.

Porter, M.E. (1990), *The Competitive Advantage of Nations*, London: Macmillan.

Porter, M.E. (1996), 'What is strategy?', *Harvard Business Review*, November–December: 61–71.

Porter, M.E. (2001), 'Strategy and the Internet', *Harvard Business Review*, March: 63–78.

Porter, M.E. (2008), 'The five competitive forces that shape strategy', *Harvard Business Review*, January: 78–93.

Porter, M.E. and Kramer, M.R. (2002), 'The competitive advantage of corporate philanthropy', *Harvard Business Review*, December: 57–68.

Porter, M.E. and Kramer, M.R. (2006), 'Strategy & society: The link between competitive advantage and corporate social responsibility', *Harvard Business Review*, December, 78–92.

Powell, W.W. (1990), 'Neither market nor hierarchy', *Research in Organizational Behaviour* 12: 295–336.

Prahalad, C.K. and Bettis, R.A. (1986), 'The dominant logic: a new linkage between diversity and performance', *Strategic Management Journal* 7: 485–501.

Prahalad, C.K. and Hamel, G. (1990), 'The core competence of the corporation', *Harvard Business Review*, May–June: 79–91.

Prahalad, C.K. and Hamel, G. (1994), 'Strategy as a field of study: why search for a new paradigm?', *Strategic Management Journal* 15: 5–16.

Prahalad, C.K. and Krishnan, M.S. (2008), *The New Age of Innovation*, New York: McGraw-Hill.

Prahalad, C.K. and Ramaswamy, V. (2004), *The Future of Competition*, Boston: Harvard Business School Press.

Prahalad, C.K., Fahey, L. and Randall, R.M. (2001), 'Creating and leveraging core competencies', in L. Fahey and R.M. Randall (eds) *The Portable MBA in Strategy*, New York: Wiley.

Priem, R.L. and Butler, J.E. (2001), 'Is the resource-based "view" a useful perspective for strategic management research?', *Academy of Management Review* 26 (1): 22–40.

Prokesch, S.E. (1997), 'Unleashing the power of learning: an interview with British Petroleum's John Browne', *Harvard Business Review*, September–October: 147–68.

Pudney, D., Van der Merwe, M. and Stockport, G.J. (2001), eBay.com – Profitability: Managing Growth from Start-up to 2000, Case No. 301-017-1, Graduate School of Management, University of Western Australia, Perth.

Quinn, J.B. (1980), *Strategies for Change: Logical Incrementalism*, Homewood Ill.: Irwin.

Quinn, J.B. (1982), 'Managing strategies incrementally', *Omega* 10 (6): 613–27.

Quinn, J.B. (1985), 'Managing innovation: controlled chaos', *Harvard Business Review*, May–June: 73–84.

Quinn, J.B. (2000), 'Outsourcing innovation: the new engine of growth', *Sloan Management Review*, Summer: 3–28.

Quinn, J.B. and Paquette, P.C. (1990), 'Technology in services: creating organizational revolutions', *Sloan Management Review*, Winter: 67–78.

Rangan, V.K. and Bell, M. (2002), Dell – New Horizons, Case No. 9-502-022, Harvard Business School.

Raynor, M.E. and Panetta, J.A. (2005), 'A better way to R&D', *Strategy & Innovation*, March–April: 3–5.

Rikert, D.C. and Christensen, C.R. (1993), Phil Knight: CEO at NIKE (1983), Case No. 9-390-038, Harvard Business School.

Roberts, E.B. (1980), 'New ventures for corporate growth, *Harvard Business Review*, July–August: 134–42.

Robbins, D.K. and Pearce, J.A. (1992), 'Turnaround: retrenchment and recovery', *Strategic Management Journal* 13: 287–309.

Rochet, J-C and Tirole, J. (2003), 'Platform competition in two-sided markets', *Journal of the European Economic Association* 1 (4): 990–1029.

Rost, J.C. (1993), *Leadership for the Twenty-First Century*, Westport Connecticut: Praeger.

Ruddiman, W. (2003) 'The anthropogenic greenhouse era began thousands of years ago', *Climatic Change* 61: 261–93.

Rumelt, R.P. (1974), *Strategy, Structure and Economic Performance*, Boston: Division of Research, Graduate School of Business Administration, Harvard University.

Rumelt, R.P. (1982), 'Diversification strategy and profitability', *Strategic Management Journal* 3: 359–69.

Rumelt, R.P., Schendel, D. and Teece, D.J. (1991), 'Strategic management and economics', *Strategic Management Journal*, 12S: 5–29.

Rutledge, J. (1997), 'Teaching things that really matter', *Forbes*, 10 March: 73.

Sakiya, T. (1982), *Honda Motor: The Men, the Management, the Machines*, Tokyo: Kodansha.

Samuelson, P. (1966), 'Science and Stocks', *Newsweek*, September: 92

Sandoz, P. (1997), *Canon: Global Responsibilities and Local Decisions*, London: Penguin.

Schawlow, A. (1982), 'Going for the gaps', *The Stanford Magazine*, Fall: 42.

Schein, E.H. (1985), *Organizational Culture and Leadership*, San Francisco: Jossey-Bass.

Schein, E.H. (1997), *Organizational Culture and Leadership*, San Francisco: Jossey-Bass (2nd Edition).

Schlesinger, A.M. (1989), *The Cycles of American History*, Middlesex: Penguin.

Schlesinger, L.A., Pelofsky, M., Pascale, R.T. and Ehrlich, S.P. (1990), The transformation at Ford, Case No. 9-390-083, Harvard Business School.

Schlender, B. (1998), 'In a meeting of incomparable minds, Buffet and Gates muse about taking risks, motivating employees, confronting mistakes and giving back', *Fortune*, July 20th: 41–7.

Schmidt, E. and Varian, H. (2005), 'Google: Ten Golden Rules', *Newsweek*, 2 December: 48–53.

Schoeffler, S., Buzell, R.D., and Heany, D.F. (1974), 'Impact of strategic planning on profit performance', *Harvard Business Review*, March–April: 137–45.

Schoemaker, P. J.H. (1997), 'Disciplined imagination: from scenarios to strategic options', *International Studies of Management & Organization* 27 (2): 43–70.

Schumpeter, J.A. (1934), *The Theory of Economic Development*, Oxford: Oxford University Press.

Schwartz, P. (1991), *The Art of the Long View: Planning for the Future in an Uncertain World*, New York: Doubleday Currency.

Senge, P.M. (1990), 'The leader's new work: building learning organizations', *Sloan Management Review*, Fall: 7–23.

Senge, P.M. (1997), 'Foreword' in A. De Geus, *The Living Company*, Boston: Harvard Business School Press.

Senge, P. and Carstedt, G. (2001), 'Innovating our way to the next industrial revolution', *MIT Sloan Management Review*, Winter: 24–38.

Senge, P., Smith, B., Kruschwitz, N., Laur, J. and Scley, S. (2008), *The Necessary Revolution: How Individuals and Organisations are Working Together to Create a Sustainable World*, New York: Doubleday.

Shearman and Sterling LLP. (2005), *Trends in the Corporate Governance Practices of the 100 largest US Public Companies*, New York: Shearman & Sterling LLP.

Sherman, S. (1993), 'A master class in radical change', *Fortune* 13 December: 40–4.

Shetty, Y.K. and Perry, N.S. (1976), 'Are top executives transferable across companies?', *Business Horizons*, June: 23–8.

Simon, H.A. (1955), 'A behavioural model of rational choice', *Quarterly Journal of Economics* 69: 99–118.

Simon, H.A. (1956), 'Rational choice and the structure of the environment', *Psychological Review* 62 (2): 129–38.

Sinetar, M. (1985), 'Entrepreneurs, chaos and creativity – can creative people really survive large company structure', *Sloan Management Review*, Winter: 57–62.

Slatter, S. (1984), *Corporate Recovery: Successful Turnaround Strategies and their Implementation*, Harmondsworth: Penguin.

Slatter, S. and Lovett, D. (1999), *Corporate Turnaround: Managing Companies in Distress*, London: Penguin.

Sloan, A. (1963), *My Years with General Motors*, New York: Doubleday.

Smircich, L. and Stubbert, C. (1985), 'Strategic management in an enacted world', *Academy of Management Review* 10 (4): 724–36.

Smock, C. (1955), 'The influence of psychological stress or the intolerance of ambiguity', *Journal of Abnormal and Social Psychology* 50: 177–82.

Southwick, K. (2000) 'Foreword', in Bunnell, D. *Making the Cisco Connection: The Story Behind the Real Internet Superpower*, New York: Wiley.

Sonnenfeld, J.A. (2004) 'A return to the power of ideas', *MIT Sloan Management Review*, Winter: 30–3.

Stalk, G., Evans, P. and Shulman, L.E. (1992), 'Competing on capabilities: the new rules of corporate strategy', *Harvard Business Review*, March–April: 57–69.

Starbuck, W.H. (1982), 'Congealing oil: inventing ideologies to justify acting ideologies out', *Journal of Management Studies* 19 (1): 3–27.

Starbuck, W. and Milliken, F. (1988), 'Challenger: fine-tuning the odds until something breaks', *Journal of Management Studies* 25: 319–40.

Starbuck, W.H., Greve, A. and Hedberg, B.L.T. (1978), 'Responding to crises', *Journal of Business Administration* 9 (2): 111–37.

Starkey, K. (2000), 'The music of organization or "some like it hot"', presented at the conference workshop, *Conception et Dynamique des Organizations: Sait On Piloter le Changement*, Ecole des Haute Etudes Commerciales, Universite de Lausanne, 17 March.

Starrat, R.J. (1993), *The Drama of Leadership*, London: Farmer Press.

Stata, R. (1989), 'Organizational learning: the key to management innovation', *Sloan Management Review*, Spring: 63–74.

Steinbock, D. (2001), *The Nokia Revolution*, New York: AMACOM.

Steiner, G.A. (1969), *Top Management Planning*, New York: Free Press.

Steiner, G.A. (1979), *Strategic Planning: What Every Manager Must Know*, New York: Free Press.

Stevens, A. (2001), *Jung: A Very Short Introduction*, Oxford: Oxford University Press.

Stewart, T.A. (1999), 'See Jack: see Jack run Europe', *Fortune*, 27 September, 66–75.

Stinchcombe, A. (1965), 'Social structure and organizations', in J. March (ed.), *Handbook of Organizations*, Chicago: Rand McNally.

Stopford, J.M. and Baden-Fuller, C. (1990), 'Corporate rejuvenation', *Journal of Management Studies* 27 (4): 399–415.

Storr, A. (1991), *The Dynamics of Creation*, Middlesex: Penguin.

Strebel, P. (1994), 'Choosing the right change path', *California Management Review*, Winter: 29–51.

Stross, R.E. (1996), *The Microsoft Way*, Reading MA: Addison-Wesley.

Sutton, R.I. (2002), *Weird Ideas that Work*, New York: Free Press.

Sykes, H.B. (1986), 'Lessons from a new ventures programme', *Harvard Business Review*, May–June: 69–74.

Tannenbaum, R. and Schmidt, W. (1958), 'How to choose a leadership pattern', *Harvard Business Review*, March–April: 95–101.

Tanriverdi, H. and Venkatraman, N. (2005), 'Knowledge relatedness and the performance of multibusiness firms', *Strategic Management Journal* 26: 97–119.

Tarnas, R. (1996), *The Passion of the Western Mind*, London: Pimlico.

Taylor, W. (1991), 'The logic of global business: an interview with ABB's Percy Barnevik', *Harvard Business Review*, March–April: 91–105.

Teece, D.J. (1986), 'Profiting from technological innovation: implications for integration, collaboration, licensing and public policy', *Research Policy* 15: 285–305.

Teece, D.J., Pisano, G. and Shuen, A. (1990), *Firm Capabilities, Resources, and the Concept of Strategy: Four Paradigms of Strategic Management*, Berkeley CA: University of California.

Teece, D.J., Pisano, G. and Shuen, A. (1997), 'Dynamic capabilities and strategic management', *Strategic Management Journal* 18 (7): 509–33.

Teerlink, R. and Ozley, L. (2000), *More than a Motorcycle*, Boston: Harvard Business School Press.

Tesluk, P.E., Farr, J.L. and Klein, S.A. (1997), 'Influences of organizational culture and climate on individual creativity, *Journal of Creative Behaviour* 31 (1): 27–41.

Thanheiser, H.T. (1972), 'Strategy and structure in German industrial enterprise', Doctoral dissertation, Harvard Business School.

Therborn, G. (2000), 'Globalizations: dimensions, historical waves, regional effects and normative governance', *International Sociology* 15 (2): 151–79.

Thomas, H. (2000), *Front Row at the White House*, New York: Touchstone.

Thomke, S. (2001), 'Enlightened experimentation: the new imperative for innovation', *Harvard Business Review*, February: 67–75.

Thomke, S. and Nimgade, A. (2000), IDEO Product Development, Case No. 9-600-143, Harvard Business School.

Tichy, N.M. and Cohen, E. (2002), *The Leadership Engine*, New York: Harper Business Essentials.

Tichy, N.M. and Devanna, M.A. (1986), *The Transformational Leader*, New York: Wiley.

Tilles, S. (1963), 'How to evaluate strategy', *Harvard Business Review*, July–August: 111–21.

TIME (1954), 'Gamble in the sky', *TIME*, 19 July: 44–9 (uncredited).

Toffler, A. (1980), *The Third Wave*, New York: William Morrow.

Toffler, A. (1985), *The Adaptive Corporation*, Aldershot: Gower.

Toynbee, A. (1972), *A Study of History*, New York: Oxford University Press.

Tushman, M.L. and Anderson, P. (1986), 'Technological discontinuities and organizational environments', *Administrative Science Quarterly* 31: 439–65.

Tushman, M.L., Newman, W.H. and Romanelli, E. (1986), 'Convergence and upheaval: managing the unsteady pace of organizational evolution', *California Management Review*, Fall: 29–44.

US National Research Council (2001), *Climate Change Science: An Analysis of Some Key Questions, Committee on the Science of Climate Change*, National Research Council, Washington: National Academy Press.

Utterback, J.M. (1994), *Mastering the Dynamics of Innovation*, Boston: Harvard Business School Press.

Utterback, J.M. and Abernathy, W.J. (1975), 'A dynamic model of process and product innovation', *Omega* 3 (6): 639–56.

Vaill, P.B. (1989), *Managing as a Performing Art*, San Francisco: Jossey-Bass.

Van Basten Battenberg, R. and Birkinshaw, J. (2002), Philips Corporate Venturing (A), Case No. 303-131-1, London Business School.

Van der Heijden, K. (1996), *Scenarios: The Art of Strategic Conversation*, Chichester: John Wiley.

Van der Heijden, K. (2005), *Scenarios: The Art of Strategic Conversation* (2nd Edition), London: John Wiley.

Van der Veer, J. (2005), 'Shell Global Scenarios to 2025: The Future Business Environment: Trends, Trade-offs and Choices', Royal Dutch/Shell Group.

Voelpel, S.C., Dous, M. and Davenport, T.H. (2005), 'Five steps to creating a global knowledge-sharing system: Siemens' ShareNet', *Academy of Management Executive* 19 (2): 9–23.

Wack, P. (1985), 'Scenarios: uncharted waters Ahead. *Harvard Business Review* 63 (5): 72–89

Waterman, R.H. (1994), *Frontiers of Excellence*, London: Nicholas Brealey Publishing.

Waterman, R.H., Peters, T.J. and Philips, J.R. (1980), 'Structure is not organization', *Business Horizons* 23 (3): 14–26.

Weick, K. (1979), *The Social Psychology of Organizing*, Reading MA: Addison-Wesley.

Weick, K. (1996), *Sensemaking in Organizations*, Newbury Park, CA: Sage.

Welch, J.F. (1988), Address at the General Electric Annual General Meeting, Waukesha, Wisconsin, 27 April.

Welch, J.F. (1989), Address at the General Electric Annual General Meeting, Greenville, South Carolina, 26 April.

Welch, J.F. (2001), *Jack: What I've Learned Leading a Great Company and Great People*, London: Headline.

Wernerfelt, B. (1984), 'A resource-based view of the firm', *Strategic Management Journal* 5: 171–80.

Westley, F. and Mintzberg, H. (1989), 'Visionary leadership and strategic management', *Strategic Management Journal* 10: 17–32.

Wetlaufer, S. (1999), 'Organizing for empowerment: an interview with AES's Roger Sant and Dennis Bakke', *Harvard Business Review*, January–February: 111–23.

Wetlaufer, S. (2000), 'Common sense and conflict: an interview with Disney's Michael Eisner', *Harvard Business Review*, January–February: 115–24.

Wetlaufer, S. (2001), 'The business case against revolution: an interview with Nestle's Peter Brabeck', *Harvard Business Review*, February: 113–19.

Whittington, R., Jarzabkowski, P., Mayer, M., Mounoud, E., Nahapiet., J. and Jouleau, I. (2003), 'Taking strategy seriously: Responsibility and reform for an important social practice', *Journal of Management Inquiry*, 12: 396–409.

Whyte, D. (1997), *The Heart Aroused: Poetry and the Preservation of the Soul at Work*, London: The Industrial Society.

Wiersema, M. (2002), 'Holes at the top: why CEO firings backfire', *Harvard Business Review*, December: 70–7.

Williamson, O.E. (1975), *Markets and Hierarchies: Analysis and Antitrust Implications*, New York: Free Press.

Wilson, E.O. (2007), *The Creation: An Appeal to Save life on Earth*, New York: W. W. Norton.

Wrigley, L. (1970), 'Divisional autonomy and diversification', DBA dissertation, Harvard Business School.

Yoffie, D. (2005), Intel Capital, 2005 (A), Case No. 9-705-408, Harvard Business School.

Zaleznik, A. (1977), 'Managers and leaders: are they different?', *Harvard Business Review*, May–June: 67–78.

Zaleznik, A. (1992), 'Managers and leaders: are they different?' (Reprinted with retrospective commentary), *Harvard Business Review*, March–April: 126–35.

Ziegler, R. (2002), 'Anyone here have any bright ideas', *Outlook*, Number 1: 51–7.

Zook, C. (2004), 'Increasing the odds of successful growth: the critical prelude to moving "beyond the core"', *Strategy & Leadership* 32 (4): 17–23.

Zook, C. (2007), *Unstoppable: Finding Hidden Assets to Renew the Core and Fuel Profitable Growth*, Boston: Harvard Business School Press.

Zook, C. and Allen, J. (2003), 'Growth outside the core', *Harvard Business Review*, December: 66–73.

Zweig, C. and Abrams, J. (1991), *Meeting the Shadow*, New York: Tarcher Putnam.

Zwicky, F. (1948), *The Morphological Method of Analysis and Construction*, Pasedena: California Institute of Technology.

index

Page spans may indicate separate mentions rather than continuous discussion. Italic page numbers indicate figures and tables.

3M, 145, 173, 184, 189, 195, 200, 211, 237
7-S framework, 177, 183, 267

'A resource-based view of the firm'
    (Wernerfelt), 139
'absorptive capacity', in innovation, 216
accountability, internal corporate venturing
    (ICV), 233–6
adhocracy, 178
AES, 32, 34, 44
Africa, globalisation, 86–8
'agency' theory, 47
Agilent, 237
agricultural society, 77
airlines, European, 237–8
Akers, John, 187
alignment, in organizational structure, 182–3
Allen, Bill, 36
Allen, J., 171
'ambidextrous organization', 231
Amo, B.W., 228
Andrews, K., 6
Ansoff, H.I., 2, 73, 171
Apple, 163
Argenti, J., 73, 227
Arnold, Thurman, 25
'art of the long view', 12
Arthur Anderson, 52–3
Asahi breweries, 271
aspiration level, 253–5
AT&T, 269, 271, 275
Athos, A.G., 267
Austin, Paul, 184
autonomous strategic behaviour, 228
autonomy, 198
    for new ventures, 229–32

Baden-Fuller, C., 269
Bakke, Dennis, 32, 34

Baks, Claude, 39
Bank of Credit and Commerce International
    (BCCI), 49
Barnevik, Percy, 186
Barney, J., 38
Bartlett, C.A., 179, 185, 187, 189–90, 211, 231
Bausch & Lomb, 131
BCG Matrix. see growth-share matrix
Beck, N., 237
Belgium, corporate governance, 55
Bennis, W., 29, 213
Berger, Gaston, 120–1
Bettis, R.A., 169, 175
BIC, 175
Biederman, P., 213
biodiversity, 92
Birkinshaw, J., 231
Black Friday, 39
Block, Z., 236
blue ocean strategy, 2, 126, 147–8
boards, 47–8, 56–8
Bobbitt, P., 82, 88
Boeing, 36
Boston Consulting Group (BCG), 130,
    132, 169
Bower, J.L., 190, 227
Boynton, A., 213
BP, 174
Branson, Richard, 20, 30–1, 34–5, 183, 195
BrightHouse, 210
'bringing the market inside', 227
Brown, J.S., 160
BTR, 175
Burgelman, R.A., 177, 223, 225, 227–8, 230
Burns, James McGregor, 30, 64
Bush, George W., 28
business concept innovation, 152
business contexts, complexity, 11–12
business leaders, priorities for, 58–9

business portfolio matrix. *see* growth-share matrix
business strategy, as distinct from corporate strategy, 13
Business Week, 170–1
businesses, portfolios, 173

Cabinet Office (UK), 82–3
Cadbury, 269
Cadbury Committee, 49–52, 55, 57
Cadbury Report. *see* Cadbury Committee
Cadbury, Sir Adrian, 55
Campbell, A., 172, 196, 224–7, 233, 237–8
Canon, 27, 141–3, 145, 170, 173, 183, 189, 276–7
capitalism, inclusive, 36–7
Capra, F., 189
Captain Kirk, 43, 45
carbon, energy/emissions, 91
Carroll, Darren, 219
Carstedt, G., 60–1
Cash Cows, 133–4
Cassano, J., 172
Cassella Wines, 149
'celebrity CEOs', 21
centralisation–decentralisation dynamic, 14
Centre d'Etudes Prospectives (CEP), 120–1
CEOs
    performance, 20
    role, 7–8, 21
    as separate from Chair of Board, 57–8
    succession and financial
Chair of Board, as separate from CEO, 57–8
Challenger, 252
Chandler, A.D., 2, 176, 196–7
Chandler–Wrigley–Rumelt studies, 177
change
    management processes for, 75–6
    in political history, 80–2
    in social history, 77–80
    structural, 99–104
    tension between drivers, 94
    typologies, 75
charisma, 31–2, 39
Charitou, C.D., 230
Chesbrough, Henry, 216, 220–1
Child, J., 269
China, 85–6, 90
Christensen, C.M., 2–3, 60, 126, 149–52, 158, 190, 230, 233, 235
Christensen, C.R., 6

Christian Church, 45–6
Chrysler, 21
Churchill, Sir Winston, 24
Ciba Vision, 231
Cirque du Soleil, 148
Cisco, 170, 216–17
Citibank, 184, 276
climate change, 91–2
CNN, 21, 34–5
co-creation of value, 2, 126, 152–4
Coates, J.F., 121–2
Coca Cola, 21, 39, 135–6, 171, 184
cognition, 70–6
cognitive ability, divergent thinking, 206–7
cognitive inertia, 71–2
cognitive schemata, 175
Cohen, E., 22
Cohen, W.M., 216
collaboration, 198
Collins, J.C., 22, 25, 36, 279
Colville, Robert, 37
competencies, portfolio of, 173
competency, 142–6, 164–5. *see also* core competency
Competing for the Future (Prahalad and Hamel), 152–4
competition
    from Eastern companies, 3
    for hearts and minds, 32–7
    network to network, 165
    shift from firm-to-firm to network-to-network, 154–64
    shift to value innovation, 146–7
competitive analysis, 12–13, 125–146
competitive positioning, 125, 137–9, 183. *see also* positioning
Competitive Strategy (Porter), 126, 164
competitive strength, and industry attractiveness, 135
competitiveness, as the focus of strategy, 2–4
complexity, of business contexts, 11–12
conceptual frameworks, development, 5, 7
Connect and Develop strategy, 218–19
constructive conflict, 184
consumer-orientation, 35–6
context
    complexity, 69
    content, culture and cognition, 71–6
    for creativity, 210–12
    importance, 70–6
    for leadership, 24

relationship between aspects, 72–3
uncertainty, 95–9
control, level of, 197
conviction, in leadership, 24–5
Coopers and Lybrand, 48–9
core competency, 2–3, 13, 125, 139–41, 144–5, 173–4. *see also* competency
core product, 141–2
Corning, 232–4
Corning Micro-array Technologies (CMT), 232–4
corporate citizenship, expanding, 59
corporate entrepreneurship, top down/bottom up debate, 227–9
corporate governance, 5–6, 45–57
corporate identity, strengthening, 35–6
corporate leadership, new agenda, 58–63
corporate management model, 167, 175, 179, 191–2, 194–6, 200
corporate management, new models of, 179–80
corporate scandals, 48–50, 52–3, 55–6
corporate social responsibility (CSR), 5, 61, 81
Corporate Strategy (Ansoff), 2
corporate strategy, as distinct from business strategy, 13
Corporate Strategy Board, 237
Courtaulds, 224
creative destruction, 127, 151, 279
creative disalignment, 183–4
creative paranoia, 184
creative personality, 205
creativity, 183
    3M, 211
    building context and culture for, 210–12
    and efficiency, 214–15
    fostering, 209–15
    as group activity, 212–13
    and innovation, 204–15
    nurturing and leading, 212–14
    psychodynamics, 207–9
    understanding, 206
credibility, in leadership, 25–8
'creeping determinism', 115
cronyism, and corporate governance, 46
cross-functional teams, 273
Cross Impact Analysis (CIA), 97–9
culture. *see also* leadership culture;
    corporate, 31–2
    for creativity, 210–12
    as a differentiator, 33–5

internal corporate venturing (ICV), 234
managerial culture
    shift from bureaucratic to entrepreneurial, 74–5
    shift from managerial to leadership, 41
    and sustainable advantage, 32
    value-rich, 38–9
curiosity, creative personality, 208–9
Cyert, R., 255–6

Dalton, C.M., 57
Dalton, D.R., 58
Davis, S.M., 184–5
Day, J.D., 186, 230
de Geus, A., 189, 243, 264, 278–80, 291–2
De Havilland, 129
de-individuation, as a theory of group action, 48
de Pree, Max, 32
dealer relations, as a core capability in Honda, 174
decentralisation, 198
decentralisation with co-ordinated control, 185
dedication, and the creative personality, 208–9
Dell, 128, 131, 138, 148, 158, 175
Deloitte and Touche, 49
democracy of ideas, 213
demographics, 88–9
Dephi method, 99–101, 103–4
Dess, G.G., 228–9
development, sustainable, 61
Dialectical Inquiry, 100
diamond, (Porter's), 2
differentiation, and corporate culture 33–5
Digital, 27
directional-growth matrix, 2, 171
discipline, and creativity, 214
discovery-driven planning, 235
disharmony, and the four Cs of strategic management, 74
Disney, 213
disruptive innovation, 2, 126, 149–52, 156
diversification, 14, 168, 170–3, 237
divine discontent, 183
divisional form, 178
Dodos, 255
Dogs, 133
dominant logic, 175
Dow Corning, 184–5

Doz, Y.L., 185
Dretler, T.D., 196
drivers, of next wave, 83–4
Drucker, Peter, 204
Du Pont, 131
duality, strategic management, 44
Dunn, Debra, 62
DuPont, 168
'dynamic efficiency', (versus 'static
    efficiency') 181
dynamism, in the environment of
    business, 179

eBay, 32, 37, 162
Ebers, M., 31
economic growth, projections, 90
'economies of experience', 130
economies of scale, 170
economies of scope, 170
Economist, 57
Edison, Thomas, 205, 212, 220
effectiveness, as dynamic interaction, 27–8
Eisenmann, T., 163–4
Eisenstat, R., 229
Eisner, Michael, 24
Eli Lilly, 219
Emerson Electric, 175
EMI, 129
emotional intelligence, 22
emphasis, shifting away from centralized
    planning, 21
employees, services to, 80
empowerment, 227
energy security, 90–1
Enron, 38–9, 44, 47, 52–3, 162
entrepreneurial orientation (EO), 228–9
entrepreneurship, 195–6, 200, 227–9
environmental factors, in determination of
    strategy, 11
environments, stable and unstable, 73–4
Ernst and Young, 49
Esler, P., 45
Europe, 55, 86, 90
'excellence crusade', 4
experience curve, 2, 125, 130–2, 164
experience effect, variation, 131–2
experience environments, 153
experience innovation/co-creation of value,
    126, 152–4
experience networks, 153

exploitation and exploration, in org. learning,
    229, 263
EXPLOR-SIM, 98

familiar, focusing on, 71–2
fear, as motivator, leadership, 40
federalism, 186–7, 189
Fellini, Federico, 208
Fiedler, E.R., 23, 96
financial control, 196–7
Fischer, B., 213
fit, internal, 182–3
five configurations, 178
Five Forces model, 2, 134–7, 165, 170
'flocking', organizational learning, 189
Florida, Richard, 291
focus, strategic outsourcing, 155
Ford Model T, 139, 148
Ford Motors, 27, 269–70, 274–5
forecasting, 95–7
foreign direct investment (FDI), 85
Foresight Group (Department of Trade and
    Industry), 107–8
'forgetting', and new business venturing,
    231–2
formulation, of strategy, 4
Foss, N.J., 167
Foster, Richard, 149, 280
founders, charismatic, 31
four Cs of strategic management, 73
France, corporate governance, 55
free trade, sustaining, 59–60
Friedman, Milton, 61
Friesen, P.H., 265–6
Fukuyama, F., 181
fun, and corporate values/culture, 32, 35

Gandhi, Indira, 28
Gardner, Howard, 25, 209
Gardner, John, 28–9, 290
Garten, Jeffrey, 57–60
Garvin, D.A., 224, 234
Gates, Bill, 24, 212–13
Gault, Stan, 24
General Electric, 21, 24–7, 43, 157, 172, 184,
    190–4, 200, 211, 237, 244, 277
General Motors, 168, 174
generalist CEO perspective on strategy, 7–8
generic strategies, 2, 134, 165, 170, 178
George, B., 22

Germany, corporate governance, 56
Geroski, P., 238
Gerstner, Lou, 21–2, 156–7, 187, 217–18, 270–2, 274–6, 278
Ghemawat, P., 131
Ghoshal, S., 179, 185, 187, 190, 199, 211, 231
Ghosn, Carlos, 270, 273–4, 276–8
Gibson, C., 231
Gillette, 151, 171
Gillette Asia, 195
Giuliani, Rudi, 25
Glass, David, 24–5
global economy, growth, 3
global scenarios, 83–92
globalisation, 58–9, 78, 84–8
globalising firms, HQ-subsidiary relationship, 196–7
Godet, Michel, 121
Goffee, R., 22
Goizueta, Roberto, 21, 24
Goleman, D., 22
Google, 211
Goold, M., 172, 196–7
Gordon, T.J., 98
Govindarajan, V., 230–2, 234–5
Gratton, L., 199
Grinyer, P., 244
group action, theories of, 47–8
'group polarisation', 48
'group think', 48
Grove, Andy, 57, 184, 213–14
growth imperative, and internal corporate venturing (ICV), 236–8
growth-share matrix, 2, 13–14, 124, 132–4, 164, 169, 184
Guilford, J.P., 206–7

Hagel, J., 160
Hall, W.K., 169
Hamel, G., 2–3, 19, 125, 139, 143–6, 152–4, 173–4, 183, 203, 216, 220, 227, 236, 272–3, 279–80, 291
Handy, Charles, 186–7
Hanson Trust, 197
Hapeslagh, Philippe, 55
Hargadon, A., 204
Harley-Davidson, 244, 271–2
harmony amongst three Cs, 74
Hart-Rudman Commission, 114
Hart, S.L., 60

Hatch, M.J., 113
headquarters, relationship with subsidiaries, 196–7
'heart-storming', not just brain-storming, 210
hearts and minds, competing for, 32–7
Heidrick and Struggles, survey of corporate governance, 55
Heifetz, R.A., 273, 278
Helmer, O., 98–9
Henderson, Bruce, 130, 132
Herbold, Robert, 215
Herman Miller, 32
Hewlett, Bill, 32
Hewlett-Packard, 32, 62–3, 237
hidden assets, and strategic renewal, 46
Higgs Inquiry, 55
Hirshberg, Jerry, 210
Hoffman, R.C., 276
homogeneity, cultural, 39
Honda, 27, 32, 34, 40, 76, 145, 170, 173–4
Honda, Soichiro, 35
hostile takeovers, 54
HQ-Subsidiary relationship, 14, 196-7
hub firms, 161
hubris, 24, 38–40, 54
Hudson Institute, 109–10
humanism, and the new industry order, 61
humanity, 293
Hyman, Bill, 54, 56

'i-community', 62–3
Iaccoca, Lee, 21, 29
Iansiti, M., 161–2
IBM, 21, 156–8, 187, 217–18, 222, 232, 237, 239, 244, 269–72, 274–8
IBM Global Services, 157
Icarus Paradox, 38, 251
ICI, 172, 269
ideas, unusual, 206–15
identification, emotional, 39
identity, strengthening corporate, 35–6
IDEO, 210, 213–14
IKEA, 31–2, 35, 148, 156, 197
Imation, 237
IMF, 52
Immelt, Jeff, 21, 191
incentives, internal corporate venturing (ICV), 235–6
India, 86, 90, 161
'individualized corporation', 231

induced strategic behaviour, 228
industrial society, 78
industry attractiveness, and competitive
    strength, 135
industry attractiveness, and market power,
    135–7
inertia, cognitive, 71–2
information and communication technology
    (ICT), 198
information society, 78
InnoCentive, 219
innovate-or-die, 184
innovation, 3, 14–15, 223, 239
    absorption, integration, invention, 215–22
    based on talent or organisation, 204–6
    closed to open, 216–22
    continuous, 75–6
    contrasting principles of closed and
      open, 222
    and creativity, 204–15
    dramatic, 76
    fostering, 209–15
    open, 215–22, 239
    thousand flowers approach, 215–22
Innovation: The Attacker's Advantage
    (Foster), 149
Institute of Chartered Accountants in England
    and Wales (ICAEW), 49
integration, 180–2, 198–200, 216, 231–2
integrity, restoring it to the financial
    markets, 59
Intel, 57, 158, 184, 205, 213–14, 224, 233
Intel Capital, 226
intellectual capital, leveraging it across the
    MBF 194
internal corporate venturing (ICV)
    autonomy of new ventures, 229–32
    corporate culture, 234
    as cyclical, 223–6
    exploration and exploitation, 229
    five main types, 226
    and growth imperative, 236–8
    incentives, 235–6
    independence and integration, 231–2
    leadership, planning and accountability,
      233–6
    risk, 225
internal processes, and growth, 4
Intuitive Logics (IL), 117–22
invention, in innovation, 216
Isdell, Neville, 21

IT industry, evolution, 158–9
Italy, corporate governance, 55

Jacobs, Jane, 291
Japan, 4, 90
Jefferson, Thomas, 27
Jobs, Steve, 30, 40
Johnson and Johnson, 36
Johnson, G., 267
Johnson, Lyndon, 29
joint stock companies, 46
Jones, G., 22
Jones, Reginald, 29, 43, 191
Jouvenal, Bertrand de, 121
Jung, C.G., 207

Kahn-based scenario planning, 110
Kahn, Herman, 109
'kaizen', 75–6
Kaku, Ryuzaburo, 27, 35, 276–7
Kamprad, Ivgar, 31, 35
Kanter, R.M., 196, 199, 227, 269, 278
Kao, 189
Kao, J., 204
Kaplan. N., 280
Kawashima, Kiyoshi, 27
Kay, John, 21
Keats, John, 208
Kelleher, Herb, 20
Kelley, David, 214
Kennedy, John F., 26
Kentucky Fried Chicken, 197
keystone firms in strategic networks, 162
Kim, W.C., 2–3, 126, 147–8, 271
kindred spirits, 34
Kingly States, 81
knowledge, 195
knowledge capital, 179
knowledge society, 79, 81–3
Kolvereid, L., 228
Kotter, J.P., 23, 29, 185
Kramer, M.R., 61–2
Krishnan, M.S., 153

La Prospective (La P), 120–1
Lafley, A.G., 218
Laggards, 254, 256
Laurie, D.L., 278
Law, Andy, 208
'law of requisite variety', 75
Lawler, E.E., 280

Lawrence, P.R., 184–5
Lay, Ken, 38–9, 47
leaders, as different from managers, 28–31
leadership. *see also* strategic leadership
  context for, 24
  conviction in, 24–5
  and corporate culture, 31
  credibility in, 25–8
  internal corporate venturing (ICV), 233–6
  and management, 11
  nature of, 22–8
  in recovery, 260
  and status, 29
  strategic impact, 8
  as strategic variable, 10–11
  traits and styles, 22
  transactional, 30–1, 64
  as transferable asset, 22–3
  transformational, 31, 64, 276–8
  value-rich, 38–9
  within living systems model, 190
leadership culture, 231. *see also* culture;
  managerial culture
  and managerial culture, 42, 42–4
  pathologies, 39
  potential pitfalls, 38–41
  as source of sustainable advantage,
    32–7
  strategy and organisation, 41–5
Leading the Revolution (Hamel), 152
Learned, E., 6
learning, in multi-business firms (MBFs),
  195–6
Lederhausen, Mats, 225
Leonard, D., 203
Levi-Strauss, 172
Levien, R., 161–2
Levinthal, D.A., 216
Levitt, T., 126–30, 171
Lewin, K., 267
Lexmark, 237
'liability of newness', 251
liberal democracy, 59, 80
liberalisation, of markets, 3
Lieberson, S., 20
Lincoln, Abraham, 27
Lincoln Electric, 131
Listwin, Don, 216–17
literature, reading widely, 291
living system model of organization, 289

logical incrementalism, 265
Lucent, 224
Lumpkin, G.T., 228–9

Maccoby, M., 39
machine bureaucracy, 178
MacKay, R.B., 115
Mackey, J., 236–7
MacMillan, I.C., 235
MACTOR, 121
management, and leadership, 11
management innovation, 152
managerial culture, 42–3. *see also* culture;
    leadership culture/managerial culture, *42*
managers, as different from leaders, 28–31
March, J.G., 205, 255–6
market power, and industry attractiveness,
    135–7
Market State, 80–3
'Marketing Myopia', 171
markets
  liberalisation of, 3
  two-sided, 163–4
  vertical, 180–1
Markides, C., 146, 230, 238
Marks & Spencer, 37
Martelli, A., 117
Masse, Pierre, 121
matrix organisation, 184–5
Matsushita, 129, 216
Mauborgne, R., 2–3, 126, 147–8, 271
Maxwell, Robert, 49
Mayo, A.J., 28
McDonald's, 224–5
McGrath, R.G., 235
McKiernan, P., 70–1, 115, 244
McKinsey, 46, 183, 267
McKnight, William, 211
mechanism of discontent, 183–4
mechanistic model of organizations, 188–9
Melville, Herman, 63
Merck, 184
Merck, George, 35
mergers and acquisitions (M&A), 58
MICMAC, 121
Microsoft, 129, 140, 158, 162–4, 205, 214–15
migrations, and the next wave of change,
    88–9
Millennium Challenge Accounts, 87
Miller, D., 38, 177–8, 182–3, 251, 265–7
mindsets, 29

Mintzberg, H., 4, 178, 185
Mirror Newspaper Group, 49
Moby Dick, 63
modernism, 113
Monsanto, 131
Montgomery, Cynthia, 7–8, 287
Moore, Geoffrey, 129–30
Moore, James F., 154
Morgan, G., 188
Morita, Akio, 39
morphological analysis (MA), 101–4
Motorola, 184
Mr Spock, 42, 45
multi-business firms (MBFs), 13–14
    added value, 167
    corporate strategy, 168–76
    federalism, 186–7
    learning and entrepreneurship, 195–6
    as living systems, 187–90
    matrix organisation, 184–5
    new model, 195–6
    organisation and competitiveness, 176–90
    as portfolio of processes, 187
    relatedness, 170–6
    resilience, 289
multi-divisional organisation, 168
multi-national corporations (MNCs), 78, 80–1
Mumford, M.D., 210, 212
mutation, for learning, 263–4
My Years with General Motors (Sloan), 2, 185

'N = 1, R = G', 153–4, 288–9
Nadir, Asil, 49
Nanus, B., 29
narcissism, and leadership, 39–40
NASA, 252
NASDAQ, 58
Nasser, Jac, 27
Nathanson, D., 172
Nation-States, 80–2
naturalism, and the new industrial order, 61
Netherlands, corporate governance, 55
networks, 153, 158–64, 182, 219
Neumair, U., 251
Neustadt, R.E., 28
new industrial order, 60
new ventures, 229–36
New York Times, 232
New York Times Digital (NYTD), 232
Newlands, Ted, 110
next wave of change, 82–92
niche players, 161–3

Nike, 155–6, 170–1, 175
Nissan, 244, 269–70, 272–4, 276–7
Nissan Design International, 210
Nixon, Richard, 24
Nohria, N., 28
Nokia, 140, 146, 156, 211, 215
Nonaka, I., 183
Normann, R., 154
nuclear family, disintegration, 78–9
Nvidia, 162

O'Connor, J.F., 20
OECD, 51–2, 85
Ohga, Norio, 39
O'Leary, Michael, 143, 145
Ollila, Jorma, 146, 156
Olsen, Ken, 27
On Leadership (Gardner), 290
open innovation, 215–22, 239
'opportunity-based organization', 229
Oracle, 231
O'Reilly, C.A., 32, 231–2
organisation
    as determinant of success, 43
    in leadership culture, 41–5
    multi-divisional, 168
    perspectives on, 178–9
    strategic significance, 5
    as strategic variable, 200
organisational advantage, building, 178–90
organisational capability, 179
organisational decline, 245–53
    aspiration level, 253–5
    causes, 248–53
    decline chain factors, 249
    diagnostics, 257
    docility of old age, 252–3
    inadequacies of youth, 251
    managerial behaviour, 255–7
    overconfidence of middle age, 251–2
    primary causes, 249–53
    recovery, 259–62
    recovery strategies, 261
    renewal, 262–5
    responses to decline, 254
    retrenchment, 258–9
    retrenchment strategies, 259
    rigidity of mindsets, 250–1
    secondary causes, 249, 250
    symptoms, 246–8, 247
    triggering action, 254
    triggers for action, 253–5

organisational effectiveness, 184–7
organisational learning, 103, 189–90, 192, 195, 200, 249, 263–5
organisational variables, 3–5
   and competitiveness, 3–4
Ornati, O., 236
Oticon, 211, 271
'outside in' paradigm, 113
outsourcing, 80, 155–9

Palmisano, Sam, 21, 157
Pandesic, 233–4
paradigm shift, in innovation, 220
Park, R., 224–5, 233, 237–8
partnerships, with Governments and NGOs, 59
Pascale, R.T., 183, 267, 273
Pauling, Linus, 212
Pearce, J.A., 258
Penrose, Edith, 139
people, emphasis on, 34, 206–15
Pepsi-Cola, 135–6
performance, strategic leadership as, 23–7
personalities, CEOs, 21
personality types, 30
perspectives, 13
   competency, core competency, 139–42, 64–5, 173
   contextual view, 27–8
   living system, 187–90
   on organisation, 178–9
   positioning, 134–9, 164, 172
   punctuated equilibrium, 266
   strategy-as-practice, 16, 287–8
   value innovation, 146–54
PESTLE (Political, Economic, Socio-demographic, Technological, Legal, Environmental) forces, 113
Peters, T.J., 4, 21, 177, 227, 267
Pettigrew, A.M., 267, 276
Pfeffer, J., 32
philanthropy, strategic, 61–3
Philip Morris, 136
Philips, 224
pitfalls, of strong leadership and culture, 38–41
planning, internal corporate venturing (ICV), 233–6
platform companies, 163
play, in creativity, 214
point forecasting, 96
Polaroid, 128

political history, change in, 80–2
Polly Peck, 48–9
population, projections, 89
Porras, J.I., 25, 36, 279
Porter, Michael, 2–3, 7, 33, 61–2, 125–6, 134, 144–5, 164–5, 170–2, 178
   competitive positioning, 137–9, 183
   Five Forces model, 135–7
   six principles of strategic positioning, 137–8
portfolio, of competencies and businesses, 173
Portugal, corporate governance, 55
positioning, 13, 134–9, 142–6, 150–1, 164, 172. see also competitive positioning
poverty, global, 59–60
Powell, W.W., 182
power, 39, 78, 80
'power of ideas', 223
Prahalad, C.K., 2–3, 125–6, 139, 141, 144–6, 152–4, 173–5, 183, 185, 216, 288
Price Waterhouse, 49
Princely States, 81
priorities, for business leaders, 58–9
Proctor and Gamble, 183–4, 218–20, 222, 239
product life cycle (PLC), 2, 125–30, 164
product realisation, 174
production learning curve, 130
professional bureaucracy, 178
profit, generating and sustaining, 125
Profit Impact of Market Strategy (PIMS) research, 2, 20, 191
psychological abuse, in leadership, 40
public outrage, excessive director compensation, 50

Question Marks, 133
questions, unresolved in new business venturing, 15
Quinn, James Brian, 4, 212, 265

radical decentralisation, 14, 187, 193, 198, 201
railroads, 171
Ramaswamy, V., 2–3
Ramirez, R., 154
RAND Corporation, 99, 109
rationalism, and management, 42–3, 61
Raynor, M.E., 230, 233, 235
recovery strategies, 244
red oceans, 148
Reed, John, 276
Regan, Ronald, 29

relatedness in the MBF, 14, 200
relationships, HQ-subsidiary, 196–7
Renault, 231
renewal, 14–16. *see also* transformation and
    renewal
    six-stage model, 16, 281
Rescher, N., 99
research, in the strategy field, 3–5, 286–7
resilience, 16–17, 278–80, 282, 288–93
resource allocation, 227–8
resource-based view (RBV), 2, 139, 172–3
resource-relatedness, 172–3
Riboud, Jean, 36
risk, 95–7, 225
'risky-shift', 47–8
rivalry, and substitutes, 135–6
Robbins, D.K., 258
Roberts, E.B., 224
Roddick, Anita, 33, 44
Rollins, Kevin, 138, 158
romanticism, and leadership, 31, 43–4
Rubbermaid, 24
Ruddiman, W., 92
Rumelt, Richard, 3, 170, 177
Rutledge, J., 37
Ryanair, 131, 135, 143, 150

Saatchi and Saatchi, 171
Samsung, 157
Samuelson, Paul, 96
Sant, Roger, 32
SAP, 233
Sarbanes-Oxley Act (SOX), 53–8
scale, 155–6, 170
scandals, 48–50, 52–3, 55–6
scenario studies, review of, 82–3
scenarios
    anticipatory, 111–12
    appearance of, 107–9
    benefits and drawbacks, 112–15
    computer programmes, 121
    conditions for use, 111–15
    development, 12
    development in France, 120–2
    drivers of change, 107–8
    European approaches, 122
    explorative, 111
    generic, 112
    global, 83–92
    history of planning, 109–11
    Intuitive Logics (IL), 117–22
    methodology, 117–22
    normative, 112
    planning, 82, 105–16
    skills needed to use effectively, 116–17
    types, 111–12
    use in combination with other
        techniques, 116
    uses for, 109
Schawlow, Arthur, 208–9
Schein, E.H., 21, 29
Schlumberger, 39
Schoemaker, P.J.H., 97
Schumpeter, Joseph, 127
Schwab, 151
Schwartz, P., 120
scope, economies of, 170, 180–2
Scott, Lee, 21
Sculley, John, 22
Securities and Exchange Commission (SEC),
    56–8
Senge, P., 60–1, 183, 188
services, to employees, 80
shadow personality, and creativity, 207–8
Shakespeare, William, 208
shared values, 199
shares, consolidation, 46
Shell, 110–11, 120, 184, 224
Shell, global scenarios, 83–92
    African futures, 86–8
    change from nation states to market
        states, 88
    demography and migrations, 88–9
    economic growth, 90
    energy and carbon industry, 91–2
    energy security, 90–1
    flags, 93
    low trust globalisation, 93
    open doors, 93
    seven predetermined variables of next
        wave, 84–92
    three drivers of next wave, 83–4
    three scenarios to 2025, 92–4, 94
    US, China and changing globalisation
        patterns, 84–6
Simonton, D.K., 210, 212
simple form, of organizational structure, 178
situational leadership, 22–3
six principles of strategic positioning,
    137–8, 170
six-stage model of decline and renewal, 16, 245
six wave globalisation hypothesis, 85
Skillings, Jeff, 39, 47
skills, location-specific, 160–1

'skunk works', 227
Sleepers, 255–6
Sloan, Alfred, 2, 30, 185
SMIC, 98, 121
Smith, C., 269
social architecture, 194
social capital, 37
social change, 77–80
social constructionism, 113
social history, change in, 77–80
social identity theory, 45–6
Sonnenfeld, Jeffrey, 222–3
Sony, 129, 140
Southwest Airlines (SWA), 20, 138, 143, 183
space, competitive, 153–4
Spain, corporate governance, 56
Sparks, Jack, 272
SPRU (Science and Technology Policy
        Unit), 107
St Augustine, 104
St Paul, 45, 63
Stalk, G., 174
Starkey, K., 256
Stars, 133–4
Stata, Ray, 132
State-Nations, 82
states, 81–2, 88
status, and leadership, 29
Steen, John, 224
Steiner, G.A., 73, 227
Sternin, J., 273
stewardship' theory, 47
Stinchcombe, A., 251
Stopford, J.M., 269
stories, and leadership, 25
Storr, Anthony, 183
strategic analysis, 126–34, 144–5
strategic behaviour, induced and
        autonomous, 228
strategic business units (SBUs), 13,
        169–70, 191
strategic control, 196–7
strategic groups, 2
strategic leadership, 23–7, 45. see also
        leadership
strategic management, 44
        four Cs, 73
strategic outsourcing, 155–8
strategic planning, 196–7
strategic repositioning, strategic outsourcing,
        156–7
strategy, 156

adaptive, 74
competency perspective, 139–42
development as discipline, 285–6
evolution of the strategy field, 2–6
key questions, 6–7
and leadership, 20–1
in leadership culture, 41–5
positioning perspective, 134–9
and structure, 3–4, 176–8, 200
teaching of, 6–10, 285
Strategy and Structure (Chandler), 2
strategy-as-practice, 16, 287–8
strategy convergence, 147
strategy matrices, 169–70, 199
'strategy oven', 19
strategy problem, changing emphasis, 2–3
Strauss, S., 203
structural change, 99–104
structural design, 182–4
structure, and strategy, 3–4, 176–8, 200
subsidiaries, relationship with headquarters,
        196–7
substitutes, and rivalry, 135–6
success, determinants, 43
'success disease', 26
sustainable development, 61
Sutton, R.I., 204
Swatch, 151
Sweden, corporate governance, 55
Switzerland, corporate governance, 55
SWOT analysis, 126

talent, as strategic resource, 206
Taurus project, 270, 274–5
teaching, of strategy, 6–10, 285
teams, cross-functional, 273
techniques and technologies, in the strategy
        field, 293
Teece, D.J., 129
telecommunications, 79
Tenneco, 272
tension, inherent in organisation, 183
Territorial States, 81
Texas Instruments, 131
Textron, 168
Thatcher, Margaret, 27
The Body Shop, 33–5
'The core competence of the corporation'
        (Prahalad and Hamel), 139
The Future of Competition (Prahalad), 152
The Future of Management (Hamel), 152, 291
The Living Company (de Geus), 278–9

The New Age of Innovation (Prahalad), 152
The Politics of Fortune (Garten), 58–9
The Theory of the Growth of the Firm
    (Penrose), 139
theories, person-focused, leadership, 23–4
theory-focused planning, 235
Therborn, G., 85
thinking, divergent and convergent, 206–7
Thomas, Helen, 26
threats, transnational, 88
three internal contradictions, 186
Tichy, N.M., 22, 191, 231
time, as three-fold present, 104
timing, getting it right in balancing creativity
    and efficiency, 215
TINA (there is no alternative), 83
Touche Ross, 48
trade dialogue, 59–60
transaction cost economics (TCE), 180–2
transactional leadership, 30–1, 64
transformation and renewal, 243–5. see also
    renewal
   crisis as necessary trigger, 275–6
   emergent nature of process, 268–9
   incremental and punctuated models of
     change process, 265–7
   leadership change, 276–8
   managing the process, 270–5
   momentum for change, 274
   organisational decline, 245–53
   process dynamics, 267–78, 281–2
   six stage model, 16, 281
   stage-by-stage characteristics, 245–65
transformation, strategic, 16
transformational leadership, 31, 64
Trend Impact Analysis (TIA), 97–9
Trimble, C., 230–2, 234–5
trust, 35–7, 181–2
trust premium, and corporate culture, 36–7
Turner. Ted, 21, 24, 34, 39, 183
Tushman, M.L., 231–2, 266–7
two-sided markets, 163–4
two-stage model of strategy, 4
Tyco, 175, 197

uncertainty, 95–9, 113
unfreeze-change-refreeze model, 267–8
Unified Planning Machinery (UPM), 110
United Kingdom, 48–50, 55–8
United States, 52–3, 55–8, 86, 90
United Technologies, 175
USA Today, 231

Valikangas, L., 223, 225, 236–7, 279–80
value chain, 2, 33, 134, 137, 165, 170
value innovation, 13, 125–6, 146–54, 165
value pioneering, 148
Van de Veer, J., 94
Van der Heijden, K., 95, 120
variables of next wave, predetermined, 84–92
venturing, new business, 222–36
vertical integration, 180–2
vertical markets, 180–1
vertical scope, 180–2
vignettes, 70–1, 81–2, 105–8
Virgin, 20, 31–2, 34–5, 37, 195, 200
Visionaries, 254, 256
vision, and leadership, 21, 25

Wack, Pierre, 110, 112, 120
Wal-Mart, 21, 25, 32, 80–1, 148, 173, 183, 205
Walsh, Mike, 272
Walton, Sam, 21, 25
Washington, George, 28
Waterman, R.A., 4, 21, 177, 227, 267
Watson, Thomas Sr., 212
wave studies, 77
wealth, sharing it in a strategic network, 163
Welch, Jack, 6, 21, 24–8, 30, 43, 172, 186,
    190–4, 237, 277
Wendler, J.C., 186
Wernerfelt, B., 139
Whirlpool, 211, 272
'white space' opportunities, 3
Whitehorn, Will, 34
Whitman, Meg, 32
Whyte, David, 208
Williamson, O.E., 177
Woodruff, Robert, 184
'Work Out', 193–4
World Bank, 52
World Trade Organisation (WTO), 86
Worldcomm, 53
Worley, C.G., 280
Wrigley, L., 177

Xerox, 128, 215, 220–1, 224

Yamaha, 40
Yamashita, Keith, 62

Zaleznik, Abraham, 29–30, 41, 64
Ziegler, R., 205
Zook, C., 146, 171, 237
Zwicky, Fritz, 101–2